P9-CJK-223

ABOUT ISLAND PRESS

Island Press is the only nonprofit organization in the United States whose principal purpose is the publication of books on environmental issues and natural resource management. We provide solutions-oriented information to professionals, public officials, business and community leaders, and concerned citizens who are shaping responses to environmental problems.

In 1994, Island Press celebrated its tenth anniversary as the leading provider of timely and practical books that take a multidisciplinary approach to critical environmental concerns. Our growing list of titles reflects our commitment to bringing the best of an expanding body of literature to the environmental community throughout North America and the world.

Support for Island Press is provided by The Geraldine R. Dodge Foundation, The Energy Foundation, The Ford Foundation, The George Gund Foundation, William and Flora Hewlett Foundation, The James Irvine Foundation, The John D. and Catherine T. MacArthur Foundation, The Andrew W. Mellon Foundation, The Joyce Mertz-Gilmore Foundation, The New-Land Foundation, The Pew Charitable Trusts, The Rockefeller Brothers Fund, The Tides Foundation, Turner Foundation, Inc., The Rockefeller Philanthropic Collaborative, Inc., and individual donors.

ABOUT MACED

The Mountain Association for Community Economic Development (MACED) is a nonprofit organization which provides opportunities and resources to help citizens build sustainable, healthy, equitable, democratic, and prosperous communities in Kentucky and Central Appalachia. Since 1976, MACED has worked with community groups and local leadership in assisting dislocated coal miners; creating new jobs through business development; improving water quality, education and housing finance; and increasing productivity and value-added manufacturing in the forest products industry.

MACED's Kentucky Local Governance Project seeks to involve Kentuckians more fully in the democratic process in order to encourage cooperation among counties, provide needed infrastructure and services, encourage sustainable development, improve the openness, responsiveness, and accountability of local government, and protect human health and the environment.

WHERE WE LIVE

WHERE WE LIVE

A Citizen's Guide to Conducting a Community Environmental Inventory

Donald F. Harker
and
Elizabeth Ungar Natter

Mountain Association for Community Economic Development

ISLAND PRESS
Washington, D.C. • Covelo, California

Artwork by Laura Dalton

Design and Desktop Publishing by Nyoka Hawkins, Tommy Dowler,
Beth Dotson, and Marilyn Wrenn Harrell

The educational maps *Portland/Vancouver: Toxic Waters* (shown as the cover background)
and *Columbia River: Troubled Waters* are available from Northwest Environmental Advo-
cates, 133 S.W. 2nd Avenue, Suite 302, Portland, OR 97204-3526, (503) 295-0490.

Library of Congress Cataloging-in-Publication Data

Harker, Donald F.
        Where we live : a citizen's guide to conducting a community
environmental inventory / Donald F. Harker and Elizabeth Ungar
Natter.
            p.   cm.
        "Mountain Association for Community Economic Development"
        Includes bibliographical references and index.
        ISBN 1-55963-377-8
        1. Environmental policy--United States--Citizen participation-
-Handbooks, manuals, etc.   I. Natter, Elizabeth Ungar.
II. Mountain Association for Community Economic Development (U.S.)
III. Title.
GE180.H37   1995
363.7 ' 00525--dc20   94-32180
                                                                    CIP

Printed on recycled, acid-free paper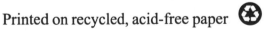

Manufactured in the United States of America

10 9 8 7 6 5 4 3 2 1

CONTENTS

FOREWORD

There is no substitute for citizens being involved in looking after their own communities. After all, it's the folks who live in a place who care the most about it. The story of a little community in Eastern Kentucky dramatically illustrates the dangers of assuming that government agencies are protecting your health and the environment.

In March of 1989 cancer-causing chemicals were found in the well that supplied drinking water to the Holiday Mobile Home Park and in fourteen private wells in Dayhoit, Kentucky.

The plant responsible for the chemicals had operated for 36 years and never had a permit to use or dispose of these chemicals. The exposure to chemical pollution in Dayhoit was also likely coming from the air, direct contact through contaminated soil, vegetables which were grown in the floodplain area, and fish from the Cumberland River.

In May of 1989, community residents and plant workers organized the Concerned Citizens Against Toxic Waste. The group has two main goals (1) to determine the extent of health problems in workers and residents that could be related to exposure to all of these chemicals and (2) to determine the full extent of the pollution.

By organizing a citizens group we have been able to teach ourselves about what is really going on in our community. We had to learn about a lot of technical data. Even though we are in the Appalachian mountains with very limited resources, we have been able to educate ourselves about the disaster in the Dayhoit community. We have also begun to look at other environmental problems throughout our county. We learned early on that the U.S. Environmental Protection Agency, local and state government, and the companies responsible for polluting were not looking out for our best interest. Through this disaster we realized that citizens have to take the initiative to find out what is going on around them.

As a result of our efforts, the Dayhoit site was listed as a Federal Superfund site in June of 1992, which means it is one of the most contaminated sites in the United States. Our work would have been a lot easier if this guide had been available when we first started. We are excited about the guide and believe it will help other communities protect themselves from environmental threats. It will also help citizens learn about their communities, make positive changes in them, and be involved in environmental decisions that affect their lives.

Oaklee Perkins, a life-long resident of Dayhoit, would like to go back to the innocence of childhood when kids played in the fields and swam in the river. Today she sees Dayhoit as a "place with poison dirt and poison water." She stays in Dayhoit because it is where her home is and she has no where else to go. With all of us working together Dayhoit will be livable again. We encourage citizens to use this *Where We Live* guide and get involved. Who knows? There may be a Dayhoit in your area.

Joan Robinett and Teri Howard
Concerned Citizens Against Toxic Waste

PREFACE

Too often environmental decisions are made without the benefit of citizen involvement, to the detriment of communities. It is clear to us that when citizens are at the decision-making table, the decisions are better for the environment and the health of the local citizens. The problem for citizens seeking to get to the table and balance the influence of vested interests is twofold: (1) decisions are made in state and federal environmental offices with only officials and company representatives in the room and (2) numerous local groups of citizens affected by a particular landfill or industrial facility make the trek to the state's capital to review the state's files on the facility and often see no one except the file room clerk. They face 9 or 12 or 15 linear feet of files containing permits, test results, notices of violations, and other technical documents. Each group must sort through the information, decide what is significant, interpret technical terms, and come to an understanding about the environment.

This guide is designed to address both of these problems. We hope that it will help citizens sort, understand, and interpret the documents they review, and that it will help them to become active participants in the environmental decisions made in their communities.

Where We Live is written for citizens. In an effort to make this guide as understandable as possible it was field tested by three citizen groups. The groups were located in Chattanooga, Tennessee (Lookout Creek watershed, including parts of Alabama and Georgia); Mt. Hope, West Virginia (Dunloup Creek watershed); and Madison County, Kentucky. The field test groups worked with the guide for approximately six months. Based upon this experience, a citizens group may want to plan a year project to do all the activities in this guide. We are deeply grateful and indebted to these groups for working with us to improve this guide. These groups found that once they announced the environmental inventory project both government officials (who seemed concerned about what might be found) and local groups and citizens wanted to help and contribute. All groups were able to attract a broad cross section of citizens who wanted to participate. The media, especially local newspapers, were very helpful in doing stories on the inventory project and advertising upcoming meetings.

Citizens also discovered they know more about their communities than the agencies that are supposedly taking care of them. For example, a member of one of the groups was amazed and disturbed to discover that a truck stop had no water discharge permit since he helped lay the discharge line to the creek. University students were involved with two of the groups. Students and others who worked on this project said it was eye-opening and educational. They enjoyed the hands-on, real world experience they got by conducting this inventory.

No single volume can cover all aspects of the environment. We hope this book will be helpful to citizens trying to protect their communities. Please send comments on the guide to the authors at 433 Chestnut Street, Berea, Kentucky 40403.

ACKNOWLEDGMENTS

The authors are deeply indebted to many people who helped with this book, and we wish to thank the following:

- Frank Taylor, President of MACED from August, 1989 until August, 1994, who read, edited, shared ideas, helped obtain grant support, encouraged, cajoled, and generally supported all aspects and efforts that culminated in this guide. His good humor and support kept us going.
- Readers of various drafts and sections of this guide, who offered many helpful suggestions. They include Jack P. Baker, Robert J. Ehrler, Tom FitzGerald, Kay Harker, Nyoka Hawkins, Lynn Hodges, Brian Holtzclaw, John E. Hornback, Susan Kiely-Bahr, Randall G. McDowell, Bob Oether, Bob Padgett, Joe Szakos, Jean True, Sally Wasielewski, Al Westerman, and Tennessee Valley Authority readers.
- The many members of the three groups who field tested the working draft of this guide and offered many helpful suggestions that improved this published version. The groups are located in Dunloup Creek Watershed in West Virginia, Lookout Creek Watershed in Tennessee, Alabama, and Georgia, and Madison County, Kentucky.
- The Woodlands Mountain Institute for conducting a work session with this guide for a group of their high school students.
- Tommy Dowler, Nyoka Hawkins, Beth Dotson, and Marilyn Wrenn Harrell for assistance with layout and design.
- Lou Martin and Van Fritts for proofreading, editing, and developing a key word index.
- Will Herrick and April Deluca for computer assistance.
- Nancy Olsen, Bill LaDue, and Jay Long of Island Press for support and help in completing this book.
- Kay Harker and Wolfgang Natter for their support and inspiration.

Funding for the Kentucky Local Governance Project, which developed and field tested this guide, was provided by the Charles Lawrence Keith and Clara Miller Foundation, Mary and Barry Bingham, Sr. Fund, Surdna Foundation, Tennessee Valley Authority/Environmental Education Division, and the W. K. Kellogg Foundation.

Members of the Kentuckians for the Commonwealth, Local Governance groups in Harlan, Hickman, Morgan, Letcher, and Union counties, and many other concerned citizens have shared with us their ideas, concerns, and insights. This book is dedicated to their efforts to protect their communities.

The authors take full responsibility for the final content of this guide.

ABOUT THE AUTHORS

DONALD F. HARKER, president of MACED and former co-director of the Kentucky Local Governance Project, received his B.S. degree in biology from Austin Peay State University and his M.S. degree in biology from the University of Notre Dame, where he studied "killer" bees in Brazil. He has recently founded (with Liz Natter and Hal Hamilton) the nonprofit Center for Sustainable Systems in Frankfort, Kentucky.

Don has been a naturalist, farmer, and environmental consultant. He spent more than ten years in Kentucky state government as director of the Nature Preserves Commission, Division of Water, and Division of Waste Management. Don's consulting and research have taken him to Alaska, Mexico, Venezuela, Ecuador, Brazil, Costa Rica, the Bahamas, and throughout the United States. Most recently he co-authored (with three others) the *Landscape Restoration Handbook*.

ELIZABETH UNGAR NATTER, director of the Kentucky Local Governance Project, received her B.A. degree in systems analysis and economics for public decision making from the Department of Geography and Environmental Engineering at Johns Hopkins University and her J.D. degree (magna cum laude) from Georgetown University Law Center. She also spent a year studying German law through the Young Lawyer's Program funded by the German Academic Exchange Service.

Liz did general litigation with the firm of Gordon, Feinblatt, Rothman, Hoffberger and Hollander in Baltimore before joining the legal staff of the Kentucky Natural Resources and Environmental Protection Cabinet. She served as branch manager in the Cabinet's Department of Law, where she worked primarily on hazardous waste, Superfund, and solid waste issues. She now works part-time for the Kentucky Resources Council, where she provides technical and legal assistance to citizens affected by environmental issues.

CHAPTER

1

INTRODUCTION

Throughout the United States, in town after town — in Dayhoit, Kentucky, in Bumpass Cove, Tennessee, in Institute, West Virginia, in Los Angeles, California, in New Bedford, Massachusetts — citizens are struggling to cope with critical environmental problems in their communities. Contaminated water supplies, polluted air, and cancer rates in children and adults are all of increasing concern. People are rejecting the notion that the government will automatically protect the environment and their health. Many citizens have concluded that government is unable — because of the influence of vested interests and the lack of resources — to properly look after their communities. People have discovered the environment is where we live and that *we* must care for it.

In many cases, citizens are turning to themselves and their neighbors for help, forming their own community groups to fight for recycling and waste reduction instead of huge landfills, for the cleanup of industrial sites, and for a halt to the dumping of toxic chemicals into local rivers and streams.

In Bumpass Cove, Tennessee, residents joined together to close a landfill that had damaged wildlife, contaminated local creeks, and polluted the community's groundwater. Without formal scientific training, but with a lot of concern for their health and that of their community, they began educating themselves about the chemicals illegally dumped at the landfill. They compiled a list of potential health effects of each chemical. Armed with their newly acquired information, they successfully challenged state health inspectors who tried to tell them the chemicals had no harmful effects.

Since you have a copy of this guide, you may already have decided to learn more about where you live so you can better participate in decisions made about your community. Decisions are being made about your community nearly every day. The decisions come in many forms, such as enforcement actions and permits for discharging pollutants into the air or water. Regulatory agency officials have immense discretion when making such decisions. For example:

- If an industry breaks the law, it can be fined from $0 to $10,000 or sometimes up to $25,000 a day per violation. Fines are often set very low and can then be easily paid by companies as a cost of doing business.
- There is lots of discretion when setting limits for how much of a pollutant will be left on a contaminated site, or in setting permit limits for discharges of pollutants.

Involved, concerned citizens can have a great effect on how this discretion is exercised. Also, most of the regulatory programs are based upon self-monitoring. This means that the industry being regulated hires a laboratory or uses its own to test its discharges. Many state governments do not certify or check laboratories. Many examples of falsified data and "fixed" samples have been investigated. Citizens can add an important layer of oversight by checking the amount of independent testing done and insisting that government do more independent testing.

Many environmental decisions are made through a process called *risk assessment and management*. This is a common method for deciding how much pollution will be allowed into your environment. Here is the way it works: a political decision is made about how much risk you should be subjected to from a chemical entering the environment. Then a technical decision is made about the human health risk posed by different levels of a particular chemical entering the environment. Let's say, for example, that an industry wants to discharge dioxin (a cancer-causing chemical) into the river. The politicians, who are likely being lobbied by the industry, decide to put the public at a 1 in 100,000 risk of getting cancer over their lifetime. A scientist determines how much dioxin can be put in the river and not exceed that risk. The industry then gets a permit, and the public is exposed to that level of dioxin through various sources such as the drinking water or fish.

Phillip Black of Pendleton County, Kentucky, says he became actively involved in solid waste issues in his community because of concerns about the water in the creek running by the landfill. In his words, "You know, my grand-parents swam in that creek, my parents swam in that creek, my wife and I swam in that creek. If one kid gets sick from swimming in that creek twenty years from now because of something I didn't do, that would be terrible."

Have you ever been asked whether you are willing to be exposed to a particular chemical so some product can be made? Every day, decisions are being made to allow the environment to be polluted. If you are not involved in these decisions in your community, then ask yourself : Who is? And why shouldn't I be?

Many people think that environmental issues are too technical or complicated for them to understand. We are led to believe that the scientific "experts" really know about such things, and more important perhaps, that we can rely on them to warn us if anything bad is happening in our communities. However, the experience of citizens in Dayhoit and Bumpass Cove, and in countless other areas, proves otherwise. We can't always trust the "experts" to protect our health and provide for our safety. "Untrained" residents often know more, and care more, about damage to their environment than people who do not live there. They have the incentive to dig out information, and are willing to develop new "technical" and "scientific" skills if that's what it takes to protect their own health and that of their community.

Technical information has an important place in making decisions about the environment, but protecting the environment is not just about technical issues. It's also about the values that people hold. It may be a technical question for a scientist to determine if a particular chemical causes cancer. It is a value judgment, however, for people to decide if they want themselves or their children exposed to that chemical.

From the Atlantic Ocean's high-tide garbage line to mountain tops studded with dying trees, there are many stark examples of our destructive impact on the earth. People everywhere are beginning to realize that the environment is not some abstract notion — it is where we live. It's the water we drink, the air we breathe, the land that grows our food, and the wild places that nurture our spirit. When we damage it, we damage ourselves.

To participate meaningfully in decisions about the environment, we need to be aware of how those decisions are made. We also must know more about the environment itself, particularly our own local environment. We hope this guide to conducting a community environmental inventory will be a valuable tool for increasing that knowledge.

An environmental inventory is a way of taking stock of ourselves as a society, of coming to a better understanding of each other and our natural world. It requires asking questions. What are the county's natural resources? How much of the land is still wild? What kind of wildlife populations exist, and where do they live? Where does the water supply come from? Where are the industrial sites? What pollutants do they release, and in what form? Where are the legal and illegal dumpsites? What are the relevant environmental regulations? What pollutants am I being exposed to?

Citizens using this guide can pursue one or all of these questions, or come up with their own questions. Whatever level of involvement you choose, this guide will help you and your neighbors form a clearer picture of your community and your environment. A sustainable society, where the environment is protected and unpolluted and where a local economy provides people a quality of life based upon their own desires, will be built one community at a time. This guide is about getting started on yours. It will help you:

- Develop a list of who is discharging pollutants into your community
- Learn what pollutants are being discharged in what amounts
- Learn whether those discharging are in compliance with environmental laws
- Inventory the natural resources (such as parks and natural areas) in your community
- Organize environmental and natural resource information on maps of your community
- Analyze the possible impacts of pollutants on human health
- Analyze whether any communities or ethnic groups receive more pollution than others
- Add to what state and federal agencies know about your community

After your group has completed this environmental and natural resource inventory of your community, you will know more about your environment than anyone else. This information will be powerful and can be used in a variety of ways. You will be able to approach your government to make it do its job, approach industries to persuade them to be good neighbors, and organize to change your community in many ways that will improve it. The resources listed in Appendix A will be helpful in follow-up projects.

Chapter 1 Introduction

THE HUMAN IMPACT ON THE ENVIRONMENT

Introduction

Can we live in our modern, highly populated society without polluting the very earth that sustains us? We must find a way to answer "yes" to that question. Year after year the soil must produce food, the seas must produce fish, the forests must produce more trees, and the air must be breathable. We can no longer afford old visions of progress and development that are built on the destruction of these natural resources. We need to embrace the idea of living in a way that can be sustained year after year and generation after generation. Environmentally and economically sustainable communities must become our vision and the very foundation of progress itself. A sustainable life-style for our children and for future generations requires new understanding of our dependence on the natural world. In this chapter we offer a brief overview of surface water, groundwater, air, and land. These are the resources that sustain all life, and these are the resources we are polluting and destroying.

We pollute these resources for a variety of reasons. As you read through the next several sections of this chapter, think about your own life-style and community. Which of the following reasons explain the pollution in your community?

1. Pollution out of ignorance and habit. An example is not considering or knowing that pouring used motor oil on the ground may pollute somebody's well.

2. Pollution caused by low regulatory standards and/or lax enforcement. Regulatory agencies have a responsibility to protect the health of citizens and the environment by establishing a regulatory framework of protective standards and seeing they are met.

3. Pollution that is blatantly illegal. "Midnight dumping" waste on the side of a road, in an old strip mine, in a river, or in the air to avoid the cost of proper disposal is blatantly illegal.

4. Pollution that occurs because of our life-style choices. Individuals can make choices such as whether to buy a container that can be reused or recycled rather than thrown away. Many choices are not easy because little or no information is available to consumers on the best choice, or the market has not provided any good choices.

Distinguishing between legal and illegal pollution will help focus on a strategy for dealing with particular problems. In one case you may need to insist upon compliance with the law; in another you may need to insist upon changing the law, or asking companies to go beyond the law and take steps to reduce pollution and be a "good neighbor." Legal or illegal pollution looks and acts the same on the environment and on your health.

Surface Water

We divide water into surface water and groundwater. Surface water is water on top of the ground in rivers, streams, ponds, lakes, and wetlands. Groundwater is water somewhere under the ground. All water is connected through a cycle. The heat of the sun evaporates water from the soil and from bodies of water, such as lakes and oceans, and pulls it into the sky. Plants also pull water from under the ground up to their leaves where it is released into the air (a process called *transpiration*). That water then falls as rain (or other precipitation such as snow) and fills our streams and also goes down through the soil becoming part of the groundwater. The cycle goes on and on. It is called the *hydrologic* or *water cycle* (Figure 2.1).

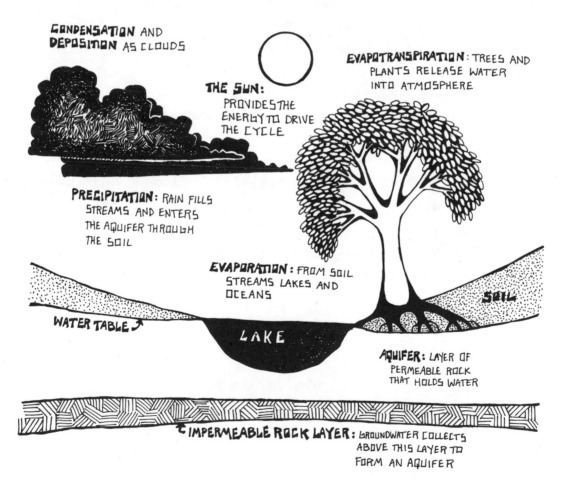

Figure 2.1 - Hydrologic Cycle

Chapter 2 The Human Impact on the Environment

Water is always on the move and everyone lives downstream. Rivers and streams are a continuum, they are connected from the mountains to the oceans. Everything going on upstream in your watershed can affect the quality and quantity of water in your community (Figure 2.2). What happens in the tiny headwater mountain stream affects the great rivers they feed. There are thousands of kinds of fish, insects, crayfish, turtles, salamanders, and plants that live in our streams. That diversity of natural creatures must be protected if streams are to stay healthy and productive.

How Is Surface Water Polluted?

Surface water is polluted in a number of ways. We have chosen to describe impacts to the surface water in four main categories:

1. point sources of pollution (these are discharges that come out of pipes and ditches);
2. polluted runoff (water coming off our farms and city streets);
3. stream modification (channelization and streamside dumping of garbage), and;
4. polluted groundwater (groundwater supplies water to many surface streams).

Point Sources of Pollution

These discharges are called point sources because the dumping usually comes out of a single point such as a pipe or ditch. Point sources of water pollution are legal and controlled by permits. Permits are used to determine the amount of legal dumping allowed into streams by industries, sewage treatment plants, and other facilities. This dumping may be legal, but it pollutes nonetheless.

Chemical pollution We put a variety of toxic chemicals, heavy metals, and other substances into our surface water through point sources. Millions of pounds of chemicals are released routinely into our rivers and streams through permitted discharges. In addition to these releases, there are illegal discharges from industries, manufacturers, auto body shops, and municipal wastewater treatment facilities which are not monitored or measured.

Organic pollution Wastewater from our kitchens and bathrooms is called organic waste and is usually discharged to a sewage treatment plant or septic system. Sewage treatment plants use different processes to break this waste down so it will not harm streams. When partially treated sewage is discharged into a stream, it continues to break down and provides food (nutrients) for the bacteria and other tiny organisms living in the stream. As the organisms begin to multiply and thrive on this food, they use up oxygen in the water — oxygen that fish need. Sometimes the organisms multiply so fast they use all of the oxygen in the stream, and cause fish kills.

WATERSHED: THE ENTIRE AREA THAT
DRAINS INTO A RIVER OR OTHER
STREAM BASIN CONSTITUTES THAT
STREAM'S WATERSHED

Figure 2.2 - Watershed

Chapter 2 The Human Impact on the Environment

Thermal pollution Another type of water pollution is heat or thermal pollution. This pollution occurs when an industry or power plant releases hot water into the streams (these are also permitted point sources). The unnatural increase in the water temperature can destroy many species of plants and animals with a low tolerance for heat. Excessive thermal discharges can leave vast areas of water lifeless.

Polluted Runoff

A second form of pollution is runoff from our farms, logging operations, city streets, strip mines, and construction sites. This is called polluted runoff, nonpoint pollution, or area pollution. The runoff can carry chemicals, fertilizer, soil, or other substances off the land into the streams. A number of on-the-land practices, called Best Management Practices (BMPs) have been developed to control this type of pollution. A BMP is something you physically do to the land, or a different way you perform the activity to prevent runoff, such as build a terrace on a slope or plant permanent grass in waterways in a field. BMPs have been developed for agriculture, construction, forestry, and other types of nonpoint pollution.

In some parts of the country nonpoint pollution is the most serious type of water pollution. Did you ever wonder what happened to the oil that drips out on the streets underneath your car? Well, it has probably washed into our streams. Why is that favorite fishing hole that used to be ten feet deep now only twelve inches deep? There may be a strip mine or a construction site located upstream that is causing soil to run off the site into the stream. The soil is called sediment when it settles in the bottom of a stream. Excessive levels of sediment in the stream can change the bottom so much that it will keep fish and other animals from living and reproducing there.

Stream Modification

Channelization, changing the shape and course of a stream, can also damage the health of a stream. Natural streams have *pools* (deeper, slower running sections) and *riffles* (shallower, faster running sections). They meander along natural bends and turns. When the stream is straightened, the pools and riffles all become the same. Trees are often removed from the bank. Without natural shade, the water becomes too warm to support many forms of life that normally live in the pools or riffles of the stream.

Streams are also modified when the floodplain is filled, built in, or used for legal and illegal dumps. These activities can result in upstream flooding, garbage washing into the stream, and increased pollution.

Polluted Groundwater

Groundwater seeps and flows into streams and rivers. This can be a large portion of their water, especially during dry times of the year. When the groundwater is polluted, it carries those pollutants with it into the surface water.

Groundwater

Groundwater is the kind of water that comes from a well or spring. It is rainwater (or any water poured onto the ground) that has made its way down through the ground until coming into contact with a layer of rock, shale, or clay that it cannot penetrate (impermeable rock layer). The water then collects in the layer of rock, gravel, or sand above that impermeable layer (Figure 2.3). The material that collects water may be a layer of gravel or sandstone rock and is called an aquifer. An aquifer is not just an underground lake or river. It can be a layer of rock with the spaces between the rock particles full of water. It's the type of rock layer you can drill a well into to get water for your house. Groundwater also supplies much of the water that flows in our streams, especially during drought conditions.

How Is Groundwater Polluted?

When a liquid is poured on the ground, it can be pulled by gravity through the soil and into the groundwater. Pollution also occurs when rainwater runs down through contaminated soil to the aquifer. Pollutants in the soil are easily picked up and carried into the groundwater. For example, if you pour some oil on the ground, it will soak in and begin to move into the soil. When it rains on that spot, some of the oil will be moved deeper into the ground. It may take many years of raining on that spot to move all the oil into the groundwater.

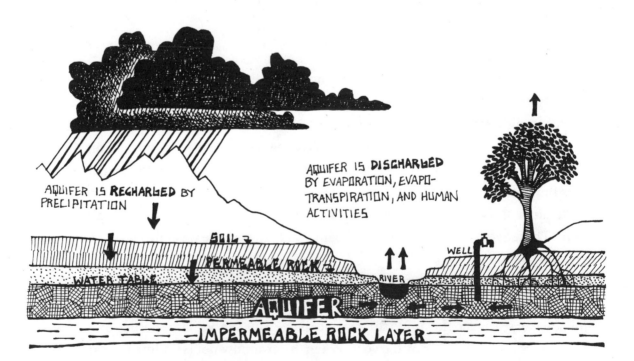

Figure 2.3 - Groundwater

Some activities can affect the flow of underground water and can pollute springs and water wells. These activities include surface mining, deep mining, oil and gas drilling, poorly drilled water wells, and road construction.

Contaminated soil can put pollutants in the groundwater for years and years. This is equally true of old, unlined solid waste landfills or "dumps." When it rains on waste that is placed directly on the ground, water runs though the waste, becomes contaminated, and then runs into the soil and eventually into the groundwater. Once polluted, groundwater is very difficult, if not impossible, to clean up.

Land

Soil is old rock that has been broken into small parts by a process called weathering. Weathering is caused by the wind and the rain, and by alternate cycles of freezing and thawing. Decaying plants add organic matter to the weathered rocks. Earthworms and other organisms begin living in the new soil and causing more changes. Soil is always being made through these processes, but it can take hundreds of years for an inch of soil to be formed.

Land grows our food and supports human life. When thinking about taking care of our land, we are concerned about a number of things. One is preventing erosion, that is, keeping the soil on the land where it is productive and out of the water where it is a pollutant. Another is preventing contamination of the soil itself so chemicals and other forms of pollution do not get carried into the surface water and groundwater or taken up by plants. Still another concern is preventing the loss of biological diversity. This means protecting the many different kinds of plants and animals that live in our forests and fields. These plants and animals are not only important to people, they are also important to maintaining the balance of nature.

How Is the Land Polluted?

Human activities create a variety of pollution threats to the integrity of the soil. Humans pollute the land in some of the following ways:

- People put things on the land, such as used motor oil, hazardous wastes, sludges from wastewater treatment plants, and pesticides that go into the soil.
- People put things into the land, such as hazardous and solid waste landfills and waste treatment lagoons.
- People put things in the air, such as mercury from coal-fired power plants, heavy metals from incinerators, and lead and other pollutants from automobile emissions, that fall back onto the land either as dust or in the rain.
- People put things in the water, such as garbage and sediment, that are deposited on the land after a flood.

Air

The air is a mixture of gases like oxygen, nitrogen, and argon (Figure 2.4). We can live without air for approximately five minutes. The air we breathe now is polluted. It has cancer-causing chemicals, metals, acids, and other human-made things in it. These pollutants are having a variety of environmental and human health effects. Environmental effects include the destruction of the ozone layer and increased levels of carbon dioxide (CO_2) which may lead to the warming of the entire earth. The human health effects range from respiratory problems to cancer. We are polluting the air far beyond anyone's ability to understand the long-term implications. For example, destroying the ozone layer allows more ultraviolet light to reach the earth. This causes skin cancer in humans. But what does it do to animals? A frog can't use sunblock and tinted glasses! There are also long-term policy questions. What are the implications of a rising sea level, disruption of ecosystems, and major agricultural impacts from global warming?

How Is the Air Polluted?

Air is polluted the same way everything else is polluted—people put things into it that should not be there. The exhaust from our cars, emissions from our power plants and industries, CFC (chlorofluorocarbon) gas which was (and in some cases still is) used in making styrofoam products, cleaning computer equipment, and in air conditioning, dust from a quarry operation, and gas used in spray cans—all these pollute the air. Air pollution also affects land and water. The Sierra Club made ecosystem protection its goal after discovering that a significant portion of the pollution in the Great Lakes came from air pollution.

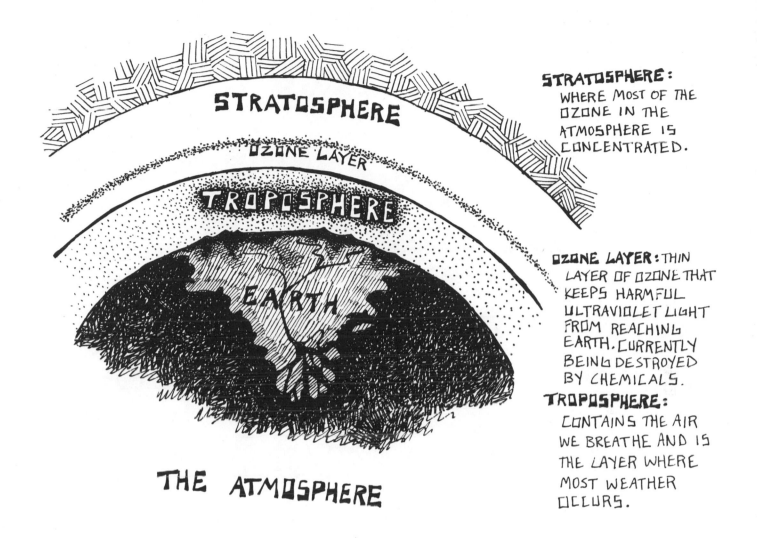

STRATOSPHERE: WHERE MOST OF THE OZONE IN THE ATMOSPHERE IS CONCENTRATED.

OZONE LAYER: THIN LAYER OF OZONE THAT KEEPS HARMFUL ULTRAVIOLET LIGHT FROM REACHING EARTH. CURRENTLY BEING DESTROYED BY CHEMICALS.

TROPOSPHERE: CONTAINS THE AIR WE BREATHE AND IS THE LAYER WHERE MOST WEATHER OCCURS.

THE ATMOSPHERE

Figure 2.4 - The Atmosphere

3 GETTING STARTED ON YOUR ENVIRONMENTAL INVENTORY

Introduction

Any individual or group can conduct an environmental inventory. This guide takes a step-by-step approach to helping you get started. Since environmental issues affect everyone in a community, we strongly recommend that a group of neighbors, friends, and local citizens organize to work on the inventory. The following section is designed to help a group get organized for an inventory. Use the Checklist of Steps at the end of this chapter to help guide you through the process.

Organizing Your Group

Everyone in your community interested in participating should have an opportunity to take part in the inventory process. This entire guide is written for the ordinary citizen who has little or no scientific background. There should be plenty of jobs available for everyone who wants to help, including young people (especially high school students). The following six suggestions might be useful in getting your group organized:

1. Form a core group. Begin by organizing a meeting of people in the community who are interested in an environmental inventory. From this meeting develop a core group who will oversee the project and meet on a regular basis to discuss progress and problems with the inventory process. The core group should choose one or more coordinators who will schedule regular meetings and keep track of the overall activity of the group. The core group can be an existing organization, which can provide structure for the group.

2. Develop a statement of purpose. The first task for the core group is to develop a statement of purpose and identify some goals for the group. A clear statement of

---

- Notify the media with either a call or a press release.
- Announce the meeting well in advance.
- Place an announcement in the local paper.
- Have the meeting announced on the radio.
- Specify time, date, and place of meeting on all announcements.
- Be as specific as possible when describing what the meeting will be about.
- Call and invite community leaders.
- Use local civic/church groups as vehicles to get the word out.
- Identify a spokesperson(s) for your project.

Figure 3.1 - Tips for Publicizing Your Meeting

---

why the group wants to conduct an environmental inventory will be important for gaining community support. Be prepared to expand or modify your purpose and goals as more people join the group. Examples of a statement of purpose might be:

- To develop a comprehensive understanding of the pollution in our community.
- To examine the extent to which our sewage treatment is protecting human health and the environment.
- To develop the first comprehensive map and listing of pollutants for our community.
- To develop a baseline of environmental information so we can judge our progress toward a cleaner environment.

3. Get the larger community together. Once the core group is formed, a public meeting should be called to tell the wider community about the inventory project, and invite them to participate. Invite local officials to your meeting. You can have a public meeting at the courthouse, church, local school, or public library. Use whatever forum best suits your situation (see Figure 3.1 for tips on publicizing your meeting).

At this meeting, ask the people attending to develop a list of every possible source of pollution known in the county, city, or whatever geographical area you are beginning to study (for examples, see Figure 3.2). As they name different sites, write each one on a blackboard, flipchart or large piece of paper put up in the front of the room so everyone can see (if you use a blackboard, make sure someone keeps notes). Who is discharging pollutants into the air or water? Who has spilled chemicals? Where are the roadside dumps? Now, look at the list that's taking shape. Already you are beginning to form a new 'picture' of the place where you live. You will be amazed at how much information you can gather about your local environment in meetings such as this one.

- Local Industry
- Car Wash
- Hog or Cattle Feeding Operation
- Mining Operation
- Logging Operation
- Dry Cleaner
- Oil and Gas Facility
- City Streets
- Landfill
- Sewage Treatment Plant
- Roadside and Sinkhole Dumps
- Auto Body Shop
- Commercial Establishments

Figure 3.2 - Possible Sources of Pollution in Your Community

4. Conduct an environmental concerns survey. This can be done either before or after the town meeting. Develop a set of questions that are relevant and important to your community and watershed area. Have a group of volunteers go around the community distributing the survey forms and picking them up. Get a volunteer from each community or neighborhood to make phone and personal follow-up contact so the group can get a maximum return of survey forms.

The group can receive professional support in conducting and analyzing a community concerns survey. The Work Group at Kansas State University (see Appendix A for address) has developed a specific process (Community Concerns Report) for conducting and analyzing the survey. The Community Concerns Report is a citizen-based method for determining what issues are important to citizens in a community. The process includes citizens selecting survey items and designing the survey, analyzing the data from the survey, and conducting a town meeting to discuss the results. The questions are structured as follows:

	How important is it to you that:	How satisfied are you that:
1. Local government is able to provide citizens with safe drinking water	0 1 2 3 4	0 1 2 3 4

The survey usually consists of 30 questions and will show the group where the major public concern is. This can be helpful in your next task of forming work groups. The survey used by a group in West Virginia is included in Appendix B.

5. *Form working groups* The most important task at the town meeting is recruiting people for working groups based on their particular area of interest. Depending on the level of detail you choose, group member's tasks could include coordinating a working group; locating maps of their study area; obtaining files from federal, state, and local government agencies; taking photographs; and contacting the media. There doesn't have to be a limit on the number of

---

Meetings Coordination - Tracking meetings of core and working groups
File Organizing - Keeping all information organized
Data Gathering - Collecting most of the information requested in this guide
Meeting Facilitation - Making meetings productive and ensuring participation
Media Contact - Distributing press releases and encouraging media to attend
    meetings
Group Spokespersons - Members who can speak on particular issues
Data Review - Putting data on summary forms
Computer Operations - Word processing and other computer tasks
Data Analysis - Analyzing the data collected
Volunteers Coordination - Recruiting and assigning volunteers
Meetings Recording - Taking minutes at meetings
Data Mapping - Mapping all information on study area maps
    *optional

Figure 3.3 - Description of Jobs for the Group or Committee Members

_____Work Group

Categories for Inventory

Environmental Concern Categories:_____

Natural Resource Categories:_____

Other Tasks:_____

Work Group Coordinator	Work Group Member
Name:_____	Name:_____
Address:_____	Address:_____
_____	_____
Phone: (home)_____	Phone: (home)_____
(Office)_____	(Office)_____
Work Group Member	Work Group Member
Name:_____	Name:_____
Address:_____	Address:_____
_____	_____
Phone: (home)_____	Phone: (home)_____
(Office)_____	(Office)_____

Activity:_____
_____
Target date:_____

Activity:_____
_____
Target date:_____

Activity:_____
_____
Target date:_____

Figure 3.4 - Work Group Form

Include the following information in each packet given to members of each
work group who do not have a copy of the entire guide:
- Introduction (Chapter 1)
- Getting Started on Your Environmental Inventory (Chapter 3)
- Mapping Your Information (Chapter 4)

If you are doing an Environmental Concerns Inventory:
- Introduction to Chapter 5 plus the specific section the work
  group has chosen
- Analysis of Pollutants (Chapter 8)

If you are doing a Natural Resources Inventory:
- Introduction to Chapter 6 plus the specific section the work group has
  chosen

Appendices
- Appendix C - List of addresses for your particular state
- Appendix D - Sample Freedom of Information request letters

Figure 3.5 - Work Group Packet

people in a working group. Members of the group can choose to attend the strategy sessions of the core group, or not, depending on how the project is designed, and what people want to do. Different tasks can be performed by individuals, or committees, or on a rotating basis. The list of job descriptions in Figure 3.3 may be helpful in defining and assigning the various areas in which people can work.

Use one copy of the Work Group Form (Figure 3.4) for each work group you want to organize. The form is set up so each work group can be named. For example, you may have a Water Work Group, a Superfund Work Group, or a Natural Areas Work Group. The form will allow you to list the work group members' names, addresses, and telephone numbers. A work group can be assigned one or more categories of environmental concern or categories of natural resources. A work group can also take on the task of auditing an individual industry, wastewater treatment plant, or drinking water plant.

Each work group coordinator should have a copy of this guide. Each member of the work group should be given either a copy of the guide or a copy of a Work Group Packet (see Figure 3.5). Each work group coordinator should go through the tasks in their category and outline specific activities for the work group members. A list of activities and target dates for completing a particular category (see Figure 3.4, Work Group Form) should be developed.

There should be a standard place where information is kept and all group members should have access to that place for filing, leaving material, working on maps, etc. Several working copies of the maps should be made available to work groups to use. The core group should decide who will map the information for a work group on the final base maps. Completion of the final set of maps should be overseen by the core group. The core group should explore the possibility of mapping several data sets on mylar (clear plastic) overlays if the information will otherwise clutter the base map.

6. Keep the public involved and informed. As your group proceeds with the environmental inventory, it is important to stay in touch with the larger community. This can be accomplished through periodic town meetings to allow other citizens to see what is being done and perhaps to become involved. You can also make regular presentations at local government meetings and civic group meetings. The press plays an important role in getting the news out about your project. Stories in the newspaper and on television and radio stimulate more participation and can provide recognition and support for people already working on the environmental inventory. The larger group should choose one person, or possibly a group of people, to work with the media to keep the public informed.

What to Inventory

When deciding what to inventory in your community, and especially when using this guide, there are several important points to remember:

1. You do not have to do everything in this guide. You can pick and choose based on your interest or concerns. You are encouraged to conduct a complete inventory of your community, if no one else has done it.

2. This guide is divided into three main sections. There is the Environmental Concerns Inventory (Chapter 5), Natural Resources Inventory (Chapter 6), and the Individual Facilities Audit (Chapter 7).

3. The Environmental Concerns Inventory and the Natural Resources Inventory are each divided into categories. For each environmental concern category you are asked to obtain information concerning who is polluting, and what pollutants are being discharged or found on sites. If the pollution is coming from a facility with a permit, find out whether they are in compliance with their permits. For each natural resource category you are asked to identify where the resource is located, how much there is, and whether it is adequately protected.

4. The Individual Facilities Audit chapter (Chapter 7) allows a group to look specifically at an individual industry, wastewater treatment plant, or drinking water plant.

5. The Analysis of Pollutants chapter (Chapter 8) provides a framework for analyzing the potential harm from the pollutants found in your inventory and who is most affected.

6. The Expanding What Agencies Know chapter (Chapter 9) provides a number of possible activities for finding information beyond what is found in government files.

If the group wants to conduct an environmental concerns inventory or a natural resources inventory, then it needs to make two decisions. First, the group needs to outline the study area (see section on Selecting Your Study Area in this Chapter). Second, the group must decide which of the 17 categories of environmental concern it wants to inventory (see Figure 3.6) and which of the nine natural resource categories it chooses to inventory (see Figure 3.7).

If the group decides to look at just one facility, it may go directly to Chapter 7 (after completing this chapter) and begin. That chapter discusses how to audit an individual industry, drinking water treatment plant, or a sewage (wastewater) treatment plant.

Sources of Information

Every section in the inventory chapters begins with a box that contains two types of information. Each box first lists the information that should be collected for that category of concern. Second, the box lists the sources for the information requested. In this guide we refer to a number of organizations that provide information to citizens. Many times the reference is general, such as the local, state or federal agency responsible for air permits in your area. In Appendix C we have included the addresses of many state and federal agencies which can be used as sources of information. One place to go for information is your regional U.S. Environmental Protection Agency (EPA) office (see Appendix C for EPA regions and addresses of regional offices). Your regional EPA should have a state contact person for any of the water, air, groundwater, hazardous waste, Superfund, or other environmental programs. Information on natural resources, floodplains, dams and other features may come from a variety of state and federal agencies. Appendix C also contains a listing of state agencies responsible for the categories listed in this guide. The addresses are listed for all agencies by state (states are alphabetical).

Government documents are an important source of information for your local environmental inventory. An alphabet soup of government agencies is responsible for regulating various aspects of the landfills, factories, Superfund sites, and other pollution sources that may pose potential environmental problems for your community. Their activities range from conducting periodic inspections to issuing permits. Under the federal Freedom of Information Act (FOIA) and the various state "Sunshine" laws, federal, state, and local agencies are required to make most government documents available to the public. While certain documents containing trade secrets or recommendations to decision-makers may be exempt from public disclosure under those laws, almost all "fact" documents must be made available to the public. For example, you should almost always be able to view documents such as inspection reports, discharge or monitoring reports, and various permit documents.

Some state and local agencies allow you to walk in off the street with a request and view their files. Other agencies require detailed written requests for specific documents (see Appendix D for a sample FOIA request letter). Almost all federal agencies require written requests. You should generally be able to request documents by mail. It is best to telephone

```
1. Toxic Chemical Releases          10. Oil and Natural Gas Facilities
2. Hazardous Chemicals              11. Underground Storage Tanks
3. Sources of Water Pollution       12. Dams and Floodplains
4. Sources of Air Pollution         13. Polluted Runoff
5. Hazardous Waste Facilities       14. Septic Systems
6. Hazardous Waste Generators       15. Drinking Water and Groundwater
7. Superfund Sites                  16. Transportation Hazards
8. Solid Waste Sites                17. Nuclear Facilities and Waste
9. Mining Sites and Facilities
```

Figure 3.6 - Categories of Environmental Concern

```
1. Rare Plants and Animals          5. Wilderness Areas
2. Natural Areas                    6. Wetlands
3. Public Parks and                 7. Scenic Vistas
   Recreation Areas                 8. Public Forests
4. Wild, Scenic, and                9. Wildlife Management
   Recreational River                  Areas
```

Figure 3.7 - Natural Resources Inventory Categories of Concern

the agency and find out the particular procedure ahead of time. Agencies usually charge a modest copying charge if your request involves more than a few pages. However, many of the "Sunshine" laws include a provision allowing agencies to forgive or "waive" copying charges for public interest organizations, so it may be worth your time to request the agency to waive copying charges.

This guide can only point you in the direction to look. It may take some work to actually find the agency or person with whom you need to talk. Be prepared to be transferred, referred, misinformed, cut off, or even told the information is not available. Persistence will likely lead you to someone who will help you. Remember this, the government does the people's business. You have a right to know anything and everything about your community. Government has a duty to provide you with that information. Following is the sequence of events from the log book one student (from one group who field tested a draft of this guide) kept while trying to get information.

- *December 20, 1992* I wrote a letter to the state EPA office in Frankfort, Kentucky for the information I needed.
- *January 12, 1993* Upon receiving nothing from the letter I wrote, I drove to Frankfort and went to the hazardous waste division of the EPA office. I talked to a person who told me what I needed. She let me fill out an open records request.
- *January 25, 1993* I received a large package through the mail with worthless information in it. A letter said the information that I needed had to be searched for by chemical name.
- *January 29, 1993* I went to the Madison County Civil Defense office. The lady there didn't have the information I needed, but she gave me a person's number in Frankfort at the state EPA. I went home and called the person. She knew exactly what I needed and said she would send it to me.
- *February 2, 1993* I received the information I needed from the person in Frankfort.

Perseverance is a must sometimes.

Selecting Your Study Area

What comes to mind when you think about your community? Is it a few houses up and down the road? Is it the city block where you live? Is it the entire county or city where you live, your watershed or bioregion? This guide is designed to address any geographic area. The area you choose may depend upon the group that has been put together, or how much work you are willing to do yourself. Where you start is no real constraint on where you end. If you start with one city block, you can add another block when you finish the first one. This geographic area of interest is your study area. You should outline this area directly on your base map (see Chapter 4, Mapping Your Information).

To understand the environmental conditions in your study area, you will sometimes need information on facilities that are geographically outside the study area's boundaries. Pollutants move from community to community, in the surface water, the groundwater, and the air. The river running through your community may be unsafe for swimming because a facility is discharging chemicals somewhere far upstream. If you wake every morning to some smell in the air that concerns you, it may not be coming from the block where you live or even the county where you live. Likewise, if there is an industry discharging pollutants to the water in your neighborhood, the effects may be felt many miles downstream. In Paducah, Kentucky, the cancer-causing organic chemical ethylene dichloride (listed by EPA as a probable carcinogen) was detected in the drinking water. A review of the upstream discharges quickly revealed the source of the chemical: a chemical plant 19 miles upstream, that was putting enough of the chemical in the Tennessee River to significantly contaminate it.

The areas of concern beyond your study area include both the upstream (or upwind for air pollution or upgradient - which is the same as upstream - for groundwater) influences on your community and downstream (or downwind or downgradient) effects from your community. For surface water you should look at facilities at least five miles immediately upstream and downstream from the edge of your study area (unless your area is a watershed). You should extend this distance if you are on a dammed portion of a river. In this situation it is possible to be impacted by any discharge (upstream or downstream) into the pool (the portion of the river that backs up from the dam), especially during times of drought and low flow. Therefore, include the entire pool or area backed up behind the dam in your review. For some issues you may be concerned about activities that are much more than five miles upstream. For example, when brine is discharged into a river from an oil and water separator, a number of pollutants are dissolved in the water. This means they stay in the water. Bromide stays in the water and is a contaminant that impacts drinking water supplies many miles downstream. There is a potential impact from any upstream discharge, but as a matter of practicality, you may want to start your data collection at five miles.

Understanding groundwater can be a complicated technical issue. As we learned earlier, groundwater is moving through a layer of rock, sand, or gravel under the ground. Determining which direction the water is moving in that layer and how fast can require considerable technical evaluation. We describe problems associated with groundwater in each appropriate place in this guide.

Determining the source of air pollutants and where they end up is problematic at best. It literally depends on which way and how fast the wind is blowing, the humidity, the temperature, and other weather factors. Specific physical aspects of the source are also important, such as what pollutants are being emitted and the height of the smokestack emitting them. Some air discharge sources ("major" sources) will have been modeled, or studied, by the permitting agency so they can predict what happens to the pollutants after they enter the air. In Chapter 5 (Environmental Concerns Inventory) under the air discharges section, we discuss how to examine the discharge and plume information (the direction and size of the area where pollutants have blown) for a particular air source. So, as you can see, selecting your study area can be tricky if you want to include all possible pollution sources impacting you. The watershed that includes your community is the best place to start if it is not too large (for example the watershed of a small creek or river is a good study area, but not the Ohio River basin). A political boundary such as a county or a city is also a good place to start.

Organizing Information

First, if possible, we recommend that the group obtain a small set of books and publications for its use. The publications listed in Appendix A will be useful in any inventory effort. There will be other references recommended in specific parts of this guide. Add those to your reference library when you are working in those specific areas. You may be able to interest your local public library in the project and have it purchase or obtain on loan the books you need for your inventory. It may also be willing to serve as a repository for your reference library.

Very likely you will be handling maps. You will need a work area or wall large enough to spread out the maps. The maps should be stored flat if possible but can be rolled or folded if necessary. See Chapter 4 (Mapping Your Information) for details on how to select, use, and develop maps.

This guide provides many forms for collecting information in a simplified and organized manner. We recommend that you keep information in files or in a loose-leaf notebook for easy addition of material as you collect it. The forms included in this guide can be photocopied.

All three groups who tested this guide recommended that a group have a place to meet, work, keep files, and display their maps. This can be a meeting room at the library, local church, school, civic group, nature center, or other public space where citizens can gather and meet comfortably.

Checklist of Steps

Identify and organize core group   Date _____

Develop a statement of purpose   Date _____

Decide on approach   Date _____

      Concerns survey   ___yes   ___no   Date _____
      Town meeting   ___yes   ___no   Date _____

Decide what to inventory

      Environmental concerns   ___yes   ___no
      Natural resources   ___yes   ___no
      Individual facility   ___yes   ___no

Select your study area for Environmental Concerns and Natural Resources Inventories

      Study area _____

Form work groups

Provide guide or information packets to work groups   Date _____

Monthly meetings of work groups scheduled   ___yes   ___no

Group reports   Date _____

Mapping information   Date _____

Analyze pollutants and who is impacted   Date _____

Expand what the agencies know (choose projects)

___Yellow pages search   ___Aerial photograph review
___Illegal dump survey   ___Question current and former employees
___Landfill truck and license checks   ___Industry background checks
___Non-reporters of TRI information   ___Taking your own samples and pictures
___Private well and spring sampling   ___Reading placards
___Household hazardous waste   ___Watchable wildlife
___Greenlinks: Connecting wildlife habitat   ___Developing a "Good Neighbor" program

CHAPTER

4

MAPPING YOUR INFORMATION

Introduction

Much of the information collected in the environmental inventory can be mapped. The study area, industries, Superfund sites, landfills, roadside dumps, parks, wildlife areas, and locations of rare plants and animals can all be shown on a map. You can also indicate stretches of river that are polluted, areas that have caves, soils that are suitable for septic tanks, areas likely to be affected by a toxic air release, or the area that provides water for the public drinking water supply.

Maps can be very powerful tools. They can help people understand that the activity on a particular piece of property is not an isolated action. For example, when we think about where a landfill should be, the word remote comes to many people's minds (except the neighbors of those remote sites). But if you map a proposed site and begin to see how many miles garbage trucks will have to travel on small back roads, other issues emerge. How much wear and tear will there be on these back roads? How safe is it for those trucks to be on those roads? In Hardin County, Kentucky, two brothers were killed less than a year apart in separate accidents with garbage trucks on small rural roads leading to a landfill. In Trimble County, Kentucky one tractor-trailer truck bringing garbage from New Jersey was involved in an accident with a school bus on a rural road, and another was hit by a train.

Maps can tell you about critical issues such as the geology and soils at a landfill site. They can also tell you about archeological sites, rare and endangered plants and animals, floodplains, wetlands, and distances from population centers, churches, and schools. Also, maps can give you a bird's-eye view of how close your own home or school is to a particular industry or discharge of pollutants.

Maps are a good way to organize information, give your group a focus for discussing potential impacts, and help you understand where things are going on in your community.

Choosing a Base Map

The base map is the map on which you will put information collected by the working groups. The most likely base maps are a U.S. Geological Survey (USGS) 7.5 minute topographic quadrangle (TQ) map with a scale of 1:24,000, and/or a county or city road map. If your study area is large, such as part of or all of a county, we recommend the USGS 7.5 minute topographic quadrangle map as the base map. It will typically take several of these maps to cover a county.

The USGS topographic quadrangle or TQ map shows where the hills, hollows, and sinkholes are, and how low or high they are. These maps show buildings, roads, bridges, streams, rivers, railroads, transmission lines, pipelines, mines, quarries, vegetation, boundaries of states, counties, cities, parks, and other types of boundaries and features. When your inventory information is placed on the topographic base map, it will be added to all the information already on the map.

You can even locate your own house on these maps. You may want to identify a number of individual houses and local landmarks so people who look at the maps will have familiar reference points for orientation.

Topographic maps may be unavailable or seem too complicated or the scale may be such that it doesn't show the houses and features in your town. For these problems two alternatives are possible. One is to get a map of your town or specific area from another source that suits your needs. Another possibility is to draw a map. It does not have to be "pretty" or to a certain scale. The question is: does it have the features you want? (see Figure 4.1). You may want to use the topographic map as your base map and supplement it with hand-drawn maps that show features that cannot fit onto the topographic map. These can even be sketches drawn during meetings to deal with concerns that do not show up on the base map.

Ordering a Map

You can order USGS topographical and geological maps from the same place. First, you need to order an index map for your state from the following address:

> National Cartographic Information Center
> Geological Survey
> 507 National Center
> Reston, Virginia 22092

(You can also call and ask where the nearest official map dealer is in your area.)

The index map shows the state divided into small areas, and each area has a name, number and date. The date tells you when the TQ was last revised (see Figure 4.2 for an example of an index map). To order the topographic quadrangle map(s) for your community, determine which quadrangles cover your area and request them by name. The index map provides a list of map dealers in your area, and also provides an address where you can order your map. The cost of each map will be in the two-to-three dollar range. (Ask for a legend at the same time you order maps. It should be provided at no charge.)

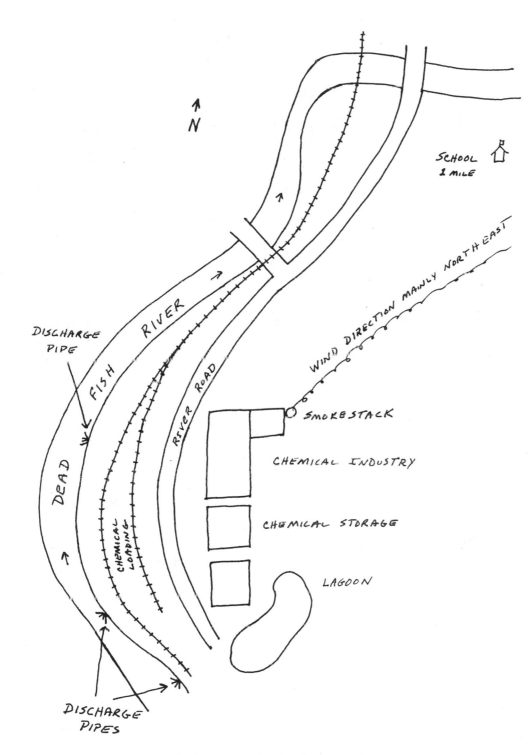

Figure 4.1 - Example of the Features of a Hand-Drawn Map

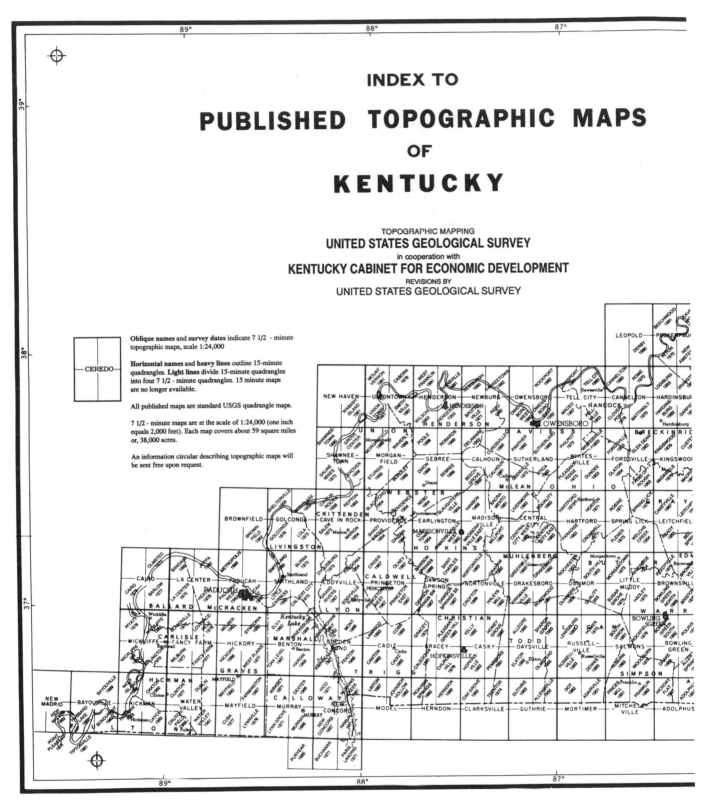

Figure 4.2 - TQ Index Map of Kentucky

Chapter 4 Mapping Your Information

Reading a Map

At first glance, the maps may seem impossible to read. But once you identify some of the basic features on the map, it begins to make sense.

The Topographic Quadrangle Map

Figure 4.3 is a partial reproduction of part of a USGS topographic map. We have identified some basic features on the map. A detailed legend (which tells you what each symbol means) is available upon request at no charge where you buy these maps. The first question to ask is, what is the scale of your base map? This means what distance on the map corresponds to what distance on the ground? The 7.5 minute topographic map is a 1:24,000 scale map. This means one inch on the map represents 24,000 inches, or 2,000 feet on the ground. Usually there is a bar scale printed on the map that gives you this information.

An important feature of the topographic map is the contour lines (the ones that give it the spilled spaghetti look). These are imaginary lines that follow a constant height (or elevation). The 7.5 minute topographic map has a contour line for every 20 feet of elevation. These lines depict the shape of the earth. You can tell if you are on a hillside and how steep it is by how close together the contour lines are (the closer the lines, the steeper the hill). The best exercise for members of the core group and those doing the mapping is to look at a portion of the map that you know, a hill behind your house or road you have driven. Then notice how that area is represented on the map. It will help you get your bearings once you identify certain basic local features on the map (see Figures 4.4 and 4.5 for an explanation of contour lines). See the box below for a mapping exercise the group can do to become comfortable with the map.

Mapping Exercise

Have each person find the following:

- His or her house
- A specific town or community
- A specific river or stream (which way is it flowing)
- A specific road
- North
- The elevation of a hill near your home

Choosing Map Symbols

You will be mapping specific types of sites and facilities that are not otherwise identified on the topographic map (Figure 4.6 shows basic topographic map symbols). Create a set of symbols for your mapping project. You can use letters such as 'S' for Superfund sites or colors for specific sites. We recommend the set of symbols in Figure 4.7 for mapping your inventory information. You should now be ready to gather information on your study area. Use the next two chapters as a reference to guide you through the mazes of environmental information important for understanding pollution and natural resources in your community.

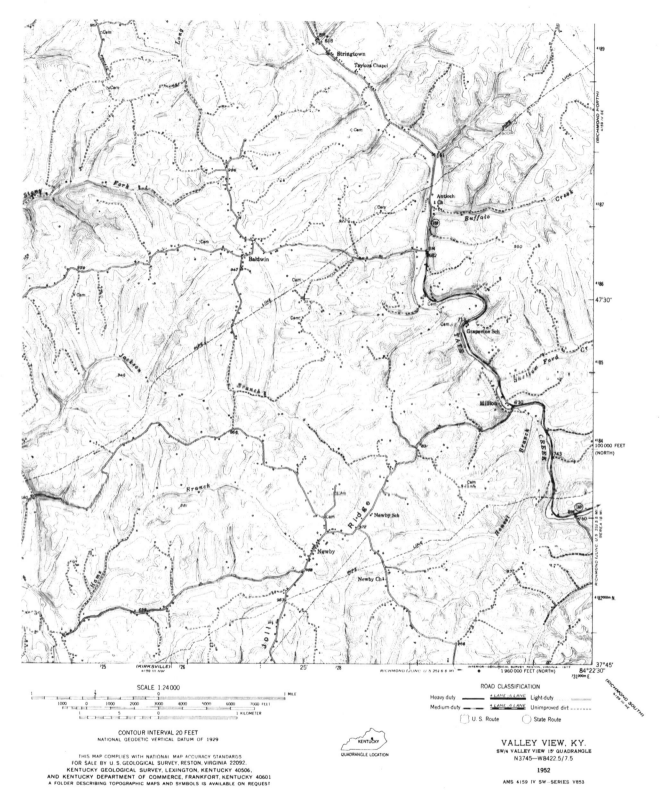

SCALE 1:24 000

CONTOUR INTERVAL 20 FEET
NATIONAL GEODETIC VERTICAL DATUM OF 1929

THIS MAP COMPLIES WITH NATIONAL MAP ACCURACY STANDARDS
FOR SALE BY U. S. GEOLOGICAL SURVEY, RESTON, VIRGINIA 22092.
KENTUCKY GEOLOGICAL SURVEY, LEXINGTON, KENTUCKY 40506,
AND KENTUCKY DEPARTMENT OF COMMERCE, FRANKFORT, KENTUCKY 40601
A FOLDER DESCRIBING TOPOGRAPHIC MAPS AND SYMBOLS IS AVAILABLE ON REQUEST

ROAD CLASSIFICATION

| Heavy duty | ——— | 4 LANE : 6 LANE | Light-duty |
| Medium-duty | ——— | 4 LANE : 6 LANE | Unimproved dirt |

☐ U. S. Route   ◯ State Route

KENTUCKY

QUADRANGLE LOCATION

VALLEY VIEW, KY.
SW/4 VALLEY VIEW 15' QUADRANGLE
N3745—W8422.5/7.5

1952

AMS 4159 IV SW—SERIES V853

Figure 4.3 - USGS Topographic Map

CONTOUR LINES

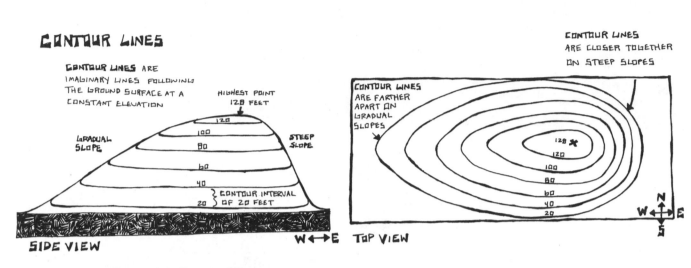

CONTOUR LINES ARE IMAGINARY LINES FOLLOWING THE GROUND SURFACE AT A CONSTANT ELEVATION

HIGHEST POINT 128 FEET

GRADUAL SLOPE

STEEP SLOPE

120
100
80
60
40
} CONTOUR INTERVAL OF 20 FEET
20

SIDE VIEW

W ←→ E

CONTOUR LINES ARE CLOSER TOGETHER ON STEEP SLOPES

CONTOUR LINES ARE FARTHER APART ON GRADUAL SLOPES

128 ✳
120
100
80
60
40
20

TOP VIEW

N
W ←→ E
S

Figure 4.4- Contour Lines

ARROWS INDICATE FLOW DIRECTION OF STREAM

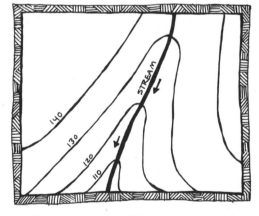

STREAM

140
130
120
110

2 DIMENSIONAL VIEW

CONTOUR LINES POINT UPHILL IN OPPOSITE DIRECTION OF STREAM FLOW

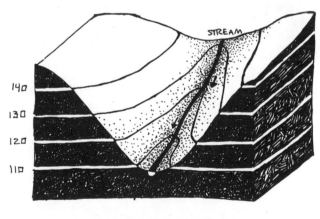

STREAM

140
130
120
110

ARROWS INDICATE FLOW DIRECTION OF STREAM

3 DIMENSIONAL VIEW

Figure 4.5 - Two and Three Dimensional Views Showing Stream Flow

ROADS AND RELATED FEATURES

Primary highway ....
Secondary highway ....
Light duty road ....
Unimproved road ....
Trail ....
Dual highway ....
Dual highway with median strip ....
Road under construction ....
Underpass; overpass ....
Bridge ....
Drawbridge ....
Tunnel ....

BUILDINGS AND RELATED FEATURES

Dwelling or place of employment: small; large ...
School; church ....
Barn, warehouse, etc.: small; large ....
House omission tint ....
Racetrack ....
Airport ....
Landing strip ....
Well (other than water); windmill ....
Water tank: small; large ....
Other tank: small; large ....
Covered reservoir ....
Gaging station ....
Landmark object ....
Campground; picnic area ....
Cemetery: small; large ....

SURFACE FEATURES

Levee ....
Sand or mud area, dunes, or shifting sand ..
Intricate surface area ....
Gravel beach or glacial moraine ....
Tailings pond ....

VEGETATION

Woods ....
Scrub ....
Orchard ....
Vineyard ....
Mangrove ....

MARINE SHORELINE

Topographic maps:
  Approximate mean high water ....
  Indefinite or unsurveyed ....
Topographic-bathymetric maps:
  Mean high water ....
  Apparent (edge of vegetation) ....

RAILROADS AND RELATED FEATURES

Standard gauge single track; station ....
Standard gauge multiple track ....
Abandoned ....
Under construction ....
Narrow gauge single track ....
Narrow gauge multiple track ....
Railroad in street ....
Juxtaposition ....
Roundhouse and turntable ....

TRANSMISSION LINES AND PIPELINES

Power transmission line: pole; tower ....
Telephone or telegraph line ....
Aboveground oil or gas pipeline ....
Underground oil or gas pipeline ....

CONTOURS

Topographic:
  Intermediate ....
  Index ....
  Supplementary ....
  Depression ....
  Cut; fill ....
Bathymetric:
  Intermediate ....
  Index ....
  Primary ....
  Index Primary ....
  Supplementary ....

MINES AND CAVES

Quarry or open pit mine ....
Gravel, sand, clay, or borrow pit ....
Mine tunnel or cave entrance ....
Prospect; mine shaft ....
Mine dump ....
Tailings ....

COASTAL FEATURES

Foreshore flat ....
Rock or coral reef ....
Rock bare or awash ....
Group of rocks bare or awash ....
Exposed wreck ....
Depth curve; sounding ....
Breakwater, pier, jetty, or wharf ....
Seawall ....

BATHYMETRIC FEATURES

Area exposed at mean low tide; sounding datum
Channel ....
Offshore oil or gas: well; platform ....
Sunken rock ....

RIVERS, LAKES, AND CANALS

Intermittent stream ....
Intermittent river ....
Disappearing stream ....
Perennial stream ....
Perennial river ....
Small falls; small rapids ....
Large falls; large rapids ....

Masonry dam ....

Dam with lock ....

Dam carrying road ....

Intermittent lake or pond ....
Dry lake ....
Narrow wash ....
Wide wash ....
Canal, flume, or aqueduct with lock ....
Elevated aqueduct, flume, or conduit ....
Aqueduct tunnel ....
Water well; spring or seep ....

GLACIERS AND PERMANENT SNOWFIELDS

Contours and limits ....
Form lines ....

SUBMERGED AREAS AND BOGS

Marsh or swamp ....
Submerged marsh or swamp ....
Wooded marsh or swamp ....
Submerged wooded marsh or swamp ....
Rice field ....
Land subject to inundation ....

BOUNDARIES

National ....
State or territorial ....
County or equivalent ....
Civil township or equivalent ....
Incorporated city or equivalent ....
Park, reservation, or monument ....
Small park ....

Figure 4.6 - Basic Topographic Map Symbols

⋇ WATER DISCHARGE SITES	OIL WELL	○ OIL	
	GAS WELL	○ GAS	
A⌒ AIR DISCHARGE SITES	REINJECTION WELL	R/○	
(HW) HAZARDOUS WASTE SITES	PIPELINE	GAS PIPELINE – – – – – – –	
▽S SUPERFUND SITES	COMPRESSOR STATION	©	
|JUNK| JUNK YARD	VALVE STATION	Ⓥ	
👓 TIRE PILE	WELL FIELD	OIL	[LABELED, IN BLACK]
♻ RECYCLING CENTER	DRILLING WASTE PIT	|DWP|	
|T| TRANSFER STATION	UNDERGROUND TANK	▣ OIL [LABEL]	
|GB| GREEN BOX	DAM	WITH LOCK / WITH ROAD	
(LF) LAND FILL			
▨LF LAND FARMING	LOCATION OF PUBLIC WATER SUPPLIES	(PWS)	
(LAGOON) LAGOONS OR SURFACE IMPOUNDMENTS	PRIVATE WELLS	JOHNSON ○	[LABELED, IN BLUE]
⋈ SURFACE MINE	FLOODPLAINS	SHOULD BE LOCATED AND COLORED IN BLUE	
◩ DEEP MINE			
⊡ COAL WASHING FACILITIES	NONPOINT SOURCES OF POLLUTION	SHOULD BE CIRCLED AND LABELED	
☀ WASTE PILE [LABEL]			
Ⓗ1 LIMITED QUANTITY HAZARDOUS WASTE GENERATOR			
Ⓗ2 SMALL QUANTITY HAZARDOUS WASTE GENERATOR	|DUMP| ILLEGAL OPEN DUMPS		
Ⓗ3 LARGE QUANTITY HAZARDOUS WASTE GENERATOR			

Figure 4.7 - Suggested Symbols for Mapping

5 ENVIRONMENTAL CONCERNS INVENTORY

Introduction

We are allowing more and more chemicals into the environment. They are destroying the protective ozone layer that surrounds the earth, causing cancer in children and adults, killing wildlife, affecting babies developing inside their mothers, and altering the genes in animal cells. Sometimes it seems the goal of environmental regulatory agencies is to legitimize pollution rather than find ways to eliminate it. In 1972, the Clean Water Act was first passed stating that: "it is the national goal that the discharge of pollutants into the navigable waters be eliminated by 1985." Today, we have failed to meet that goal. Even worse, we have decided to pollute the waters.

Environmental protection is beginning to resemble a lottery. Decisions on how much of a chemical will be allowed into the environment are made based on the odds of a person being adversely affected. Think about it like this: if a person puts enough arsenic in a glass of water to kill one person living in a city of 100,000, he or she would be tried for murder. However, if the government allows enough arsenic in the water to kill one person in a city of 100,000, then it is okay. What if that one person is your child, spouse, or friend? Since cancer can take 20 years or longer to develop, the effects of exposure to a cancer-causing chemical may not be known for a long time. Adults who are exposed may never get sick. However, young children, because they are smaller in comparison to the exposure and growing rapidly, and have the potential to be exposed over a longer period, can be at very high risk. There is also a portion of the population that is more vulnerable than others. We don't always know who they are! Some people say this is the price we willingly pay for our consumer lifestyle. Unfortunately, many of the people who pay the greatest price are the same people who get the least benefit from our high-consumption lifestyle (see section on Patterns of Pollution in Chapter 8).

It is estimated that 63,000 chemicals are commercially used or produced in the United States, and as many as 1,000 new chemicals are introduced each year. New chemicals are controlled under the federal law called the Toxic Substances Control Act (TSCA). When a company wants to begin using a new chemical, it submits required information (testing is not required) to the U.S. EPA. The agency has 90 days to react to the company's request or it is automatically approved.

The politics of pollution heavily favor the polluter. The government and the polluters have frequent discussions about what levels of pollution to subject people to. The people who are most affected are rarely involved in these discussions. The government needs to hear from the people whose water, land, and air are being polluted and not just from those who make money polluting.

You should read the following introductory material before starting your inventory. Each category of Environmental Concern begins with a Collecting Information box that basically divides the work into four steps:

- *Step One* Request a list of all industries, sites, or individuals in the category of environmental concern.
- *Step Two* Obtain copies of permits or information listing all pollutants at the site or facility.
- *Step Three* Determine if the regulated facilities or sites are in compliance with the law and their permits.
- *Step Four* Map the appropriate information on your base map.

Included in the Collecting Information box is a set of directions for "Where to Get the Information." Appendix C contains addresses and phone numbers for state and federal agencies mentioned in these directions. Following each Collecting Information box is a discussion of that particular environmental category. If you are unfamiliar with a particular environmental category, please read the discussion first.

Step One: Who Is Polluting or Causing the Environmental Concern?

Step One is designed to create a list of all pollution sources and potential environmental problems within your study area known by the environmental agencies. This list will include the name and location of all the different places that may be polluting the environment, including landfills, water discharges, Superfund sites, factories, and places that handle hazardous waste. A group may think that a Superfund site is their biggest problem until they look at the entire list of pollution sources in their neighborhood. Therefore, we recommend that Step One be completed for all categories to establish a broad understanding of the pollution sources in your community.

The seventeen categories of environmental concern are based upon how the environment is generally regulated in the United States. The categories represent the way regulatory programs and information are generally organized at the U.S. Environmental Protection Agency and in most states. The major federal laws regulating the environment are referenced and summarized in Appendix E of this guide. It may take some persistence to obtain data from government agencies (see Appendix D on open records). Your state may have additional regulatory programs.

Either the core group or one of the working groups should fill out the Pollution Source Summary Form (page 40). On the form you will list all of the industries or facilities found under each category of investigation. An individual industry might have several types of discharges or problems, such as a water discharge permit, air permit, Superfund site, hazardous waste facility, and landfill. For that industry you should check all appropriate columns. This form will allow you to track the complete list of potential pollution sources in your study area.

Step Two: What's Being Discharged?

In Step One a complete list of who is discharging pollutants into the environment was developed. The completion of Step Two will provide lists of which pollutants are being discharged at what quantities and the status of certain facilities. This step requires looking at applications, permits, site studies, and discharge reports. For each of the 17 categories of Environmental Concern, the group will develop a list of pollutants, quantities of discharge, and status of facilities such as dams.

Step Three: Environmental Compliance

Once you know what facilities are in your study area, and what pollutants they are legally permitted to emit, discharge, or dump, you need to know whether they are complying with the terms of their permits. Are they continually in violation of their water discharge permit? (Many facilities operate pursuant to compliance orders that give them months or years to improve their process to meet legal limits — in the meantime they get some kind of "relaxed" standards.) Are they operating a landfill with an expired permit, or no permit? Have they dumped or spilled chemicals in the past that they are now required to clean up? Do they have a record of building additions to the plant without applying for the required construction permits for air discharges? Have there been many complaints from the public about chemical odors, dead fish in the stream, or other problems in your study area?

This is the kind of information you can obtain through a review of agency files. You will learn whether the company has a history of compliance with environmental laws or a history of violating environmental laws. Of course, you will only learn what the agencies already know. It is not necessarily a complete picture of what's going on at the facility. Other sources (for example, current and former plant employees) may be even more valuable. See Chapter 9 "Expanding What Agencies Know" for more discussion. The Environmental Compliance Summary Form (page 46) can generally be used in step three of each section in this inventory to record compliance information.

Pollution Source Summary

Industry or facility name	Reports under section 313 Right-to-know law	Stores extremely hazardous materials	Water discharge permit	Pre-treatment permit	Air permit	Hazardous waste facility	Hazardous waste generator	Superfund sites	Landfills	Other solid waste	Lagoons	State specific permits

The public files on an individual facility will contain the following types of documents and reports that should be examined:

- *Permits* Copies of all construction, operating and discharge permits, and permit applications for that facility
- *Self-Monitoring Reports* Reports of the compliance sampling performed by the facility
- *Inspection Reports* Inspections performed by the regulatory agency
- *Laboratory Reports* Sampling and analysis performed by the regulatory agency (see Reading a Lab Report in box below)
- *Spill Release and Malfunction Reports* Reports called in or filed by the facility relating to discharges or spills that violated their permit limits
- *Notices of Violation (NOVs)* These are notices given by an inspector of violations found during an inspection (NOVs have different names in different states)
- *Administrative and Court Orders* These are official orders coming from an enforcement action that include fines and schedules for complying with the law.

Reading a Lab Report

One important thing to note about discharge monitoring reports (also called DMRs) and results of environmental samples in general is what is called the detection limit. When a report comes back and says zero concentration of a certain pollutant is found, it does not actually mean zero — it means less than whatever the laboratory instrument could detect (for this reason instead of zero, many labs use < (less than) whatever the detection limit was, or "nd," for "not detected" in their reports). Detection limits vary from lab to lab, test to test, and from sample to sample, but you will want to compare the detection limit with the permit limitation or regulatory standard. Some substances are regulated in quantities smaller than those in which they are normally measured. For example, the federal guideline for PCBs in water is 14 parts per trillion, but many labs will only find it if present at a level over 2,000 parts per trillion (for a discussion on parts per million, billion, and trillion see page 42).

Another thing you will notice are sample analysis reports labelled "field blank" or "lab blank." In order to test whether laboratory techniques are causing contamination of samples (for example, residues of chemicals used to clean laboratory glassware), samples of distilled water ("lab blanks") are analyzed using the same equipment and instruments. The field blank (also called "trip blank") is similar, but makes the trip with the sample containers that contain the real samples (so that if chemicals from the air get into the samples taken, they should also show up in the field blanks). If a chemical is found in the lab or field blank, it means finding it in the sample from the site does not prove it is at the site. It does not mean that the chemical is not at the site, it just means you can't prove it based on that round of sampling.

Conversions and Parts Per Million, Billion, and Trillion

m^3 = cubic meter
kg = kilogram = 2.2 pounds
g = grams = .001 kilograms
mg = milligrams = .001 grams
µg = micrograms = .000001 grams
ng = nanograms = .000000001 grams.

ppm = parts per million
ppb = parts per billion
ppt = parts per trillion
1 ppm = 1000 ppb
1 ppb = 1000 ppt

mg/kg = milligrams per kilogram = ppm
mg/1 = milligrams per liter = ppm
µg/kg = micrograms per kilogram = ppb
µg/1 = micrograms per liter = ppb
mg/m^3 = milligrams per cubic meter = ppm (varies with substance)
µg/m^3 = micrograms per cubic meter = ppb (varies with substance)

1 part per million =
for water: 1mg/1 = 1 milligram per liter of water
for soil: 1mg/kg = 1 milligram per kilogram of soil
for air: 1mg/m^3 = varies with substance

1 part per billion =
for water: 1µg/1 = 1 microgram per liter of water
for soil: 1 µg/kg = 1 microgram per kilogram of soil
for air: 1 µg/m^3 = varies with substance

1 part per trillion =
for water: 1 ng/1 = 1 nanogram per liter of water
for soil: 1 ng/kg = 1 nanogram per kilogram of soil
for air: 1 ng/m^3 = varies with substance

The state files will contain copies of the permit and permit application, which were obtained in Step Two. They will also contain the self-monitoring reports of the facility. These are reports that must be sent in by the facility or its agent (such as a lab employed by the facility).

The state files will also contain inspection reports. From these, you can tell how often the state has inspected the facility for compliance with environmental laws. In many states the air, water, waste, and employee safety programs are all separate; the waste inspector will not be looking for water quality violations, or vice versa. You should find out what violations were observed on inspections, and whether those same conditions continued or were fixed (abated) by the time of the next inspection.

The files will also contain any reports of sample analyses performed by the agency's lab. These will tell you how often the agency has done sampling and analysis and how the results compare to those from the company's own lab.

The file will also contain documents relating to violations and enforcement actions. Once a violation is discovered (either through an inspection, or from a review of self-monitoring reports, for example) some notice to that effect will be sent to the company. It might be called a Notice of Violation or a Demand for Penalty and Remedial Measures, or an order might be issued requiring the company to stop violating the law, called a Cessation Order, Abatement Order, or Abate and Alleviate order. Whatever it is, such a document will spell out the violation, and often list remedial measures to be performed or even order some operations to shut down until the problem is fixed. Sometimes it will also ask for a specific penalty amount. After this point, many violations are settled through an Agreed Order (also called Consent Order or Consent Decree).

An Agreed Order is just that, an agreement between the company and the regulatory agency settling a particular violation. It is also an official, enforceable order, usually with specific penalties for its violation. It will usually contain a promise by the company to perform certain tasks (such as ceasing the discharge which violates the law, performing activities to discover the source of the problem, paying a penalty, etc.). In addition to specifics about the particular violation, it will also contain some legal gobbledegook, called "boiler plate," and provisions about what happens if the company violates the order.

If the case is not settled with an agreement at this stage, there may be court proceedings. The polluter can be sued in state or federal court, or by the agency before its own administrative court. Some of the court documents you might find in the files are the following:

- *Complaint or administrative complaint* This is the document that initiates the lawsuit. It should list the violations and the basic facts alleged by the agency, as well as the action (remedial measures and/or penalty) sought by the agency.
- *Discovery* Discovery is the stage of the proceeding where the parties find out what facts the other side knows and may present at trial. Discovery can be done through several means, including interrogatories (written questions the other side has to answer in writing under oath); depositions (where a witness is required to appear and answer questions under oath, before a court reporter who usually then prepares a transcript); and subpoenas or requests for production of documents or to inspect land (where one side makes a written request for the other to produce documents relating to the case or to inspect a facility and take samples).
- *Other pretrial proceedings* You may find motions (these are legal requests for the judge or hearing officer to decide certain issues prior to trial). These frequently relate to discovery, evidence, or issues of law that can be decided without resolving

---

Principles of Self-Monitoring and Self-Reporting

Many environmental regulatory programs depend on self-monitoring, or self-reporting for their implementation. Rather than frequent inspections, sampling, or monitoring, the system depends on the polluter to report a spill, discharge, release, or malfunction to the state. It also relies on the discharger to test its own wastewater for compliance with permit limitations. Obviously, such a program will not work unless there is an effective system for dealing with false information. Such a system must include a high probability of detection of violations, a high probability of enforcement, and a penalty that costs more than the company saves by violating the law.

As you go through this compliance review, pay attention to the questions, "How likely is it that someone can get away with polluting?" "How frequently is the facility inspected?" "How often does the agency take and analyze its own samples for compliance with the permit?" "When someone is caught, is the penalty high enough so they won't be tempted to risk getting caught again?" You might want to ask if the agency has inspectors who make surprise inspections on nights and weekends. If you know any employees at the plant, you should ask if regular inspections are done on an announced or unannounced basis.

In reviewing the self-reported compliance records, such as the discharge monitoring reports (DMRs), keep in mind that there are companies that have lied in their reports. What is perhaps more frightening is the question of who looks at the reports. One study, done in the state of New York, found a surprisingly high percentage of reports were either not filled out, or not filled in completely, and no enforcement action was taken. Be sure to look for signs that your environmental agency maintains an active presence in detection and enforcement.

disputed factual issues. In some particularly serious cases, an agency will seek a restraining order or injunction to stop immediate harm.

- *Final judgment or order* A case can be resolved by an agreed order, or by a final order of the agency, issued after hearing (like a trial), or if it's in a court, by a judgment. If the case is not resolved by agreement, check the file for indications that one side has appealed the final order (for example, a notice of appeal).

Many environmental regulatory agencies are plagued with a high level of political interference in the enforcement process. For example a medium sized company in northern Kentucky took a portable pump to its wastewater holding area and pumped waste to the creek. A state inspector sneaked in through the woods and caught them. The company not only avoided criminal prosecution but got off with a very low fine. They saved a lot of money by polluting. What's their incentive for not polluting? In this case, the head of the company had donated to the governor's election campaign. You have to wonder if this influenced the enforcement action.

Environmental Compliance Summary

Facility name _____

Number of inspections in the last two years _____

Number of Agreed orders/Court orders _____

Fines levied _____

Compliance schedule? _____

Amount of time to reach compliance? _____

Number of notices of violation during last two years _____

Number of violations that question the accuracy of self-reports _____

Number of spill and complaint reports _____

Current unresolved violations (list): _____

Increased discharge limits if compliance schedule changed permit

Number of violations that indicate excess over permitted limits

Number of State sample analyses

Number of self-reported analyses

Permit limits

Individual violations (list)

1. Toxic Chemical Releases (TRI Data)

Step One: Who should report?
- Request a list (name and address) of every industrial facility in your study area that is required (under the Emergency Planning and Community Right-to-Know Act of 1986) to report its releases of toxic chemicals into the environment.

Step Two: List of toxic chemicals released
- Ask for a complete list of chemicals and the amounts being released or transferred by each facility in your study area.
- Request an additional list, one that is organized by chemical name (that is, lists all the industries in your study area releasing, for example, benzene, or all the industries releasing dioxin, etc.). This is particularly useful if you live in an area where there are multiple industrial plants.

Step Three: Compliance information
- Request copies of all records of enforcement activities regarding toxic chemical releases in your study area.

Step Four: Mapping locations of facilities reporting
- Map the location of each reporting facility on your study area maps, usually the address is sent with the original data collected.

Where to get the information
- The state environmental protection agency will probably have a division or office just for hazardous waste.
- The regional office of the U.S. Environmental Protection Agency (EPA).

The Toxics Release Inventory (TRI) Reporting Center is the national repository for all TRI reports submitted to EPA. Their address is EPCRA Reporting Center, P.O. Box 23779, Washington, D.C. 20026-3779, Attn: Public Inquiry. Include the name and address of the facility or county you are interested in with your request.

A private source for this information is the RTK Network, a computerized network that works with citizens and environmental groups. Their address is RTK Net, 1731 Connecticut Avenue, NW, Washington, DC 20009.

In 1986, a new federal law was enacted that begins to recognize that citizens have a right to know what toxic chemicals are being released into their communities. That law is officially called the Emergency Planning and Community Right-to-Know Act of 1986 (see Appendix E). This law is also referred to as Title III of the Superfund Amendments and Reauthorization Act

(SARA Title III). Industries in 20 categories (those categories are listed in Appendix E and are the Standard Industrial Classification codes 20-39) must report to the U.S. Environmental Protection Agency and to the state their total use and disposition of some 325 very toxic chemicals (see Figure 5.1 for reporting requirements). In 1991 in the United States alone there were 7,251,154,642 pounds of these very toxic compounds released or transfered. Figure 5.2 shows how much of these chemicals go into the air, water, land and underground. Figure 5.3 gives the total chemical transfers by state.

Citizens are using the TRI information to bring public pressure on industries and government. In many cases, citizens armed with this information are having more success getting industries to reduce emissions than the environmental enforcement agencies are achieving. One company in Kentucky reduced its releases of one cancer-causing chemical by 70% after the Toxics Release Inventory (TRI) information became public. That reduction was done with technology that had been available for several years.

A company must submit TRI information on a special form call an "EPA Form R" (see Appendix F). Many companies are not required to report, such as facilities producing, storing, or handling less than 25,000 pounds per year of the listed chemicals, and commercial hazardous waste incinerators. The law also covers only 300 or so of the most toxic chemicals (there are more than 65,000 chemicals reportedly in use).

The U.S. Environmental Protection Agency and the state have authority to enforce violations of the TRI reporting requirements. They should have records of enforcement actions they have taken in your study area. In addition, there should be records of any investigative activity they have performed to find nonreporting violators, or any auditing activities performed to see if reports were accurate.

Who Has To Report?

Factories and facilities that meet the following standard industrial classification:

- Standard Industrial Classification (SIC) codes 20-39 (see Appendix G)
- Have 10 or more full time employees
- Manufacture, import, or process over 25,000 pounds of a listed chemical over the course of a year
- Use over 10,000 pounds of the listed chemical in a year

Figure 5.1 - Toxic Release Inventory Reporting Requirements

State	Fugitive or Non-point Air Emissions	Stack or Point Air (lbs)	Surface Water Discharges (lbs)	Underground Injection (lbs)	Releases to Land (lbs)	Total Releases (lbs)
Alabama	16,580,199	82,578,637	4,264,358	7,988,920	6,662,537	118,074,651
Alaska	582,728	12,643,715	4,795,953	150	4,132	18,026,678
American Samo	22,000	0	0	0	0	22,000
Arizona	4,487,344	5,022,927	32,960	0	53,310,818	62,854,049
Arkansas	9,072,344	22,347,516	2,424,306	14,031,499	1,692,933	49,568,598
California	31,444,873	35,856,384	10,232,335	1,944,661	8,722,943	88,201,196
Colorado	2,754,475	3,318,751	195,424	500	514,465	6,783,615
Connecticut	6,870,076	9,388,954	3,902,429	50	3,345	20,164,854
Delaware	1,496,345	4,380,793	349,040	0	155,180	6,381,358
Florida	14,797,254	23,444,346	3,147,409	13,728,636	32,737,051	87,854,696
Georgia	13,526,226	44,514,716	4,728,313	0	1,155,194	63,924,449
Hawaii	438,180	141,478	17,029	235,199	81,200	913,086
Idaho	974,270	5,151,603	119,934	0	3,880,780	10,126,587
Illinois	27,542,663	54,164,438	6,438,552	16,199,676	18,591,746	122,937,075
Indiana	38,159,600	58,165,907	1,723,434	2,360,830	36,009,003	136,418,774
Iowa	6,407,397	28,701,215	2,001,525	0	1,789,953	38,900,090
Kansas	8,485,733	19,372,658	921,578	44,938,711	1,235,203	74,953,883
Kentucky	11,385,737	27,200,204	682,699	22,000,000	1,645,414	62,914,054
Louisiana	21,845,216	76,977,192	161,287,666	196,607,237	1,850,432	458,567,743
Maine	2,451,528	11,541,829	813,197	0	876,354	15,682,908
Maryland	4,478,187	7,078,279	682,953	0	1,293,351	13,532,770
Massachusetts	6,412,932	10,020,869	396,842	0	167,019	16,997,662
Michigan	18,598,896	51,851,274	944,817	6,699,997	13,943,692	92,038,676
Minnesota	7,350,164	32,030,987	838,399	0	1,432,241	41,651,791
Mississippi	13,746,569	42,198,692	2,173,830	48,371,556	5,607,356	112,098,003
Missouri	10,605,454	24,431,418	1,230,337	0	23,823,821	60,091,030
Montana	1,552,443	808,406	147,484	0	38,533,803	41,042,136
Nebraska	3,769,064	11,008,508	385,629	0	395,026	15,558,227
Nevada	447,056	543,444	250	0	2,435,160	3,425,910
New Hampshire	1,861,622	3,442,431	44,361	0	38,328	5,386,742
New Jersey	8,239,096	13,822,245	493,623	1	547,802	23,102,767
New Mexico	601,965	1,697,575	9,992	750	37,670,985	39,981,267
New York	21,158,898	43,526,898	1,656,018	38	1,742,285	68,084,137
North Carolina	20,133,754	63,499,937	781,249	0	23,599,855	108,014,795
North Dakota	582,348	1,214,279	79,557	0	22,750	1,898,934
Ohio	33,214,660	66,996,655	6,055,535	29,417,995	35,462,806	171,147,651
Oklahoma	5,398,061	18,428,487	509,137	2,597,370	8,366,323	35,299,378
Oregon	4,937,250	12,557,412	386,156	0	1,331,309	19,212,127
Pennsylvania	28,452,750	38,363,869	1,225,774	0	7,832,148	75,874,541
Puerto Rico	8,690,832	7,981,641	119,408	250	130,650	16,922,781
Rhode Island	2,668,383	1,682,723	121,277	0	24,147	4,496,530
South Carolina	17,463,068	44,452,404	1,210,766	0	1,069,601	64,195,839
South Dakota	377,674	2,261,739	9,038	0	32,790	2,681,241
Tennessee	53,306,877	86,310,304	3,622,533	69,568,902	2,417,820	215,226,436
Texas	79,402,956	89,520,877	2,889,837	225,032,087	13,767,951	410,613,708
Utah	5,000,623	69,550,357	120,656	0	23,722,951	98,394,587
Vermont	298,726	611,615	44,250	0	57,189	1,011,780
Virgin Islands	794,692	315,396	394,318	0	15,610	1,520,016
Virginia	17,716,400	49,592,240	2,251,200	0	2,022,165	71,582,005
Washington	10,392,763	15,738,122	4,355,925	5	156,331	30,643,146
West Virginia	10,359,757	16,758,644	1,436,226	0	354,546	28,909,173
Wisconsin	8,114,196	29,012,764	712,079	25	2,324,940	40,164,004
Wyoming	927,092	1,950,915	106,175	8,652,092	166,710	11,802,984
Total	626,379,396	1,384,174,669	243,513,772	710,377,137	421,428,144	3,385,873,118

Figure 5.2- Toxic chemical releases by state, 1991

State	Transfers to POTWs (lbs)	Transfers to Treatment	Transfers to Disposal (lbs)	Tranfers to Energy Recovery	Transfers to Recycling (lbs)	Other Off-Site Xfers	Total Transfers (lbs)
Alabama	945,395	9,456,286	5,841,317	45,325,310	39,335,023	148,902	101,052,233
Alaska	0	1,036	20	0	0	0	1,056
American Samoa	0	0	0	0	0	0	0
Arizona	475,907	1,138,509	80,969	815,522	23,873,872	42,191	26,426,970
Arkansas	576,892	2,246,527	2,292,016	3,520,143	30,854,407	4,124	39,494,109
California	28,349,693	6,329,931	8,906,422	13,625,824	131,519,474	312,378	189,043,722
Colorado	460,138	1,805,943	1,059,679	1,323,698	6,895,802	165,500	11,710,760
Connecticut	1,566,744	6,324,365	1,041,153	3,586,484	22,581,871	191,209	35,291,826
Delaware	2,344,905	806,462	28,741	1,186,088	7,045,571	0	11,411,767
Florida	13,860,357	7,112,699	2,590,989	4,855,937	15,097,568	18,154	43,535,704
Georgia	8,353,426	3,361,216	8,762,511	6,874,235	53,318,134	258,138	80,927,660
Hawaii	26,253	20	12,388	185	42,781	0	81,627
Idaho	1,246,330	61,501	5,065	283,187	475,283	0	2,071,366
Illinois	59,457,320	15,510,816	20,810,237	26,383,842	75,500,327	346,944	198,009,486
Indiana	5,761,241	35,159,725	10,435,579	19,408,585	294,438,283	1,378,073	366,581,486
Iowa	8,313,212	2,525,595	1,832,804	4,163,659	16,115,605	43,392	32,994,267
Kansas	1,951,405	3,017,996	43,694,705	1,548,678	32,746,921	1,660	82,961,365
Kentucky	1,942,905	6,698,250	7,184,087	5,351,092	59,278,568	807,733	81,262,635
Louisiana	112,305	9,381,126	4,317,925	5,127,982	28,730,868	9,627	47,679,833
Maine	794,917	474,453	1,081,428	298,665	2,589,437	9,600	5,248,500
Maryland	4,589,080	2,058,549	725,963	1,624,448	24,973,328	4,483	33,975,851
Massachusetts	5,708,676	4,993,072	2,358,484	6,707,841	15,797,249	199,355	35,764,677
Michigan	14,692,799	22,427,390	22,974,160	60,116,674	75,910,180	659,742	196,780,945
Minnesota	4,834,431	2,120,595	966,720	3,566,433	19,361,828	24,730	30,874,737
Mississippi	1,200,612	1,921,390	709,018	3,724,518	44,557,507	93,194	52,206,239
Missouri	26,111,983	6,317,491	2,110,458	9,753,464	31,805,124	134,441	76,232,961
Montana	10,650	156,360	78,681	184,211	2,874,853	0	3,304,755
Nebraska	1,295,342	3,875,356	4,098,986	1,004,157	13,640,100	6,866	23,920,807
Nevada	8,612	16,234	40,583	8,274	387,776	800	462,279
New Hampshire	451,079	1,601,771	391,659	329,446	3,633,242	38,650	6,445,847
New Jersey	44,204,143	17,653,135	2,458,127	22,512,174	93,159,759	176,797	180,164,135
New Mexico	90,891	60,776	31,920	147,996	198,644	25,444	555,671
New York	11,311,332	8,928,910	5,900,633	9,847,093	41,997,009	157,452	78,142,429
North Carolina	5,465,648	7,586,054	3,960,381	8,311,606	109,326,810	195,628	134,846,127
North Dakota	108,820	38,860	5,070	36,120	31,750	399	221,019
Ohio	45,038,807	44,941,803	22,650,421	26,439,909	319,626,185	189,512	458,886,637
Oklahoma	156,243	1,929,808	13,090,567	1,303,266	16,986,379	250	33,466,513
Oregon	4,133,808	949,589	4,059,878	457,922	8,109,370	56,016	17,766,583
Pennsylvania	15,505,272	33,660,701	17,192,967	16,703,984	210,783,647	231,317	294,077,888
Puerto Rico	6,206,477	7,977,747	461,490	6,400,370	11,914,110	250	32,960,444
Rhode Island	678,929	734,009	336,988	462,785	6,877,389	16,602	9,106,702
South Carolina	3,646,939	7,075,642	3,006,742	6,774,721	82,274,965	355,874	103,134,883
South Dakota	199,789	32,626	41,771	207,533	216,054	21,150	718,923
Tennessee	17,489,150	5,011,931	17,851,458	8,522,817	30,097,377	1,753,189	80,725,922
Texas	30,863,548	42,273,079	35,621,960	71,008,321	165,505,214	1,287,370	346,559,492
Utah	572,366	929,934	2,305,443	379,910	28,835,045	12,000	33,034,698
Vermont	35,707	673,321	29,477	73,460	2,158,192	4,400	2,974,557
Virgin Islands	0	173	0	0	376,488	0	376,661
Virginia	20,831,067	3,097,201	2,028,579	10,341,187	25,320,804	45,845	61,664,683
Washington	383,361	1,745,436	843,120	804,281	67,675,647	4,311	71,456,156
West Virginia	1,840,770	2,416,754	2,951,693	7,404,858	25,564,125	3,684	40,181,884
Wisconsin	7,528,307	7,813,947	9,778,535	9,382,150	33,707,641	112,503	68,323,083
Wyoming	173,115	1,068	2,484	4,297	0	0	180,964
Total	411,907,098	352,433,168	299,042,451	438,225,342	2,354,123,586	9,549,879	3,865,281,524

Figure 5.3- Toxic chemical transfers by state, 1991

2. Extremely Hazardous Chemicals

Step One: Who is storing extremely hazardous chemicals?
- Request a list of the facilities in your study area storing "extremely hazardous" chemicals that have reported under the Emergency Planning and Community Right-to-Know Act of 1986.

Step Two: What chemicals are being stored and is there an emergency plan?
- Ask for a list of the chemicals stored and their quantities.
- Ask for a list of the members on your Local Emergency Planning Committee (LEPC).
- Request a copy of the emergency plan for your community.

Step Three: Are all facilities in compliance and is the plan workable?
- Review the local emergency response plans for your study area.
- Determine if the plans are workable and done in accordance with regulations.
- Ask citizens living near a facility that stores hazardous chemicals to evaluate and comment on the plan.
- Check to see if the companies that store hazardous chemicals in your area are in compliance with the law.

Step Four: Mapping the facilities storing chemicals
- Map the location of each facility storing these hazardous chemicals on your study area map.

Where to get the information
- This information should be available from your Local Emergency Planning Committee, the State Emergency Response Commission, or the regional office of the U.S. Environmental Protection Agency.

You may not be aware of it, but the warehouse or industry down the street from you may have hundreds or thousands of drums or other containers of extremely hazardous chemicals stored on site. The Emergency Planning and Community Right-to-Know Act of 1986 (see Appendix E) requires the following:

- Local Emergency Planning Committees be created to develop an emergency plan for the community.
- Governors appoint State Emergency Response Commissions (SERCs) that will establish emergency planning districts and appoint, supervise, and coordinate Local Emergency Planning Committees (LEPCs).

- Facilities notify SERCs and LEPCs if they have extremely hazardous substances present above threshold planning quantities and participate in emergency planning.
- Facilities notify SERCs and LEPCs of accidental releases. The SERCs and LEPCs must in turn make this information available to the public on request.
- Facilities must submit Material Safety Data Sheets (MSDSs) to SERCs and LEPCs.

The local emergency plan covers emergencies such as spills, or fires caused or aggravated by stored hazardous substances. Each local emergency response plan must include:

- a list of facilities required to report and transportation routes used for hazardous substances
- methods and procedures for responding to an emergency release
- procedures for notification of emergency releases
- list of community and facility emergency coordinators
- methods for determining the occurrence and severity of a release, and the sites and populations affected
- description of facilities within a community and their emergency equipment
- evacuation plans
- training programs

The only real test of whether the emergency plan will work would be a real emergency. But who wants that! The next best thing is simulation or a practice-run of the plan. If this has not occurred in your community, you may have to review the plan and make your best judgment about whether it will work.

3. Sources of Water Pollution

Step One: Who is discharging to streams and rivers?
- Request a list of all the facilities in your study area that have a permit (or multiple permits) to discharge pollutants into the water.

Step Two: Review the discharge permits
- Review the NPDES (National Pollutant Discharge Elimination System) water discharge permits for each facility discharging pollutants into the water in your study area. Use the permit information to fill out a *Water Discharge Summary Form* (page 58) for each facility.
- Review the pretreatment permits (permits that allow facilities to discharge pollutants into the local sewage system) for each facility.
- Send a letter to the following agencies (see Appendix C for addresses) asking for water quality information on stream segments within your study area:
    - State regulatory agency for water
    - U.S. Geological Survey
    - Tennessee Valley Authority
    - State geological survey
    - U.S. Army Corps of Engineers
    - Water Watch or Stream Watch groups (see the 1992 River Consevation Directory in reference list)
- Summarize the water quality information you receive on the *Ambient Water Quality Data Summary Form* (page 59).

Step Three: Check on compliance
- Complete the *Environmental Compliance Summary Form* (page 46).

Step Four: Map the discharge locations
- Map the locations of all of dischargers on your study area map. You should map both the location of each facility and the discharge points on the river, stream, lake, wetland, or reservoir. There should be a latitude/longitude listed for the discharge point in the permit. Generally, agencies map this information on topographic maps. You can copy the locations onto your map.

Where to get the information
- For NPDES permits, contact the state agency in charge of water quality, or the regional office of the U.S. Environmental Protection Agency. You can either request that copies of permits be sent to you by mail, or you can go to the agency's central or regional office to review the permits. For POTW (publicly owned treatment works) permits, pretreatment permits, and compliance files, contact the local sewage treatment plant or the state agency.

The federal Clean Water Act (see Appendix A) generally prohibits anyone from discharging anything into a river, stream, lake, or wetland without a permit. That permit is obtained either from the U.S. Environmental Protection Agency or the state in which you live. The permit program is called the National Pollutant Discharge Elimination System or NPDES. Sometimes the word national is replaced with the name of the state that is running the program (like KPDES in Kentucky). Even though this program has been around since 1972, there are still companies discharging without a permit. In the mid 1980s, in Bowling Green, Kentucky, a number of industries were discovered discharging without a permit directly into the Lost River that runs through a cave system beneath Bowling Green. A school there had such high levels of fumes it had to be vented with explosion-proof fans. The fumes were coming up through the ground into the school from the cave system.

A permit is permission to release a certain level of pollution. Obtaining a permit begins with an application. The conditions of the permit are usually negotiated between the industry that wants the permit and the government agency that oversees the program. The public is rarely involved in the process at all and almost never involved in the early stages of permit development.

An NPDES water discharge permit allows certain levels of pollutants to be discharged into the water. The company's permit application should tell you what chemicals they propose to discharge and what industrial processes produce them. The permit will list concentration limits and discharge amounts, and will give you the monitoring requirements including the frequency and chemicals for monitoring. It is important to remember that the agency has a great deal of discretion, and probably will not set limits for every chemical that may be discharged.

To find out what is being put in the water, you will need to review copies of these permits. The information of interest to you includes the following:

BOD These letters stand for Biochemical (or biological) Oxygen Demand. Natural organic waste, like human waste in sewage, is broken down by bacteria in a process that uses oxygen. The more organic waste in the water, the more oxygen is used by the bacteria that break it down. BOD is a measure of how much oxygen it will take to degrade the natural organic waste that is in the water. The higher the BOD, the more polluted the water. Water permits place a limit on the BOD. It is expressed in terms of mg/l (milligrams per liter) of oxygen over time. It is important to limit this number because the more oxygen that gets used by the bacteria to break down the waste, the less oxygen is available for fish and other marine life. The regulatory agency decides what this number should be by using an elaborate computer model that looks at the low-flow conditions (volume of water, temperature, velocity) of the stream.

Suspended Solids How cloudy or murky is the water being discharged? It depends on the level of solids (dirt) suspended in the water. There is a permit limit on the amount of suspended solids that can be discharged. This limit does not address amounts of specific toxic chemicals, such as metals, that may be in the suspended solids.

Fecal Coliform Sewage can contain many harmful viruses, bacteria, and parasites. Fecal coliform is bacteria that grows in the intestine of mammals (including humans). A test for how much fecal coliform bacteria remains in the water after treatment will indicate how effectively harmful organisms have been destroyed. A water discharge permit will have a limit on fecal coliform.

Dissolved Oxygen (DO) Dissolved oxygen is not a pollutant. Actually, it is something that you want in the water. Aquatic organisms like fish must have certain levels of dissolved oxygen if they are going to live. The permit limit sets a minimum level of DO in a discharge.

Nitrogen and phosphorus compounds Too much nitrogen or phosphorus in the water leads to excessive algae growth and is harmful to the natural balance of aquatic life. These compounds are partially removed by secondary treatment, but are most effectively removed by tertiary treatment (see chapter 7). Water permits limit these compounds. Many states have reduced the phosphorus problem by banning phosphate detergents.

The above items represent what most sewage treatment plants are designed to control if they are only taking domestic sewage (waste from households is primarily organic but increasingly includes more hazardous chemicals from cleaning products, paint, drain cleaner, and other household hazardous materials). Industrial discharges are very different and can contain any number of pollutants. Depending on the industry, toxic metals, organic solvents, acids, or corrosives might be discharged. An industry can have its own treatment facility or it can send its waste to the local public treatment facility. In general, companies submit applications for a water discharge permit to either the state (for a direct discharge to a waterway) or the local government running the sewer plant (for a discharge to a publicly owned treatment works). The permit application is supposed to list all the pollutants expected to be present in the discharge.

When industries are part of a public sewer system, the possible amounts and kinds of pollutants going into the publicly owned treatment works (POTW) is significantly changed. Not only do you have the wastewater from the toilets and cafeteria at the factory, but you can have waste from many different industrial processes. Publicly owned treatment works that have industries discharging to them must have a *pretreatment* program in place that has been approved by the regulatory agency. *Pretreatment* is treatment that is done by the industry before the wastewater is discharged to the POTW. The pretreatment program requires the POTW to look at the industrial discharger and be sure the waste coming to the treatment plant meets the following three conditions:

- It will not kill the biological organisms (bacteria and other microorganisms) living in the treatment plant that are essential for breaking down the waste.
- The waste will not contaminate the sludge that is left after treatment to the level that it would be considered a hazardous waste. For example, the level of the metal cadmium coming to the plant from an industry and settling in the sludge cannot be in a concentration that causes the sludge to be classified as a hazardous waste (see section 6).
- There will not be a pass-through of pollutants in the discharge of the POTW that make it fail to meet its own permit conditions.

Sometimes the POTW actually acts as a treatment facility for an industry. The regulatory agencies seem quite tolerant of a variety of relationships between the industries and the POTW. In some cases 90% of the waste coming to a POTW is from industry, but the primary responsibility for treatment, and primary liability for violations is borne by the local government. As part of the pretreatment program each POTW must have its own program for monitoring and permitting the industrial dischargers to the system. Discharges sometimes have many different pollutants in them. It is difficult to know what the combined effect of low levels of many different pollutants will be on a particular stream. A biomonitoring test has been developed for these complex discharges. Basically you take some of the discharge, dilute it, and see what happens when you put aquatic organisms like fish and water fleas in it. If the animals die, then the discharger is supposed to find out which pollutants are the problem and reduce them.

The pollutants discharged by sewage treatment plants or industries are regulated by concentration (in the effluent or discharge) and by amount. In other words, the total amount of the discharge (in liters) times the concentration of the pollutant in the discharge (in milligrams per liter) will give you the total amount of that pollutant released into the water in the given time period (that is called pollutant loading) by that facility.

Pollutant concentration   x   Total discharge   =   Total pollutant loading

That total pollutant loading is related back to the total volume of water flowing in the stream, and must be added to the amount of the pollutant already in the stream from other sources to reveal a maximum or total allowed concentration of the pollutant in the stream. This is important, because the regulatory standards are set based on the toxicity of a given concentration of a pollutant either to humans or aquatic life. Toxicity can be chronic (causes harm over a long period of time, like long-term exposure to a small amount of a cancer-causing chemical) or acute (causes injury or death after a brief exposure). You need to know the highest concentrations that will occur, and how long they will last. These numbers can be compared to the standards each state sets for allowable concentrations of pollutants in surface water (see Appendix H).

In general, your state environmental agency will have a department responsible for enforcing the water pollution laws. That agency should keep files relating to all companies that have NPDES or state permits to discharge pollutants into the waters of your state. If you have a public sewage treatment plant in your study area, and the local government has a pretreatment program for local industrial discharges, the local government entity administering that program will also have files of interest on the individual facilities that discharge to the POTW (see Chapter 7 for more information on auditing an individual sewage treatment plant and how those plants work).

The state files will contain discharge monitoring reports (DMRs) which are required to be filed by facilities that have NPDES permits. You will want to know how often the facility submits DMRs, how many violations they show, and whether and how often the state has performed independent sampling and analysis. The local POTW will have compliance and pretreatment records on file.

The only problem with looking at all that water discharge information is that it doesn't always tell you about the actual water quality in the stream or river. Aside from the fact that permit limits are not always complied with, and that agencies often rely on self-monitoring (see Box on page 120), there is little actual independent analysis of water quality. There is some water quality monitoring going on in the streams, rivers, lakes and wetlands, but even this data normally measures only a few of the potential water quality problems. This monitoring is often called ambient water quality monitoring. Ambient means the water in the environment that is actually running in the streams and lakes.

A review of the Minnesota water permitting program from 1987-1989 found the following:

- 100% of industrial major dischargers violated their permits
- 97% of industrial minor dischargers surveyed violated their permits
- 96% of municipal major dischargers violated their permits
- 52% of municipal minor dischargers violated their permits

These permit violations were just a small part of the inadequacies found in a complete audit that the Project Environment Foundation performed on the Minnesota Water Quality Division. There is no reason to believe that similar comprehensive audits in other states would be substantially different.

Water Discharge Summary

Discharger Name _____

Location or address _____

How often is facility
self monitored?   ☐ Weekly   ☐ Monthly   ☐ Quarterly   ☐ Other _____

How many state or federal sample analyses taken in the last year? _____

Permit Requirements

What's monitored	Concentration (permit limit)	X	Total discharge	=	Total pollutant loading

Ambient Water Quality Data

Stream Segment _____

River Mile Index _____

What's monitored	Agency	Last date monitored	Highest concentration (Lowest for DO)	Average concentration

Comments:

4. Sources of Air Pollution

Step One: Who is discharging air pollutants?
- Request a list of all facilities in your study area that have either registered as an air contaminant source or have applied for permits (either construction or operating permits) for releasing pollutants into the air.
- Request a list of all nonattainment areas or areas that do not meet the basic ambient air quality standards (ambient air refers to the air all around you as opposed to what is being directly discharged from an industry) located within your study area. Ambient air is usually tested for the pollutants listed on p. 64.
- Request local climatic information for your area to create a wind rose (diagram of local wind patterns, see Figure 5.4) for your area.

Step Two: What pollutants are going into the air?
- Examine all registrations, and construction and operating permits (and applications) for facilities in your study area discharging pollutants into the air. Fill out the *Air Permit Summary Form* (page 65) for each facility.
- Request all ambient air monitoring data for your area. Summarize this information on the *Ambient Air Quality Data Form* (page 66).

Step Three: Are companies in compliance with their permits
- Complete the *Environmental Compliance Summary Form* for each facility on the air permit list (page 46).

Step Four: Mapping air pollution sources
- Map the locations of all the facilities on your study area map.
- Map the nonattainment areas on your study area map.

Where to get the information
- Permit and compliance information and ambient air monitoring data are available from the state agency or local authority responsible for air quality control, or the regional office of the U.S. Environmental Protection Agency.

Climatic information for your area is available from your local airport or the:
> National Climatic Data Center
> Federal Building
> Asheville, NC 28801-2696

The federal clean air law was passed in 1963 and changed in 1970 and in 1990 (see Clean Air Act Summary in Appendix E). Unfortunately, we still have lots of air pollution with us. The *stationary sources* (things such as factories that don't move around) of air pollution must have a permit. Different states have different types of permitting programs for stationary sources.

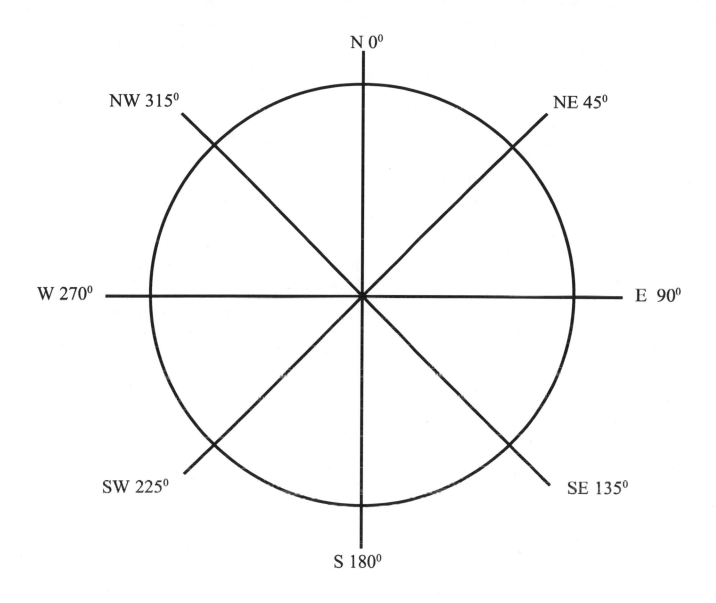

Figure 5.4 - Wind Rose

The wind rose provides information that is useful in determining which areas potentially suffer the greatest impact from a particular source. Mark the degrees for the average annual wind direction. This point represents the direction the wind is coming from. From this point draw a line through the center of the circle. This line represents the direction the wind is blowing. You may be able to get averages for each season, as well as an overall average. The more complicated wind rose you will find in various agency files has bars of different lengths pointing in different directions. The length of the bar represents the amount of time per year that the wind blows from that direction.

Generally there are two types of air permits. One is the construction permit which is required before a facility (e.g., factory with an air emission) is built. The other is the operating permit which is required within a certain period of time after operations begin.

Mobile sources (those that move around) of pollution such as cars and trucks can be significant sources of air pollution, especially in crowded cities. The pollution gets worse in the morning and afternoon with rush-hour traffic.

Air permit information can be a very poor indication of what is actually happening with the air discharge in your community. The whole air permitting system depends on calculations of emissions, based on chemical reactions and amount of product produced and raw materials used. Unless the agency does a very thorough job, it may not discover increased emissions due to lower-than-expected production efficiencies (which could result in more raw materials being used to produce the same amount of product and more emissions) or lower than expected efficiencies of pollution control devices that are assumed to filter out some percentage of emissions. (Of course, the whole system assumes an honest company reporting accurately its production rate). In addition, the exposure analysis performed by the agency usually assumes a certain percentage of emissions go out the stack and are more widely dispersed than the ground-level (fugitive) emissions. If the operation is less efficient than anticipated, or control of fugitive emissions is less effective than anticipated, people living near the plant can suffer greater exposures, even from the same total amount of pollution.

Also, the quality of the air on any particular day depends to a great extent on the local weather conditions. The permit analysis or administrative record will give you the agency's calculation of what you are receiving in the way of long-term and short-term exposures to particular pollutants. In order to determine ambient pollution levels, the regulatory agency may go out into the community near an air pollution source and put up a monitor for particulates, sulphur dioxide, or other pollutants.

Part of the new Clean Air Act amendments strengthened regulation of toxic air pollutants (see Appendix E). This portion of the law is called Title III and expands the National Emission Standards for Hazardous Air Pollutants (NESHAPs). Any existing or new source of one of these listed toxic chemicals discharging more than ten tons per year of a single chemical or twenty-five tons per year of more than one chemical must have a permit. These 189 toxic chemicals (see Appendix H, List of Regulated Air Pollutants) are of particular concern because of their potential impact on human health and the environment. Industries should be making special efforts to reduce the discharges of these toxics.

The National Ambient Air Quality Standards are outlined in Figure 5.5. These are the standards used to determine whether the local air quality meets the law. When the level of one or more of these pollutants is exceeded for a total of ten days during the year, the area is designated a nonattainment area.

There are two kinds of emissions from stationary sources: stack or source (point source) emissions, and fugitive emissions. The first type comes out of stacks, vents, or other mechanical devices designed to release pollutants to the atmosphere. The second, fugitive emissions, are those coming from something other than the permitted source, such as a leaky valve or storage tank, and include activities that cause dust, smoke, gases or other matter to be released without reasonable control measures.

The agency responsible for enforcing the air pollution laws has specific responsibilities relating to individual facilities. For one thing, it has the responsibility of permitting facilities. Any operation that will emit specified pollutants or contaminants into the air is required to register with the state. If it will emit more than a certain amount, it is required to apply for a construction permit before beginning construction. The construction permit sets limits for the facility's emissions. Once built and operating, the facility is required to do tests to prove compliance with the construction permit and to receive an operating permit.

In addition to enforcing violations of permit limits, the air pollution agency enforces laws relating to open burning, fugitive emissions, and in some states, odor violations (there is actually a device called a scentometer for using the human nose for sniffing out an odor violator).

As discussed in the introduction to this chapter, there will be inspection reports, notices of violation, Agreed Orders, and court documents for enforcement cases. For air pollution facilities, you should carefully examine what conditions (parameters) are monitored. For example, many companies are tested once to see what chemicals are coming out of the stack, and after that only inspected for "opacity"—how black the smoke is. Since only particulate matter (dust, dirt, some metals) adds to the blackness of the smoke, many people feel this method neglects dangerous organic chemicals that are released from the stacks of many facilities. In addition, opacity cannot normally be checked at night or on cloudy days.

Larger facilities may be required to monitor a variety of things that indicate how well the process is working, and therefore indirectly what might be coming out of the stack. Examples of indirect monitoring include the temperature of a reactor or combustion chamber, amount of carbon monoxide (CO) in the stack, pH of scrubber liquid, or air pressure in a baghouse. Scrubbers and baghouses are two types of air pollution control devices: baghouses force the polluted air through bags, like filters, that collect the dust or chemicals; scrubbers often pipe the air through liquid that, because of its chemical properties, catches some of the pollutants. Then the scrubber liquid must be cleaned so it can do its job again. The gunk that comes out of it is called scrubber sludge.

Major Regulated Air Pollutants and Their Sources

Criteria Air Pollutant	Primary Standard	Pollutant Source
Sulfur Dioxide	Annual average 80 μg/m³ (0.03 ppm) 24 hr. max 365 μg/m³ (0.14 ppm)	fossil fueled electric generation, and industrial plants
Nitrogen dioxide	Annual average 100 μg/m³ (0.053 ppm)	40% from motor vehicles, 30% from fossil fuel burning, 10% other sources
Particulates	Annual average 50 μg/m³ 24 hour average 150 μg/m³	coal combustion and industry
Ozone Producing Chemicals	Maximum hourly average 235 μg/m³ (0.12 ppm)	by-product of motor vehicles chemical discharges from industry
Carbon Monoxide	8 hr. average 10 mg/m³ (9 ppm)	motor vehicles
Lead	Quarterly average 1.5 μg/m³	leaded gasoline and incinerators

Figure 5.5 - National Ambient Air Quality Standards

Malfunctions and Release Reporting

Sometimes equipment will malfunction, and air pollutants are released at levels higher than the permit allows. Companies are required to report such malfunctions to the regulatory agency within 72 hours. Unless the agency can demonstrate that such malfunctions are part of a pattern indicating poor design, construction or operation, these malfunctions are legal. Critics say that this constitutes a big loophole in the air pollution limits contained in permits. In one case, a Kentucky company operated with malfunctioning air pollution equipment for eight days and released more sulfur dioxide in that time period than its permit would allow in a year. It should be noted that only the pollutants listed in figure 5.5 are monitored. The air toxics defined by EPA and chemicals listed under the Toxics Release Inventory (see section two) are not usually monitored.

Air Permit Summary

Discharger Name _____

Location _____

Chemicals discharged and permit conditions	Permit limits	Reported operational levels	Direct or indirect monitoring	Monitoring frequency

Ambient Air Quality Data

Air monitor location _____

_____

What's monitored	Agency	Last date monitored	Highest concentration	Average concentration

Comments:

5. Hazardous Waste Facilities

Step One: Which industries are hazardous waste facilities?
- Request a list of all hazardous waste TSD (treatment, storage, and disposal) facilities in your study area.

Step Two: What hazardous wastes are on site?
- Request the permit and permit application for each hazardous waste facility in your study area.
- Request a list of all places at each hazardous waste facility where chemicals have spilled or leaked. These places are referred to as SWMU's (Solid Waste Management Units).
- Ask for a list of all known hazardous constituents at the site and data indicating whether those hazardous constituents are in the air, land, groundwater, or surface water.
- Organize the information you receive for each site on the *Hazardous Waste Facility Summary Form* (page 72).

Step Three: Are the hazardous waste facilities in compliance?
- Complete the *Environmental Compliance Summary Form* for each facility (page 46).
- Complete the *RCRA Corrective Action Summary Form* for each facility (page 73).

Step Four: Map the locations of all facilities
- Map the locations of these facilities on your study area map. Each permit you obtained during data collection should have an address for the facility. Use that address and local knowledge of a facility's location to map it.

Where to get the information
- Information about these facilities can be obtained from the state agency responsible for regulating hazardous waste, or from the regional office of the U.S. Environmental Protection Agency. Ask about the cost of photocopying. Since a hazardous waste permit can be thousands of pages, it will often be too bulky and expensive to get copies by mail. You may have to visit the agency to inspect the permits for hazardous waste facilities.

In 1980 a federal hazardous waste law was passed known as the Resource Conservation and Recovery Act, or RCRA (see Appendix E). One might think that such a law would include everything that is toxic or poisonous. That is not the case. First of all, the law only covers materials once they become wastes; it does not cover the storage or handling of hazardous chemicals, products or substances until they are discarded. This section deals only with facilities that are permitted to treat, store, or dispose of hazardous waste. Companies that produce hazardous waste are called generators. Section 6 deals with generators, who also store, and sometimes even treat, hazardous waste without a permit.

Basically there are two ways something becomes classified as hazardous waste and therefore becomes regulated under the hazardous waste law. The first way is for the substance or product to be listed. A listed hazardous waste is one that is found somewhere on the long RCRA list. Some chemicals are listed by name, but many are listed by the process that produces them (for example, sludges from creosote wood-preserving activities). A second way is for a substance or product to be characteristic. A characteristic hazardous waste is one that meets one of the four following tests:

- Ignitability This applies to substances that will ignite at 140 degrees Fahrenheit. Gasoline meets this test.
- Toxicity - This is determined through a test called the T.C.L.P. (toxicity characteristic leach procedure). In this test acid water is run through a waste, such as an industrial sludge or incinerator ash, to see if any listed heavy metals (lead, mercury, cadmium, etc.) or organic chemicals (chemicals such as benzene, PCBs, and polyvinyl chloride) come out with the water in amounts greater than certain standards (see Appendix H for standards). This test is designed to prevent wastes with the potential to leach toxic materials into groundwater from going to solid waste landfills.
- Corrosivity A substance that will corrode metal. This includes strong acid and strong alkaline materials (pH less than 2 or greater than 12.5).
- Reactivity Some wastes will react if they come in contact with water or air. The reaction may be an explosion or it may be a silent reaction that gives off toxic gases. (A waste like aluminum dross from an aluminum plant gives off ammonia gas when water is put on it.)

There are a lot of waste products that are as toxic as the currently listed wastes but are not themselves listed as hazardous wastes. Depending on what they are, wastes not officially considered hazardous waste, can be treated as solid waste, special waste, or exempted altogether from regulation. Some can go to a regular municipal solid waste landfill, others have to go to a landfill specially designed for the waste, and still others, exempted altogether, can go virtually anywhere.

One problem from the community's point of view is not knowing the location of hazardous waste sites. In one small Western Kentucky community, children whose homes were near a lead-contaminated hazardous waste site had bicycle paths through the site. In Ashland,

Kentucky, the owner of a warehouse that had been used to store hazardous waste rented it to another company for the storage of food.

Hazardous waste sites and facilities range from small areas where hazardous waste was spilled to entire industrial facilities. A hazardous waste or RCRA permit can be thousands of pages and multiple volumes.

Agency files on hazardous waste treatment, storage and disposal facilities (TSDs) will be thick and complicated (see box below for types of TSDs). Hazardous waste TSDs are required to go through a long complicated permitting process, including submitting engineering drawings, bonds or other financial assurance, and liability insurance. When hazardous waste facilities were first regulated, they were normally grandfathered in under a temporary permit (which lasted for 5 to 10 years for many facilities). This is called interim status. The facilities were under obligation to obtain a full hazardous waste permit or convert their hazardous waste management activity to one that was exempt under the regulations. (The form filed for obtaining interim status, which is just the name, location, and a summary of the waste-handling activities, is called a Part A Hazardous Waste Permit Application. The full permit application, with engineering drawings and narrative is called the Part B.)

The permit application should tell you what kinds of wastes are being handled, and what type of treatment, storage or disposal is being provided. There should be maps or drawings of the waste-handling areas and equipment. If the facility is required to have a groundwater monitoring program, the plan for it should be part of the permit application unless it was

---

Types of Treatment, Storage and Disposal Facilities (TSDs)

Any facility that treats, stores, or disposes of hazardous waste (and is not exempt from regulation) is a TSD facility. Disposal facilities are any facilities that place hazardous waste on land or in water in such a way that constituents of the waste can enter land or water. Hazardous waste landfills, lagoons, or piles can be disposal facilities. Treatment is defined as any process which changes the waste (physically or chemically) to render it less hazardous or easier to handle. Incineration (burning) of hazardous waste is considered **thermal treatment**. Some other types of treatment are **solidification** of liquid hazardous wastes and **distillation** of used solvents to purify them. Storage facilities include any place where hazardous waste produced somewhere else is stored, or where generators exceed their allowed time limit (generally 90 days) for storage. There are two types of TSDs. "Captive" or on-site TSD facilities are located at or near factories that produce some product or chemical and are used to treat, store, or dispose of the company's own waste. Commercial hazardous waste facilities are built to treat, store, or dispose of other companies' wastes, such as a hazardous waste incinerator or landfill.

instituted later in response to some problem. The file should also contain any groundwater monitoring results and may include correspondence related to interpreting those results.

Some TSD facilities treat, store, or dispose of only their own waste. Others are commercial TSDs that accept waste from off-site and treat or dispose of it at the facility. Both types of facilities have to file annual reports with the state or federal hazardous waste agency showing all wastes that have been treated, stored, or disposed.

Compliance information for TSDs can include all reports and documents that were mentioned in the introduction to this section.

In addition, TSD facilities are now required to clean up any mess that was made by sloppy waste handling in the past (this is called corrective action). This means that the agency, or sometimes a contractor, is required to do a RCRA Facility Assessment (RFA), which is a review of records and a walk through the site to look for areas where there may have been a release of some particular hazardous constituents (this refers to a specific list of chemicals used by RCRA).

These areas of potential contamination are called solid waste management units or SWMUs (pronounced "smoos"). These are all the places at a hazardous waste site where it is possible that hazardous chemicals (officially called hazardous constituents) have spilled or leaked on the ground. These would be places like loading docks, lagoons, burn pits (where chemicals were poured on the ground and burned), chemical and drum burial sites, and drum storage areas. Sometimes there are hundreds of these sites on the property of a single hazardous waste facility. The RFA usually results in the conclusion that some areas need no further action (usually because they were completely contained). Other areas may need further investigation.

This additional investigation is done through a RCRA Facility Investigation, or RFI which can involve several stages. You should look for an RFI workplan — laying out the tasks to be done as part of the RFI (very important!) — or an RFI Report, which gives the results of the investigation and involves mapping, sampling, and analyzing the waste management units, and can also involve groundwater investigation, stream water, or sediment sampling.

The next step in the process is a Corrective Measures Study (CMS) (again you may see a workplan for this study) which is supposed to analyze alternatives for dealing with the contamination.

The final stage is Corrective Measures Implementation (CMI) (there may be a plan and a report relating to this also) which is the actual carrying out of the corrective measures approved by the agency.

Corrective Action

- *Step one* RFA - RCRA Facility Assessment

- *Step two* RFI - RCRA Facility Investigation

- *Step three* CMS - Corrective Measures Study

- *Step four* CMI - Corrective Measures Implementation

Common Problems With Corrective Action

Environmental investigations many times follow an approach of: "if you don't look for it, you won't find it." This means that there may be areas that are contaminated but not identified as such. Often, employees or former employees have useful information about contamination in areas that are not being studied or investigated.

Other problems with corrective action plans include the use of high detection limits for the chemicals tested, not analyzing for all the right compounds, not sampling the full extent of contamination, taking too few samples, not sampling deep enough into the ground, and not sampling all media (water, groundwater, and stream sediments).

Hazardous Waste Facility Summary

Facility Name _____

Type of TSD _____ Permit Status _____ Number of SWMUs _____

Status of Cleanup _____

List of pollutants	Pollutant found in air, land, or water?	Pollutant amount	Groundwater monitoring for each pollutant?	Level of groundwater contamination for each pollutant?

RCRA Corrective
Action Summary

Site or facility name	RCRA Facility Assessment (RFA)	Number of SWMU's	RCRA Facility Investigation (RFI)	Corrective Measures Study (CMS)	Corrective Measures Implementation (CMI)

6. Hazardous Waste Generators

Step One: What companies are generating hazardous waste?
- Request a list of names and generator ID numbers for all hazardous waste generators in your study area.

Step Two: What kinds of hazardous waste are being generated?
- Request copies of hazardous waste generator annual reports for the last two years for all generators in your study area.
- Fill out the *Waste Generator Summary Form* (page 77) indicating the quantity and type of waste reported by each generator in your area.

Step Three: Are generators in compliance?
- Fill out the *Environmental Compliance Summary Form* (page 46).

Step Four: Mapping your information
- Map the location of all companies generating hazardous waste on your study area map.

Where to get the information
- Write to the state agency in charge of hazardous waste generators, or the regional office of the U.S. Environmental Protection Agency.

If a facility disposes of hazardous waste, treats it, or stores it for over a certain period of time (usually 90 days), then it becomes a TSD (treatment, storage, or disposal) facility and needs a RCRA permit to operate. The state agency responsible for hazardous waste should have a list of TSDs (TSDs are dealt with in section 5).

RCRA, the federal hazardous waste law, is designed to keep track of hazardous waste from "cradle to grave." This means companies that generate or initially create hazardous waste always have some responsibilities under the law for the waste they create.

Within your study area, you will probably find some companies that produce waste as a result of manufacturing, servicing, or cleaning activities. Each company must determine if its wastes are hazardous. If the wastes are hazardous, the company is a hazardous waste generator. Hazardous waste generators are required to meet a number of requirements designed to make both spills and illegal disposal of hazardous waste less likely. These requirements include: training workers that come in contact with hazardous waste in protective procedures; keeping detailed records; time limits on how long hazardous waste is stored before being sent to a licensed treatment or disposal facility; inspecting storage containers regularly and ensuring they do not leak; cleaning up spills immediately; labeling as hazardous, and dating all stored hazardous waste; and preparing and updating a contingency plan (how to respond in an emergency); making sure the waste goes to a proper facility for disposal; and making sure that all shipments of hazardous waste are accompanied by a special shipping paper, called a manifest.

Hazardous waste generators are required to register with the state (or federal EPA) and obtain an identification number. Usually, this number is required before a legal hauler or disposal site will accept hazardous waste. The registration will tell you what kind of hazardous waste the company expects to generate and how much. Generators are also required to file annual reports explaining how much of what types of hazardous waste they generated and how they disposed of it.

Hazardous waste generators are also required to describe their waste minimization efforts. Watch for activities that may reduce the waste but have other adverse environmental effects (for example, leaving cans of waste paint or solvents open to evaporate into the air, leaving less waste to be disposed of).

These requirements may apply differently to different size generators. Agency files on a hazardous waste generator will include the following:

- generator registration form (all hazardous waste generators must renew their certificate of registration annually)
- annual reports of how much waste was generated and where it was disposed
- summary of the company's efforts with regard to waste minimization or waste reduction.

The files may also contain notices of violation or other enforcement documents discussed in the introduction to this chapter.

Most state laws regulate three types of generators (names may vary for each state) by how much they produce:

- Large quantity or full quantity generators are those that produce more than 1,000 kilograms of hazardous waste in any one month (that's about 2,200 pounds). Examples of large quantity generators are large manufacturing plants.
- Small quantity generators produce between 100 kilograms and 1,000 kilograms in any one month (220 pounds to 2,200 pounds). Examples of small quantity generators might be small manufacturers, dry cleaners, printing shops, and pest control companies.
- Conditionally exempt or limited quantity generators are those which produce less than the 100 kilograms of hazardous waste per month (that's roughly half of a 55 gallon drum, or less than 220 pounds in any one month). Examples are the local gas station, body shop, or small dry cleaner.

When it comes to regulating the generators, some states are more stringent than others. In Kentucky, for example, the limited quantity generator (less than 100 kilograms per month) does not have to be registered with the state and can send its hazardous waste to solid waste landfills. The large and small quantity generators must be registered and have to follow federal and state laws in manifesting (filling out a form that tracks the waste from where it is made to where it is disposed) their hazardous waste to an approved hazardous waste facility. Some hazardous waste gets recycled and some is disposed of by incineration or landfilling in hazardous waste landfills.

Hazardous waste generators may be inspected by the regulating agency's waste inspectors once a year, or less if they only produce a small amount of waste. They may also be inspected more often. Kentucky, for example, has proposed inspecting full-quantity generators every six months.

In filling out the Environmental Compliance Summary Form, questions to keep in mind include: Have they submitted annual reports? Has the facility made progress on waste reduction from year to year? Have there been noncompliances or violations? Any that might have caused contamination, such as land disposal, failure to clean up a spill, or failure to maintain containers so as to prevent releases? How often have they been inspected?

Look carefully at generators who have big discrepancies from year-to-year, or plants that have been in production for many years but have only recently registered. A big decrease (or no reports for several years, when production was continuous) can mean illegal disposal. A big increase can mean spill cleanup or old dumpsite cleanup. Special consideration should be given to any generators who generated a particular waste only one time. This might be an indication of a spill or cleanup of an old dumping area. A common scenario is: someone buys a plant site, finds an area of contaminated soil, and digs up the dirt to ship off and dispose of. If it tests hazardous, the company is supposed to register as a hazardous waste generator, but they may not report the cleanup of the contaminated area. Because regulatory agencies are generally understaffed and overworked, they do not always have the opportunity to check up on whether there is site contamination that should have been reported. You will want to know whether there has been groundwater monitoring, whether the area around (and below) the cleanup area has been sampled, and what the results were, as well as how long ago the spill occurred.

Waste Generator Summary

Name of Industry _____

SIC Code _____

Type of waste	Annual total	Where does waste go?	Reported waste minimization activity

Comments:

7. Superfund Sites

Step One: Obtain a list of state and federal sites
- Request a list of the state and federally designated Superfund sites in your study area. (These sites may be called CERCLA, hazardous substance, or uncontrolled sites.) Ask for the lists by county, and alphabetically by company or site name. Request the location and address for each site in your study area.

Step Two: Examine site records
- Examine the files on each state or federal Superfund site in your study area.
- As you examine the files, fill out the Superfund Site Summary Form (page 83).
- Request a site map that shows the areas of contamination, areas where testing has been conducted, and the locations of groundwater monitoring wells.

Step Three: Are all sites in compliance with the law?
- Check the files for each state or federal Superfund site for consent decrees, agreed orders, 106 orders, and court enforcement actions. The federal EPA will need to be contacted for NPL sites.
- Fill out the Superfund Action Checklist (page 84) for each of the state and federal Superfund sites in your study area.

Step Four: Map all sites
- Map the location of the Superfund sites on your study area map.

Where to get the information
- Request the files and maps from the agency responsible for Superfund sites in your state, or the regional office of the U.S. Environmental Protection Agency. Depending on the procedures in your state and the length of the files and cost for photocopying, you may be able to get some files by mail, or you may have to go to the state agency to examine them.

In Bullitt County, Kentucky, three families were using a spring for their drinking water source. It was clean water bubbling out of the ground and had been used for years and years. What no one apparently realized was that the improper disposal of industrial waste near the spring had contaminated it with cancer-causing chemicals. One mistake at this site was the disposal, but a second one occurred when the government investigated the site, found the chemicals in the water and did not tell the families who were drinking the water. This and similar stories provide evidence that citizens need to be involved in what is going on in their community. Do not assume that because your community does not have a famous Superfund site such as New York's "Love Canal" or Kentucky's "Valley of the Drums" that you are not at risk from toxic chemical contamination.

Superfund sites are places where hazardous wastes were dumped before November 1980 (when RCRA hazardous waste laws became effective), and some hazardous waste sites where owners are bankrupt or unwilling to comply with the hazardous waste laws. Many sites are contaminated with chemicals as bad as (or the same as) those at hazardous waste sites. The official Superfund law is called the Comprehensive Environmental Response, Compensation, and Liability Act or CERCLA (see Appendix E).

The Superfund program works from the hazardous substance list. This is a different, longer list, than the RCRA hazardous waste list. One simple example is copper, which is not a hazardous waste, but is considered a hazardous substance on the Superfund list because it can wipe out fish and wildlife if too much gets into a stream.

There is a list of Superfund sites for every state. There are usually at least two categories of sites. One category consists of sites considered to be a national priority and are on the federal National Priorities List (NPL). The second category is state sites that do not, or do not yet, rank as a national priority. These may be called something other than "Superfund" sites, such as "uncontrolled sites," "abandoned sites," or "hazardous substance sites." They should be on a list called the CERCLIS (Comprehensive Environmental Response, Compensation and Liability Inventory System list). There is a specific ranking process that sites go through for the NPL. Classifying these sites into two kinds can be misleading, since in some cases there are sites on the state list much worse environmentally than sites on the federal list. Examples of state listed sites not on the NPL include those being evaluated for listing and sites where only a few people are exposed to contaminants.

Many sites on state Superfund lists are simply old dumpsites where it is unknown exactly what chemicals were dumped. These sites may include everything from old dumps to areas behind factories where chemicals were poured on the ground in the days before there were any laws, to places where chemicals were spilled as a result of a wreck, or even places where contaminated oil was sprayed on roads to prevent dust from blowing.

The federal Superfund provides two ways sites can be addressed. The "Superfund sites" we normally think of are remedial action sites. These are sites that have been evaluated and scored for how bad they are, and have made it on the list of the worst sites in the country (NPL). EPA can also use the Superfund to conduct emergency actions (removing wastes that might explode, for example) called removal actions, where just enough is done to address the temporary threat of disaster.

State law requirements vary widely as to what kind of sites have to be cleaned up, how and how well they have to be cleaned up, and who is responsible for cleaning them up. Private parties are allowed to use the Superfund law to clean up sites and then sue those responsible for putting the waste there for the money, but, other than that, the ability to get sites cleaned up depends on government action and varies widely across the country.

It is also important to note here that you may have problem sites in your community that have not yet been discovered by the authorities. Your concern about them is valid without regard to any national ranking. The advantage of federal ranking is that NPL sites are in line for federal cleanup money, but just because sites in your community are not on the NPL does not mean they do not pose serious threats. The state Superfund list may overlap with other lists like the hazardous waste site list, solid waste site list, and underground storage tank list. For example, many Superfund sites are old landfills leaking chemicals regulated under the Superfund law.

Once you know where the Superfund sites are in your study area, and what contaminants are in the air, soil, water and groundwater, the question is — what has the government or responsible parties (those who made the site and should clean it up) done about the site? Have the sites in your community been properly investigated? Have requirements placed upon the responsible parties been satisfied?

Every site listed in your community should have a file detailing what action has been taken there. There are many levels of action possible, from "none" to "cleaned up." The important points here are: What pollutants were dumped at the site? Are those pollutants confined to the site? Are people being exposed to them through evaporation into the air, contact with the soil, or migration of contaminants into the ground or surface water? Is anything being done to clean up the site? You should be aware that sites are still being discovered where houses have been built on top of the old disposal site and where people nearby are using untested wells for their drinking water.

Review the general files for your area, at least for some time back for citizen complaints (complaints made to the agency about illegal dumping, odors, dead fish, discolored streams, or other suspicious activity,) and see what follow-up investigation has been done by the agency. In addition, there should be files where reports of chemical spills or releases (or overflows of wastewater, or malfunctions that cause releases into the air) are kept. You will want to review these for companies' records of spills and releases. You should also ask for the list of "reportable quantities" of chemicals in your state. This is the list that sets forth the amount of a chemical that has to be reported (if someone spills less than that amount, they don't have to report it). For example, under federal law, the reportable quantity for PCBs is one pound. That doesn't sound like much, but if a company spills 10,000 pounds of oil containing 50 parts per million PCBs, that's only a half pound of pure PCBs, so they don't have to report the PCB spill. Find out how your state applies reportable quantities to mixtures, too.

Your state will have a long list of sites that have some potential for contamination (in Kentucky it is about 550). These are sometimes called "uncontrolled sites" (by comparison, say, to a hazardous waste landfill, which is supposedly controlled). At all of these sites a Preliminary Assessment/Site Investigation (PA/SI) is performed (sometimes just a PA is done, though most times, the two are done together). The federal Office of Technology Assessment has estimated that for every site we know about, there are 12 more we do not know about.

The PA/SI consists of examining available state records about the site, and a brief "look-see" by an inspector at the site conditions and surroundings. Based on this information, the site is "scored" according to what is called the Hazard Ranking System (HRS) which takes into account such things as the amount and toxicity of the materials disposed at the site, the number of people living close by, nearby drinking water sources, and proximity to streams. Sites that score 28.5 or greater on the HRS2 (the latest version of the HRS) are proposed by the federal government for listing on the National Priorities List. At that time a notice is published in the Federal Register and interested parties (like the companies who are on the hook) can challenge EPA's decision. If the listing becomes final, then the site is eligible to be cleaned up with money from the Superfund. Public money is not used unless the responsible parties cannot be made to pay for a cleanup.

Once a site is listed on the NPL, it goes through a Remedial Investigation (RI). This is often done together with the next step, which is called the Feasibility Study (FS). In general the Remedial Investigation is supposed to determine what kinds of chemicals are present at the site, and how contaminated the land, streams, groundwater, and air are. The Feasibility Study is supposed to evaluate the different choices (called Remedial Alternatives) that might be made to clean up the site (or more often, close up the site so nothing more is supposed to leak into the environment). Reports of the Remedial Investigation and Feasibility Study are prepared. Together, these are sometimes called the RI/FS Report (or RI/FS for short). When the RI/FS is done, it, together with a "proposed plan" for cleanup, is put out for public comment (a newspaper advertisement is published and a public hearing scheduled). After the public comment period is over, the EPA issues a Record of Decision (ROD) which is the EPA's final decision about what to do at the site.

Perhaps the most important thing to keep in mind for these remedial action Superfund sites is that they are exempt from many state law requirements that would apply to all other sites in the state. Instead of going through the state's permitting process, EPA is required to list and apply all the appropriate environmental requirements (these are called ARARs) in the Record of Decision (ROD) that it writes describing the remedy. Then those standards listed by the EPA (for example, the creek next to the site should not be polluted in excess of 5 parts per billion ethylene dichloride — see Chapter 8 for more detail on chemicals and standards) in the ROD will be the ones used to determine whether the remedy is working, or whether EPA or the responsible parties will have to go back and do further cleanup. In recent years, some states, including Kentucky, have sued EPA for not including strict enough requirements. In other words, the states have argued that EPA was allowing for or authorizing remedies that illegally pollute the environment.

You might think that's all there is to it — but there is more. Next, a Remedial Design, which is the detailed design of the remedy, is prepared. Naturally, there is a Remedial Design Report (RD report). Then there is the Remedial Action Plan (RA). Of course, throughout the process there are workplans (like the RI/FS workplan, or the RD/RA workplan), comments from the state to the Federal EPA, or from the state and the Federal EPA to the contractor. The contractor may work either for the EPA or for the companies who are paying for the cleanup (potentially responsible parties—PRPs—or—RPs—responsible parties).

Help is available to you in understanding and interpreting all the reports you read through. Your group can apply for a technical assistance grant of up to $75,000 from EPA. This grant allows citizens' groups dealing with a federal Superfund site to hire its own expert to read all the fine print and then summarize it for you.

If there is a federal Superfund site in your study area, you will need to check the records to see what stage of the process the site is in. If the site is a removal site (removal means an initial response action at a site which is limited to $2 million dollars and must be completed in 12 months), there may be some plan or report available regarding the removal. If the site is a remedial action site (NPL or National Priorities List), it will go through the following process:

Remedial Action Site Process

PA/SI - Preliminary Assessment/Site Investigation
HRS - Hazard Ranking System
Proposed NPL - National Priorities List
Final NPL - National Priorities List
RI/FS - Remedial Investigation/Feasibility Study
ROD - Record of Decision
RD/RA - Remedial Design/Remedial Action

Under Superfund, everyone who produced, hauled, touched, owned the site, or brokered the waste is potentially responsible for the costs of cleanup. If a site proves an immediate danger, EPA has the authority to issue orders to responsible parties, requiring them to engage in cleanup activity or be subject to three times the cost of cleanup and penalties (section 106 orders). In addition, many companies voluntarily agree to pay for Superfund investigations and cleanups, because they think they can do it cheaper, or with less waste, or to have more control over what remedy is selected and how it is implemented. This responsibility is assumed by companies by means of a "consent decree." A consent decree is a court judgment, signed by the judge (legally called entered) not requiring a trial because the parties agree to it. Section 106 Orders or consent decrees can relate to all or part of a remedial action. If they object to the decree, citizens, local groups, or local governments not party to the decree may ask the court for the right to intervene in the consent decree action, and place their objections before the court for a decision.

Superfund Site Summary

Site name _____

Location _____

Contaminants found	Where? Soil(S) Groundwater(GW) Surfacewater(SW)	Concentration or amount of contamination

Comments:

Superfund Action Checklist

Check off with a yes or no and enter the date where possible for each of the steps in the Superfund process. See text for explanation of Steps.

	Next action required to be taken	Consent Decrees/106 Orders/Court Orders	Remedial Action Plan	Remedial Design Report	Record of Decision	Feasibility Study	Remedial Investigation	NPL Final	NPL Proposed	HRS Score	PA/SI	Site name

8. Solid Waste Sites

Step One: Identifying solid waste sites in your study area
- Write for a list of all permitted solid waste facilities in your area including landfills, landfarming sites, and other solid waste disposal sites.

Step Two: Review files and organize information
- Review the files for all the solid waste landfills in your study area. As you review the files, fill out the *Landfill Summary Form* (page 92).
- Make a list of the different sources for the waste at each landfill site. Fill out the *Waste Sources and Types Form* (page 93). On the form, note the chemicals coming to the landfill in industrial waste.
- Review the files for all other solid waste sites with permits in your study area. Fill out the *Solid Waste Sites Form* (page 94).
- See if there are any registered or permitted landfarming facilities in your study area. For each permitted landfarming facility, determine what the sludge is tested for, whether there is groundwater monitoring, soil monitoring, and what provisions there are to limit surface runoff. (For more information on figuring out what contaminants might be in the sludge, see Chapter 7 on sewage treatment plants.)
- If there are no permitted landfarming facilities in your study area, ask the local sewage treatment plant manager what they do with the sludge generated at the plant.

Step Three: Are permit limits and conditions being met?
- Complete the *Environmental Compliance Summary Form* (page 46) and the Solid Waste Sites Form (page 94) for each solid waste site or facility, permitted, registered or for which there is a file.
- Some regulatory agencies maintain what they call a "general file" for a particular area like a county. Look at the file for records of complaints about or inspections of solid waste facilities that do not specifically require a permit.

Step Four: Map all solid waste facilities
- Map the location of each solid waste facility and site on your study area map.

Where to get the information
- Most of the files will be available from the state agency responsible for solid waste. In some states, landfarming, sludges, and lagoons are regulated by the state agency responsible for water; in this case, you will have to deal with both the solid waste and the water agencies to complete this activity. Because of their length, files may not be available by mail; you may have to go to the agency (or agencies) to examine them.

What is solid waste? Think of it as anything (including liquids or gases in containers) a person throws away that is not officially hazardous waste. That is not a regulatory definition. It is a common-sense definition. A solid waste site is then any site where someone has thrown away some solid waste. Many states have a problem with improper and illegal disposal of solid waste. In one Kentucky county the top elected official said he had counted 112 illegal roadside dumps. A local group took on the task of doing an inventory and discovered that the county actually had over 400 illegal dumps on roadsides and stream banks.

The type of solid waste facility that usually comes to mind first is the county dump or municipal landfill. If you have a solid waste landfill in your community, find out what is going into it, what's coming out of it, and how good the plans for the future are (including who's going to take care of it after it closes). However, there are many other types of solid waste sites or facilities. Essentially, EPA has the job of deciding which wastes are dangerous enough to be regulated as hazardous wastes from "cradle to grave." In 1980 the federal hazardous waste law, RCRA, was passed (see section 5, Hazardous Wastes). This law required much of what was called solid waste to be treated as hazardous waste. In most states everything else falls into a lesser regulated category of nonhazardous solid waste. Besides landfills, other types of solid waste facilities that are of interest in determining the health of the environment are:

- Waste storage areas, like waste piles
- Recycling or materials recovery facilities (MRF)
- Waste incinerators, or electric boilers that burn waste for fuel
- Pits, ponds, and lagoons, for wastewater treatment or settling
- Garbage transfer stations
- Landfills or pits for utility fly ash, bottom ash, and scrubber water lagoons
- Plants that process garbage into Refuse Derived Fuel (RDF)
- Mining and drilling wastes
- Utility fly ash ponds and other special waste facilities
- Roadside, stream bank, sinkhole, or other open dumps
- Old spill sites or contaminated dump sites (also see section 7 on Superfund)
- Landfarming sites where municipal and industrial wastewater treatment sludges are spread on the ground

Landfills

Many people are concerned about landfills. In the old days, people buried their trash and figured it would just go back to dirt (what we now call "biodegrade"). But in the old days they didn't have plastics (which decay very slowly or not at all), and they didn't throw away so many batteries, paints, chemicals, and pesticides which can get in the groundwater and poison people and the environment. Even after we started using (and throwing away) large quantities of these

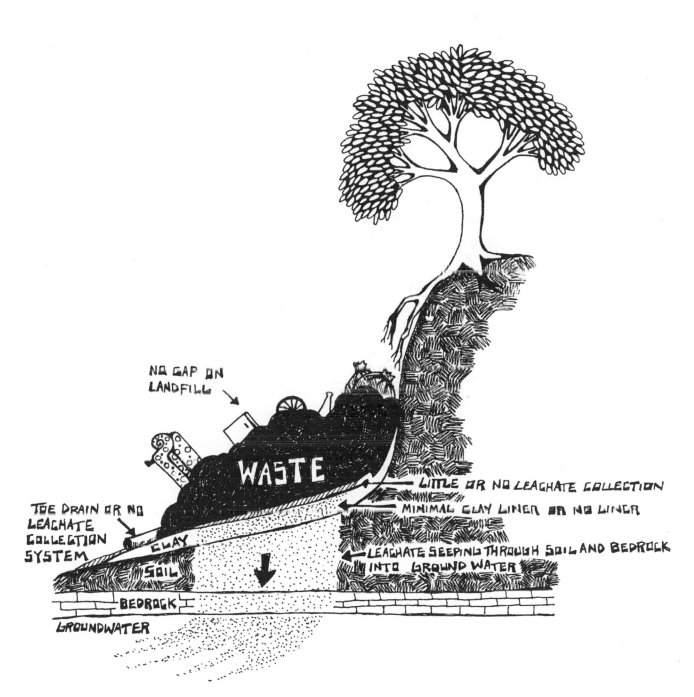

Figure 5.6 - Old-Fashioned Landfill

toxic chemicals, we continued to bury our trash in holes in the ground (see Figure 5.6). When it rains, water gets in through the soil, seeps through the buried trash and forms a toxic garbage juice called leachate (pronounced leech-ate). The garbage juice keeps moving down through the soil until it hits the groundwater, contaminates it, and flows with it until it hits somebody's well, a spring, a creek, or a river.

A significant percentage of the sites on the Superfund list are old garbage dumps. Modern landfills are supposed to be designed like a big underground baggie that will seal up the waste and not let water in. The design features are discussed below. The problem according to EPA (*Federal Register* February 5, 1981, July 26, 1982, May 26, 1981) is that even the best landfills are doomed to leak. Just as the forces of nature eventually crack the sidewalk, landfills are continually attacked by those forces and will eventually leak. Better built landfills with good leachate collection systems will last longer and may cause fewer problems over the long haul. However, we still need to reuse, recycle, and reduce our waste and get the toxics out of the waste stream (what we throw away). And we need to make sure that the landfills we do have will be taken care of—for generations.

The elements of a landfill (see Figure 5.7) are the liner, leachate collection system, and cap. The liner is a layer underneath the garbage, which is supposed to keep the leachate from seeping out. The leachate collection system is a network of pipes with holes in them in a sand or gravel layer. It is supposed to collect the leachate as it reaches the bottom of the landfill and carry it into a tank. The leachate is then taken from the tank, treated and discharged to a stream, or hauled to a sewage treatment plant. The final cap, or cover, is supposed to prevent water from penetrating into the buried waste. Since the waste may settle over time, rigid materials like concrete might crack. For this and other reasons, the best cap material appears to be grass and soil on top of denser layers like clay and plastic, with a sand or gravel drainage layer in between. It is important to keep grass on top. If there are no plants, erosion is likely to wear through the cap. However, the grass must be carefully maintained. If trees are allowed to grow on the cap, their roots may eventually penetrate into the buried garbage and get into the landfill.

Landfills are also usually required to have groundwater monitoring systems to detect pollutants seeping into the groundwater around the landfill. If contamination above a certain level is discovered, most states require that a system be installed for cleaning up (or at least slowing down) the groundwater contamination.

Methane gas must also be monitored at the landfill. Methane gas is produced as a result of biodegradation (breaking down) of the waste by bacteria, and can cause disastrous landfill fires, or even explosions if it seeps into buildings on or near the landfill. Methane control measures or remediation can also be required. This can involve anything from burning off the methane to collecting it for use as an energy source.

Most landfills are required to obtain permits from the state agency responsible for solid waste. The files on a landfill are likely to be several feet thick, and will take quite a while to go through, especially if it is an old landfill dating back to the 1960s when many states started to keep records and require some kind of permit for so-called "sanitary landfills." If you have time, read through the entire file. But if you're short of time, there are specific things you will want to seek out.

- Does the site have groundwater monitoring?
- What tests are run on the groundwater samples? What are the results?
- Has the state raised any questions about the adequacy of the groundwater monitoring system? (If you have a geologist or hydrogeologist in your group or teaching at a nearby high school or college, you may want an independent assessment of the groundwater plan.)
- If there is contamination, or if there is no groundwater monitoring, have nearby wells or springs been tested?

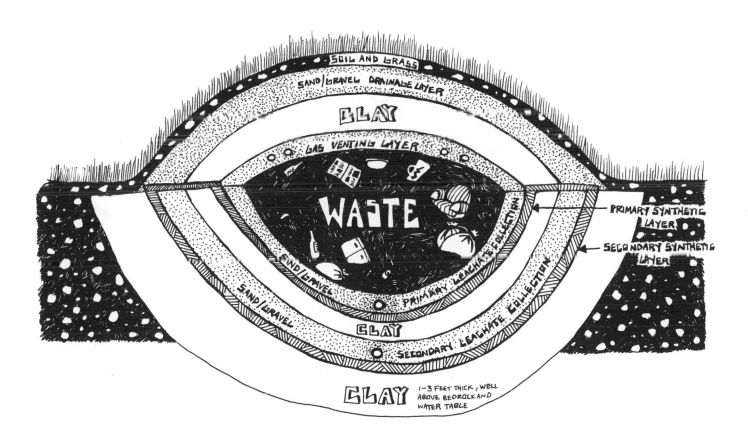

Figure 5.7 - Anatomy of a Modern Landfill

- How is rainwater managed at the site?
- Are diversion ditches (to keep water out of the landfill) in place and well maintained?
- Are there reports of leachate outbreaks at the site?
- What is done with the leachate generated at the site?
- What type of liner does the landfill have?
- What types of waste does the landfill take? Is it just waste from home pickup, or industrial waste?
- What types of industrial waste? Is there a testing program for the industrial waste? How many chemicals are they required to test for?

Answering the questions listed above will give you a better understanding of potential problems at the landfill.

A landfill's compliance with its permit may say little about its ability to protect the environment. For example, some states have very weak landfill construction regulations. Other states have strong regulations for new landfills, but sometimes new landfill regulations grandfather in the old landfills, thus allowing them to continue operating for years under old standards.

One landfill in Kentucky had a requirement that it collect the leachate (see Figure 5.6 for description) at the toe of the landfill and treat it in a wastewater treatment plant. The only problem was the landfill never seemed to produce any leachate. The landfill had no liner so the leachate was going out the bottom and into the groundwater. The landfill was not technically considered in violation of regulations, but neither was it protecting the environment from contaminants in the waste.

Information about the landfill and the types of waste it takes can be summarized on the *Landfill Summary Form* and *Waste Sources and Types Form*. The group will need to examine the files for answers to these questions: What do the permit or design documents say about the groundwater monitoring system? What type of liner (if any) does the landfill have? How many acres are permitted? How many acres are planned to be filled? Are there applications for expansions on file? Given current and proposed sources of waste, what is the remaining life of the landfill? What type of cap is required? What is the amount of the bond, and what does it cover? What kinds of chemicals are being dumped at the landfill in industrial waste?

Bonds are often required before a landfill permit is issued. The bond is established to protect the state (taxpayer) in the event the operator goes bankrupt or walks away from the site. It should be enough to properly close the site as provided by law. Bonds may also be required for post closure activities. In many states, this is the 30 or more years of groundwater monitoring and other care that may be required after the landfill closes. Some states also require a remedial action bond to clean up the water if and when it is contaminated.

Landfarming

Landfarming is an odd term for a rather odd practice. It does not involve farming land at all, but disposing of contaminated sludge by spreading it on the land. The sludges can come from wastewater treatment plants, drinking water plants, or food processing or manufacturing plants. The hope is that the toxic heavy metals and other contaminants in the sludge will be minimal and will bind to the clay in the soil and do no harm. Landfarming is regulated differently in each state.

Generally, sludges are classified based on the amount of certain metals in them. Those with the most metals are usually required to have a permit. The permit should specify groundwater monitoring (not required for all kinds of sludges) to determine if the practice is polluting the groundwater. It should also specify surface runoff controls and surface water monitoring (sampling nearby streams, lakes, or rivers), and periodic testing of levels of contamination in the soil. The use of this land should also be controlled. For example, vegetables should not be grown on landfarming areas.

Other Solid Waste Sites

Solid waste sites are the ones most likely to be ignored or unregulated in your area. These sites include landfills, landfarming sites (where sewage or other sludge is spread), junkyards, tire piles, recycling centers, and garbage transfer stations. Federal guidelines are issued for some of those sites, but they are generally regulated at the state and/or local level.

Garbage transfer stations are places where small garbage trucks transfer garbage to larger trucks. The larger trucks haul it to landfills. Transfer stations may or may not be regulated in your state. One concern is that "cocktailing" of waste can go on at these sites. Cocktailing is the illegal mixing of hazardous waste with the garbage as it is compacted into the larger trucks.

Lagoons

Lagoons are often used to treat waste. They are generally more poorly regulated than other types of facilities, and are serious potential sources of groundwater contamination. It is not always clear which agency regulates lagoons. Sometimes the water agency permits the discharge and approves the design, but does not perform an in-depth evaluation, except to look at capacity or size. The waste agency may or may not regulate the liner and other design needs based upon what is in the lagoon.

Before 1980, there was no such thing (legally) as "hazardous waste," and solid waste facilities handled wastes that are today considered hazardous. Laws and regulations governing solid waste sites differ from state to state. From your Step One and Step Two activities you should have a list of all waste facilities permitted or registered. Some solid waste facilities do not require either. In Chapter 9 we offer suggestions of how to get more information on the unpermitted sites.

Landfill Summary

Landfill Name _____

Location _____

Bond amount _____ Bond covers _____ Closure _____ Post Closure _____ Remedial Action

Permit status _____ New _____ Expansion _____ Existing _____ Expired _____ Application pending

Projected remaining life of landfill _____ Size: acres permitted _____ acres planned _____

Type of liner _____ Type of cap _____

Groundwater Monitoring ☐ Yes ☐ No Total number of monitoring wells: upgradient _____ downgradient _____

Upgradient well concentrations

Well Number	Concentration

Highest downgradient well concentration

Well number	Concentration

What's monitored

Waste Sources and Types

Landfill name _____

Location _____

Total tons per month _____

Type of waste	Source of waste	Amount of waste (tons per month)

Solid Waste Sites (except landfills)

Site name and type	Permit status Current Expired Revoked Not required	Testing on site Y/N				Known contaminants (by medium)	Permit limits (by medium)
		surface water	groundwater	soil	sediment		

9. Mining Sites and Facilities

Step One: Who is mining and what are they mining?
- Request a list of all sites and companies with active mining permits for both deep mining and strip (surface) mining in your study area.
- Request a list of all sites and companies in your study area that are not currently active but were issued permits and operated after the 1977 federal strip mining act took effect (and thus were required by federal law to reclaim the land).
- Request a list of all abandoned mined land sites (and companies responsible for them) in your study area. These are the ones that operated before the federal strip mining act took effect.

Step Two: What pollutants are coming from the mining sites?
- Review the files for each mine site that has a permit in your study area.
- Review the files for each abandoned mined site in your study area.
- As you review the files, fill out the *Mining Sites Summary Form* (page 98).

Step Three: Are all mining operations in compliance?
- Review the files on each of the mining facilities that you listed in Step One. Review the compliance record of each of the sites and compare the violations cited by the state agency with what was cited by the federal agency.
- Fill out the *Mining Compliance Summary Form* (page 99).

Step Four: Map all mining sites and facilities
- Map the locations of all of the above on your study area map.

Where to get the information
- Contact the state or federal agency in charge of mining in your state. Different agencies may be responsible for hardrock mining, deep mining, surface mining, air, water, or blasting on a particular site. If the files are too bulky, or too expensive to photocopy, you may have to go to the agencies to examine them. It will be very helpful to contact citizen groups that work on mining issues. These include the Mineral Policy Center (hardrock mining), Citizens Coal Council, and the National Coal Project of the Kentucky Resources Council (see Appendix A for addresses).

This section will be of interest primarily if you are in a major mining area, such as a copper mining, coal mining, or phosphate mining area. There can also be locally significant quarrying activities, such as for limestone. Some of these sites may show up in your other lists. For example, these sites may also have a water or air permit for discharging pollutants. Quarries and strip mines are sometimes used for landfills. Since these activities are major land disturbing activities, primary concerns are how much land has been disturbed, how much is likely to be disturbed, and how is it being reclaimed, and effects on the water from materials washing into it through runoff, or groundwater sources being destroyed through digging and earth moving.

Mining activities in many areas are destroying prime agricultural land, damaging private property through subsidence (where the surface falls into the mined area below), and landslides impairing the visual quality of areas, destroying wetlands, and degrading the quality and quantity of both surface water and groundwater. More than 50% of our valuable wetlands nationwide have been destroyed by mining, agriculture, and other practices. These are areas that provide valuable habitat for plants and animals, hold water that would otherwise cause downstream flooding, release that water to the streams over a period of time, and remove pollutants from the water before it enters the stream.

Deep mine sites, especially old and abandoned sites, can be significant sources for acid mine drainage (this is the acid water that runs from these sites and turns streams orange and kills all or most of the life in the streams).

Under federal surface mining laws (see Appendix E), all pre-1977 surface mines are required to be inventoried under the Abandoned Mined Lands (AML) program. If they have not been properly reclaimed, federal money is available for reclamation. In certain cases, post 1977 abandoned mines may be eligible for the AML program

There are four major pollutants associated with coal mining operations: iron (total and total recoverable), manganese (total), total suspended solids, and pH (alkalinity and acidity).

Iron Too much iron in a stream can destroy the aquatic life. Check your state's water discharge permit for the total and total recoverable iron discharge limits.

Manganese This is another metal commonly found in the runoff of mine sites. Check your state's water discharge permit for the discharge limits.

Suspended solids This is one of the most persistent problems with coal and other mining operations. Because mining is a land-disturbing activity, it exposes soil to rain. Rainwater running off mined sites can have 1,000 times greater sediment load than water running off an unmined site. Suspended solids can adversely affect aquatic life, increase the cost of drinking water treatment, and particles can also carry other pollutants such as heavy metals.

pH This is a measure of how acid a liquid is. Water from a mine should be between a pH of 6 and 9. A pH of 7 is considered neutral, with 1 being most acidic and 14 being most alkaline.

Water discharge permits associated with these mine sites usually have limits on these four pollutants. Other pollutants associated with coal mining include arsenic and aluminum. Other types of mining operations have other types of pollutants associated with them, such as heavy metals. Contaminants not properly regulated include waste oil drained and dumped on mining sites and solvents from equipment cleaning and repair.

The post-mining land use determines what type of reclamation is required on a site. Sites have to be returned to approximate original contour (AOC) unless an alternate post- mining land use plan is requested and approved. One example of a post-mining use is wildlife habitat. In this case, a plan has to be submitted for what is to be planted, and where ponds, or other areas that may benefit wildlife will be left or created.

Bonds have to be provided by a mining company to cover reclamation costs in the event the company goes bankrupt or walks away without reclaiming the site. In Kentucky and other coal states, these bonds have often proved to be too little to cover reclamation. This problem is the result of low bond calculations and lack of enforcement.

For a surface mine, the most important issues relating to environmental protection are whether the mine site is discharging pollutants to the water, whether it is destroying or disturbing a zone that is important for groundwater flow, disposal of excess spoil and overburden in large fills (long-term stability and public safety issues), and how well the site is being reclaimed. For deep mines, discharges of water from the mine, subsidence, disposal of coal refuse in impoundments, and safety issues are the most critical. A review of the compliance history will help determine if the mining company is attempting to obey the law. When there is both state and federal oversight, a comparison between the two agencies' activities on the site may provide insight into the state's willingness to regulate this industry.

Hardrock mining and mining not covered by the surface mining laws is under considerable discussion, especially related to public lands in the west. For these issues contact a local group working on them, or the Mineral Policy Center (see Appendix A).

Mining Sites Summary

Site name	Permitted or abandoned	Total acres/ acres mined	Post-mining land use (after reclamation)	Bond amount per acre	Priority for reclamation (abandoned sites)

Mining Compliance Summary

Mine or facility name	Facility type	No. of environmental violations cited by state	No. of environmental violations cited by federal government	No. of safety violations cited by state	No. of safety violations cited by federal government

10. Oil and Natural Gas Facilities

Step One: Obtain a list of oil and gas facilities
- Determine whether you have any pipelines running through your area. Find out who owns the pipelines. Request a list of transmission facilities including pipeline compressor stations, and pipeline valve and meter stations.
- Determine whether your study area is in an oil and natural gas field. You can do this by looking at a topographic map or asking local officials or citizens.
- If you are in an oil and natural gas field, request a list of all the oil and gas facilities operating in your study area. This list should include oil and gas production wells, oil and brine water separators, and reinjection well operations.

Step Two: Obtain all permits relating to oil and gas facilities
- Check for water discharge permits and hazardous waste generator information.
- Find out what kind of testing has been done at oil and gas well drilling sites, service areas, or compressor stations.

Step Three: Checking compliance
- Examine the files of all the oil and natural gas companies in your study area that you listed in Steps One and Two. Determine which have been cited for violations or have had enforcement actions taken against them for other than water discharge violations. Ask the cause for taking the enforcement action and the penalty.
- Fill out the *Environmental Compliance Summary Form* (page 46).
- Request information on unplugged oil and gas wells that have been abandoned. These wells can be sources of groundwater contamination.

Step Four: Map all facilities in your study area
- Map the locations of all oil and gas facilities on your study area map. Include the unplugged well locations described in Step Three.

Where to get the information
- For a list of oil and gas facilities or abandoned oil and gas wells in your study area, write to the state environmental protection agency (the division that regulates oil and gas), or the regional office of the U.S. Environmental Protection Agency. In some states, the oil and gas regulatory group is outside the environmental protection agency. You can contact the oil and gas companies directly to request a complete listing of their transmission facilities (compressor facilities, valve and meter stations, etc.). To question whether a facility has a proper water discharge permit, contact the state agency responsible for water pollution control.

This section is generally about oil and natural gas production and transmission facilities. Examples of these facilities are oil and gas production wells, oil and gas field reinjection wells (for reinjecting the brine water that was pumped up with the oil), abandoned wells, oil and brine separator facilities, drilling pits, gas pipeline compressor stations, gas pipeline cleanouts, and valve and meter stations. Refineries and other types of facilities are covered in the air, water, and groundwater sections of this manual.

PCBs (polychlorinated biphenyls) are chemicals that cause environmental and human health problems. They have been banned by the U.S. Environmental Protection Agency (for all except some closed system uses) for many years, but there are areas that are seriously contaminated with PCBs. For example, there is a farm in Kentucky that was contaminated with PCBs from runoff from a natural gas compressor station next to the farm. When animals such as cows eat grass contaminated with PCBs, it tends to collect in their fatty tissue. The milk and the meat become contaminated. Some cows were found with such high levels of PCBs in their fatty tissue that they would have to be classified as PCB waste if they died.

Many natural gas pipelines used PCBs (polychlorinated biphenyls) over the years. These chemicals are toxic and very persistent in the environment. You should determine whether PCBs and organic chemicals have been tested for at compressor stations or other facilities related to pipelines.

In Kentucky's oil fields there are a number of streams that are dead from the high levels of brine or chlorides (salt) that are discharged into the streams from the oil/water separators at oil wells. Some wells are pumping a half a barrel of oil a day and 10 barrels of brine. The discharge of this brine water, along with oil spills and erosion from the roads and oil well sites, causes serious stream pollution.

Oil and gas drilling operations have been notorious for operating outside of the law. Wildcat drillers go around drilling wells without permits or concern for the environmental effects of their activity. There is improper closing or plugging of drilled wells when they stop producing or go dry. The small bonds that are paid before drilling are forfeited to the state. There may not be enough money in the bond for the state to properly plug and secure the well. This varies considerably from state to state so the group will need to review the adequacy of the law in their state.

Most oil and gas facilities related to drilling have a brine discharge associated with them. Comparing the list of water dischargers to the oil and gas facilities in your area will give you an opportunity to be sure each facility has a valid permit. You cannot be sure that the regulatory agencies are cross checking lists between agencies. If the facility does not have a permit, it may have an illegal discharge, or it may not produce any discharge at all. You may want to see if there are any files that indicate whether these sites have ever been inspected for discharges, and alert the agency to their existence, if they have not been (also see Chapter 9 — Expanding What Agencies Know).

Other problems have shown up at oil and gas drilling facilities. Radioactive material that occurs naturally below the ground can be brought to the surface by the drilling and become a health and environmental threat. This went on for years in Martha's oil field in Kentucky without testing or action taken. According to an Associated Press report a cleanup will be required of mercury contamination at abandoned oil and gas drilling sites in the west. Other issues that have come up in recent years include road building, erosion, contamination of water supplies, unplugged abandoned wells, and a need for reclamation of drilling sites.

11. Underground Storage Tanks (UST)

Step One: Who has underground storage tanks?
- Obtain a list of all the registered underground storage tanks in your study area.

Step Two: Compile basic information on each underground storage tank
- Fill out all except the last column on the *UST Summary Form* (page 105).

Step Three: Are all tanks in compliance?
- Identify which underground storage tank (UST) facilities have received notices of violation or been the subject of enforcement and why.
- Fill out the last column on the *UST Summary Form* (page 105) that you began filling out in Step Two.

Step Four: Map the locations of all tanks
- Map the locations of all facilities with underground storage tanks on your study area map.

Where to get the information
- Write the state environmental protection agency (the department responsible for underground storage tanks). This program may be in the water quality section, groundwater section, or waste management. The Regional EPA manages this program in their groundwater section and may be contacted for information if you are not successful at the state level.

If there is a classic example of the old adage "out of sight, out of mind," it is the story of the underground storage tank. How convenient and seemingly safe it is to take a tank full of gasoline and bury it in the ground; put a pump on it and pump up what you need, when you need it. It seemed like such a good idea that we buried thousands and thousands of tanks all over the place. Now tanks buried in the great burying spree of 20 to 30 years ago are aging and showing signs of wear. The tanks are rusting and gasoline, diesel fuel, and oil are seeping into our drinking water.

The little community of Custer, Kentucky, learned this the hard way. In Custer, everybody used well water. Most of the well water came from a shallow aquifer. Residents began reporting odors when they ran water in their kitchens or bathrooms. Testing revealed that the water was contaminated with gasoline from a leaking underground storage tank at the corner gas station. Families in Custer had been drinking cancer-causing chemicals from gasoline in their water for many years.

There are new laws that require tanks to be registered, tested, and removed from service if they are of a certain age or cannot pass a pressure test (this is a test which pressurizes the underground storage tank and pipes leading to the gas pumps to reveal leaks).

The EPA has estimated that 25% of the tens of thousands of underground storage tanks have leaked gasoline, diesel fuel, or oil into the ground. Probably most of those have also contaminated the groundwater. The most likely contaminants are benzene, toluene, ethyl benzene, xylene, and lead. The first four together are sometimes referred to as BTEX. UST sites of immediate concern are those in areas where people use groundwater for drinking.

There are a number of reasons for an enforcement action to be taken against an owner of a UST. They may have failed to register their tanks, to pressure-test their system, to clean up contaminated soil properly, or to monitor groundwater after contamination was found.

The cleanup standards for contaminated sites vary from state to state. Many tanks belong to Mom and Pop stores (many tanks were sold to them by the big oil companies for $1 just before the UST laws came into effect). Because of this, some state programs have been adopted to help them pay for cleaning up the contamination, and some states have put in place very weak standards so these facilities would not have to clean up.

UST Summary

UST facility	Number of tanks	Age of oldest tank	Known contamination of soil (list chemicals)	Level of contamination left in soil	Groundwater monitoring (list chemicals)	Under enforcement

12. Dams and Floodplains

Step One: Are there dams and floodplains in the study area?
- Request a list of all the regulated dams in your study area.

Step Two: What permits have been issued for dams and floodplain filling?
- Request a list of all floodplain construction and filling permits issued in your study area. Ask if the Department of Transportation permits are included on the list, and if not, where that list might be obtained.
- Ask for any floodplain maps that have been done for your study area.
- Request maps of the areas below the dam that would be flooded if a high-hazard dam breaks. Map those areas on your study area map.

Step Three: Which dams and floodplain fills are out of compliance?
- Request a list of the dams in your study area that are not complying with regulations. Your request should also specifically ask about dams related to mining activity.
- Request a list of any violations issued for dams or construction in the floodplain.
- Review the enforcement file for each facility to find out the outcome of any enforcement action that was taken.

Step Four: Map the dams and floodplains
- Map the locations of all regulated dams on your study area map.
- Map the 100-year floodplain on your study area map.
- Identify any problem dams on your map.

Where to get the information
- Write the state environmental protection agency (the department responsible for dams and floodplains). The Federal Emergency Management Agency (FEMA) also has this information. If you are in a mining area, ask whether those impoundments are regulated separately and by whom. Obtain the information related to mining impoundments from the appropriate agency.

Everyone knows what a dam is. What you may not know, however, is the condition of the dam just upstream from your house. Do not think that all the dams out there meet good engineering standards; they don't! One problem is that some dams do not have a large enough spillway to pass the water from even a moderate rainstorm. The spillway is an area specifically designed and constructed to carry excess water from the impounded area behind the dam to the stream below (see Figure 5.8). It should be large enough that even in large storms the impoundment will not fill up and begin running over the top of the dam (overtopping). When a dam overtops it can wash away and collapse.

Most states regulate dams that are 25 feet high or higher. There are three categories of dams that will be of interest to you. One category is *high-hazard dams*. These are the ones that will likely cause a loss of life if they collapse. The second classification is the *moderate-hazard dam*. This is one that could cause property damage (like washing out a road) if it collapses. The last class is the *low-hazard dam*. These are usually located where there is no expected loss of life or property if they collapse. If, however, someone builds a house below a low or moderate-hazard dam, it then becomes a high-hazard dam and must be upgraded to the higher standards. Dams built to create silt ponds for mining activity are sometimes regulated separately from other dams in a state. If you are in a mining area, you may have to seek information from the agency that regulates mining for information. In Kentucky, there are thousands of these mining-related dams and impoundments.

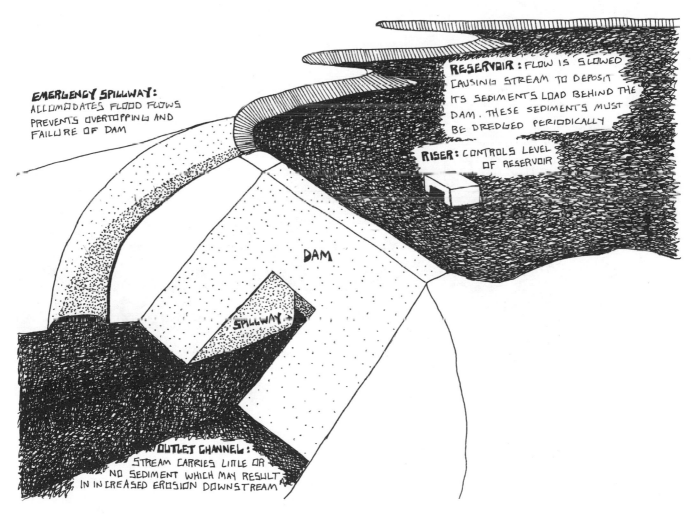

Figure 5.8 - Dam Construction

The *floodplain* (see Figure 5.9) is the land along rivers and streams that periodically floods. It is divided into several sections. One is called the floodway. This is the part of the floodplain next to the river that allows most of the floodwater to pass. Sometimes we talk about the 10-year floodplain (statistically likely to flood every 10 years). Then there is the 100-year floodplain. This is the one of greatest regulatory significance. Things like landfills usually cannot be built in the 100-year floodplain. If you want to fill an area or build something in the 100-year floodplain, you have to have a permit. If you decide to move into the 100-year floodplain thinking you will likely be dead and gone before the next flood, think about this: Frankfort, the capital of Kentucky, has had three 100-year floods in the last 10 years.

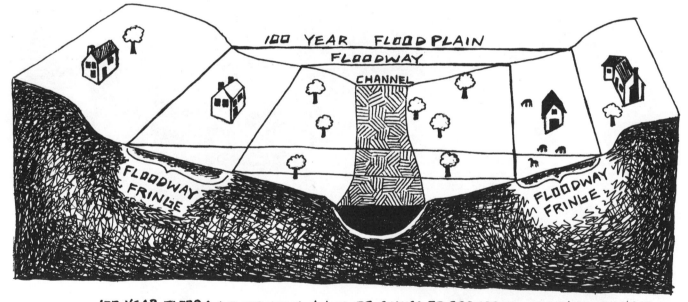

100 YEAR FLOOD: A FLOOD HAVING A 1 IN 100 CHANCE OF OCCURRING IN ANY GIVEN YEAR

FLOODPLAIN: LAND THAT LIES ALONG THE RIVER THAT IS FLOODED PERIODICALLY

FLOODWAY: PART OF THE FLOODPLAIN NEXT TO AND INCLUDING THE RIVER CHANNEL THAT ALLOWS MOST OF THE FLOODWATER TO PASS

FLOODWAY FRINGE: THAT PART OF THE FLOODPLAIN OUTSIDE OF THE FLOODWAY BUT STILL SUBJECT TO FLOODING

Figure 5.9 - Floodplain

Most states regulate the building of dams and construction in the floodplain. The most common floodplain violations include construction without a permit and failure to follow plans in the construction permit. The most common violations for dams include failure to properly maintain (such as trees growing on face of the dam) or improper spillway design for the class of dam.

The enforcement of floodplain construction laws has generally been weak. Many states have more unpermitted filling of the floodplain than permitted. Also, transportation departments are often exempt from floodplain regulations, or they abide by their own regulations.

13. Polluted Runoff

Step One: Collecting permit and discharge information
- Send the *Polluted Runoff Survey* (page 112) to each of the following agencies:
    - state water pollution control agency
    - state forestry agency
    - state conservation agency
    - federal Soil Conservation Service
    - agricultural extension service (state land grant university)
    - Tennessee Valley Authority (for states served by TVA)

Step Two: Review of nonpoint problems
- Obtain a copy of the 305b report and review it for any nonpoint pollution problems in your study area.
- If there are any nonpoint pollution problems, map those segments of the affected streams on your study area maps.

Step Three: Check compliance
- If you are in a state that regulates nonpoint pollution, request a list of enforcement actions that have been taken.

Step Four: Mapping your information
- Map the forest land, pasture land, crop land, and developed land in your study area. This will give you some idea of where polluted runoff is occurring.
- Determine the source of the nonpoint pollution for the polluted segments of the streams (for example, row-crop land on slopes). Identify these areas on your map.

Where to get the information
- The 305b report is available from the state water quality agency or the regional office of the EPA. Addresses for the other agencies listed above are available in Appendix C. Compliance information is most likely available from the state water agency.

Polluted runoff is often called *nonpoint* or *area sources* of pollution. There are two types of polluted runoff: One is the point source discharge that may or may not require a permit. This might be a stormwater discharge from a city or existing industry. Stormwater is sometimes thought of as "just rain," but depending upon what that rainwater runs over on the ground, it can be very polluted.

A second source of polluted runoff is from farms, logging operations, construction sites, and parking lots. A number of states have developed BMPs or Best Management Practices for controlling nonpoint runoff. Some states regulate nonpoint sources of pollution, while others seek voluntary implementation of BMPs. Agriculture and silviculture are most often exempted from regulation. The Soil Conservation Service is the federal agency most involved in preventing erosion of farm land. Keeping the topsoil in place preserves both the farmland it nourishes and the streams it would pollute.

Polluted runoff (nonpoint pollution) programs are probably the most diverse of any of the water pollution control programs. Most states have voluntary programs. Information can be sketchy. Responsibilities for nonpoint pollution are scattered among several agencies. Those agencies include the state agency responsible for water pollution control, state forestry agency, state conservation agency, federal Soil Conservation Service, and the land grant university extension service.

Most polluted runoff or nonpoint programs are voluntary so there will be no enforcement history for a site or problem. You can, however, request a copy of the 305b Water Quality Report to Congress. This report is done every two years by every state, or by EPA, and lists stream segments that are impaired due to nonpoint pollution.

Polluted Runoff Survey

Agency completing form:_____

Address:_____

_____

(phone)

Contact person:_____

Does your agency promote nonpoint pollution control?

Is your program regulatory or voluntary?

If regulatory, how many violations have been issued in our study area: (see attached map)

Do you have a BMP (Best Management Practices) manual?

Do you have a cost share program for implementing BMPs?

How much money has been spent in our study area on BMPs?

What is your assessment of nonpoint problems in our study area?

List any written reports or information you have on nonpoint pollution in our study area.

Return this form to: _____

_____

_____

_____

14. Septic Systems

Step One: Where are the septic systems located?
- Contact each regional sewer system and request a map of the area they serve.
- Examine your list of water permits for small package plants. Identify the likely small subdivisions or developments they serve.

Step Two: Are there local problems with septic systems?
- Conduct an interview with the health or water official responsible for issuing permits for septic systems in your study area. Ask about the types of septic system problems in your area; ask if there are any local laws for siting septic systems.

Step Three: Are permit limits being met?
- Find out if any complaints were filed or enforcement actions taken for failing septic systems.

Step Four: Mapping your information
- All parts of your study area not served by a treatment plant should be served by individual septic systems or individual sewage treatment systems.
- Map these areas on your study area map.
- Obtain a soil map for your study area. Find out which soils are adequate for septic systems; map the areas with those soil types on your study area maps.
- Identify known failed systems on your study area map.

Where to get the information
- The most likely sources for this information are the local sewer plant operator and the local health department. For information on the locations of package plants, you may need to write to the state agency responsible for water quality control (you may already have this information from your Step One activities on Sources of Water Pollution, section 3).
- The agency responsible for issuing septic system permits will either be the local health department or the state environmental protection agency. Contact the state health or water agency responsible for permitting septic systems for criteria they use to permit septic systems. A soil map for your study area is available from the county office of the federal Soil Conservation Service.

Studies have shown that on average half of the septic systems in a given area are failing. There are a variety of reasons for this—they were improperly installed, they are old, they are plugged up, they have not been pumped out lately, or the surrounding soil simply will not support septic systems. These failing systems can result in the direct release of pollutants to surface and groundwater.

A lot of isolated housing developments use package plants (these are small self-contained treatment systems that are brought in to serve a group of homes developed away from a municipal sewer system). Package plants generally are poorly managed sewage treatment systems that degrade the streams into which they discharge. Developers often fail to provide for the long-term management of the package plant. A possible solution to the problems caused by package plants is to develop regional sewer systems that serve areas on package plants and areas with failing septic systems. There are also models for using composting toilets and alternate septic system designs like artificial wetlands for individuals or areas with failing systems.

It is sometimes difficult to obtain information about how many failing septic systems there are in an area. The best way to obtain information is to interview the local health or water official who is actually responsible for permitting septic systems.

15. Drinking Water and Groundwater

Step One: Collecting permit and water withdrawal information
- Request a list of all public water supplies in your study area including addresses, and location of the supply and the source for the water (well water, surface water, etc.). If you want to audit your drinking water plant, see chapter 7.
- Request a list of Underground Injection Control (UIC) permit holders.

Step Two: Checking the quality of your drinking water
- Request copies of groundwater quality and quantity studies done in your study area or sample results of tests on wells and springs.
- Obtain a list of what is being injected into the ground through the UIC permits.
- As you review records, fill out the *Well and Spring Summary Form* (page 118).
- Request a topographical map showing the aquifers and the recharge area for the springs in your study area (see Figure 5.10 for a sample map of a recharge area supplying groundwater).

Step Three: Are permit limits being met?
- For each contaminated well or spring identified in Step Two, compare the pollutants in the well or spring water with the pollutants being discharged (by industrial facilities or other sources of pollution) near the aquifer or recharge area. Begin by looking at pollution sources in a one-mile radius around the contaminated well. Include hazardous waste sites, Superfund sites, spill areas, and any industrial dischargers in your review.
- Request compliance information concerning any UIC permit holders.

Step Four: Mapping your information
- Mark on your study area map the areas served by public water supplies. The areas that remain unmarked can be assumed to be supplied by private springs, wells, or cisterns. Map the locations of public water intakes.
- Map the aquifers and recharge areas on your study area map.
- Map the location of all UIC injection wells.

Where to get the information
- The list of public water supplies is available from the state health agency, or the state environmental protection agency (whichever is responsible for regulating drinking water). A description of the area served by a water supply can be obtained by writing the individual water suppliers. Groundwater and UIC information can be obtained from the state or federal environmental protection agency responsible for groundwater, the U.S. Geological Survey, or the state geological survey. You might also get useful information by interviewing your local water well drillers.

In order to use what has historically been considered the purest water, we generally look for a spring where groundwater is coming up out of the ground or drill a well and pump water from beneath the earth. Wells and springs are the source of both public and private water supplies. Anyone who operates a publicly or privately owned public water supply (serving more than a certain number of people, depending on your state's rules) must test and treat that water to ensure that it is safe for the user. However, if you drill a well and use that groundwater for yourself, you do not have to test it. In most parts of the U.S. a majority of the rural people depend upon groundwater. What part of your study area is being served by a public water line and in what part do the people depend upon a spring, well, or cistern for their water?

Doubtless, more groundwater contamination has occurred than has actually been discovered. Springs and wells can be good indicators of what contamination is occurring in the recharge area of the aquifer where you get water. If this information is available for your area, it may be included in the files for the individual facilities that have caused the contamination. You may have to develop it yourself (see Chapter 9, Expanding What the Agencies Know). If wells and springs are sources of a public water supply, there should be results of tests run on the water.

If any contaminated wells or springs were discovered you can begin to make some guesses as to the sources of the pollution. Most likely, the source of bacterial contamination is local and may be the result of surface water getting down a well. If a well is contaminated with agricultural pollutants or lawn chemicals, then the pollutants may be seeping in from the ground. This may indicate the well was improperly constructed. If the contaminants are chemicals that can be found in gasoline, then the most likely source is an underground storage tank. This exercise just takes a little detective work. You will need to compare pollutants from a possible source with pollutants in your well or spring. A contaminant can work as a tracer back to the source.

In some states a variety of toxic chemicals, hazardous waste, and brine water (pumped up from oil wells) are injected into the underground through wells. A permit is required for all injection wells. Some states are in charge of the Underground Injection Control (UIC) program, however the U.S. EPA may be the agency which issues the permits.

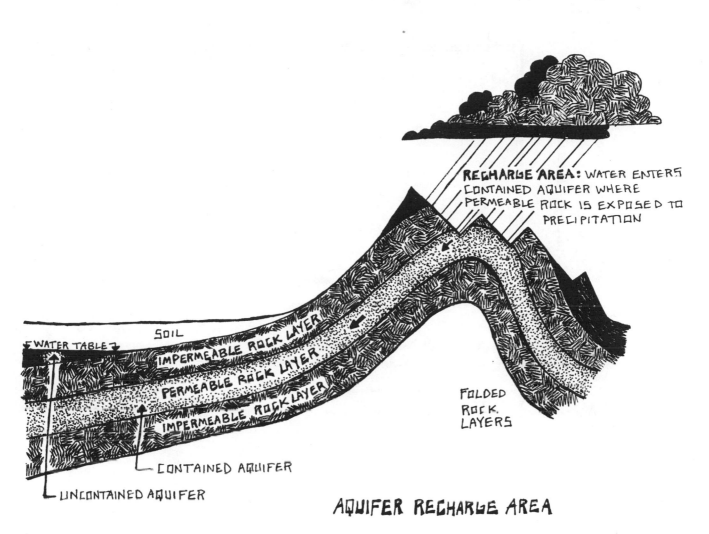

RECHARGE AREA: WATER ENTERS
CONTAINED AQUIFER WHERE
PERMEABLE ROCK IS EXPOSED TO
PRECIPITATION

SOIL

WATER TABLE

IMPERMEABLE ROCK LAYER

PERMEABLE ROCK LAYER

IMPERMEABLE ROCK LAYER

FOLDED
ROCK
LAYERS

CONTAINED AQUIFER

UNCONTAINED AQUIFER

AQUIFER RECHARGE AREA

Figure 5.10 - One Example of a Groundwater Recharge Area

Well and Spring Summary

Well location and owner's name	Drilled or hand dug?	Bacteria count (fecal coliform)	Other pollutants found in the water (organic chemicals and metals)	
			Name	Amount

16. Transportation Hazards in Your Community

Step One: Collecting hazardous material transport information
- Request a list of all hazardous waste transporters in your area.
- Request a list of any survey information the state Department of Transportation has on the shipment of hazardous materials in your study area.
- Ask the local fire department or local disaster and emergency office for any information they have collected on the transport of hazardous materials through your study area.
- Write to the railroad company that uses the tracks in your community. Ask for a list of type and quantity of hazardous materials that have moved through your community in recent years.
- Write for a copy of *Community Teamwork*, a guide to helping local communities develop a hazardous materials transportation safety program.

Step Two: Identify what is hauled and where
- Identify the major traffic routes in your study area used for hauling hazardous materials. Make a list of the materials being hauled on each major route over a one year period.

Step Three: Check accident reports
- Request any accident reports involving hazardous waste or chemical spills that have occurred in your study area.

Step Four: Mapping your information
- Map all major hazardous materials routes onto your study area map.

Where to get the information
- Information on hazardous waste transporters is available from the regional office of the U.S. EPA, or from the state agency in charge of hazardous waste generators. Check with the state agency to see if hazardous waste transporters must be registered with the agency. For example, in Kentucky the transporter must register with the agency and have a valid EPA identification number. The lists from these agencies will only include haulers of hazardous waste that fall under RCRA (Resource Conservation and Recovery Act, see Appendix E). Many of the chemicals being transported through your community are not regulated under that law. Contact the state department of transportation, the state environmental emergency response agency, and the state police in your area for Step Two and Three information. Also see section 2, Hazardous Chemicals, in this chapter. The *Community Teamwork* guide is available free from the Department of Transportation, Research and Special Programs Administration, Washington, DC 20590.

This section will offer the group some information on how to find out what is being transported to, from, and through your community. This is not an easy task. There is no list of what is being hauled on the roads at a particular time. Although hazardous waste transporters have an origin and destination, they are not required to file their routes with anyone. And what if you have a railroad track running through your community, or you live on the river where barges and ships move hazardous and toxic chemicals? In Kentucky there were 530 truck and train wrecks reported to the state environmental response office in 1991. One of those train wrecks resulted in the evacuation of an entire city; others required evacuations of neighborhoods (or smaller areas).

Using whatever information you can, identify the major traffic routes in your study area used for hauling hazardous materials. The best information may be from the environmental inventory you are conducting. If a company is reporting the release of benzene in the right-to-know reports (see Section One), you can bet they are having benzene delivered by truck, train, or barge to their facility or having it hauled away from their facility. All railroads and waterways with barge traffic are used for hauling hazardous materials. It can generally be assumed that the following roads are being used for hauling hazardous materials in your study area:

- All interstate highways
- Secondary roads leading to manufacturing facilities and RCRA facilities
- Secondary roads used for truck traffic between smaller cities
- Roads that lead to your large and small generators of hazardous waste

A good way to determine if there have been any spills or releases of hazardous material in your study area from transport is to look at accident reports. You may also want to look at places in your community that are high accident areas to see if they are routes for the transport of hazardous materials.

17. Nuclear Facilities and Waste

Step One: Are there nuclear facilities or waste sites in your study area?
- Request a list of nuclear facilities licensed or permitted from the following agencies:
  - Nuclear Regulatory Commission (NRC)
  - U.S. Environmental Protection Agency (EPA)
  - U.S. Department of Energy (DOE)
  - State office for nuclear waste or radiation control
- Request information concerning approved routes and past shipments of nuclear waste in your area, from the U.S. Department of Transportation.

Step Two: What are the permit or license conditions?
- Send any licensed or permitted facilities in your study area the *Nuclear Facility Questionnaire* on page 125. If they will not respond, then send it to the appropriate regulatory agency. If the agency is unresponsive, you may have to review the file. Files for these facilities are generally so large it is a problem to get through them and find what you need.

Step Three: Are facilities in compliance with the law?
- The Nuclear Facilities Questionnaire sent out in Step Two includes questions about compliance. If there is no response to the questionnaire, you will have to review the official file.

Step Four: Map the nuclear facilities
- Map the location of all nuclear facilities and waste sites in your study area.

Where to get the information
- The Nuclear Regulatory Commission (NRC), U.S. Environmental Protection Agency, U.S. Department of Energy, and the state office of nuclear facilities and waste or the state office of radiation control all have roles in regulating the nuclear industry.

Nuclear material is used to produce energy and is used in research, medicine, manufacturing, and weapons production. Nuclear material and nuclear waste are of concern because they emit radiation, which can harm humans and the environment. A lot of nuclear waste is also mixed with harmful chemicals.

Radiation can cause harm because its rays or particles can collide with important parts of cells and cause damage. High doses of radiation exposure result in radiation sickness, which can be fatal. Even low level exposures can result in damage to DNA that can cause cancer or birth defects. Nuclear radiation, also called ionizing radiation, is a result of unstable elements decaying, and releasing particles, or gamma radiation. (Other types of radiation, called nonionizing radiation, are not covered in this guide. One example is electromagnetic radiation or fields (EMF) produced by power lines and electrical appliances.)

Types of radiation

- *Alpha radiation* Alpha radiation consists of a particle made up of parts of an atom. (Two protons and two neutrons). This is very harmful but can be easily blocked by as little as a sheet of paper. It can cause serious problems if inhaled, eaten, or it enters the body through a cut in the skin.
- *Beta radiation* Beta particles (are equal in mass to an electron) are more penetrating than alpha. They can penetrate the skin, but are most harmful when inhaled or eaten.
- *Gamma radiation* Gamma is similar to X-rays and has the greatest penetrating power. Gamma and beta are commonly emitted together.

Measuring radiation

The amount of radiation emitted by a source can be measured in rads or curies. The actual effect varies with the type of radiation and is better expressed in rems. Rems refer to the effect of radiation on humans, and express the "dose" received by a person. (A millirem is one thousandth of a rem.) Curies refer to the rate of radioactive emissions. The standard for radon in your basement is 4 picocuries per liter of air (A picocurie is one trillionth of a curie).

Two common classifications for nuclear waste are high-level and low-level. High-level nuclear waste generally refers to highly radioactive waste from the reprocessing of uranium and plutonium and other wastes from the nuclear fuel cycle including spent fuel from power plants. Low-level nuclear waste is everything not classified as a high-level waste. This includes a lot of medical, industry, and research waste. It takes many forms, such as clothes, trash, and medical equipment.

There are several problems associated with nuclear energy:

- *Hazards from emissions and leaks* Nuclear power necessarily involves the release of low levels of radioactivity into the environment (and may involve higher level releases). In addition, the generation of nuclear power and the processing of fuel create highly toxic high level radioactive waste. Radioactivity and other wastes can impact human health and the environment.

- *Obligation to maintain* Plutonium, a highly toxic element found in the waste from nuclear power plants, has a half life of more than 24,000 years. (That means that after that period, half of the material has decayed to a degradation product). Does the current generation have the right to make electricity for itself and create a waste that will require future generations to manage at great expense? This is a serious issue of intergenerational equity.
- *Accidents* Although the probability of a serious accident is said to be low, the potential catastrophic effects mean these risks must be taken seriously. In addition, many people feel the probability of accidents is understated. Accidents at Three-mile Island and Chernobyl clearly demonstrate that serious accidents, releasing radiation and endangering humans and the environment, do happen.
- *Security* One of the by-products of nuclear fission is plutonium. This is the critical ingredient in a nuclear bomb. How can plutonium be kept out of the wrong hands?

There are numerous steps and several types of nuclear facilities associated with the nuclear fuel cycle. They include the following:

- *Uranium mining* Most uranium ore in the United States is found in natural deposits in New Mexico, Texas, Utah, Wyoming, Arizona, and Colorado. The environmental problems associated with mining include the release of radon gas and uranium dust.
- *Uranium milling* Uranium ore is crushed and ground, chemically treated, and made into an intermediate product called "yellowcake." Radioactive waste or "tailings" are left from this process. The process creates mostly waste since 2000 pounds of ore yield only 1-5 pounds of uranium.
- *Uranium conversion* Yellowcake is processed into uranium hexafluoride (UF_6). The emissions from the different conversion processes include radioactive sludges, radioactive gas, and radioactive liquids.
- *Uranium enrichment* This is a process by which uranium hexafluoride is purified to different levels. The level of enrichment depends on the final use.
- *Fuel fabrication* Uranium hexafluoride is chemically converted into uranium dioxide metal. This metal is used to make fuel rods for nuclear power plants. Waste products from this process include radioactive gas and liquid.
- *Nuclear plant licensing* A nuclear power plant uses the heat of a nuclear reaction in the fuel rods to heat water that runs a turbine and makes electricity. Both a construction and an operating permit are required. Also an environmental impact statement is required if significant environmental impacts will occur.

• *Nuclear waste* The disposal of nuclear waste is an unsolved problem. As of yet, we have no mechanism for isolating these wastes from humans and the environment for thousands of years. There are disposal sites for low-level nuclear waste. Siting new ones is a difficult process. The Nuclear Waste Policy Act set a deadline of January 31, 1998 for initial operation of a permanent disposal site for high-level nuclear waste. The Department of Energy is also looking at possible sites for a monitored retrievable storage facility (MRS). This will be a "temporary" storage site until a permanent site can be developed. Communities are concerned about hazards and about how long they might be stuck with the waste. In addition to the nuclear fuel cycle described above, radioactive material is also used in certain industries. These industries have the problems of releases, accidents, and disposal.

All of the above steps represent some type of facility. All citizens should be concerned about these facilities, but if you have one in your community or one proposed for your community, you should be especially concerned. The authors are familiar with two sites in Kentucky. One is a Department of Energy uranium enrichment plant. This site is among the most polluted sites in Kentucky, if not the most polluted. The other site is called Maxey Flats. This was a low-level nuclear waste dump. It is now a closed Superfund site leaking radioactive material into the air, streams, and groundwater. This site will have to be managed for hundreds and perhaps thousands of years and will require millions of dollars. It should be noted that having this site in Kentucky was once heralded as a great economic development strategy.

The following agencies regulate nuclear facilities:

Nuclear Regulatory Commission (NRC)
Office of Nuclear Material Safety and Safeguards
1 White Flint North
Mail Stop 5E4
Washington, DC 20555
(301) 504-3432

U.S. Environmental Protection Agency
Office of Radiation Programs
401 M Street, SW
Mail Code ORP6601J
Washington, DC 20460
(202) 233-9320

U.S. Department of Energy
Office of Civilian Radioactive Waste
   Management
1000 Independence Avenue, SW
Washington, DC 20585
(202) 586-6842

See Appendix C for addresses of state offices controlling nuclear facilities and waste.

NUCLEAR FACILITY QUESTIONNAIRE

Please provide the information requested on this form for the following described area.

1. List any facilities your agency has permitted, licensed, under review, or proposed. Please provide any important dates such as date permitted or dates for public comment.

2. Please provide a copy of a map showing the location of each facility and a description of what type of nuclear facility it is.

3. List all pollutants being discharged by the listed facilities and the permit or license conditions that apply to them.

4. List any non-compliances or notices of violation that have been issued to the facilities.

5. Describe any spills or accidents that have occurred at the facilities.

Name of person filling out this form _____

Telephone number _____

CHAPTER

6 Natural Resources Inventory

Introduction

Throughout the centuries, humans have been degrading the earth. As our numbers have increased, the amount of natural resources used has increased. Unfortunately, we are using more resources than our resilient earth can replace. In the name of progress, we have learned ways to more quickly and completely log forests, make way for roads, and mine nonrenewable resources. New chemicals and machines have created a petroleum-based agriculture which is not sustainable. We have used up more of the earth this century than in all the previous centuries combined.

But since we have so drastically modified the earth, we are now left the task of somehow identifying and protecting what natural resources we have left. It is time for people to take a hard look around and decide which natural resources they want to remain as part of their community and as part of their children's heritage.

Natural resources play an important role in our communities. A forest may, if managed correctly, provide sustainable timber production, wildlife habitat, and wilderness. Natural areas can offer people and wildlife a sanctuary from the relentless march of humanity.

This inventory is designed to help you identify nine kinds of natural resources in your community: rare plants and animals; natural areas; public parks and recreation areas; wild, scenic and recreational rivers; wilderness areas; wetlands; scenic vistas; public forests; and wildlife management areas. These categories are based on designations created by government. In *Step One*, you will identify what you have, and in *Step Two*, you will evaluate how it's cared for and project what you need. *Step Three* is to map the natural resources defined in each category on your study area map.

Each of the specific natural resources being inventoried represents a potentially important part of your community's heritage. They also represent places and areas you enjoy, utilize, and want to remain part of your community. Doing a natural resources assessment by looking at how the resources are being used, and whether they are protected will provide a basis for future planning with regard to managing and protecting those resources.

You will be completing a form describing the resources in each category you inventory. You should fill out each of the specific natural resources inventory forms. Under each of the resource areas (such as wildlife management area, natural area, or wilderness) you should include sites that your group thinks are potential candidates for the particular designation.

For each of the natural resource categories you will be making two judgments. One concerns the level of protection a resource currently receives. Suggestions are offered under each category for making this assessment. The second judgement to be made concerns the *area use pattern*. This assessment will require an individual or the group to make a best guess about how much an area (or resource) is being used. Four use classifications are suggested:

(N) *not used* This classification is appropriate for areas not used publicly or privately.

(O) *overused* This classification is for areas used by people to the extent that it is crowded, vegetation is worn down, erosion problems appear, or the area is trashed.

(S) *sustainable* This classification should reflect a moderate use that appears to be acceptable and is not degrading the resource.

(U) *underused/sustainable* This classification is for areas only lightly used and where there is clearly no threat to the resource.

1. Rare Plants and Animals

Step One: Which species are protected in your study area?
- Request a list of the rare and endangered species of plants and animals for your study area. The list will have both federally listed species and state listed species.

Step Two: Is this resource protected?
- Has there been a systematic search for rare plants and animals in your study area? Are the areas where rare plants and animals are located protected from development and other types of disturbance? List the species identified in Step One in the first column of the *Rare Plants and Animals Form* on page 131. For each species, use your best judgment to fill out the relevant information in the other columns. The following categories might be helpful in determining the level of protection for column #3:

  High Species located in areas publicly or privately owned that are protected from development, including protection from condemnation by the state for use as a road or other non-protected use.
  Medium Species located in privately owned areas that have been registered as protected areas or species in publicly owned sites that are not fully protected, such as natural areas in state or federal forests that are open to logging.
  Low Species located in privately owned areas where no action has been taken for protection.
  Vulnerable Species in any category where a known threat, such as a road or other development, is going to destroy all, or a portion, of them.

Step Three: Mapping your information
- Determine where these species are located in your study area and map the locations on your study area map.

Where to get the information
- Contact either the state agency (natural heritage program, natural areas program, or wildlife agency) responsible for endangered species or The Nature Conservancy, a private nonprofit organization now operating in all states.

Buffalo clover has big, nutritious leaves (for animals), and was once eaten by buffalo. This plant was thought extinct in Kentucky until a botanist from the Kentucky State Nature Preserves Commission discovered a small patch in a Kentucky county. The agricultural experts have since become interested in obtaining some plants and seeds for research purposes. Maybe this plant could once again be an important crop. If it had been allowed to become extinct, we would not have the chance we now have to explore its potential.

Some people are concerned about extinction because they believe that all species of plants and animals have an inherent right to exist. Others are concerned because we could be losing something of value to us or to future generations. Still others worry that if a person or society does not care about a rare plant or animal today and allows or causes its extinction, then at what point, and for which species, will the person or society begin to care? For whatever reason, taking inventory of rare and endangered plants and animals in your community will be the first step in making sure human-caused extinction of plants and animals will stop.

Rare Plants and Animals

Species of plant or animal	Area where species is located	Level of protection: High, Medium, Low, Vulnerable	Area use pattern: (N) not used; (O) over used; (S) sustainable; (U) underused /sustainable

Comments, plans for future action:

2. Natural Areas

Step One: What natural areas do we have?
- Develop a list of natural areas, both public and private, in your study area.

Step Two: Are natural areas protected?
- To evaluate the status of natural areas in your study area, fill out the *Natural Areas Form* on page 133. In column #2, define the resource (rare plant, geologic feature, old growth forest, etc.) being protected. The following categories might be helpful in determining the level of protection for column #4:

High Areas publicly or privately owned that are protected from development, including condemnation by the state.
Medium Privately owned areas that have been registered with an official federal, state or private organization and recognized as natural areas. Also publicly owned sites that have not been designated as natural areas, such as state or federal forests that are open to logging.
Low Private sites where no action has been taken for protection.
Vulnerable Sites in any category where a known threat (road, development, etc.) is going to destroy all, or a portion, of them.

Step Three: Mapping Your Information
- Map the location of these areas on your study area map.

Where to get the information
- Contact the state agency in charge of natural areas, or The Nature Conservancy, a private nonprofit organization now operating in all states.

What is a natural area? One definition is that it is the area that provides the *habitat* for rare and endangered species. To some it's an old growth or virgin forest (one never logged). A *natural area* may be more broadly defined as an area that is relatively undisturbed or retains its natural character and provides habitat to native plants and animals. Native plants and animals mean the ones that should naturally be there. We generally have to settle for the relatively undisturbed because of the heavy imprint of human activity on nature. Areas completely pristine and unaltered by humans are nowhere to be found.

Most states now have natural area programs and a list of natural areas. These include areas owned by government and areas owned, and sometimes officially registered, by private landowners. Environmental organizations (especially The Nature Conservancy) also own natural areas and maintain lists of natural areas.

Natural Areas

Natural areas	Resources being protected (include plant, animal, geology, water, scenic)	Size of area: acres/miles	Level of protection: high, medium, low, vulnerable	Area use pattern: (N) not used; (O) over used; (S) sustainable; (U) under used/ sustainable

Comments, plans for future action:

3. Public Parks and Recreation Areas

Step One: What public parks do we have?
- Develop a list of all parks and recreation areas in your study area.

Step Two: Do we have enough parks?
- To assess the need for parks and recreation areas you should interview the manager of each park and recreation area identified in your study area. Get copies of any *use reports* that have been done on the areas. With these two sets of information you should be able to fill out column #4 on the *Public Parks and Recreation Areas Form* on page 136. Anytime you determine that a particular category is overused, you are probably dealing with a need for more of that kind of park or recreational opportunity. Information about the need for more sites may also come from the interview. Include this information in the "comments, plans for future action" section of the form. To evaluate the public parks and recreation areas in your study area, complete the form on page 136. The following categories might be useful in determining the level of protection in column #3:

High Publicly owned site that is located in an area unlikely to be taken by development.
Medium Publicly owned site in an area of rapid development, or a private site in an underdeveloped area.
Low Privately owned site that exists as a business for someone (like a campground) and could be sold for other types of development. This category could also include a public area that has a river running through it that is polluted from sources upstream.
Vulnerable Site where a known threat to its continuation exists.

Step Three: Mapping your information
- Map the locations of all of the public parks and recreation areas in your study area on your study area map.

Where to get the information
- Most federal parks, state parks, and recreation areas should be on current topographic maps of your area. For newer parks or recreation areas contact the state and local government agencies responsible for parks. There are also a number of federal agencies in addition to the U.S. Park Service that may own and manage parks and recreation areas. These include the Tennessee Valley Authority, U.S. Forest Service, Bureau of Land Management, U.S. Fish and Wildlife Service and the U.S. Army Corps of Engineers. Your local county property tax assessor or county planning office may also have this information.

Chapter 6 Natural Resources Inventory

Federal, state, and local public parks and recreation areas can be of great importance to a community. This can be especially true in communities of high growth, where important land can be taken for development without any consideration of the eventual need for green space and recreation. Knowing where your public parks are and how they are used is important. Furthermore, many state and federal parks and recreation areas are developed around an important or outstanding natural feature or recreational site such as a lake or stream. These facilities can be important to long-term tourism development. Recreation areas are places like picnic areas, boat ramps, roadside parks, swimming beaches, and other public areas.

Public Parks and Recreation Areas

Parks and recreation areas	Size: acres/miles	Level of protection: high, medium, low, vulnerable	Area use pattern: (N) not used; (O) over used; (S) sustainable; (U) under used/ sustainable

Comments, plans for future action:

4. Wild, Scenic, and Recreational Rivers

Step One: What wild rivers do we have?
- Obtain the lists of designated and proposed wild, scenic, and/or recreational rivers in your study area.
- Obtain a list of study rivers (rivers that are being reviewed and considered for wild, scenic, and/or recreational designation).

Step Two: Are the wild rivers protected?
- The particular law that protects these designated stream segments is the most important factor in determining the protection level. In addition, the ownership is important. The stream segment is also not being protected unless the water itself is being protected. You may have information from your water quality work (Chapter 5) that suggests the water quality is impaired from some activity upstream. Obtain a copy of the laws governing these rivers and interview the person in charge of your state's program. Review the ownership patterns for the designated portion of the stream segment in your study area. Complete the *Wild Scenic and Recreational Rivers Form* on page 139.

Designations - In column #2, enter the appropriate official designation: "federal," "state," "proposed federal," "under study," or "none." Use information in the files and the 305b report to make a judgement about the quality of the water in the river segment. Use the following categories for column #3:

      A - Good, with no serious upstream threats to the water quality
      B - Good, but threatened by upstream activities or discharges
      C - Impacted

Categories that may help determine the level of protection (column #5) are:
High Federally designated river and good water quality with no upstream threats.
Medium Segment protected by state law and/or under study for federal designation. Water quality good with no serious upstream threats.
Low Water quality impacted. Segment identified on river assessment, but not given official protection.
Vulnerable Water being seriously polluted from upstream source. No protection to segment.

Step Three: Mapping Your Information
- Identify any river segments (from 1 or 2 above) on your study area map.

Where to get the information
- Most states have a wild rivers program in the water agency or natural resources agency. The federal program is in the Department of Interior. See Chapter 5, section 3 for how to obtain water quality information and the 305b report.

Free-flowing rivers with good water quality are becoming rare. Most of our rivers have had their course altered by dams or channelization and many suffer from pollution problems. Some rivers and streams have been officially designated as wild, scenic and/or recreational. Sections of rivers or streams can be designated under either state or federal law. The state and federal laws have specific criteria that must be met before a segment of stream or river is designated. The criteria generally include water quality and the type of land use and other activities in the corridor. The corridor refers to some designated section of land along the stream or river. In Kentucky the wild river corridor is 2,000 feet on either side of the stream, or the visual horizon. This corridor is protected when the river is designated wild or scenic. Once designated, certain kinds of activity—logging, building, etc.—may not be allowed, especially if the activity will adversely affect the wild or scenic river. Protection of the corridor serves several purposes: it protects water quality by limiting the activity near the bank, protects the vegetation that shades the water (so fish can survive), and protects the scenic view from the river for boaters, swimmers, and others.

Even though the corridor may come under official protection, it can be difficult to make that protection work. For example, in Kentucky the U.S. Forest Service has actually clear-cut (timber harvest method where everything is cut) portions of state-designated wild river corridors that are under Forest Service ownership. Sometimes the corridors are privately owned. This can cause problems if the landowners are opposed to the designation and wish to develop something such as logging within the corridor. Usually a permit is required for any land disturbing activities in the corridor.

Chapter 6 Natural Resources Inventory

Wild, Scenic, and Recreational Rivers

Rivers	Length of protected segment	Designation: Federal State Proposed federal Under study None	Water Quality: (A) Good - no serious upstream threats (B) Good - but threatened by development upstream (C) Impacted	Level of protection: high, medium, low, vulnerable	Area use pattern: (N) not used; (O) over used; (S) sustainable; (U) under used /sustainable

Comments, plans for future action:

5. Wilderness Areas

Step One: Do we have any wilderness areas?
- Request a list of designated wilderness or proposed wilderness areas in your study area.

Step Two: What is the condition of wilderness in our area?
- You should request a copy of any evaluations done on potential wilderness areas in your study area. Conduct your own review of the site(s). Interview local individuals and groups interested in the area. Your own effort may yield new information about a potential site that will help in its evaluation.

- To assess the status of wilderness areas in your study area, complete the *Wilderness Areas Form* on page 142. Include any wilderness study sites that you identified in your Level One activities. Include sites regardless of whether they have been designated as wilderness, and any sites that your group believes will meet the basic wilderness criteria.

  High Site officially designated as wilderness.
  Medium Site under study or consideration for wilderness designation.
  Low Privately owned or publicly owned and not designated. No apparent or immediate plans for mining or logging.
  Vulnerable Privately owned or publicly owned and not designated. Good timber or other resources (such as coal) on site for extraction.

Step Three: Map the wilderness areas
- Map the wilderness areas on your study area map.

Where to get the information
- Contact the federal agencies (Department of Interior, Bureau of Land Management, and U.S. Forest Service) that hold wilderness land in your state. If you don't know, write to each of the above agencies.

"Wilderness" is a designation for federal land. There are specific criteria to be met, but basically wilderness areas are wild, remote, and relatively undisturbed places. There are restrictions for what can be done in wilderness areas. Henry Thoreau said, "In wilderness is the preservation of the world." Even though most people will never enter a wilderness, they want to know there are undisturbed areas out there somewhere. The idea that humans could destroy the last wilderness is deeply unsettling to the human spirit.

Wilderness can serve as an important barometer for what humans are doing to the earth. Wilderness areas are refuges for plants and animals, especially large animals that need large undisturbed areas for survival. All wilderness areas are natural areas, but not all natural areas are wilderness.

The Wilderness Act states that wilderness is "an area where the earth and its community of life are untrammeled by man, where man himself is a visitor who does not remain." Wilderness is further defined as "an area of undeveloped federal land retaining its primeval character and influence . . . and which (1) generally appears to have been affected primarily by the forces of nature, with the imprint of man's work substantially unnoticeable; (2) has outstanding opportunities for solitude or a primitive and unconfined type of recreation; (3) has at least 5,000 acres of land or is of sufficient size as to make practical its preservation and use in an unimpaired condition, and (4) may also contain ecological, geological, or other features of scientific, educational, scenic, or historical value."

Wilderness Areas

Wilderness area Designated or undesignated?	Size: Acres	Level of protection: high, medium, low, vulnerable	Area use pattern: (N) not used; (O) over used; (S) sustainable; (U) under used /sustainable

Comments, plans for future action:

6. Wetlands

Step One: Where are the wetlands?
- Identify the known wetlands in your study area. Include tidal and coastal areas.
- The U.S. Fish and Wildlife Service is conducting a National Wetlands Inventory throughout the United States. Find out if the U.S. Fish and Wildlife Service has completed the wetlands mapping in your study area and obtain the wetlands map if available (see Figure 6.1 for an example of a wetlands map).
- If the U.S. Fish and Wildlife Service has not completed the wetlands mapping in your study area, then visit your local Soil Conservation Service office and ask them to help identify wetlands on the latest soil survey maps for your study area.

Step Two: What is the status of your wetlands?
- To assess the status of wetlands in your study area, complete the *Wetlands Form* on page 146. The following categories for assessing the level of protection in column #3 might be useful:

  High Areas publicly or privately owned that are protected from development, including development through condemnation by the state. The water quality should be good and not threatened.
  Medium Privately owned areas that have been registered and recognized as natural areas. Also publicly owned sites that have not been designated as natural areas, such as state or federal forests that are open to logging. The water quality should be good and not threatened.
  Low Private sites where no action has been taken for protection. Wetlands with water quality impacted are in this category.
  Vulnerable Sites in any category where a known threat (road, development, etc.) is going to destroy all or a portion of them. Water quality is seriously impacted.

Step Three: Map your wetlands
- Map wetlands identified from the sources listed above on your study area maps.

Where to get the information
- For information on wetlands, contact the state water agency, the state and federal fish and wildlife agencies, and the state natural areas program. Soil survey maps are available from the county office of the federal Soil Conservation Service. For further information on wetlands, refer to the following publication: *A Citizens' Guide to Protecting Wetlands* - March 1989, National Wildlife Federation, 1400 16th Street, N.W., Washington, D.C. 20036-2266, (404) 876-8733

Wetlands are one of America's most maligned natural resources. Usually called swamps or marshes, they conjure up visions of mosquitoes, alligators, snakes, and quicksand that will swallow you up. There are many different kinds of wetlands from cattail marshes to cypress swamps. Wetlands serve many valuable functions for society. It is one of the most productive wildlife systems on earth. Many fish, shellfish, waterfowl, and plants depend upon wetlands for some part of their life cycle. Wetlands hold water and therefore reduce downstream flooding, recharge the groundwater that feeds streams in summer, and remove pollutants from the water. These are all features of value to the public. However, these features are rarely perceived as valuable to property owners. Private landowners with wetlands on their property have little incentive to preserve, rather than fill, their wetlands. The policy of the U.S. government is to not allow any further loss of wetlands. This "no net loss" policy does allow mitigation (take a wetland one place, replace it somewhere else) for wetland "taking" or elimination. There are many unresolved issues about mitigation. How well can we actually restore the functional aspects of a wetland? How far away from the site eliminated can mitigation occur? Does the same type of community have to be restored?

About Figure 6.1

Each of the letters or combinations of letters represents a particular wetland type. Wetlands such as **PFO1A** have been delineated on the USFWS map (fig. 6.1). For this code the **P** means palustrine; **FO** means forested; **1** means broad-leaved deciduous; **A** means temporarily flooded. The codes for how the particular wetland is classified will be provided with the wetland maps. If the area is in agricultural use, it is not mapped as wetland by the USFWS. Therefore, the wetlands are the hydric soils remaining in natural vegetation. For more information on the classification system you can order a copy of *Photointerpretation Conventions for the National Wetlands Inventory* from the National Wetlands Inventory National Office (see Appendix A for address).

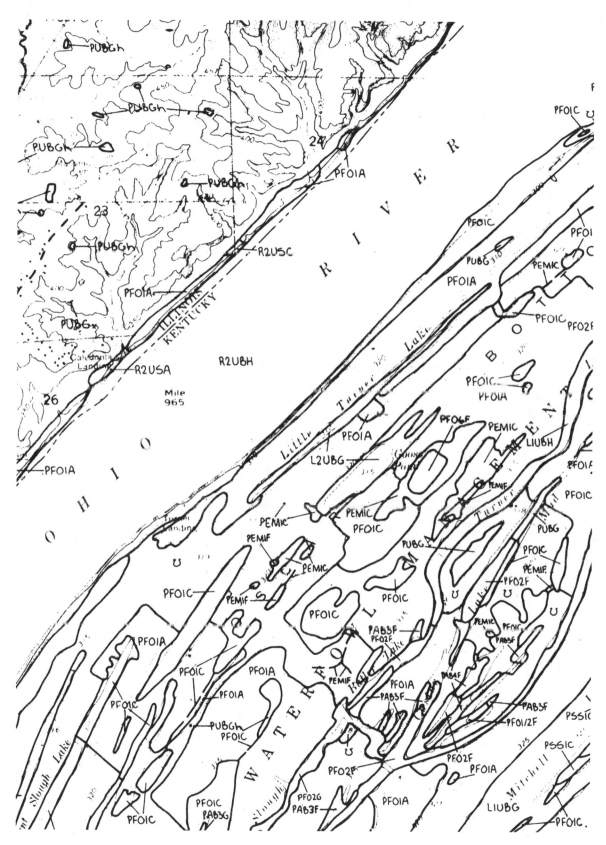

Figure 6.1 - Wetlands Map

Wetlands

Wetland sites	Size: Acres	Level of protection: high, medium, low, vulnerable	Area use pattern: (N) not used; (O) over used; (S) sustainable; (U) under used /sustainable

Comments, plans for future action:

7. Scenic Vistas

Step One: Where are our scenic vistas?
- Conduct a visual survey of your study area. This survey can be accomplished in two ways:

  (a) Ask people to send in photos of their favorite scene or view in the study area (or hold a contest).

  (b) Assign a group to drive all the roads in the study area and photograph all of the outstanding vistas they find (following the criteria in Figure 6.3 on page 149). The group should also walk any trails and bike paths to look for vistas (you can also consider vistas from boats). Then have an evaluation team review all the photos to compile a list of the outstanding and significant views in your study area. Ask the local newspaper and tourism group to work with you on this project. Some vistas will be especially scenic at certain times of the year, such as during autumn foliage.

Step Two: Are your scenic vistas protected?
- Write to the state road department and ask about any road plans and specifically for any plans that include roadside pullouts for scenic vistas. If any new parks, walking/running trails, or bike paths are being considered, there may be opportunities for scenic vistas to be developed.
- To assess the status of scenic vistas in your study area, fill out the *Scenic Vistas Form* on page 152. Using the information you gathered in Step One, estimate the acreage covered by each scenic view and enter the totals in column #2. It will not be easy to determine the level of protection (column #3) for a scenic vista. See Figure 6.2 for suggestions on how to judge whether scenic vistas are protected.

  To determine the use pattern (column #4), consider the number of people driving by a vista and whether there is a pullout for stopping, observing, and taking pictures. It is hard to imagine that a "scene" could be overused. "Overused" does not mean that too many people are looking at it, but rather that a pull-off cannot handle the cars and visitors that want to use it.

Step Three: Map your scenic vistas
- Map the entire area that is part of the viewshed (this is the area that can be seen from a particular point) in each photo judged outstanding or significant.

It is hard for some people to believe that the quality of their life results in large part from the visual quality of the everyday environment. When you drive to town, do you go by some especially pleasing view of the valley or mountain side? This may be a well known place where a scenic overlook has been designated or provided, or it may just be a particular curve in the road which yields an aesthetically pleasing view when you round it. Aesthetics can be very personal. The person who owns the coal in a mountain may claim that seeing it mined is much more aesthetically pleasing than viewing the mountain in its natural state. Some people think a pig farm smells like money! Notwithstanding these anomalies of the senses, you will discover the areas your community finds most visually pleasing by conducting a visual survey (see Figure 6.3 for visual quality criteria).

Determining Protection Status of Scenic Vistas

The following criteria might help you or your group reach a common judgement about the protection level:

- Amount of land in a land use plan that is zoned in such a way that it will protect the vista quality.
- Amount of land in public ownership that protects vista quality.
- Amount of development in the vista area.
- Type of growth in the vista area.

Following is a suggested matrix for determining the level of protection:

	High	**Medium**	**Low**	**Vulnerable**
Zoned land	80-100%	50-80%	0-50%	No zoning
Public land	80-100%	50-80%	0-50%	No public land
% Developed	0-20%	20-50%	50-100%	Mostly developed
Type of growth	No growth	Slow	Moderate	Rapid

Determining the protection status is a judgment call, it may be little more than a best guess. The group will need to consider all categories in the matrix together. For example, if 80% of the viewshed is in public land (say national forest) and the other 20% is wide open for any type of development, then the viewshed may be vulnerable. If the forest land can be clearcut, it may also be vulnerable even if it is public land. The group making this judgment will need to discuss all aspects of what can destroy a view and try to arrive at a consensus about how well a particular area is protected.

Figure 6.2 - Determining Protection Status of Scenic Vistas

Chapter 6 Natural Resources Inventory

Scenic Quality Inventory/Evaluation
Rating Criteria and Score
Modified from the Bureau of Land Management

Landform	Vegetation	Water	Color	Adjacent Scenery	Scarcity	Cultural Modifications
High mountains, cliffs, or massive rock outcrops; sand dunes or other detail features dominant and striking. (5)	A variety of vegetative types in interesting forms, textures, and patterns; overall state of naturalness should be a factor. (5)	Clear and clean appearing, still, or cascading white water, any of which are a dominant factor in the landscape. (5)	Rich color combinations, variety or vivid color; or pleasing contrasts in the soil, rock, vegetation, water or snow fields. (5)	Adjacent scenery greatly enhances visual quality. (5)	One of a kind; or unusually memorable; or very rare within region. Consistent chance for exceptional wildlife or wildflower viewing. (5)	Free from aesthetically undesirable or discordant sights such as strip mines, forest clear-cut areas, and road cuts. (5)
Rolling hills, isolated knob hills and interesting topographic relief. Detail features not dominant or exceptional. (3)	Some variety of vegetation, but only one or two types. (3)	Flowing or still, but not dominant in the landscape. (3)	Some intensity or variety in colors and contrast of the soil, rock and vegetation, but not a dominant scenic element. (3)	Adjacent scenery moderately enhances overall visual quality. (3)	Distinctive though somewhat similar to others within the region. (2)	Scenic quality is somewhat depreciated by inharmonious intrusions, but not so extensively that they are entirely negated, or modifications add little or no visual variety to the areas. (0)
Flat landscape with few detailed landscape features. (1)	Little or no variety or contrast in vegetation. (1)	Absent, or not noticable. (0)	Subtle color variations, contrast or interest; generally muted tones. (1)	Adjacent scenery has little or no influence on overall visual quality. (0)	Interesting within its setting, but fairly common within the region. (1)	Modifications are so extensive that scenic qualities are mostly nullified or substatially reduced. (-4)

Figure 6.3 - Visual Quality Criteria

Priority Rating
A = 19 or more points
B = 12-18 points
C = 11 or less points

Scenic Quality - Explanation of Rating Criteria

Modified from the Bureau of Land Management's Manual H-8410-1
"Visual Resource Inventory"

Landform

Topography becomes more interesting as it gets steeper or more massive, or more severely or universally sculptured. Outstanding landforms may be monumental, as the Grand Canyon. When you look at your own region, you will be looking at differences on a smaller scale. The Great Smoky Mountains in the east are spectacular. When you get into Eastern Kentucky for example, places like Natural Bridge, Red River Gorge, Raven Rock and Bad Branch Falls are examples of scenes that rate a 5 on a scale of 1 to 5, with one being less interesting, and 5 being the most interesting. In a coastal area you might rate a sand dune 5 or a rugged coastline as a 5.

Vegetation

Give primary consideration to the variety of patterns, forms, and textures created by plant life. Consider short-lived displays, such as fall colors or spring wildflowers, when they are known to be recurring or spectacular. Consider also smaller scale vegetational features which add striking and intriguing detail elements to the landscape (e.g., gnarled or wind-beaten trees, and heath or rhododendron balds).

Water

Water is the ingredient which adds movement or serenity to a scene. The degree to which water dominates the scene is the primary consideration in selecting the rating score. Waterfalls, lakes, and cascading rivers all rate high.

Color

Consider the overall color(s) of the basic components of the landscape (e.g., soil, rock, vegetation, etc.) as they appear during seasons or periods of high use. Key factors to use when rating "color" are variety, contrast, and harmony. Remember the spectacular display of fall colors in the eastern deciduous (trees lose leaves) forests.

Continued next page

Chapter 6 Natural Resources Inventory

Adjacent Scenery

Such factors as topography and vegetation as far away as five miles in an adjacent area can enhance the visual quality of the area being rated and increase its score. Likewise, the view of a nearby polluting factory can decrease the area's score.

Scarcity

With the scarcity score, you can give added importance to scenes and scenic features that appear to be unique or rare within a region. A one-of-a-kind scene or feature would score a five (on a scale of one to five with five being unique), while a feature that is interesting within its setting, but fairly common within the region would receive a lower score.

Cultural Modifications

Cultural modifications (changes that people make) of the land, waterways, vegetation, and man-made structures should be taken into consideration. These modifications may detract from the scenery, or, in some cases, complement or improve the scenic quality of a particular area. Strip mines, forest clear-cuts and road cuts, for example, can significantly detract from a scene. On the other hand, a man-made lake could increase the scenic quality.

Visual inventories can be conducted in many ways. The Bureau of Land Management's Visual Resource Inventory provides descriptions and criteria useful for ranking areas of scenic value. Once you have identified spots of scenic value in your study area, you may want to use the scores to prioritize which areas should be protected through such mechanisms as zoning. The ranking could also help you pinpoint areas where the Department of Transportation (or the county, depending on the type of road) could provide scenic overlooks or trails. Feel free to develop your own criteria or just have your group vote on which scene they like best. This is not a science; it is an art. The bottom line is that the scenic quality of your area can add greatly to your quality of life.

Scenic Vistas

Scenic vistas	Size of viewshed: acres/miles	Level of protection: high, medium, low, vulnerable	Area use pattern: (N) not used; (O) over used

Comments, plans for future action:

8. Public Forests

Step One: Where are your public forests?
- Find out where the state forests and national forests in your study area are located.
- Request copies of any resource management plans or other plans on these forests.

Step Two: How are the forests used?
- To evaluate the status of public forests in your study area, fill out the *Public Forests Form* on page 155. In column #3, identify the types of uses permitted for the forests in your area. The forestry plan you obtained in Step One will contain information about different kinds of permitted uses including:

  Logging How many acres of the forest area are open to logging?
  Hunting How much of the forest land is open to some type of hunting?
  Off Road Vehicles Is any part of the forest open to this use? How much?
  Recreation Are areas of the forest open to picnicking and camping?

  Complete the use information for each permitted activity. Interviews with managers and specific site studies could be conducted to determine use patterns.

Step Three: Map your forests
- Map the forest boundaries on your study area map.

Where to get the information
- Contact the state forestry department and/or the U.S. Forest Service.

Trees are one of the greatest, most useful renewable natural resources we have. They provide food, lumber, fuel, paper, oxygen and shade. Forests are habitat for plants and animals, take in carbon dioxide and give off oxygen, and protect our hillsides and stream banks and river banks from eroding. Public forests also provide retreats for people who want to experience nature up close. Most state and national forests are open to hikers, campers, and tourists. There is no one whose life is not affected by, and improved by, trees.

Forests are more threatened today than ever before. The demands of an ever increasing population are seriously affecting our forests. The fragmentation (breaking large tracks into small pieces) is negatively affecting wildlife. Some forestry practices reduce the naturalness and biodiversity (this means all the plants and animals living in a forest) of a forest in order to enhance the production of particular species of trees and sometimes only one species of tree.

A forest is an *ecosystem*. This means it is a complex community of plants and animals that live together. There are many interactions between these plants and animals that humans do not understand. The best management is *ecosystem management*, which attempts to make use of the forest without destroying the ecosystem. In Chapter 9 there is a section on developing a Greenlinks program (connecting wildlife habitat) in your study area. This will help your group examine the fragmentation and greenspace issue in your area.

Forests can be managed as a sustainable resource. Broad public involvement is essential to ensure that the U.S. Forest Service and state forestry agencies properly manage this public resource.

Public Forests

Public forests	Size: acres/miles	Types of uses permitted	Area use pattern: (N) not used; (O) over used (S) sustainable; (U) under used /sustainable

Comments, plans for future action:

9. Wildlife Management Areas

Step One: Where are the wildlife management areas?
- Identify the wildlife management areas in your study area that are owned or managed by the U.S. Fish and Wildlife Service or the state fish and wildlife agency.
- Ask for a list of the species of plants or animals they are managing.
- Ask for information on their nongame wildlife program and/or watchable wildlife program.

Step Two: What is the status of your wildlife management areas?
- State and federal wildlife management areas and refuges are important wildlife areas for many species of plants and animals. To evaluate the status of wildlife management areas in your study area, fill out the *Wildlife Management Areas Form* on page 158. All designated wildlife management sites are considered protected unless some adjacent activity is threatening them with pollution or the site has a severed mineral estate which might allow mining or drilling. Include any information about threats in the comments section of the form.

  Potential sites include large tracts of wetlands and forest that are relatively undisturbed and have some type of special wildlife value. Many times the land adjacent to an existing area is an important potential site. That land may have the same wetland or other value as the wildlife area, or it may be important to buffer the wildlife area from the encroachment of surrounding development. Contact the local managers of these sites in your study area and ask for information on potential sites. Also request information on the level of use or copies of any use reports for the area. Contact the state and federal wildlife agencies and request information on any potential wildlife areas under consideration by them. Include all potential sites on your form.

Step Three: Map the wildlife management areas
- Map the boundaries of the wildlife management areas on your study area map.

Where to get the information
- Contact the U.S. Fish and Wildlife Service and the state fish and wildlife agency.

Both the state and federal fish and wildlife agencies own and manage wildlife management areas. Also, land owned by other federal agencies, such as the Tennessee Valley Authority, U.S. Army Corps of Engineers and the Forest Service is designated for wildlife management. In addition, private land owners can designate wildlife management areas through cooperative agreements with state and federal agencies.

Many progressive wildlife agencies have nongame wildlife (wildlife not hunted) programs and watchable wildlife programs. Just as forestry programs are going to ecosystem management, so are wildlife programs moving to ecosystem management. This means protecting entire ecosystems so all wildlife benefits and thrives, not just the hunted species.

The watchable wildlife programs usually involve providing areas where particular species like Bald Eagles, waterfowl, or Prairie Chickens can be observed. Chapter 9 has a section describing how to develop a watchable wildlife program.

Wildlife Management Areas

Wildlife management areas	Size: acres/miles	Types of uses permitted	Area use pattern: (N) not used; (O) over used (S) sustainable; (U) under used /sustainable

Comments, plans for future action:

CHAPTER 7

EXAMINING AN INDIVIDUAL FACILITY

Introduction

In this section we use the term "audit" for learning about an individual facility. There are a number of ways to do an environmental audit. Citizens do not, however, have the access to a facility to conduct the type of audit that an engineer or scientist hired by the owner might. This means that citizens must rely on information contained in public records or facts which a private facility will voluntarily provide. Following the process outlined here will give a person, group, or public official a good idea of how well a particular facility is operating according to government records.

The three types of facilities discussed in this section are the individual industry, the drinking water plant, and the wastewater treatment plant. Think about the individual industry audit in terms of your own checkbook. (No, we don't mean that it's empty!) You would like to be able to account for what's coming in and what's going out of the facility. This is especially true of all the chemicals being used. If a company buys a million gallons of benzene, it should be able to say where it went: how much went out as product, how much was converted by some chemical reaction to something else, how much was spilled, how much escaped into the air, how much was sent for recycling and disposal, and how much went out with the wastewater. A good audit will also tell a company whether it is in compliance with environmental laws. A great audit will tell a company how to minimize, reduce, and stop producing wastes that end up being discharged into the environment. The audit outlined here will only begin to raise all the right questions about these issues.

Auditing the Individual Industry

When looking at an individual industry, you have to do many of the tasks discussed for the environmental concerns inventory in chapter 5. It is possible just to deal with the air, water or land portion of an industry, but we recommend that all aspects of a site be reviewed. If you are most concerned about your well water, you could just look at the groundwater. But remember, several things can affect the groundwater quality such as disposal of chemicals on the land, the use of lagoons for waste treatment, disposal of chemicals down a well, leaking sewer pipes, leaks from open ditches used to move waste around an industrial site, and spills.

What to Do: Contact and Survey the Industry

Your first activity is to contact the industry and inform them you are reviewing their environmental record. Ask for a tour of the facility and have them fill out the Individual Facility Survey Form on pages 162-163. The individual facility survey form includes a request that the company provide copies of all permits and other documents relevant to reviewing their environmental performance. If you receive all the information requested, you will get a copy of their environmental permits, find out what they are discharging, and be able to check their environmental compliance record. After you receive the completed survey you should then follow the worksheet entitled Individual Industry Audit Worksheet on pages 164. This worksheet will direct you to the appropriate section of this manual for further work and summary forms that you can use. If you do not receive the information requested, or want to check that information then, follow the Individual Industry Audit Worksheet. For example, if the industry has a water discharge permit, you will follow the steps under water pollution sources in the Environmental Concerns Inventory section of this manual. When you have collected necessary data and completed the appropriate summary forms, you can examine what the discharge levels mean to your community by completing steps outlined in Chapter 8.

One major task in this section differs from what has been thus far recommended as part of the overall community review: conducting a right-to-know audit of chemicals that are used at a company but not covered by that law. As discussed in the right-to-know section on page 47, that law only covers 320 acutely toxic chemicals in certain industries above certain levels of use or production. There are over 60,000 chemicals in use, many of which have unknown human health and environmental effects. We are recommending an audit on all the chemicals used at a facility. Superfund sites exist today because of how chemicals were used and discarded in the past. The question is, "How are all of the chemicals a company is using being handled today?

Steps for an Individual Industry Audit

In summary, here are the steps you should follow for an individual industry audit:

- Identify the industry
- Send questionnaire and request a visit
- Obtain copies of all necessary documents, records, permits, etc.
- Fill out all appropriate data summary forms. Follow the individual Industry Audit Worksheet
- Make your findings known to the industry, community, and regulators

---

A second major task to perform in this section is the review of waste minimization and reduction efforts that have been made by the company. This waste minimization audit can be performed in the following way:

1. Make a list of the wastes being generated by the facility.
2. Write to one of the following for information on known waste reduction methods for that type of industry:

   • U.S. Environmental Protection Agency
   • Your state agency responsible for hazardous waste
   • Tennessee Valley Authority

Ask them to send you information that relates specifically to the waste streams identified, or the particular type of industry you are reviewing (such as dry cleaners). You should review this information and send a copy to the industry with recommendations for reduction goals and time tables, or request a meeting with the industry and your group to discuss waste reduction.

Individual Facility Survey Form

Facility Name _____

Contact Person _____

Address _____

_____ (Phone) _____

1. Do you have or have you submitted an application for :

- ☐ Water discharge permit (NPDES #_____)
- ☐ Storm water discharge (permit #_____)
- ☐ Air construction (permit #_____)
- ☐ Hazardous waste generator registration (#_____)
- ☐ Hazardous waste (RCRA) permit (#_____)
- ☐ TSD facility (Type_____)
- ☐ Solid waste landfill permit (#_____)
- ☐ Pits, ponds, and lagoons (permit #'s (if applicable)_____)

2. Are you now, or have you ever been a RCRA treatment, storage, or disposal facility?

Yes ☐   No ☐

Please check the following that are appropriate

- ☐ Corrective Action program underway
- ☐ RCRA part B permit issued (Date)_____
- ☐ RCRA Facility Assessment complete
- ☐ Number of SWMU's_____
- ☐ RCRA Facility Investigation complete
- ☐ Corrective Measures Study complete
- ☐ Corrective Measures Implementation plan complete

3. Does your facility contain a state or federal Superfund site or other uncontrolled site?

Yes ☐   No ☐

If yes, check the following that are applicable

- ☐ PA/SI complete
- ☐ HRS score_____
- ☐ NPL proposed
- ☐ NPL final listing
- ☐ Remedial Investigation complete
- ☐ Feasibility Study complete
- ☐ Record of Decision final

- ☐ Remedial Design report complete
- ☐ Remedial Action plan complete
- ☐ Consent decrees/106 orders/court orders
- ☐ Next action required_____
  _____
- ☐ State cleanup plan underway
  Phase_____

4. Do you have any of the following on the property where your facility is located:

Yes	No	Don't know	
☐	☐	☐	Dams
☐	☐	☐	Wetlands
☐	☐	☐	Floodplains
☐	☐	☐	Wildlife management areas
☐	☐	☐	Rare plants or animals
☐	☐	☐	Natural areas
☐	☐	☐	Ash ponds
☐	☐	☐	Water treatment lagoons
☐	☐	☐	Pits

5. Have you ever conducted an environmental audit at your facility? Yes ☐ No ☐

6. Do you have an ongoing program for waste reduction? Yes ☐ No ☐

7. Have you ever conducted a waste reduction or minimization audit? Yes ☐ No ☐
   If yes, when?

8. Do you handle or store chemicals on the 313 list below the reportable quantities?
   Yes ☐ No ☐   **If yes, please list:**

   Chemicals   **Quantities**

9. Will you provide our group with copies of the following information on your facility?

Yes	No	
☐	☐	Environmental permits and applications
☐	☐	Inspection reports
☐	☐	DMRs (Discharge Monitoring Reports)
☐	☐	Waste reduction audits
☐	☐	Environmental audits
☐	☐	List of all chemicals used at your facility and MSDS sheets for them?
☐	☐	TRS submittal
☐	☐	Groundwater monitoring well results

Individual Industry Audit Worksheet

1. If you received the information requested on the survey form and are comfortable it is complete and accurate, go to the "forms" column below to find which forms to fill out. Where it says "no form," then no summary form exists.

2. If the industry would not cooperate and provide information, work your way through the appropriate sections of chapter 5. This should get you the same information you requested on your survey form to the industry.

3. The suggested steps in the individual sections of chapter 5 are directed toward the study area. You will need to revise the suggested steps slightly so they can apply to the individual facility. (For example, under "Superfund Sites," the suggested activity is to examine files on Superfund sites in your study area. For this section, however you will need to change this to a study of Superfund sites at your particular facility). An industry is likely to have discharges or regulatory responsibilities in any of the following sections of Chapter 5.

Section	Forms
1. Reported toxic chemical release	No Form
2. Extremely hazardous chemicals	No Form
3. Sources of water pollution	Water Discharge Summary
	Environmental Compliance Summary
4. Sources of air pollution	Air Discharge Summary
	Environmental Compliance Summary
5. Hazardous waste facilities	Hazardous Waste Facility Summary
	Environmental Compliance Summary
6. Hazardous waste generators	Environmental Compliance Summary
7. Superfund sites	Superfund Site Summary
	Superfund Action Checklist
8. Solid waste sites	Landfill Summary
	Waste Sources and Types
	Environmental Compliance Summary
9. Mining sites and facilities	Mining Sites Summary
	Mining Compliance Summary
10. Oil and natural gas facilities	Environmental Compliance Summary
11. Underground storage tanks	UST Summary
12. Dams and floodplains	No Form
13. Polluted runoff	No Form
14. Septic systems	No Form
15. Springs and wells	No Form
16. Transportation hazards	No Form

After data has been collected and all appropriate summary forms filled out, go to Chapter 8 for how to analyze the pollutants.

Auditing the Public Water Supply

Few responsibilities of government are as important as ensuring a safe public water supply. Elected officials, managers in charge of drinking water facilities, and the public are all concerned with this issue. People do not want to have second thoughts about turning on the tap and drinking a glass of water or cooking with it or giving it to their children. So how safe is your drinking water?

The answer is, you have to check. Unless you do, you could be drinking anything. Sometimes you can see what's in the water and sometimes you can't. Water from public water supplies has been known to contain gasoline, trihalomethanes, bacteria, dirt, heavy metals, and a variety of organic chemicals. There was even one public water supply in eastern Kentucky where the citizens would periodically have live worms (midge fly larvae) coming out the tap. This posed an interesting problem for the regulators since worms were not listed as a pollutant in the law and it probably would not hurt to drink them. There are worse pollutants in our water, but just try to convince someone with worms coming out of the tap of that!

From 1971 to 1974, there were 99 reported and documented waterborne-disease outbreaks in the U.S. that affected 16,950 people. The outbreaks involved typhoid fever, bacterial diseases (causing intestinal problems), chemical poisoning, and parasites. A 1982 Government Accountability Office report found that of 146,000 violations on record in 1980, only 16,000 were publicly reported and very few were acted upon by a state regulatory agency. Our suggested audit is one that citizens can do and is based on public records. It is not the type of audit done by a team of experts who go into a facility and examine it from top to bottom (which is rarely done). From this audit, however, you should get a good idea of how well your facility is operating, according to government records and requirements.

Purifying Water

Purifying surface water requires a more extensive treatment process than for groundwater. Steps include settling out the dirt and other particles in the water, treating with chlorine, ozonation or ultraviolet light to kill harmful bacteria and other organisms, filtering, and maintaining a distribution system that does not pollute the purified water.

For well and spring water the treatment can be simplified. This is because there are usually no particles (dirt) in the water to be settled out. In some cases this water can be pumped, disinfected, and distributed. People in rural areas have been pumping and using well and spring water for years without disinfection.

What to Do: Contact and Survey the Drinking Water Plant

Begin by sending the Drinking Water Supply Survey (pages 168-169) to the local drinking water plant. If the drinking water plant officials are unwilling to complete the survey, then you should request all of the information on the survey form through a freedom of information or open records request (see Appendix D for a sample letter).

Determine the service area for the water system. Map that information on a study area map (see Chapter 4 for mapping information). From the records of the water company determine how many households and individuals are being served.

What contaminants are tested for by your drinking water plant and with what frequency? Appendix H contains the list of contaminants which are the chemicals that large plants are required to measure. Smaller plants may be exempt from much of this testing, depending on your state's program. Find out what your drinking water plant is measuring. Compare these two sets of information. If, for example, the supply is not testing for organic chemicals, then you do not know if it is safe. Some potential drinking water contaminants are carcinogens (cancer causing). These chemicals may have a standard (Maximum Contaminant Level), which allows some level of chemical in drinking water, and a federal goal (Maximum Contaminant Level Goal — or MCLG) which is set at zero. This is the federal government's recognition that zero exposure to carcinogens is desirable, since any exposure amounts to some amount of risk. The standards (MCLs) are set taking economics and feasibility into consideration.

Follow the steps in Chapter 8 to analyze the chemicals in your drinking water. Fill out the Chemicals of Concern Form (page 183) based on all of the known chemicals in your finished drinking water. Add to that list all chemicals that should be, but are not being tested for in your supply. This list should minimally be all chemicals in Appendix H. Other chemicals that should be tested for are those in the raw water supply. Look at the information collected in Chapter 5, section 3, Sources of Water Pollution for additional chemicals in the water.

How much water is available for my community?

We have been talking about the quality of our drinking water so far, but quantity of water is another concern—whether or not you have enough water available to serve your community. This is an especially significant issue if you are in a growing area. Kentucky is water-rich with an estimated 90,000 miles of streams and rivers, but many miles of those streams dry up every summer. In the drought of 1987, ten Kentucky water supplies ran out of water and 20 became vulnerable and had to go on some type of conservation program, including the large city of Lexington, KY. Even the city of Atlanta, Georgia has had water conservation imposed during recent dry summers.

In order to determine if you have enough drinking water, or more importantly, to determine if you will have enough in the future, you need to know the following:

Demand Past records can be used to project the demand for water. This figure can then be adjusted for new growth. One thing you need to remember about water use is that when it doesn't rain there are new demands, such as irrigation of crops and watering of lawns. See the Water Availability Worksheet to examine your local water situation.

Raw Water Supply The amount of water available really means how much is available during a drought. The term low flow is used for describing the flow in streams during certain conditions. A common term is 7Q10. This refers to the low flow for a seven day period on a frequency of every ten years. 3Q20 is the three day low flow on a 20 year frequency. Different states use different baselines for low flow. Droughts can be more severe than the low flow conditions.

Well Water To calculate the water available from your well you will need to do a pump test. This can be accomplished most accurately by pumping a specific amount of water out of your well while monitoring what happens to the water levels in two or more nearby wells. If your supply is on a well, ask the manager if a pump test has been conducted and request a copy of the results.

Storage Capacity How much water can be stored in the system (includes water tanks, reservoirs, and lines) if the water source is contaminated or breaks down and is temporarily shut off? For what period of time can that storage supply the community?

Surface Water The amount of water available from some sources is simply not an issue. If your intake is the Ohio River, Mississippi River or a large reservoir, you will not need to make any calculations. For many communities this is not the case. A small stream with low seasonal flow, into a small impoundment is all that serves many communities.

Conservation Because of our extravagant use of water in the U.S., there is much to be saved through conservation. For example, it is estimated that an easy 30 percent can be saved with water-saving showerheads and commodes. Be aware that many systems have leaks and that means water not paid for and wasted. Many systems have as much as 30 percent loss. When thinking about water availability and water needs, we should first think conservation.

What are they doing with their backwash?

Water treatment plants not only take water in, they also have a discharge. That discharge comes from the backwashing of filters that washes out the dirt and suspended solids originally taken in. If discharged directly back to the river or stream in this concentrated form, these pollutants can be a water quality problem. The drinking water plant should have an NPDES water discharge permit and a system of lagoons designed for the backwash. Request a copy of the discharge permit.

Drinking Water Supply Survey

Facility name _____

Contact person _____

Address _____

_____(Phone)_____

1. What is the source of your raw water supply?

2. How many households do you serve?

3. How many gallons of water per 24 hours is your plant rated to deliver?

4. What was you average demand for each of the last 12 months?

Jan_____ Feb_____ Mar_____ Apr_____ May_____ Jun_____

Jul_____ Aug_____ Sep_____ Oct_____ Nov_____ Dec_____

5. Have you received any notices of violation for your operations in the last year?

6. Are you under any type of enforcement orders (including administrative orders, agreed orders, court orders)?

7. What are the possible sources of pollution that directly impact the raw water supply?

8. Does the drinking water plant have enough certified water plant operators?
   ☐ Yes ☐ No
Do they have the proper certification and do they attend the required update classes to keep their licenses current?   ☐ Yes ☐ No. Please give the names of your certified operators and their certification numbers.

9. Do you run the compliance tests required by the Safe Drinking Water Act or are the tests run by outside labs?

10. Have the managers of the water supply visited the laboratory they contract with and are they familiar with these tests, or do they rely entirely on the laboratory to select and evaluate the methods?

11. Does the water supply have an emergency plan for droughts, emergencies, plant breakdown, and spills?

12. Does the water plant have granulated activated carbon (GAC) on-hand to absorb organic chemicals?

13. Does the state do split samples with commercial laboratories on compliance samples?
    Date of last split sample analysis: _____

14. Does the water plant have a cross-connection prevention program to ensure that untreated water does not enter the system from private wells or other sources?

15. What is being done to control corrosion in the system?

16. Is there a regular flushing and cleaning program for the lines?
    Frequency_____   Date of last flushing_____

17. Are old lines replaced as needed?
    Date of last replacement_____ Location_____

18. Is there a regular maintenance of storage tanks and hydrants?

19. Is there proper water pressure through the system to prevent back siphoning of contaminants and provide for fire protection?   ☐ Yes ☐ No. What is the lowest pressure in the system? _____ psi. Where does that occur?

20. Do you have a map of the distribution system?

21. Are dead end lines equipped to be flushed?

What contaminants are tested for in the raw and/or finished water?

Chemical	Raw Water	Frequency	Finished Water	Frequency

Water Availability Worksheet

Rated treatment capacity of the plant _____ gallons/day

Average daily demand _____ gallons/day
(if data is given monthly, divide the total gallons consumed during the month of highest demand by the number of days in that month).

Lowest flow of source _____ gallons/day

Number of days the low flow has lasted _____

Sustained capacity of well _____ gallons/day

Capacity of reservoir _____ gallons

Available capacity _____
 (60% x capacity of reservoir = available gallons)

Is siltation a problem and has it reduced available capacity? If yes, what is the % reduction?

If low flow is zero: $\dfrac{\text{available gallons}}{\text{demand per day}}$ = days reservoir will last

If low flow is less than demand: $\dfrac{\text{Available gallons in reservoir}}{\text{Demand - low flow}}$ = days reservoir will last

Days reservoir will last _____

If the demand is 80% or more of the rated treatment capacity (gallons per day) of the plant, you already have a problem if your service area is still growing. This demand level should trigger additional planning.

80% x rated treatment capacity (gallons/day) = _____ gallons/day

Auditing the Sewage Treatment Plant

When you have a concentration of people, you need a sewage treatment plant to handle all of the waste produced. Sewage treatment plants that are publicly owned (called POTWs - publicly owned treatment works) are usually designed to decompose and digest organic material. This is primarily domestic waste from the bathroom, laundry, and kitchen. A sewage treatment plant is just a concentrated form of nature. When animals die or defecate in the woods, tiny organisms like bacteria break the waste down into harmless water and carbon dioxide. In a sewage treatment plant there are a lot of these tiny organisms working on the waste. Of course, there can also be many toxic chemical pollutants in sewage, either from industry or from toxic household products, like insecticides, paint and paint thinners, and even toxic cleaning products. See Chapter 9 for how to make your household less toxic. Figure 7.1 shows the basics of how a sewage treatment plant is designed to work.

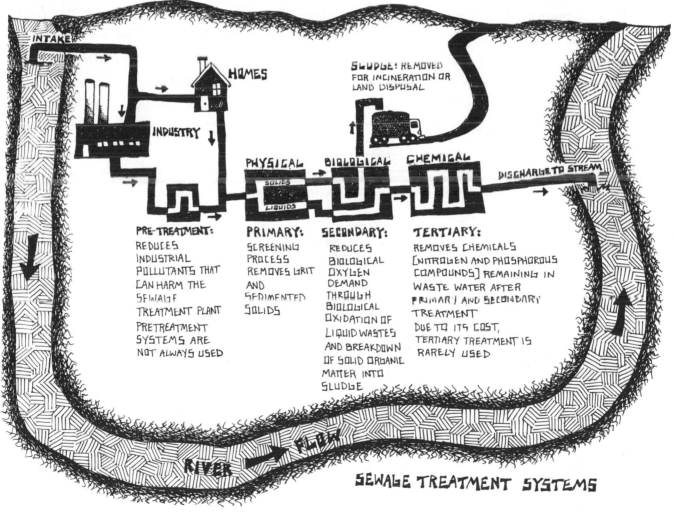

Figure 7.1 - Sewage Treatment Systems

Basically, you have sewage coming in the front of the plant, and water (still containing some pollutants) and sludge (the solids left over after the tiny organisms have digested what they can) coming out the end of the plant. The concern is with the quality of the water being discharged back to the environment and the quality of the sludge which may be spread on a farm or go into a landfill.

Sewage treatment is divided into three categories: primary, secondary, and tertiary. Primary treatment is when the large particles are screened or settled out. The sewage goes into a tank called a "clarifier," and the flow is slowed so the particles will settle to the bottom. This portion then becomes part of the sludge. The sewage then goes on for secondary treatment. This is where the bugs go to work on it. The bugs are all of those bacteria and other microscopic organisms that eat up the organic material in the water. After the bugs have done their work, the sewage goes into another clarifier where more sludge is removed. There are three types of secondary systems. One is the *activated sludge process* where the sewage and bugs are actively mixed with lots of air. Another system is the *trickling filter* where the bugs live in a bed of rocks and the sewage trickles over them. There is also the *lagoon system* where sewage is pumped into what looks like a pond or lake. The bugs break down the organic material in these open water systems.

Another type of system that works well for domestic sewage is the *artificial wetland*. The artificial wetland contains a carefully designed and graded wetland that allows raw sewage to enter at one end and flow through the roots of growing plants such as cattails. The bacteria and other organisms living in the wetland and on the roots of plants degrade the organic waste. Clean water comes out the end of the wetland.

The third level of treatment (tertiary) is for removing nitrogen and phosphates and further reducing organics and suspended solids. Nitrogen and phosphates are usually limited in nature. Organisms such as algae thrive on these compounds. Extra nitrogen and phosphates can cause algae to grow so fast and use so much oxygen that fish and wildlife in lakes and rivers die, so it is important to remove as much as possible from the water being introduced back into the environment. Tertiary treatment is also used to remove organic (industrial) chemicals that need charcoal filtration. More sewage treatment systems are being required to have tertiary treatment in order to protect the environment. Unfortunately, very few sewage treatment plants have tertiary treatment.

The final step after treatment is disinfection, usually through chlorination and dechlorination. This involves the use of chlorine to kill all of the pathogens like bacteria and viruses that are in sewage and are not affected by any of the other levels of treatment. The chlorine must be taken out before the water is discharged because it is harmful to fish and other aquatic life. Ultraviolet light, which avoids the environmental problems that chlorine can cause, can also be used to kill pathogens in the discharge. If it is to be used, sand filters are often required to ensure that the water subjected to the ultraviolet light is free of particles that will prevent the light from reaching all of the water.

How do you know if the sewage plant is working?

The discharge from the sewage plant (where the treated water is coming out the pipe to the environment) must have a permit. The permit is called an NPDES permit (that stands for National Pollutant Discharge Elimination System. The word "national" may be replaced with the name of your state). That permit usually comes from the state, but can be issued by the U.S. Environmental Protection Agency.

In order to determine how well the sewage treatment plant is working, you should request a tour of the facility and ask that the Wastewater Treatment Plant Survey (pages 174-176) be completed. If the facility refuses to fill out the survey you should request the documents containing the same information under a freedom of information (open records) request (see Appendix D for sample letter). All of the information you are requesting is public information.

Are there industries on the sewage system?

This is a very important question because the waste coming to a sewage treatment plant from industries can be very different from household sewage. Industrial waste can contain heavy metals like the very toxic cadmium, organic chemicals (a number of which can cause cancer), salt, and dyes. If industries discharge to your sewage system, the city or sewage authority should have a pretreatment program in place. See Chapter Five, section three (Sources of Water Pollution) of this guide for what information to obtain about the pretreatment program.

Wastewater Treatment Plant Survey

Facility name _____

Contact person _____

Address _____

_____ (phone)_____

1. How many households do you serve?

2. How many total people do you serve?

3. How many gallons of sewage per 24 hours is your plant rated to treat?

4. What organic loading is your plant rated to treat?

5. What was your average flow for each of the last 12 months?

Jan_____ Feb_____ Mar_____ Apr_____ May_____ Jun_____

Jul_____ Aug_____ Sep_____ Oct_____ Nov_____ Dec_____

6. Have you received any notices of violation for your operations in the last year?

7. Are you under any type of enforcement orders (including administrative orders, agreed orders, court orders)?

8. What are the industrial waste sources connected to the treatment plant?

9. Do you have an approved pretreatment program?

10. How many certified plant operators do you have?

Do they have the proper certification and do they attend the required update classes to keep their licenses current? ☐ Yes ☐ No. Please give the names of your certified operators and their certification numbers.

11. Do you run the compliance tests required by your permit, or are the tests run by outside labs (if outside please give name and location of lab)?

12. Have the managers of the treatment plant visited the laboratory they contract with and are they familiar with the tests or do they rely entirely on the laboratory to select and evaluate the methods?

13. Does the state split samples with commercial laboratories on your compliance samples?
        Date of last split sampling _____
    Does the state split samples with industrial dischargers to your plant?
        Date of last split sampling _____

14. Does the wastewater plant have an emergency plan for plant breakdown or spills? If yes, are copies of the plan available?

15. Does the plant have an I/I (inflow/infiltration) prevention program?

16. Does the sewer system have combined stormwater and sewer lines?

17. Are old lines replaced as needed? _____ Date of last replacement _____

Location_____

18. Do you have a map of the collection system?

19. Describe how you handle sludge.

Will you provide our group copies of the following information on your facility?

Yes	No	
☐	☐	Environmental permits and applications
☐	☐	Pretreatment ordinances
☐	☐	Pretreatment permits issued
☐	☐	Rate structure
☐	☐	Discharge Monitoring Reports (past 12 months)
☐	☐	Environmental audits
☐	☐	Sludge handling permits (landfarming, etc.)
☐	☐	Sludge characterization tests

What contaminants are tested for in the discharge from the plant?

Discharge

Chemical	Frequency of testing

What contaminants are tested for through the pretreatment program?

Pretreatment

Facility	Contaminants tested	Frequency of testing

8 ANALYSIS OF POLLUTANTS

Environmental and Human Health Concerns

By now, you probably have some idea what chemicals are present in your community's land, air, and water. This chapter is intended to help you decide what those results mean. There are a number of ways to categorize the effects of chemicals on human health and the environment. One is by how fast a person or animal is likely to be killed or poisoned by exposure to certain levels of a chemical. *Acute toxicity* is when some type of *immediate* harm will likely be caused to a person or the environment. *Chronic toxicity* is when harm comes if a person or wildlife is exposed over a long period of time. Another way to categorize chemicals is by the particular type of health or ecological effect they have. Some chemicals are regulated because they cause acid rain, global warming, ozone depletion, or some other type of environmental problem that may not be covered in the analysis outlined in this chapter.

Much of our time and energy is spent worrying about how certain chemicals can harm humans. But what about the fish, deer, insects, mice, birds, and plants? Most people have concluded from their own common sense that a world that can't support plants and animals will not support humans. Our environmental laws are as much about protecting the total environment as about only protecting human health. Our water quality standards have been developed to protect the animals that live in the water. Appendix H gives the federal water quality standards.

You should be aware that the federal standards are minimal standards for the entire United States. They were not designed to be sufficiently protective for all types of environments; that's why states are allowed to pass more stringent standards. They may not be sufficient to protect your state or community and clearly have not been sufficient for many. In Kentucky, for example, discharges of brine from oil field operations were killing all life in some streams and rivers. There was no federal standard, so Kentucky had to develop its own. In many states people who have a financial stake in polluting try to keep their state from being any more stringent than the federal government, even in the face of inadequate federal regulation.

For the toxic chemicals listed in Appendix I, the following categories of potential adverse human health effects are the most commonly used:

Carcinogens (C) Chemicals in this category are those that can cause cancer in humans, like benzene (which can cause leukemia), and those that are thought possibly to cause cancer in humans because they cause cancer in other animals.

Genetic and Chromosomal Mutagens (GC) These are chemicals that can cause the genes (DNA) in a sperm or an egg to be mutated or changed. Those changes can then be passed along to a baby. Changes to other cells in the body, such as cells in your liver, can also occur.

Developmental toxicity (DT) These are chemicals that affect the development of a baby inside its mother. Being exposed to such chemicals can cause miscarriages and physical defects to the baby.

Reproductive toxicity (RT) These are chemicals that can damage the ability of men and women to reproduce.

Acute Toxicity (AT) Short term exposures, either through the lungs, mouth, or skin, can cause death.

Chronic Toxicity (CT) Exposure over a long period can cause damage other than cancer, such as lung, liver, or kidney problems.

Nervous System Toxicants (N) These include chemicals such as solvents and glues that cause problems with the brain and nervous system. These effects can be either temporary or permanent.

Ecological and environmental concerns relate to how a chemical harms wildlife and plants, whether a chemical stays in the environment, and whether it accumulates in the food chain. There are three categories for the chemicals listed in Appendix I.

Environmental Toxicity (ET) These chemicals can harm wildlife when released to the water, air, or onto the land.

Bioaccumulative (B) This means a chemical becomes more and more concentrated in the food chain. For example, an insect will have a low level of chemical, a mouse that eats insects will have a higher level, and the hawk that eats mice will have an even higher level.

Persistent (P) This means that it is stable and does not break down very easily once it enters the environment.

How do we take pollutants into our bodies?

Different pollutants get into our bodies in different ways. Certainly we breathe in anything that is in the air. When you smell gasoline, you are taking some amount of benzene into your body. We also eat many chemicals. They are on our food because they were put on as a pesticide or preservative. They are in our food because the chemicals are in the environment and have been taken up by the plants or animals. They are in the water we drink because lots of chemicals are being discharged into our streams and rivers. Most public drinking water systems are not equipped to remove organic chemicals.

Which Chemicals are of Concern?

The simple answer is that all of them are of concern. But from the regulatory point of view, there are specific lists that are regulated under different environmental laws:

Emergency Planning and Community Right-to-Know (SARA Title III) This is a list of 320 of the most toxic chemicals that must be reported under the law.

TSCA This is the longest list. These are all of the known chemicals in use. The regulatory significance of this list is minimal. TSCA has a short list of regulated chemicals including PCBs.

Hazardous Waste (RCRA list) This is a list of chemicals regulated under RCRA as hazardous waste. There is also a RCRA list of "hazardous constituents," which are the chemicals that must be cleaned up at RCRA facilities, even if they did not come from "hazardous waste."

Superfund (CERCLA) The Superfund list is different from the others. Any chemicals on this list (called hazardous substances) that were improperly disposed can be cleaned up as part of the Superfund program.

There are also a number of chemicals that have specific limits for how much can be put into the air, water, or drinking water. They usually relate to a specific law:

Drinking Water Standards For the protection of human health, certain chemicals are regulated in drinking water. See Appendix H for the drinking water standards.

Water Quality Criteria These are the minimum standards necessary to protect living organisms in the stream, and human health from drinking, swimming, and eating fish. (See Appendix H).

Air Standards Air discharge limits have been set for a few pollutants. They are listed in Appendix H.

Relative Comparison of Pollution Impact

List all of the chemicals found in your study area by source

Fill out the *Chemicals of Concern Form* on page 183. For each source, list on this form all the chemicals found in your Environmental Concerns Inventory (Chapter 5) or from your Individual Facilities Audit (Chapter 7). The following list corresponds to the columns on the form:

Source List the name of the company or site discharging the chemicals. Use individual forms for each source.

Chemical List any chemical being discharged that you discovered in your inventory.

Media For each chemical and source, list whether it is the land, air, or water being contaminated.

Likely Exceeding Permitted Limits For each chemical, source, and medium, identify the amount, or a "yes" or "no" if you think the permit limits are being exceeded. Information obtained for each category in Step Three of Chapter 5 will give you a good sense of this.

Unpermitted or Uncontrolled Discharges or Contamination This would be a "yes" or "no." If there are fugitive emissions, malfunctions, or spills, place a "yes" in this column.

TIP Score The TIP stands for Toxicity Index Profile. It represents a measure of how many different types of potential toxic effects a chemical has, based upon the different impact categories into which it falls. Look up each chemical on the list of Chemicals of Concern in Appendix I. Write the TIP score from the table on your form. Note for yourself the different effects a particular chemical can have. Each chemical is given a score of 1-10. A score of 10 means that it has the highest potential number of types of adverse human health and ecological effects. It is important to note that the TIP Score is just one indication of the potential harm caused by a chemical -- it does not provide any measure of how dangerous the chemical is. For example, a really dangerous cancer-causing substance, dangerous in tiny quantities, could have the same score as a cancer-causing substance that was dangerous only in larger quantities.

If a particular chemical is not on the list in Appendix I, that does not mean that it is not a problem. EPA is currently considering doubling the chemicals that must be reported under the Right-to-Know law. Place a "U" in the TIP score column if you do not know the chemicals effect. If you want more information on chemicals, then obtain either a MSDS or a New Jersey Data Sheet on the chemical (see below for how to obtain this information).

Pounds of Chemical Enter the total pounds of the chemical from the TRI information collected in Chapter 5, section one (Toxic Chemical Releases). If you have this information for other chemicals from other sections in Chapter 5, you can also enter that here. If this is unknown then enter a "U" in this column.

Potential Relative Exposure (PRE) The Potential Relative Exposure for each chemical is the TIP score multiplied by the number of released pounds of that chemical (TIP x Pounds = PRE). Then, add up the PRE's scores for all chemicals to obtain the total PRE for the facility. You may then compare different sources to one another.

Making Comparisons

Use the total PRE score to make comparisons between facilities. For this score add all the PRE scores for a particular facility or source. This approach gives a way to begin thinking about the pollution impacts in your community. This is obviously just a relative ranking system. The totals arrived at do not necessarily reflect actual exposures. Also all chemicals are not equal in potency. You can, however, begin with such an approach. The method described in the above steps is modified from procedures developed by Dr. John R. Stockwell and colleagues at the U.S. Environmental Protection Agency.

Where to get additional information

Most of the information is available in your own work sheets and from the list of Chemicals of Concern in Appendix I. To obtain additional information about the effects of a particular chemical, you can go to several sources:

Material Safety Data Sheets (MSDS) Under the Occupational Health and Safety Administration (OSHA) there is a requirement to provide information on every chemical used in the workplace. That information is provided on Material Safety Data Sheets (MSDS) (see Appendix F for a sample). These may be obtained from individual industries or from OSHA.

New Jersey Data Sheets These sheets cover all of the chemicals on the Superfund list. These may be obtained from the following two sources:

Right-To-Know Project
Department of Health
CN 368
Trenton, New Jersey 08625-0360
(609) 984-2202

RTK Network
1731 Connecticut Avenue, NW
Washington, DC 20009

Patterns of Pollution

There is considerable evidence that there is a concentration of the highest polluting industries in low-income communities and communities with a high percentage of people of color. Once society decides it wants or needs a particular product, there are many possible ways to deal with the pollution from making that product. One way would be to distribute the pollution equally to everyone who benefits from the product. The second option is to ensure that no pollution levels exist that can degrade the quality of life where the industry exists and spread the cost of achieving that to all those who benefit from the product. Unfortunately, it seems our society disproportionately puts the burdens of pollution on those who are discriminated against in other ways, or those who can ill afford protective measures such as adequate health care, buying bottled water, or moving out of the polluted neighborhood.

It is a worthwhile exercise to examine your own community for evidence of environmental racism or classism. Divide your study area into separate regions based upon race and/or income. Your map might show Indian reservations, ethnic communities, income groups, colonias, or communities of Appalachians who migrated to an area. The groupings need to make sense for your own community. Overlay this "map of people" with the map you developed that shows the sources of pollution in your community. Do you see any patterns or relationships that lead you to conclude that some people in your community are being exposed to high levels of pollution?

You can also just draw a one mile or half mile circle around each pollution source and use the total PRE score obtained in the previous exercise to compare those sites. Determine if the "worst" pollution is in particular communities or neighborhoods.

There are two sources for the information needed to make your maps. It is completely acceptable for you to use the knowledge of people in your group to generally outline on a map the different groups you are concerned about. Your group can also use the U.S. Census Bureau information for your community to determine where particular groupings occur. If you are using the Census Bureau data, select some level to look for, such as over 50% African-American or any other ethnic group. You can also select income levels, such as under $20,000 income or the poverty level. Identify which census tracts fit your criteria.

Chemicals of Concern

Facility/site name

Chemical	Where found? land, air, or water	Discharges likely exceeding permitted limits?	Unpermitted or uncontrolled discharges or contamination?	TIP Score	Pounds of chemical	Potential Relative Exposure (PRE)	Total PRE

* PRE = TIP score x pounds of chemical

9 Expanding What The Agencies Know

Introduction

Many times individuals know more than what is in the official files of the government agencies. There are many examples of companies that have been overlooked, examples of illegal and improper practices that have gone unnoticed, whole communities of people who have been subjected to high levels of pollution, and pollution that has gone unreported. Sometimes new laws and regulations are needed, sometimes enforcement of existing laws is needed, and sometimes public pressure on the industry, local government, or the regulatory agency is needed. Before anything can be done, someone who cares has to be aware of what is going on. This section offers several ways that citizens can find out more about what's going on in their community.

Yellow Pages Search

In the community of Dayhoit, Kentucky, serious groundwater contamination was discovered. The source was a company that had been using a solvent for cleaning coal mining equipment parts. Since that company had been overlooked by the regulatory agency, others like it could also have been overlooked. Looking up that type of business in the Yellow Pages of the phone book could reveal other similar businesses in the area. If you have dry cleaners, auto body shops, service stations, or other types of businesses on your hazardous waste generator list, check to see if all facilities representing each type in your area are listed. Once you learn about a specific company, send a letter of inquiry to the state or federal agency most likely responsible for regulating them and ask if they have been inspected and, if not, why they are not being regulated.

Illegal Dump Survey

It is illegal everywhere to throw your garbage on the side of the road, in a sinkhole, or in a creek. Drive every road in your study area and catalog all of the dumps. Use a county road map or USGS topographic map and actually record the location of every dump. You will have to drive every back road, dirt road, and dead-end road. You may want to even collect any discarded mail found at a dump so you can identify who is using the site. Conduct your survey when the leaves are off the trees if possible. You can see a lot more and a lot farther.

Aerial Photograph Review

Looking at photographs taken from the air can be quite revealing. You can find illegal dumpsites, drums of chemical waste, waste lagoons, eroded areas, places where tanker trucks are parked, and bare areas where no vegetation is growing. All of these indicators of possible pollution can lead to an on-the-ground review of just what is going on at these sites. Two good sources for aerial photographs are your local ASCS (Agriculture Stabilization Conservation Service) office and the state department of transportation.

In the "cave country," sinkholes are often used for dump sites. Surveying these sites may be a bit trickier since many of them are on the "back forty" of someone's farm. Record as many as you can see from the road. You may be able to identify many on aerial photos.

Questioning Current and Former Employees

The employees at a company know if chemicals are being dumped out the back door, down a well, or down the sewer in the middle of the night. Many times the best leads a regulatory agency gets are anonymous calls from employees. Generally they fear for their job and are reluctant to have their names used. The information you get from them must be used carefully so that the company cannot learn the source. However, a number of state and federal laws protect such "whistle blowers" from retribution.

If possible, try to independently verify information received from an anonymous source. Sometimes the only thing to do with this information is pass it on to the regulatory authorities and wait (or hope) for some type of official action to take place before you make it part of the environmental inventory. Once the regulatory agency has acted, or if the information can be independently verified so the source will not be identified, you should add the information to the appropriate part of your environmental inventory.

Landfill Truck and License Checks

Sitting outside a landfill counting trucks entering and checking license plates can tell you how much is coming to a landfill and from where. Use the *Landfill Deliveries Form* (page 194) for tracking what is coming to your landfill. Compare this information with the official records collected in the landfill section from earlier chapter 5, section 8.

Industry Background Checks

Who really owns and operates the local landfill or industry that is polluting your environment? What is their environmental record in other states? You can take the following basic steps to learn more about a company:

- In most states, deeds are kept in the county courthouse. Find out who owns the land that the plant is located on.

- Request a copy of the company's incorporation filing. First check in your state. The company should be registered to do business in your state even if its home state is elsewhere. The incorporation records can also be requested from the secretary of state in the company's home state.

- Obtain a Dunn and Bradstreet information sheet on the company. To do this you will have to locate someone who is a subscriber (check with your local newspaper reporter). Some large public libraries offer this service. The Dunn and Bradstreet report will tell you who the principals, officers, and affiliated companies are. There are also other data bases that contain this information. Check with your local librarian.

- Request information from all states where the company and principals are operating concerning environmental violations in those states.

- If the company is publicly traded (on the stock exchange), it must file in-depth reports with the Securities and Exchange Commission in Washington, D. C. Request the company's 10 (K) annual report.

Non-reporters of TRI Information

The Toxic Release Inventory (TRI) data can easily overlook an industry that fails to report. Review the complete list of industries included in SIC codes 20-39 (Appendix G). If you have any of the types of industries listed and they are not on your TRI inventory obtained in chapter 5, section one, then send a letter to the state agency responsible for TRI information and ask why the particular industry is not on the list.

Taking Your Own Samples and Pictures

There are many environmental watch, water watch, stream watch and other volunteer environmental monitoring programs in the United States. A listing of these organizations is provided in Appendix A (see the 1992 River Conservation Directory in the Reference List). We recommend becoming involved with one of these programs if your group is seriously interested in monitoring some aspect of the environment.

You may just want to take a few samples to spot check some discharge in your community. If you have a budget, hire a laboratory, or consultant to take some samples for you. Be careful how you select the consultant. Most firms survive by working for industry, and they may be reluctant to work for citizens.

Citizens need to be on the alert seven days a week and after working hours to document pollution. Often it is a Saturday or after working hours when the river turns purple or the smokestack turns black. Copies of photographs and videotapes taken by citizens can be given to a regulatory agency, used as evidence in a lawsuit, or to confront a company about their practices. This can also be the necessary encouragement for the regulatory agency to do its job. A camera that marks the date and time on the photograph is helpful, but not necessary. Be sure to take careful notes regarding the pictures or video you take (date, exact time, exact place you were standing, etc.).

Private Well and Spring Sampling

Groundwater is one of our least understood resources. Private wells are rarely regulated or tested for contamination. However, many states will test private wells, at least for bacterial contamination. Call your health department or environmental agency responsible for groundwater and see what type of program they have for testing private water supplies. Organize a private well and spring testing program in your study area. If you can show a potential for contamination based upon the information you collected in your Environmental Concerns Inventory, the state agency responsible for groundwater or the health department should be willing to participate in such a study. If these agencies will not provide help, you may need to pay for a consultant or private lab to sample for a list of organic industrial pollutants, pesticides, and metals.

Reading Placards

Any truck that is transporting hazardous materials must display a placard telling what they are hauling. For a complete listing of what each placard number means, obtain a copy of the Department of Transportation's Emergency Response Guidebook. This book also gives information about what action needs to be taken if a spill of any one of hundreds of chemicals occurs. You can obtain the guidebook by writing:

> Office of Hazardous Materials
> Research and Special Programs Administration
> U.S. Department of Transportation
> Washington, D.C. 20590
> 1-800-752-6367

Your group could set up a watch program at a busy intersection in your community and record how many trucks come by that point. Record this information on the *Road Survey Form* on page 195. By doing this at several different times and recording the placard number or symbol, you can get an idea of the quantity and type of chemicals being transported through your community. If you have a Department of Transportation weigh station in your study area, you could seek their cooperation in determining what comes through during a particular period.

Household Hazardous Waste

Household hazardous waste or toxic chemicals have become much more common in the home waste stream. Cleaners, throwaway batteries, used oil, paint, paint thinners and strippers, oven cleaner, and pesticides are examples of the products that contain toxic chemicals (see table 9.1 for a more complete list).

Conduct a toxic products audit of your home by listing all the products in all the rooms of your home that have toxic chemicals in them.

The next step is to reduce the use of toxic products. The best way to do this is through selection and use of non-toxic alternative products. By reducing their use, you reduce indoor air pollution and your own exposure and eliminate the impact to the environment from disposal. Table 9.2 gives suggestions for alternatives to toxic products.

For additional information on household hazardous waste write:

Concern, Inc.
1794 Columbia Rd., NW
Washington, D.C. 20009
(202) 328-8160

Environmental Hazardous Management Institute
P.O. Box 932
Durham, NH 03824
(800) 446-5256

Watchable Wildlife

You may be able to talk your state fish and wildlife agency into developing a watchable wildlife program or area in your region, or maybe there already is one. There is a growing interest in viewing and photographing wildlife. Providing watchable wildlife areas expands the recreation, education, and conservation opportunities for citizens. A local watchable wildlife area can be an economic benefit to local merchants.

If you are interested in developing a watchable wildlife program you can do the following:

- Contact your state fish and wildlife agency and see what type of program exists. Ask if guides are available.
- Determine if an opportunity exists locally for a watchable wildlife area.
- Obtain a copy of *NatureWatch*, a publication of the Defenders of Wildlife. It is available from Falcon Press, Helena, Montana. This is a comprehensive publication about all aspects of a watchable wildlife program. It will allow you to help start a new program or judge an existing program in your own state.

Hazardous Contents of Common Household Products

Household Cleaners

Air freshener: Alkyl phenoxy polyethoxy ethanol; Isobutane; Propane

Ammonia based cleaner: Ammonia; Ammonium hydroxide; Diethylene glycol; Ethoxylated alcohol; Phenols; Sodium hypochlorite; Surfactants; Xylenols

Drain opener: Hydrochloric acid; Potassium hydroxide; Sodium hydroxide

Floor finish: Ammonia; Diethylene glycol; Petroleum solvents

Laundry soap, dishwashing detergent: Ethylene glycol; Methanol chloride; Perchloroethane; Sodium hypochlorite; Surfactants; Tetrachloroethylene

Polish: Denatured ethanol or isopropanol; Mineral spirits; Oxalic acid; Petroleum distillates; Petroleum solvents; Phosphoric acid; 1,1,1-Tricholoroethane

Toilet bowl cleaner: Chlorinated phenols; Sodium acid sulfate or oxalate or hydrochloric acid; Trichloro-s-triazinetrione

Oven cleaner: Sodium or potassium hydroxide

Household Maintenance

Glue: Acetone; Asbestos fiber (asbestos cement); Hexane; Methylene chloride; Methyl ethyl ketone; Toluene

Paint: Halogenated aromatic hydrocarbons; Methylene chloride; Mineral spirits; Toluene; Xylene

Paint thinner and stripper: Alcohols; Chlorinated aliphatic hydrocarbons; Chlorinated aromatic hydrocarbons; Esters; Ketones; Toluene

Varnish/sealant: Benzene; Lead; Methyl and ethyl alcohol; Methylene chloride; Mineral spirits; Pentachlorophenols; Petroleum

Automotive Maintenance

Antifreeze/coolant: Ethylene glycol; Methanol; Auto wax; Petroleum distillates

Engine treatment: Methylene chloride; Mineral spirits; Petroleum distillates; Toluene; 1,1,2-Trichloroethylene; Xylenes

Oil and transmission fluid: Lead; Petroleum distillates

Batteries: Lead; Sulfuric acid

Pesticides and Yard Maintenance

Fertilizer: Ammonia; Nitrogen; Phosphorus; Potassium (concentrated)

Herbicides: Chlorinated phenoxys; Dipyridyl; Nitrophenols

Pesticides: Aromatic petroleum hydrocarbons; Carbamates; Chlorinated hydrocarbons; Coumarin; Naphthalene; Organophosphorus; petroleum distillates; Triazine base; Uracil; Urea; Xylene

Pet treatment (flea and tick): Carbaryl; Chlordane; Dichlorophene; Other chlorinated hydrocarbons

Table 9.1 - Source: U.S. Environmental Protection Agency. Report to Congress. Solid Waste Disposal in the United States. EPA/530-SW-88-011B, Vol. II, Oct. 1988.

Alternatives to Toxic Products Used in the Home

Instead of this	Use this
Ammonia-based cleaners	Vinegar, salt, and water mixture; baking soda and water
Abrasive cleaners	1/2 lemon dipped in borax
Floor or furniture polish	1 part lemon juice, 2 parts olive or vegetable oil
Silver cleaners	Boiling water with baking soda, salt, a piece of aluminum
Toilet cleaners	Baking soda, toilet brush
Disinfectants	1/2 cup borax in 1 gallon water
Drain cleaners	1/4 cup baking soda and 1/4 cup vinegar in boiling water; use a plunger
Rug/upholstery cleaners	Dry cornstarch
Moth balls	Cedar chips, lavender flowers
Enamel or oil-based paints	Latex or water-based paints
Furniture strippers	Sandpaper
House plant insecticide	Dishwater or bar soap and water

Table 9.2 - Adapted from: Household Hazardous Waste Wheel. Environmental Hazards Management Institute, P.O. Box 932, Durham, NH 03824. (800) 446-5256.

Greenlinks: Connecting Wildlife Habitat

You have identified and mapped the natural areas, public forests, parks, streams, and other natural resources in your area. If these are connected by green corridors that allow for wildlife to move between them, the biodiversity of the landscape can be protected and enhanced. In other words, the whole of your natural areas, parks, forests, and greenspaces, if connected, can be much more than the sum of the disjointed parts.

Connections, or corridors, are also important for allowing animals to migrate between areas. For example, a small woodland will have more birds in it if it is somehow connected to a larger forest. That connection can be along a wooded stream or fencerow. By naturalizing or revegetating a stream bank with native plants, you protect the stream from erosion and provide shade to the water and animals that live there.

The first task is to look for ways to connect your parks, natural areas, forests, and other greenspaces together along streams, roads, fencerows, old railroad right-of-ways, ridgelines, or steep slopes that cannot be otherwise developed. Try to link areas that deserve protection, areas that have scenic value, and areas that protect rare plants and animals. Identify on your map those corridors between areas that will make good bike paths and walking paths, which provide the opportunity for recreation and environmental education.

Your proposed set of green links can be called a greenspace plan. Share your greenspace plan for the area with the landowners who will be affected, public officials, and the public. Thoroughly develop your ideas for why greenspace is important to your community.

Part of your greenspace plan will address specific managed areas or parcels of land. If a local park has two isolated patches of woodland on it, include in your plan a link between them. If a particular area can be made a better natural area or park by including an adjacent wooded area, include that recommendation in your proposal. Sometimes the habitat for rare plants can be protected by providing a buffer area around where they live.

If you want to do more to enhance the wildlife habitat in your area, you could develop a "Greenlinks" program. Chapter Two of the *Landscape Restoration Handbook, Harker et. al.*, offers more information on such programs. Connections can be made by naturalizing (planting or revegetating with native plants) or expanding the vegetated area along stream banks, fencerows and roadsides. A Greenlinks program has three basic parts: 1) working with landowners in the region to link more and more greenspaces and natural areas together in a regional context; 2) developing a detailed naturalization plan for particular managed sites; and 3) linking the public to the idea of naturalizing the landscape through a strong education program.

Developing a "Good Neighbor" Program

The Good Neighbor Handbook by Sanford J. Lewis and others is a comprehensive guide for assessing a local industry and developing a good neighbor agreement to help assure the industry meets the communities' standards. Citizens can and should advise companies of their expectations of neighborliness. In many cases, organized local citizens may be able to achieve greater reductions in pollutants through agreements than the regulatory agencies can achieve.

The Good Neighbor Handbook is comprehensive and looks at such things as toxics reduction and pollution prevention, industry assessment procedures, success stories, negotiating procedures, how to forge neighbor-labor alliances, model good neighbor agreements, and how to build community power. *The Good Neighbor Handbook* complements and supplements this guide and provides a comprehensive approach for the follow-up activity of obtaining good neighbor agreements with industrics of concern.

The following quote is from the Good Neighbor Handbook:

Many citizens' groups are seeking opportunities to thoroughly evaluate safety risks or pollution from a particular local plant. Some of these organizations are concerned with the risks to their health from a potential accident; in other cases, their members may have already been exposed to a recent accident. Still other groups want to evaluate the extent of ongoing "chronic" pollution to their local community. Underlying most of these groups' inquiries is the question of whether the firm is doing all that it can to actively reduce pollution and accident hazards. Unfortunately, environmental laws do not make it "simple" for a local citizens group to answer this question. For instance, they don't grant citizens easy access to all of the information, facilities and experts needed to provide the answers. But some citizens groups have pioneered a way to attain these rights and resources by getting a firm to enter into a "Good Neighbor Agreement," which allows a citizen inspection of the facility and an in-depth audit of company documents.

The Good Neighbor Handbook suggests the following seven steps:

1. Decide whether a particular industry is one that you want to evaluate in depth
2. Gather information before contacting the company
3. Contact the company
4. Negotiate access
5. Inspect the industry
6. Prepare a follow-up report
7. Negotiate a good neighbor agreement

For more information and to order a copy of the handbook, write or call:

The Good Neighbor Project
P.O. Box 79225
Waverly, MA 02179
(617) 489-3686

Landfill Delivery Form

Landfill Name _____ Date _____

Recorder _____

| Time | Vehicle | | | Placard Type | Placard Number |
	Type*	Tons	License Number		

* 1. 18 Wheeler (semi tractor-trailer)
  2. Small 13 ton packer
  3. Large 20 ton packer
  4. Pickup truck
  5. Other

Road Survey Form

Location _____

_____

Date _____ Recorder _____

Time	Vehicle Type		Placard Type	Placard Number
	Non-Tanker	Tanker		

10 ENVIRONMENTAL DECISION MAKING IN YOUR AREA

Evaluating Sites for Industrial Facilities

Ask yourself this basic question: do you have anything to say about the types or locations of facilities that come into your community? The following conditions must be present if you are to answer "yes". First, you must know what facilities are planned or are being recruited to your community. Second, there must be a process by which you are able to evaluate the facility. This evaluation should include what the proposed facility does, where it is from, what materials it uses and produces, what discharges it will have, and its past record of following environmental laws. Third, there must be a process by which you can affect the decision about whether the facility will or will not locate in your area. Establishing such a process could be achieved through your local governing body, a planning and zoning process, or an industrial or economic development board that is sensitive to environmental issues as part of its recruitment process.

Certain states and communities are being targeted for high risk and heavy polluting industries. A California study conducted for the waste industry recommended that low income, under-educated, rural, and minority areas be targeted for the unwanted facilities because, among other things, these areas had no political clout.

The first task for your group is to figure out the local process for siting a new facility (see Figure 10.1 for characteristics of a good approach). Identify what groups of elected and non-elected people are involved. Also identify when the public is made aware of the plans. Try to find out what type of evaluation goes on beyond the usual determination of how many jobs will be created, and find out whether there is any real way to influence the decision.

Your second task is to develop procedures for the deficient areas in the process. We recommend a siting process which genuinely involves the public in the decision making. The public needs to consider the long-term future of the community, including the effects on the water supply and water quality, air quality and waste issues (see Figure 10.2 for questions). Other considerations include the usefulness and sustainability of the products the facility produces (will it produce styrofoam cups or durable wood furniture). Ask yourself if the facility will exploit your community or build the kind of community you want. A responsible company will not be deterred from becoming part of a community because that community cares about its future and the role that company plays in it.

- The economic development group formed to evaluate the facility is representative of the community (Includes non-elected officials, women, minorities, environmentalists, small business, etc.).
- Through a public process (town meetings, etc.) a vision for the community is formed, including what types of facilities to attract. This occurs before major recruiting. This process should include a sustainability analysis.
- Alternatives to industrial recruiting are considered, including putting money into expanding existing local businesses and developing and assisting small businesses.
- A screening process for all proposed facilities includes an extensive environmental review and background check, including full public disclosure. This process concludes with a public meeting and report of the economic development group.
- All incentive packages are submitted for public scrutiny and comment. No public officials or anyone involved with recruiting should benefit directly or indirectly from the deal.
- A process for true citizen input should be implemented, including public meetings (widely advertised, well in advance) with company representatives.

Figure 10.1 - Characteristics of a Good Approach

- Are infrastructure needs (public utilities, water, sewer, roads, etc.) currently available?
- Will the new facility disrupt or displace existing industries?
- What financial incentives (such as buildings, tax breaks, water, sewer, and other utilities rate reductions and services, training, and roads) is the facility expecting?
- How many jobs will be created immediately and at what pay? How many jobs are promised later? How many jobs will be full-time? What benefits will employees receive?
- Is the facility compatible with the community's vision and idea of sustainable development?
- Is this a "dirty" industry with significant water or air discharges, or landfill requirements?
- What is the environmental record of the facility? Where are the parent company and other branches located?
- Is the company likely to have longevity in the community? Does it have a stake in the community?
- Is the facility relocating from another community, or expanding operations? If relocating, how long was the facility at its last site? How often and how many times has it moved?
- If a relocation, under what conditions did the facility leave the last community?

Figure 10.2 - Some Questions About a New Facility

The Environmental Permitting Process

It is important to understand that permits are one way we as a society legitimize and actually legalize pollution. The permitting process gives citizens one way to voice their concerns about polluters. Every state's process is different. Remember, the person or industry trying to obtain the permit has likely been working to get the most lenient permit possible. The agency giving the permit has a very large amount of discretion in deciding what conditions and discharge limits go into the permit. Public involvement provides some of the essential balance that can make the government agency do its job better. For example, it is startling to find the degree to which the state depends on industry for monitoring. The regulatory agency sets the frequency of the monitoring. The facility may be required to sample its discharge daily, monthly, quarterly, or annually. The state regulators may sample an industry only once a year to check compliance with their permit, or not at all, as in many air permits. Citizens can help determine how frequent an industry is sampled. The permitting process works better and is more protective of the health and welfare of the community when the public is involved.

Most environmental laws require a rather unsatisfactory method of public notice for alerting citizens that a permit is to be issued. The public notice must be published in a local newspaper. If you miss seeing it, too bad. Some regulatory agencies attempting to avoid a public controversy have been known to publish the permit notice at a time such as Christmas Eve, when the public will likely not notice it. More responsible programs have outreach to concerned citizens and groups, notifying when actions are to be taken in their areas.

Water Permits

There are two aspects for permitting a facility: one for construction, and one for discharge. These may be handled in one or two permit actions. Also, different rules may apply to how these permits are handled. The discharge permit is part of the federal clean water act (NPDES program) and therefore has certain requirements the states must meet. The construction permit is usually a state action (there is no federal oversite for construction permits). In some states, the plant can be built while the discharge permit is pending. Sometimes states will issue a "general" permit which covers all activities of a particular type, such as stormwater discharges from parking lots or discharges from surface mines. Here is an outline of the discharge permitting process:

1. A permit application must be filled out by anyone intending to discharge pollutants into the environment. This application will request a variety of information including what the applicant wants to discharge and where. There is no federal requirement that the public be informed that this application has been filed.

2. The responsible regulatory agency will develop a draft permit. This draft permit will include all of the requirements the agency is proposing for the discharger.
3. A public notice will be published in the local newspaper stating that the draft permit has been issued and is available for review. The public generally has thirty days to comment on the permit and ask for a public hearing.
4. If a public hearing is requested, the permitting agency will publish a notice stating where and when the hearing will be held. The agency will conduct the meeting. Most likely the public will only be allowed to comment at the meeting, with no real give and take. After listening to the comments, the agency will respond to them in a written document, and incorporate the changes they accept into a new permit.
5. The new permit is issued (or in exceptional cases, is denied). The public then has 30 days to challenge the permit on legal grounds. If challenged, the parties appeal in an administrative hearing (which is like a court within the regulatory agency). If either party is dissatisfied with the administrative process, then the matter can be taken to court.

Hazardous Waste Permits

Like the water permit process, the hazardous waste treatment, storage, or disposal facility permit process begins with a permit application. Before the permit becomes final, a draft permit must be prepared, the public must be notified, and public comments must be accepted and responded to. In addition, the public can request a public hearing on the draft permit, (or in Kentucky, at least an administrative hearing). The local government may have the power to veto or approve the siting of the hazardous waste facility based on social and economic impacts such as property values, the emotional costs connected to having a hazardous waste facility in the community, and its compatibility with local planning. Check your state and local laws (including planning and zoning laws) for any special treatment of hazardous waste facilities. When special state or local laws exist, there will likely be additional opportunities to voice concerns about a facility.

Hazardous Waste Generators

There is no permit process for hazardous waste generators, although most will need air and/or water discharge permits. Hazardous waste generators are required only to file a registration.

Solid Waste Permits

This is an area that the federal government has left mostly to the states. The U.S. Environmental Protection Agency has developed some minimal regulations in this area. Most states have developed an independent set of regulations for solid waste. Some states have taken a progressive and protective approach to the problem of solid waste and some have all but ignored it. See chapter 5, section 8 for a discussion of different types of solid waste facilities.

States may or may not have regulations requiring them to publish notice of draft permits and take comments before issuance of final permits. Many types of solid waste facilities are not required to have permits at all. You need to obtain a copy of solid waste regulations for facilities in your state. Different types of solid waste facilities have different public notice requirements.

404/401 Permits (filling in wetlands)

The protection of floodplains and wetlands is primarily accomplished through the section 404 permitting process of the Clean Water Act. This section is jointly administered by the Corps of Engineers and the U.S. Environmental Protection Agency. In addition to the Federal 404 permit, states have the power to restrict the discharges of "dredged or fill material" into wetlands. This state process is called the 401 certification process. A 404 permit cannot be issued unless the state certifies it meets water quality standards through the 401 process. See Figure 10.3 for an overview of the 404 permitting process.

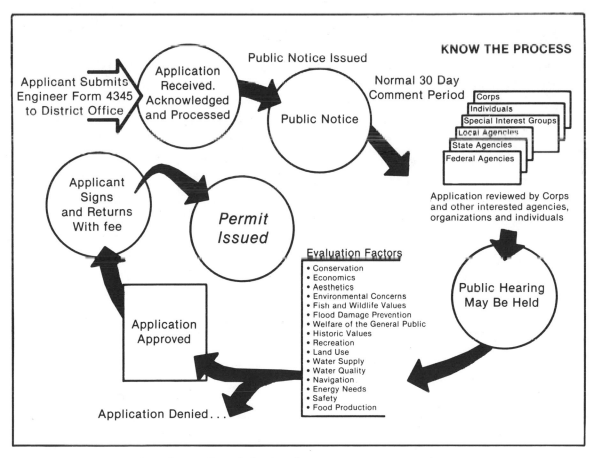

Figure 10.3 - Corps of Engineers Permit Review Process
Source: U.S. Army Corps of Engineers

Air Permits

The air pollution permit process, like water and hazardous waste, is largely controlled under guidelines set by the federal EPA. For any "major" source of air pollution, the permit will have to go through the public notice and comment process. Permits for so-called "minor sources," less than a specific tonnage of any individual pollutant to be emitted, are not required under federal law to be subjected to public comment before issuance, but states can provide for this kind of public participation if they wish.

Other Ways Citizens Can Be Involved

Legislative Process Legislative committees hold hearings on environmental laws that are proposed for enactment.

Rulemaking Process Environmental regulatory agencies enact regulations, which are designed to give necessary details for how laws are to be implemented. For example, a law might say streams must be fishable. A regulation will then set the dissolved oxygen level at 7 ppm to support fish. Regulations go through a public process, where citizens can comment.

Citizen Complaints Formal complaints can force a regulatory agency to take action. Document complaints with photos, samples, and videotape.

Citizen Suits Most environmental laws allow for citizens to sue a polluter when the regulatory agencies are not doing their job. Citizens can also intervene in actions between an industry and the regulatory agency.

Good Neighbor Negotiations Citizens can be involved in direct discussions with industries in their community. Citizens should not be timid about expressing what they consider acceptable standards in their community. See discussion in chapter 9.

APPENDIX

A RESOURCES AND REFERENCES

Hotlines and Organizations

Hotlines:

RCRA HOTLINE. A U.S. EPA sponsored information line for answers to questions about the Resource Conservation and Recovery Act, the basic law regulating hazardous waste. (800) 424-9346.

SARA 313 COMMUNITY RIGHT-TO-KNOW. A U.S. EPA sponsored information line for answers to questions about Section 313 of the SARA laws (this is the part of SARA pertaining to Form R and toxic emissions). (202)479-2449 or (800) 535-0202.

SUPERFUND, SOLID WASTE, AND UNDERGROUND STORAGE TANKS. (800) 424-9346.

DRINKING WATER. (800) 426-4791.

EMERGENCIES (NATIONAL RESPONSE CENTER, U.S. COAST GUARD AND EPA). (800) 424-8802.

PESTICIDES. (800) 858-7378.

WASTE WATER. (800) 624-8301

WETLANDS. (800) 832-7828.

Organizations: There are many local and state organizations that can be of help to groups. Find out what organizations are working in your area.

CITIZENS CLEARINGHOUSE FOR HAZARDOUS WASTE, P O Box 926, Arlington VA 22216, (703) 276-7070. An information clearinghouse for toxics activists, founded by the people who fought and won at Love Canal. Offers a large assortment of low price reports on topics of interest to community activists, as well as direct advice on organizing to win. CCHW can also refer you to other helpful contacts in your area.

ENVIRONMENTAL RESEARCH FOUNDATION, P O Box 3541, Princeton NJ 08543-3541, (609) 683-0707. Co-producers of this manual with Greenpeace, ERF sponsors computer databases with information on toxics and publishes the weekly newsletter on toxics issues, "Rachel's Hazardous Waste News."

GREENPEACE ACTION, 1436 U St. NW, Washington DC 20009, (202) 462-1177 (many regional offices). Sister organization to Greenpeace U.S.A., this branch of the international Greenpeace movement handles grassroots lobbying and public education about environmental issues in the United States.

GREENPEACE U.S.A., 1436 U St. NW, Washington DC 20009, (202) 462-1177 (many regional offices) Sister organization to Greenpeace Action in the United States, Greenpeace campaigns on toxics, disarmament, and wildlife issues.

WORKING GROUP ON COMMUNITY RIGHT-TO-KNOW, Paul Orum, Coordinator, 215 Pennsylvania Ave. SE, Washington DC 20003, (202)546-9707. Publishes monthly newsletter. A collaboration of about 12 national environmental organizations working to supply information to toxics activists on right-to-know.

THE GOOD NEIGHBOR PROJECT, P.O. Box 79225 Waverly, MA 02179, (617) 489-3686. Publication available on developing good neighbor agreements.

LEAGUE OF WOMEN VOTERS, 1730 M Street, NW, Washington, DC 20036, (202) 429-1965. The League has many local groups working on environmental issues.
INSTITUTE FOR GLOBAL COMMUNICATIONS, 18 De Boom Street, San Francisco, CA 94107, (415) 422-0220. This organization operates several worldwide computer networks including EcoNet.

SIERRA CLUB, 730 Polk Street, San Francisco, CA 94109, (415) 776-2211

INSTITUTE FOR LOCAL SELF RELIANCE, 2425 18th Street, NW, Washington, DC 20010, (202) 232-4108

MINERAL POLICY CENTER, 20 W. Chapman Street, Alexandria, VA 22301, (703) 683-0506

KENTUCKY RESOURCES COUNCIL, NATIONAL COAL PROJECT, 311 Wilkinson Street, Frankfort, KY 40601, (502) 875-2428

ENVIRONMENTAL HAZARDOUS MANAGEMENT INSTITUTE, P.O. Box 932, Durham, NH 03824, 800-446-5256.

CONCERN, INC., 1794 Columbia Rd. NW, Washington, DC 20009, (202) 328-8160

RTK NETWORK, 1731 Connecticut Avenue, NW, Washington, DC 20009.

NATIONAL WILDLIFE FEDERATION, 1400 16th Street, NW, Washington, DC 20036-2266, (404) 876-8733.

THE JOBS AND ENVIRONMENT CAMPAIGN, 1168 Commonwealth Avenue, Boston MA 02134, (617) 232-5833

HIGHLANDER CENTER, 1959 Highlander Way, New Market, TN 37820, (615) 933-3443

CITIZENS ENVIRONMENTAL LABORATORY, 1168 Commonwealth Avenue, Boston, MA 02134, (617) 232-5833

USPIRG, 215 Pennsylvania Ave, SE, Washington, DC 20003, (202) 546-9707

References

A citizen's guide to clean water. n.d. Izaak Walton League of America. Arlington, VA: Izaak Walton League of America.

A citizen's guide to promoting toxic waste reduction. 1990. Kenworthy, L. and E. Schaeffer. New York, NY: Inform, Inc.

A citizen's toxic waste audit manual. 2nd ed. 1990. Gordon, B., P. Montague. Washington, DC: Greenpeace U.S.A.

Citizens' guide for environmental issues: a handbook for cultivating dialogue. 3rd ed. 1993. Charleston, WV: National Institute for Chemical Studies and US EPA.

Communities at risk: environmental dangers in rural America. 1989. Fritsch, A. Washington, DC: Renew America.

Conducting a health survey. 1984. Gibbs, L. M., S. Lester, and contributors. Falls Church, VA: Citizen's Clearinghouse for Hazardous Wastes.

Drinking water: a community action guide. 1991. Boyd, S., et. al. Washington, DC: Concern, Inc.

Environmental science: living within the system of nature. 1993. Kupchella, C. and M. Hyland. Englewood Cliffs, NJ: Prentice Hall.

Environmental testing?? 1988. Lester, S. and L. M. Gibbs. Falls Church, VA: Citizen's Clearinghouse for Hazardous Wastes.

From poison to prevention: a white paper on replacing hazardous waste facility siting with toxics reduction. 1989. Lewis, S. M. Kaltofen. Boston, MA: The National Toxics Campaign Fund.

Household ecoteam workbook. 1992. Gershon, D. and R. Gilman. Woodstock, NY: Global Action Plan for the Earth

Landscape restoration handbook. 1993. Harker, D., S. Evans, M. Evans, and K. Harker. Boca Raton, FL: Lewis Publishers.

Making connections: service training for environmental progress. 1992. Nashville, TN: (STEP): Center for Health Services, Vanderbilt University.

National directory of citizen volunteer environmental monitoring programs. 3rd ed. 1990. Lee, V. and E. Ely. Washington, DC: Environmental Protection Agency.

Putting the scientists in their place: participatory research in environmental and occupational health. 1989. Merrifield, J. New Market, TN: Highlander Research and Education Center.

Resource guide to state environmental management. 1989. Brown, R. S. and K. Marshall. Lexington, KY: The Council of State Governments.

Risk communication about chemicals in your community: a manual for local officials. 1989. Environmental Protection Agency. Washington, DC: EPA.

1992 river conservation directory. 1992. U.S. Department of the Interior - National Park Service. Washington, DC: American Rivers, Inc.

Saving America's countryside: a guide to rural conservation. 1989. Stokes, S. Baltimore, MD: The Johns Hopkins University Press.

Solid waste action project guidebook. 1987. Connett, P. and P. Montague. Arlington, VA: Citizens Clearinghouse for Hazardous Wastes.

Strip mining handbook. 1990. Squillace, M. Washington, DC: Environmental Policy Institute and Friends of the Earth.

The citizens toxics protection manual. 198?. National Campaign Against Toxic Hazards. *The environment: issues and choices for society.* 1988. ReVelle, P. and C. ReVelle. Boston, MA: Jones and Bartlett Publishers.

The nuclear waste primer. 1993. Wiltshire, S. League of Women Voters Education Fund. New York, NY: Lyons and Burford.

Toxic and hazardous substances, title III and communities: an outreach manual for community groups. 1989. Environmental Protection Agency. Washington, DC: EPA.

Volunteer water monitoring: a guide for state managers. 1990. Environmental Protection Agency. Washington, DC: EPA.

Waking a sleeping giant: a citizen's guide to toxic chemical releases reported under section 313 of the emergency planning and community right-to-know act. 1989. Kentucky Resources Council. Frankfort, KY: Kentucky Resources Council.

Waste: choices for communities. 1988. Boyd, S., B. Lapham, and C. McGrath., editors. Washington, DC: CONCERN, Inc.

Wetlands protection: a handbook for local officials - environmental planning information series report #7. Department of Environmental Resources Commonwealth of Pennsylvania. 1990. Washington, DC: Environmental Law Institute.

B ENVIRONMENTAL CONCERNS SURVEY

Sample Environmental Concerns Survey / pages 209-213

Instructions: In the first column, circle the number that shows how important each issue is to you. In the second column, circle the number that shows how satisfied you are with your community's efforts to address the issue. If you find an item that does not apply to you, leave both columns blank.

EXAMPLE:	Importance of the issue	Satisfaction with the community's efforts
	not very	not very
1. There are enough restaurants in the community.	0 1 2 3 4	0 1 2 3 4

In the example, the person filling out the survey saw the restaurant issue as very important and was only somewhat satisfied with the community's efforts to address this issue.

Please circle the importance and satisfaction for each of the items that follow.

	Importance of the issue	Satisfaction with the community's efforts
	not very	not very
1. Government officials work closely and cooperatively with private citizens.	0 1 2 3 4	0 1 2 3 4
2. Citizen groups are actively involved in improving this community.	0 1 2 3 4	0 1 2 3 4
3. Residents care about making this community a nice place to live.	0 1 2 3 4	0 1 2 3 4
4. Dunloup Creek Water is free of disease-carrying organisms.	0 1 2 3 4	0 1 2 3 4
5. Dunloup Creek is a good place to fish.	0 1 2 3 4	0 1 2 3 4
6. Dunloup Creek is a good place to wade and swim.	0 1 2 3 4	0 1 2 3 4
7. People can walk and ride bicycles safely and conveniently to areas around Dunloup Creek.	0 1 2 3 4	0 1 2 3 4
8. Local training for environmental jobs is available.	0 1 2 3 4	0 1 2 3 4
9. The quality of drinking water is good.	0 1 2 3 4	0 1 2 3 4
10. Adequate environmental protection services are provided.	0 1 2 3 4	0 1 2 3 4

Appendix B

	Importance of the issue	Satisfaction with the community's efforts
	not very	not very
11. Houses are hooked up to public sewers.	0 1 2 3 4	0 1 2 3 4
12. Water in Dunloup Creek is clean.	0 1 2 3 4	0 1 2 3 4
13. Dunloup Creek is clear and free from mud and silt.	0 1 2 3 4	0 1 2 3 4
14. Log and construction sites prevent mud and silt from entering Dunlop Creek.	0 1 2 3 4	0 1 2 3 4
15. Household sewage is adequately treated before reaching Dunloup Creek.	0 1 2 3 4	0 1 2 3 4
16. Coal mine water is adequately treated before reaching Dunloup Creek.	0 1 2 3 4	0 1 2 3 4
17. Sewage treatment is affordable.	0 1 2 3 4	0 1 2 3 4
18. Surface mining laws are enforced.	0 1 2 3 4	0 1 2 3 4
19. Surface mining companies adhere to mining regulations.	0 1 2 3 4	0 1 2 3 4
20. Residents keep their communities clean.	0 1 2 3 4	0 1 2 3 4
21. Everyone has garbage pick-up.	0 1 2 3 4	0 1 2 3 4

	Importance of the issue					Satisfaction with the community's efforts				
	not			very		not			very	
22. Environmental education is available to residents.	0	1	2	3	4	0	1	2	3	4
23. Government agencies respond to environmental complaints.	0	1	2	3	4	0	1	2	3	4
24. Adequate flood control is available along Dunloup Creek.	0	1	2	3	4	0	1	2	3	4
25. People along Dunloup Creek like the way it looks.	0	1	2	3	4	0	1	2	3	4
26. Communities along Dunloup Creek are attractive.	0	1	2	3	4	0	1	2	3	4
27. Environmental laws are adequately enforced.	0	1	2	3	4	0	1	2	3	4
28. Residential garbage collection is handled in a way that insures the sanitation and neatness of the area.	0	1	2	3	4	0	1	2	3	4
29. People can get help in paying for sewage hook-up.	0	1	2	3	4	0	1	2	3	4
30. Overall, quality of community life is good.	0	1	2	3	4	0	1	2	3	4

Appendix B

Personal Information

1. What community do you live in?

2. Are you a registered voter?

       Yes _____

       No _____

3. Are you employed?

       Yes _____

       No _____

4. How many people are in your household?

5. What outdoor hobbies and recreational activities does your family participate in?

6. Is your house connected to a public sewer system?

       Yes _____

       No _____

7. Is your house connected to a septic system?

       Yes _____

       No _____

8. What is your household water source?

APPENDIX C

ADDRESSES

FEDERAL OFFICES

Regional Offices of the U.S. Environmental Protection Agency /
    pages 215-216

Regional Offices of the U.S. Fish and Wildlife Service / page 217

Regional Offices of the U.S. Army Corps of Engineers /
    pages 218-219

Other Federal Offices / page 220

> Federal Soil Conservation Services
> U.S. Army Corps of Engineers
> United States Geological Survey (USGS)
> Tennessee Valley Authority
> National Wetlands Inventory

Federal Office of Surface Mining (state offices) / page 221

STATE ENVIRONMENTAL OFFICES / pages 222-277

State offices are arranged from left to right with environmental offices listed alphabetically after each state. This information is from the *Resource Guide to State Environmental Management* by Steve Brown and Karen Marshall and published by The Council of State Governments.

Regional Offices of the U.S. Environmental Protection Agency

Region 1
(CT, ME, MA, NH, RI, VT)
Environmental Protection Agency
John F. Kennedy Federal Bldg.,
Room 2203
Boston, MA 02203-0001
(617) 565-3932

Region 2
(NJ, NY, Puerto Rico, Virgin Islands)
Environmental Protection Agency
26 Federal Plaza, Room 906
New York, NY 10278
(212) 264-2525

Region 3
(DC, DE, MD, PA, VA, WV)
Environmental Protection Agency
841 Chestnut St.
Philadelphia, PA 19107-4431
(215) 597-9800

Region 4
(AL, FL, GA, KY, MS, NC, SC, TN)
Environmental Protection Agency
345 Courtland St. N.E.
Atlanta, GA 30365
(404) 347-4727

Region 5
(IL, IN, MI, MN, OH, WI)
Environmental Protection Agency
77 West Jackson Blvd.
Chicago, IL 60604
(312) 353-2000

Region 6
(AR, LA, NM, OK, TX)
Environmental Protection Agency
First Interstate Bank Tower
 at Fountain Place
1445 Ross Ave., Suite 1200
Dallas, TX 75202-2733
(214) 655-2100

Region 7
(IA, KA, MO, NE)
Environmental Protection Agency
726 Minnesota Ave.
Kansas City, KA 66101
(913) 551-7006

Region 8
(CO, MT, ND, SD, UT, WY)
Environmental Protection Agency
999 18th St., Suite 500
Denver, CO 80202-2466
(303) 293-1603

Region 9
(AZ, CA, HI, NV, American Samoa,
Guam, Trust Territories of the Pacific)
Environmental Protection Agency
75 Hawthorne St.
San Francisco, CA 94105
(415) 744-1087

Region 10
(AK, ID, OR, WA)
Environmental Protection Agency
1200 Sixth Ave.
Seattle, WA 98101
(206) 553-4016

Map of U.S. Environmental Protection Agency Regions

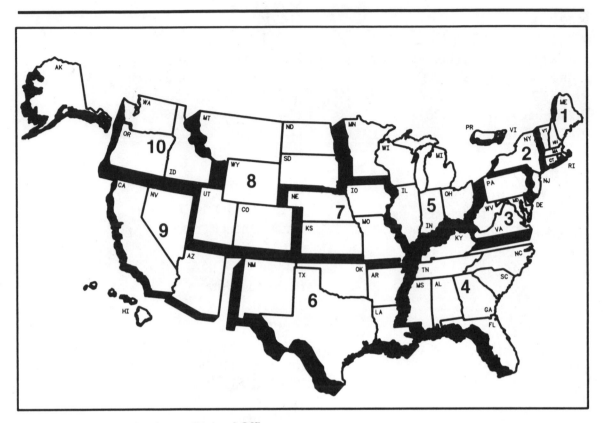

Environmental Protection Agency Regional Offices
U.S. Environmental Protection Agency

Regional Offices of the U.S. Fish and Wildlife Service

Region 1
(CA, HI, ID, NV
OR, WA, Guam)
U.S. Fish and Wildlife Service
911 N. E. 11th Ave.
Portland, OR 97232-4181
(503) 231-6118

Region 2
(AZ, NM, OK, TX)
U.S. Fish and Wildlife Service
500 Gold Ave. S. W.
P.O. Box 1306
Albuquerque, NM 87103
(505) 766-2321

Region 3
(IL, IN, IA, MI, MN, MO,
OH, WI,)
U.S. Fish and Wildlife Service
Whipple Federal Bldg.
1 Federal Drive
Fort Snelling, MN 55111
(612) 725-3502

Region 4
(AL, AR, FL, GA, KY, LA, MS,
NC, SC, TN, Puerto Rico, Virgin
Islands)
U.S. Fish and Wildlife Service
Richard B. Russell Federal Bldg.
75 Spring St. S.W., Room 1200
Atlanta, GA 30303
(404) 679-7319

Region 5
(CT, DE, ME, MA, MD, NH, NJ, NY, PA,
RI, VA, VT, WV)
U.S. Fish and Wildlife Service
300 Westage Center Dr.
Hadley, MA 01035-9589
(413) 253-8200

Region 6
(CO, KS, MT, ND, NE, SD, UT, WY)
U.S. Fish and Wildlife Service
134 Union Blvd.
Lakewood, CO
(303) 236-7920
    Mailing address:
    P.O. Box 25486
    Denver Federal Center
    Denver, CO 80225

Region 7
(Alaska)
U.S. Fish and Wildlife Service
1011 E. Tudor Rd.
Anchorage, Alaska 99503
(907) 786-3486

Regional Offices of the U.S. Army Corps of Engineers

Missouri River Division (CEMRD-CO-O)
P.O. Box 103 Downtown Station
Omaha, NE 68101

New England Division
Regulatory Branch
424 Trapelo Road
Waltham, MA 02254

North Atlantic Division (CENAD-CO-OP)
90 Church Street
New York, NY 1007

North Central Division (CENCD-CO-MO)
536 S. Clark Street
Chicago, IL 60605

Lower Mississippi Valley Division
P.O. Box 80
Vicksburg, MS 39180

North Pacific Division
P.O. Box 2870
Portland, Oregon 97208

Ohio River Division (ORDCO-OF)
P.O. Box 1159
Cincinnati, OH 45201

Pacific Ocean Division (CEPOD-CO-O)
Regulatory Branch
Building 230, Fort Shafter
Honolulu, HI 96858

South Atlantic Division (CESAS-CO-O)
77 Forsyth Street, SW
Atlanta, GA 30303

South Pacific Division (CESPD-CO)
630 Sansome Street, Room 1218
San Francisco, CA 94111

Southwestern Division (CESWD-CO-R)
1114 Commerce Street
Dallas, Texas 75242

Map of U.S. Army Corps of Engineers Regions

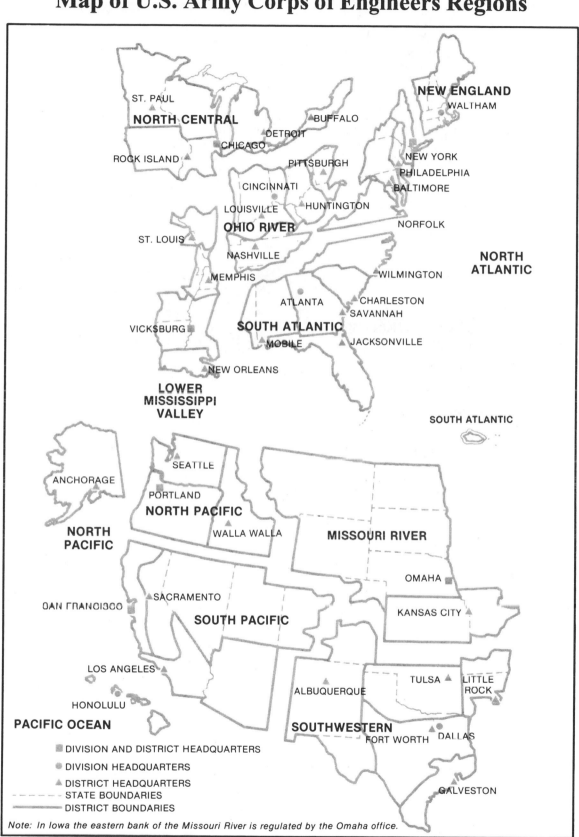

Note: In Iowa the eastern bank of the Missouri River is regulated by the Omaha office.

Other Federal Offices

Soil Conservation Service
P.O. Box 2890
Washington, D.C. 20013

U.S. Army Corps of Engineers
20 Massachusetts Ave. NW
Washington, D.C. 20314

United States Geological Survey
Geological Survey Bldg.
12201 Sunrise Valley Dr.
Mail Stop 101
Reston, VA 22092

Tennessee Valley Authority
400 W. Summit Hill Dr.
Knoxville, TN 37902

National Wetlands Inventory
National Office
Suite 101, Monroe Building
9720 Executive Center Drive
St. Petersburg, FL 33702
(813) 893-3624

Office of Surface Mining Field Offices (Federal)

OSM Headquarters
1951 Constitution Ave., NW
Washington, DC 20240
(202) 208-4006

Albuquerque Field Office
(CA, CO, NM, UT, Navajo, Hopi)
505 Marquette Ave., NW, Suite 1200
Albuquerque, NM 87102
(505) 766-1486

Big Stone Gap Field Office (VA)
P.O. Drawer 1216
Big Stone Gap, VA 24219
(703) 523-4203

Birmingham Field Office
(AL, GA, MS)
135 Gemini Circle, Suite 215
Homewood, AL 35209
(205) 290-7282

Casper Field Office
(AK, ID, MT, ND, SD, WY, OR, WA)
100 East B St., Rm. 2128
Casper, WY 82601

Charleston Field Office (WV)
603 Morris St.
Charleston, WV 25301
(904) 347-7158

Columbus Field Office
(OH, MI)
4480 Refugee Rd.
Columbus, OH 43232
(614) 866-0578

Harrisburg Field Office
(MA, MD, PA, RI)
Harrisburg Transportation Center
3rd Floor, Suite #C
4th and Market Streets
Harrisburg, PA 17101
(717) 782-4036

Indianapolis Field Office (IN)
575 North Penn St., Rm. 301
Indianapolis, IN 46204
(317) 226-6700

Kansas City Field Office
(IA, KS, MO)
934 Wyandotte St., Rm. 500
Kansas City, MO 64105
(816) 374-6405

Knoxville Field Office
(GA, NC, TN)
530 Gay Street, S.W., Suite 500
Knoxville, TN 37902

Lexington Field Office (KY)
2675 Regency Road
Lexington, KY 40503
(606) 233-2896

Springfield Field Office (IL)
511 West Capitol Ave., Suite 202
Springfield, IL 62704
(217) 492-4495

Tulsa Field Office
(AR, LA, OK, TX)
5100 East Skelly Dr., Suite 550
Tulsa, OK 74135
(919) 581-6430

State Environmental Offices

ALABAMA

Coastal Zone Management:
Mobile Field Office
Field Operations Division
2204 Perimeter
Mobile, AL 36615
205 479 2336

Drinking Water:
Water Supply Branch
Water Division
1751 Congressman W.L. Dickinson Drive
Montgomery, AL 36130
205 271 7773

Flood Plain Management:
Office of Water Resources
Department of Economic and Community Affairs
3465 Norman Ridge Road, P.O. Box 2939
Montgomery, AL 36105
205 242 5499

Groundwater:
Groundwater Branch
Water Division
1751 Congressman W.L. Dickinson Drive
Montgomery, AL 36130
205 271 7832

Mined Land Reclamation:
Alabama Surface Mining Commission
P.O. Box 2390
Jasper, AL 35502
205 221 4130

NPDES:
Industrial Branch
Water Division
1751 Congressman W.L. Dickinson Drive
Montgomery, AL 36130
205 271 7852

Solid Waste:
Solid Waste Branch, Land Division
Department of Environmental Management
1751 Congressman W.L. Dickinson Drive
Montgomery, AL 36130
205 271 7988

Air Pollution Agency:
Air Division
Department of Environmental Management
State Capitol
Montgomery, AL 36130
205 271 7861

Community Right-to-Know:
Field Operations
Department of Environmental Management
1751 Congressman W.L. Dickinson Drive
Montgomery, AL 36130
205 271 7931

Emergency Response:
Field Operations
Department of Environmental Management
1751 Congressman W.L. Dickinson Drive
Montgomery, AL 36130
205 271 7931

Forestry:
Alabama Forestry Commission
513 Madison Avenue
Montgomery, AL 36130
205 240 9304

Hazardous Waste:
Compliance Branch, Land Division
Department of Environmental Management
1751 Congressman W.L. Dickinson Drive
Montgomery, AL 36130
205 271 7736

Natural Resources Agency:
Department of Conservation and Natural Resources
64 North Union Street, Room 702
Montgomery, AL 36130
205 242 3486

Nuclear Waste/Nuclear Safety:
Division of Radiation Control
Department of Public Health
434 Monroe Street
Montgomery, AL 36130
205 242 5315

Superfund, Federal:
Special Projects, Permits and Services Division
Department of Environmental Management
1751 Congressman W.L. Dickinson Drive
Montgomery, AL 36130
205 271 7939

Climatology:
K.E. Johnson Environmental and Energy Center
University of Alabama
Huntsville, AL 35899
205 895 6257

Dam Safety:
Plans Division
Emergency Management Agency
560 South McDonough Street
Montgomery, AL 36130
205 280 2200

Fish and Wildlife:
Division of Game and Fish
Department of Conservation and Natural Resources
64 North Union Street, Room 720
Montgomery, AL 36130
205 242 3465

Geological Survey:
Geological Survey of Alabama
Oil and Gas Board
420 Hackberry Lane, P.O. Drawer O
University, AL 35486
205 349 2852

Industrial Pre-Treatment Program:
Industrial Branch
Water Division
1751 Congressman W.L. Dickinson Drive
Montgomery, AL 36130
205 271 7830

Nature Preserves Commission:
Friends of Forever Wild Committee
Alabama Nature Conservancy
2821 C Second Avenue, South
Birmingham, AL 35233
205 251 1155

Parks:
Division of Parks
Department of Conservation and Natural Resources
64 North Union Street, Room 720
Montgomery, AL 36130
205 242 3334

Superfund, State:
Special Projects, Permits and Services Division
Department of Environmental Management
1751 Congressman W.L. Dickinson Drive
Montgomery, AL 36130
205 271 7939

Underground Storage Tanks (UST):
Groundwater Branch
Water Division
1751 Congressman W.L. Dickinson Drive
Montgomery, AL 36130
205 271 7830

ALASKA

Coastal Zone Management:
Coastal Zone Management Program
Department of Environmental Conservation
410 Willoughby Ave., Suite 105
Juneau, AK 99801
907 465 5308

Drinking Water:
Drinking Water
Office of Waste Water and Water Treatment
410 Willoughby Street, Suite 105
Juneau, AK 99801
907 465 5301

Flood Plain Management:
Department of Community and Regional Affairs
333 West Fourth Avenue, Suite 220
Anchorage, AK 99501
907 269 4500

Groundwater:
Office of Water Quality Management
3601 C Street, Suite 1350
Anchorage, AK 99503
907 465 5300

Mined Land Reclamation:
Division of Mining
Department of Natural Resources
P.O. 7016
Anchorage, AK 99510
907 762 2162

NPDES:
Wastewater and Water Treatment
Office of Water Quality Management
410 Willoughby Street, Suite 105
Juneau, AK 99801
907 465 5300

Waste Management Agency:
Land Division
Department of Environmental Management
1751 Congressman W.L. Dickinson Drive
Montgomery, AL 36130
205 271 7730

Air Pollution Agency:
Air Quality Management Section
Department of Environmental Conservation
410 Willoughby Avenue, Suite 105
Juneau, AK 99801
907 465 5100

Community Right-to-Know:
Division of Spill Prevention and Response
Department of Environmental Conservation
410 Willoughby Avenue
Juneau, AK 99801
907 465 5220

Emergency Response:
Division of Spill Prevention and Response
Department of Environmental Conservation
410 Willoughby Avenue
Juneau, AK 99801
907 465 5220

Forestry:
Division of Forestry
Department of Natural Resources
3601 C Street, Suite 11058, Box 107005
Anchorage, AK 99510
907 762 2501

Hazardous Waste:
Hazardous Waste Program
Solid and Hazardous Waste Mgt Program
410 Willoughby Avenue
Juneau, AK 99801
907 465 5150

Natural Resources Agency:
Department of Natural Resources
P.O. Box M, 400 Willoughby Ave., 3rd Fl.
Juneau, AK 99801
907 465 2400

Nuclear Waste/Nuclear Safety:
Solid Waste Program
Solid and Hazardous Waste Management Program
410 Willoughby Avenue
Juneau, AK 99801
907 465 5150

Water Agency:
Water Division
Department of Environmental Management
1751 Congressman W.L. Dickinson Drive
Montgomery, AL 36130
205 271 7823

Climatology:
Alaska Climate Center
AEIDC/University of Alaska
707 A Street
Anchorage, AK 99501
907 279 4523

Dam Safety:
Dam Safety
Department of Natural Resources
P.O. Box 107005, 3601 C St., Suite 822
Anchorage, AK 99501
907 762 2680

Fish and Wildlife:
Department of Fish and Game
P.O. Box 3-2000
Juneau, AK 99802
907 465 4100

Geological Survey:
Division of Geological and Geophysical Surveys
Department of Natural Resources
3700 Airport Way
Fairbanks, AK 99709
907 451 2760

Industrial Pre-treatment:
Office of Water Quality Management
410 Willoughby Street, Suite 105
Juneau, AK 99801
907 465 5300

Nature Preserves Commission:
Division of Parks and Outdoor Recreation
Department of Natural Resources
3601 C Street, Suite 1200, P.O. 107001
Anchorage, AK 99510
907 762 2602

Parks:
Division of Parks and Outdoor Recreation
Department of Natural Resources
3601 C Street, Suite 1200, P.O. 107001
Anchorage, AK 99510
907 762 2602

Solid Waste:
Solid Waste Program
Office of Solid and Hazardous Waste Management
P.O. Box O
Juneau, AK 99811
907 465 2671

Underground Storage Tanks (UST):
USTs, Spill Prevention and Response Division
Department of Environmental Conservation
410 Willoughby Street
Juneau, AK 99801
907 465 5250

ARIZONA

Community Right-to-Know:
Emergency and Remedial Section
Office of Waste Programs
2005 North Central Avenue
Phoenix, AZ 85004
602 392 4085

Emergency Response:
Emergency Response Coordination Unit
Office of Waste Programs
2655 East Magnolia
Phoenix, AZ 85034
602 392 4085

Forestry:
Forestry Division
State Land Department
1616 West Adams
Phoenix, AZ 85007
602 542 4625

Hazardous Waste:
Hazardous and Solid Waste Section
Office of Waste Programs
2005 North Central Avenue
Phoenix, AZ 85004
602 257 2331

Natural Resources Agency:
Natural Resources Division
State Land Department
1616 West Adams
Phoenix, AZ 85007
602 542 4626

Superfund, Federal:
Contaminated Sites Section, CERCLA
Department of Environmental Conservation
410 Willoughby Avenue, Suite 105
Juneau, AK 99801
907 465 5220

Waste Management Agency:
Solid and Hazardous Waste Management Program
Department of Environmental Conservation
410 Willoughby Avenue
Juneau, AK 99801
907 465 5150

Air Pollution Agency:
Office of Air Quality
Department of Environmental Quality
2005 North Central Avenue
Phoenix, AZ 85004
602 257 2308

Dam Safety:
Engineering Division
Department of Water Resources
15 South 15th Avenue
Phoenix, AZ 85007
602 542 1541

Fish and Wildlife:
Department of Game and Fish
2222 West Greenway Road, P.O. Box 9099
Phoenix, AZ 85023
602 942 3000

Geological Survey:
Department of Mineral Resources
Mineral Building
Fairgrounds
Phoenix, AZ 85007
602 255 3791

Industrial Pre-treatment Program:
Waste Management
Department of Environmental Quality
2005 North Central Avenue
Phoenix, AZ 85004
602 392 4001

Nature Preserves Commission:
Nongame Branch
Game and Fish Department
2222 West Greenway Road
Phoenix, AZ 85023
602 942 3000

Superfund, State:
Solid and Hazardous Waste Management Program
Department of Environmental Conservation
410 Willoughby Avenue
Juneau, AK 99801
907 465 5150

Water Agency:
Office of Water Quality Management
Department of Environmental Conservation
410 Willoughby Street, Suite 105
Juneau, AK 99801
907 465 5300

Climatology:
The Laboratory of Climatology
Arizona State University
Tempe, AZ 85287
602 965 6265

Drinking Water:
Drinking Water Compliance Unit
Office of Water Quality
2005 North Central Avenue
Phoenix, AZ 85004
602 257 2209

Flood Plain Management:
Nonstructural Measures Branch
Department of Water Resources
99 East Virginia Avenue
Phoenix, AZ 85004
602 255 1566

Groundwater:
Groundwater Section
Office of Water Quality
2005 North Central Avenue
Phoenix, AZ 85004
602 257 6805

Mined Land Reclamation:
Department of Mineral Resources
Mineral Building, Fairgrounds
Phoenix, AZ 85007
602 255 3791

NPDES:
Plan Review and Permits Section
Office of Water Quality
2005 North Central Avenue
Phoenix, AZ 85004
602 257 2140

Nuclear Waste/Nuclear Safety:
Arizona Radiation Regulatory Agency
4814 South 40th Street
Phoenix, AZ 85040
602 255 4845

Superfund, Federal:
Superfund/WQARF Coordination Unit, Emergency
and Remedial Section
Office of Waste Programs
2005 North Central Avenue
Phoenix, AZ 85004
602 257 6841

Waste Management Agency:
Office of Waste Programs
Department of Environmental Quality
2005 North Central Avenue
Phoenix, AZ 85004
602 207 2381

Air Pollution Agency:
Air Division
Department of Pollution Control and Ecology
P.O. Box 9583
Little Rock, AR 72219
501 562 7444

Dam Safety:
Soil and Water Conservation Commission
One Capitol Mall, Suite 2-D
Little Rock, AR 72201
501 682 1611

Fish and Wildlife:
Game and Fish Commission
2 Natural Resources Drive
Little Rock, AR 72205
501 223 6305

Geological Survey:
Geological Commission
3821 West Roosevelt Road
Little Rock, AR 72204
501 371 1488

Industrial Pre-treatment Program:
Water Division
Department of Pollution Control and Ecology
P.O. Box 9583
Little Rock, AR 72219
501 562 7444

Parks:
State Parks
800 West Washington Street, Suite 415
Phoenix, AZ 85007
602 255 4174

Superfund, State:
Emergency and Remedial Section
Office of Waste Programs
2005 North Central Avenue
Phoenix, AZ 85004
602 257 4085

Water Agency:
Office of Water Quality
Department of Environmental Quality
3033 North Central Avenue
Phoenix, AZ 85012
602 207 2305

Climatology:
Department of Geography
University of Arkansas
Carnall Hall 104
Fayetteville, AR 72701
501 575 3159

Drinking Water:
Division of Engineering
Department of Health
4815 West Markham Street
Little Rock, AR 72205
501 661 2623

Flood Plain Management:
Soil and Water Commission
One Capitol Mall, Suite 2D
Little Rock, AR 72201
501 371 1611

Groundwater:
Water Division
Department of Pollution Control and Ecology
P.O. Box 9583
Little Rock, AR 72219
501 562 7444

Mined Land Reclamation:
Mining and Reclamation Division
Department of Pollution Control and Ecology
P.O. Box 9583
Little Rock, AR 72219
501 562 7444

Solid Waste:
Hazardous and Solid Waste Section
Office of Waste Programs
2005 North Central Avenue
Phoenix, AZ 85004
602 257 2331

Underground Storage Tanks (UST):
UST Compliance Unit, Compliance Section
Department of Environmental Quality
2005 North Central Avenue
Phoenix, AZ 85004
602 257 2369

ARKANSAS

Community Right-to-Know:
Administration Division
Department of Pollution Control and Ecology
P.O. Box 9583
Little Rock, AR 72219
501 562 7444

Emergency Response:
Emergency Response
Department of Pollution Control and Ecology
P.O. Box 9583
Little Rock, AR 72219
501 370 2108

Forestry:
Forestry Commission
3821 West Roosevelt Road
P.O. Box 4523 Asher Station
Little Rock, AR 72214
501 664 2531

Hazardous Waste:
Hazardous Waste Division
Department of Pollution Control and Ecology
P.O. Box 9583
Little Rock, AR 72219
501 562 6533

Natural Resources Agency:
Department of Arkansas Heritage
225 East Markham Street, Room 200
Little Rock, AR 72201
501 371 1639

Nature Preserves Commission:
Research Section
The Heritage Center
225 East Markham, Suite 200
Little Rock, AR 72201
501 371 1706

Parks:
State Parks Division
1 Capitol Mall
Little Rock, AR 72201
501 682 2535

Superfund, State:
Superfund Branch
Hazardous Waste Division
P.O. Box 9583
Little Rock, AR 72219
501 370 2127

Water Agency:
Water Division
Department of Pollution Control and Ecology
P.O. Box 9583
Little Rock, AR 72219
501 562 7444

Climatology:
Division of Flood Plain Management
Department of Water Resources
P.O. Box 388
Sacramento, CA 95802
916 445 5800

Dam Safety:
Division of Safety of Dams
Department of Water Resources
P.O. Box 942836
Sacramento, CA 94236
916 653 7007

Fish and Wildlife:
Fish and Game Department
Resources Agency
1416 9th Street, 12th Floor
Sacramento, CA 95814
916 653 7667

Geological Survey:
Division of Mines and Geology
Department of Conservation
1416 9th Street, Room 1341
Sacramento, CA 95814
916 445 1923

NPDES:
NPDES Branch
Water Division
P.O. Box 9583
Little Rock, AR 72219
501 562 7444

Solid Waste:
Department of Pollution Control and Ecology
P.O. Box 9583
Little Rock, AR 72219
501 562 7444

Underground Storage Tanks (UST):
Underground Storage Tanks Division
Department of Pollution Control and Ecology
P.O. Box 9583
Little Rock, AR 72219
501 562 7444

CALIFORNIA

Coastal Zone Management:
Coastal Commission
Resources Agency
45 Fremont Street
San Francisco, CA 94105
415 904 5200

Drinking Water:
Sanitary Engineering Branch
Department of Health Services
714 P Street, Room 600
Sacramento, CA 95814
916 323 6111

Flood Plain Management:
Flood Plain Management Branch
Department of Water Resources
P.O.Box 942836
Sacramento, CA 94236
916 653 7007

Groundwater:
Division of Local Assistance
Department of Water Resources
P.O. Box 942836
Sacramento, CA 94236
916 653 7007

Nuclear Waste/Nuclear Safety:
Division of Radiation Control and Emergency
Management
Department of Health
4815 West Markham Street
Little Rock, AR 72205
501 661 2574

Superfund, Federal:
Superfund Branch
Hazardous Waste Division
P.O. Box 9583
Little Rock, AR 72219
501 370 2127

Waste Management Agency:
Department of Pollution Control and Ecology
P.O. Box 9583
Little Rock, AR 72219
501 562 7444

Air Pollution Agency:
Air Resources Board
Environmental Protection Agency
P.O. Box 2815
Sacramento, CA 95812
916 322 5840

Community Right-to-Know:
Public Information Office
Integrated Waste Management Board
1020 9th Street, Suite 300
Sacramento, CA 95814
916 255 2182

Emergency Response:
Emergency Response Unit
Toxic Substances Control Program
714 P Street
Sacramento, CA 95814
916 323 1782

Forestry:
Forestry & Fire Protection Department
Resources Agency
P.O. Box 944246
Sacramento, CA 94244
916 445 3976

Hazardous Waste:
Environmental Health Section
Department of Health Services
714 P Street
Sacramento, CA 95814
916 322 2308

Industrial Pre-treatment Program:
Water Quality Division
Water Resources Control Board
P.O. Box 100
Sacramento, CA 95801
916 445 9552

NPDES:
Division of Water Quality
Water Resources Control Board
P.O. Box 100
Sacramento, CA 95801
916 445 9552

Superfund, Federal:
Integrated Waste Management Board
1020 9th Street, Suite 300
Sacramento, CA 95814
916 322 3330

Waste Management Agency:
Integrated Waste Management Board
Environmental Protection Agency
1020 9th Street, Suite 300
Sacramento, CA 95814
916 255 2182

Air Pollution Agency:
Air Pollution Control Division
Office of Health and Environmental Protection
4300 Cherry Creek Drive South
Denver, CO 80222
303 692 3115

Dam Safety:
Dam Safety Branch
Division of Water Resources
1313 Sherman Street, Room 818
Denver, CO 80203
303 866 3611

Fish and Wildlife:
Division of Wildlife
Department of Natural Resources
6060 Broadway
Denver, CO 80216
303 291 7208

Geological Survey:
Colorado Geological Survey
Department of Natural Resources
1313 Sherman Street, Room 715
Denver, CO 80203
303 866 2611

Mined Land Reclamation:
Division of Mines and Geology
Conservation Department
1416 9th Street, 13th Floor
Sacramento, CA 95814
916 445 1923

Parks:
Wildlife Conservation Board
1416 Ninth Street
Sacramento, CA 95814
916 445 8448

Superfund, State:
Site Mitigation Branch
Toxic Substances Control Program
714 P Street
Sacramento, CA 95814
916 324 3773

Water Agency:
Department of Water Resources
Resources Agency
P.O. Box 942836
Sacramento, CA 94236
916 653 7007

Climatology:
Colorado Climate Center
Department of Atmospheric Science
Colorado State University
Fort Collins, CO 80523
303 491 8545

Drinking Water:
Drinking Water Unit
Water Quality Control Division
4300 Cherry Creek Drive South
Denver, CO 80222
303 692 3546

Flood Plain Management:
Flood Control and Flood Plain Management
Water Conservation Board
1313 Sherman Street
Denver, CO 80203
303 866 3311

Groundwater:
Groundwater Section
Division of Water Resources
1313 Sherman Street, Room 818
Denver, CO 80203
303 866 3763

Natural Resources Agency:
Resources Agency
1416 9th Street, Room 1311
Sacramento, CA 95814
916 653 5656

Solid Waste:
Integrated Waste Management Board
Environmental Protection Agency
1020 9th Street, Suite 300
Sacramento, CA 95814
916 255 2182

Underground Storage Tanks (UST):
Clean Water Division
Water Resources Control Board
P.O. Box 100
Sacramento, CA 95801
916 657 2390

COLORADO

Community Right-to-Know:
Solid Waste and Incident Management Section
Hazardous Materials and Waste Management
4300 Cherry Creek Drive South
Denver, CO 80222
303 692 3445

Emergency Response:
Solid Waste and Incident Management Section
Hazardous Materials and Waste Management
4300 Cherry Creek Drive South
Denver, CO 80222
303 692 3022

Forestry:
Forest Service
203 Forestry Building
Colorado State University
Fort Collins, CO 80523
303 491 6303

Hazardous Waste:
Hazardous Materials and Waste Management
Office of Health and Environmental Protection
4300 Cherry Creek Drive South
Denver, CO 80222
303 692 3359

Industrial Pre-treatment Program:
Permits and Enforcement Section
Water Quality Control Division
4300 Cherry Creek Drive South
Denver, CO 80222
303 692 3608

Nature Preserves Commission:
Natural Areas
Parks and Outdoor Recreation Division
1313 Sherman Street, Room 718
Denver, CO 80203
303 866 3311

Parks:
Division of Parks & Outdoor Recreation
Department of Natural Resources
1313 Sherman Street, 6th Floor
Denver, CO 80203
303 866 2884

Superfund, State:
Superfund Program, Remedial Programs Section
Hazardous Materials and Waste Management
4300 Cherry Creek Drive South
Denver, CO 80222
303 692 3398

Water Agency:
Division of Water Resources
Department of Natural Resources
1313 Sherman Street, Room 818
Denver, CO 80203
303 866 2243

Climatology:
Department of Renewable Resources
University of Connecticut
1376 Storrs Road, Room 308 WBY Building
Storrs, CT 06268
203 486 2840

Dam Safety:
Dam Safety/Flood Management Program
Inland Water Resources Management Division
165 Capitol Avenue
Hartford, CT 06106
203 566 7245

Fish and Wildlife:
Fisheries Division, Natural Resources Bureau
Department of Environmental Protection
165 Capitol Avenue, Room 254
Hartford, CT 06106
203 566 3424

Mined Land Reclamation:
Mined Land Reclamation Division
Department of Natural Resources
1313 Sherman Street, Room 423
Denver, CO 80203
303 866 3454

NPDES:
Permits and Enforcement Section
Water Quality Control Division
4300 Cherry Creek Drive South
Denver, CO 80222
303 692 3610

Solid Waste:
Solid Waste and Incident Management Section
Hazardous Materials and Waste Management
4300 Cherry Creek Drive South
Denver, CO 80222
303 692 3440

Underground Storage Tanks (UST):
Solid Waste and Incident Management Section
Hazardous Materials and Waste Management
4300 Cherry Creek Drive South
Denver, CO 80222
303 692 3453

CONNECTICUT

Coastal Zone Management:
Office of Long Island Sound Programs
Department of Environmental Protection
165 Capitol Avenue
Hartford, CT 06106
203 566 3740

Drinking Water:
Water Supply Section
Department of Health Services
150 Washington Street
Hartford, CT 06106
203 566 1251

Flood Plain Management:
Dam Safety/Flood Management Program
Inland Water Resources Management Division
165 Capitol Avenue
Hartford, CT 06106
203 566 7245

Natural Resources Agency:
Department of Natural Resources
1313 Sherman Street, Room 718
Denver, CO 80203
303 866 3311

Nuclear Waste/Nuclear Safety:
Enforcement and Inspection Section
Hazardous Materials and Waste Management
4300 Cherry Creek Drive South
Denver, CO 80222
303 692 3359

Superfund, Federal:
Superfund Program, Remedial Programs Section
Hazardous Materials and Waste Management
4300 Cherry Creek Drive South
Denver, CO 80222
303 692 3398

Waste Management Agency:
Hazardous Materials and Waste Management
Office of Health and Environmental Protection
4300 Cherry Creek Drive South
Denver, CO 80222
303 692 3313

Air Pollution Agency:
Air Management Bureau
Department of Environmental Protection
165 Capitol Avenue, Room 144
Hartford, CT 06106
203 566 7854

Community Right-to-Know:
Chemical Spills Branch
Department of Environmental Protection
165 Capitol Avenue
Hartford, CT 06106
203 566 4856

Emergency Response:
Oil and Chemical Spills Response Division
Waste Management Bureau
165 Capitol Avenue
Hartford, CT 06106
203 566 4633

Forestry:
Forestry Division, Natural Resources Bureau
Department of Environmental Protection
165 Capitol Avenue, Room 260
Hartford, CT 06106
203 566 5348

Geological Survey:
Natural Resources Center
Department of Environmental Protection
165 Capitol Avenue, Room 553
Hartford, CT 06106
203 566 3540

Industrial Pre-treatment Program:
Site Remediation and Closure Division
Waste Management Bureau
165 Capitol Avenue
Hartford, CT 06106
203 566 5486

NPDES:
Site Remediation and Closure Division
Waste Management Bureau
165 Capitol Avenue
Hartford, CT 06106
203 566 5486

Solid Waste:
Waste Management Bureau
Department of Environmental Protection
165 Capitol Avenue
Hartford, CT 06106
203 566 5847

Underground Storage Tanks (UST):
Pesticides Division
Waste Management Bureau
165 Capitol Avenue
Hartford, CT 06106
203 566 5148

DELAWARE

Coastal Zone Management:
Coastal Management Program
Division of Soil and Water Conservation
89 Kings Highway, P.O. Box 1401
Dover, DE 19903
302 739 4411

Drinking Water:
Health Systems Protection
Division of Public Health
Cooper Building, P.O. Box 637
Dover, DE 19903
302 739 4731

Groundwater:
Water Compliance Unit
Department of Environmental Protection
165 Capitol Avenue
Hartford, CT 06106
203 566 3496

Natural Resources Agency:
Department of Environmental Protection
165 Capitol Avenue
Hartford, CT 06106
203 566 2110

Nuclear Waste/Nuclear Safety:
Monitoring and Radiation
Air Management Bureau
165 Capitol Avenue
Hartford, CT 06106
203 566 5134

Superfund, Federal:
Site Remediation and Closure Division
Waste Management Bureau
165 Capitol Avenue
Hartford, CT 06106
203 566 5486

Waste Management Agency:
Waste Management Bureau
Department of Environmental Protection
165 Capitol Avenue
Hartford, CT 06106
203 566 8476

Air Pollution Agency:
Air Resources Section
Division of Air and Waste Management
89 Kings Highway, P.O. Box 1401
Dover, DE 19903
302 739 4791

Community Right-to-Know:
Air Resources Section
Division of Air and Waste Management
89 Kings Highway, P.O. Box 1401
Dover, DE 19903
302 739 4791

Emergency Response:
Emergency Response Branch, Waste Management Section
Division of Air and Waste Management
89 Kings Highway, P.O. Box 1401
Dover, DE 19903
302 739 3694

Hazardous Waste:
Engineering and Enforcement Division
Waste Management Bureau
165 Capitol Avenue
Hartford, CT 06106
203 566 6682

Nature Preserves Commission:
Council on Environmental Quality
165 Capitol Avenue
Hartford, CT 06106
203 566 3510

Parks:
Bureau of Outdoor Recreation
Department of Environmental Protection
165 Capitol Avenue, Room 267
Hartford, CT 06106
203 566 2304

Superfund, State:
Engineering and Enforcement Division
Waste Management Bureau
165 Capitol Avenue
Hartford, CT 06106
203 566 5486

Water Agency:
Water Management Bureau
Department of Environmental Protection
122 Washington Street
Hartford, CT 06106
203 566 2110

Climatology:
Department of Geography
University of Delaware
Newark, DE 19716
302 451 2294

Dam Safety:
Division of Soil and Water Conservation
Dept. of Nat. Resources & Environmental Control
89 Kings Highway, P.O. Box 1401
Dover, DE 19903
302 739 4411

Fish and Wildlife:
Division of Fish & Wildlife
Dept. of Nat. Resources & Environmental Control
89 Kings Highway, P.O. Box 1401
Dover, DE 19903
302 739 5295

Flood Plain Management:
Beach Preservation Branch
Division of Soil and Water Conservation
89 Kings Highway, P.O. Box 1401
Dover, DE 19903
302 739 4411

Groundwater:
Groundwater Quality Branch
Water Supply Branch, Division of Water Resources
89 Kings Highway, P.O. Box 1401
Dover, DE 19903
302 739 4860

Natural Resources Agency:
Dept. of Nat. Resources and Environmental Control
89 Kings Highway, P.O. Box 1401
Dover, DE 19903
302 739 4403

Nuclear Waste/Nuclear Safety:
Office of Radiation Control
Division of Public Health
Cooper Building, Capital Square
Dover, DE 19903
302 739 3839

Superfund, Federal:
Superfund Branch, Waste Management Section
Division of Air and Waste Management
715 Grantham
New Castle, DE 19720
302 323 4540

Waste Management Agency:
Division of Air and Waste Management
Dept. of Nat. Resources & Environmental Control
89 Kings Highway, P.O. Box 1401
Dover, DE 19903
302 739 4764

Air Pollution Agency:
Division of Air Resources Management
Department of Environmental Regulation
2600 Blairstone Road
Tallahassee, FL 32399
904 488 0114

Community Right-to-Know:
Bureau of Waste Cleanup
Division of Waste Management
2600 Blairstone Road
Tallahassee, FL 32399
904 488 0198

Forestry:
Forestry Section
Dept. of Agriculture
2320 S. DuPont Highway
Dover, DE 19901
302 739 4811

Hazardous Waste:
Hazardous Waste Branch, Waste Management Section
Division of Air and Waste Management
89 Kings Highway, P.O. Box 1401
Dover, DE 19903
302 739 3689

Nature Preserves Commission:
Delaware Natural Heritage Inventory
Division of Parks and Recreation
89 Kings Highway
Dover, DE 19903
302 739 5285

Parks:
Division of Parks and Recreation
Dept. of Nat. Resources & Environmental Control
89 Kings Highway, P.O. Box 1401
Dover, DE 19903
302 739 4401

Superfund, State:
Superfund Branch, Waste Management Section
Division of Air and Waste Management
715 Grantham
New Castle, DE 19720
302 323 4540

Water Agency:
Water Resources Division
Dept. of Nat. Resources & Environmental Control
89 Kings Highway, P.O. Box 1401
Dover, DE 19903
302 739 4860

Climatology:
Department of Meteorology
Florida State University
Tallahassee, FL 32306
904 644 3417

Dam Safety:
Laboratory and Special Programs Bureau
Department of Environmental Regulation
2600 Blairstone Road
Tallahassee, FL 32399
904 488 0131

Geological Survey:
Delaware Geological Survey
University of Delaware
Delaware Geological Survey Building
Newark, DE 19716
302 831 2833

Industrial Pre-treatment Program:
Surface Water Management
Division of Water Resources
89 Kings Highway, P.O. Box 1401
Dover, DE 19903
302 739 4411

NPDES:
Surface Water Management
Division of Water Resources
89 Kings Highway, P.O. Box 1401
Dover, DE 19903
302 739 5731

Solid Waste:
Solid Waste Branch, Waste Management Section
Division of Air and Waste Management
89 Kings Highway, P.O. Box 1401
Dover, DE 19903
302 739 3820

Underground Storage Tanks (UST):
Underground Storage Tanks Branch, Waste Management Section
Division of Air and Waste Management
89 Kings Highway, P.O. Box 1401
Dover, DE 19903
302 739 4588

FLORIDA

Coastal Zone Management:
Coastal Zone Management
Department of Community Affairs
2740 Centerview Drive
Tallahassee, FL 32399
904 488 8466

Drinking Water:
Bureau of Drinking Water and Groundwater Resources
Division of Water Facilities
2600 Blairstone Road
Tallahassee, FL 32399
904 487 1855

Emergency Response:
Emergency Response
Division of Waste Management
2600 Blairstone Road
Tallahassee, FL 32399
904 488 0190

Forestry:
Division of Forestry
Department of Agriculture and Consumer Services
3125 Conner Boulevard
Tallahassee, FL 32399
904 488 4274

Hazardous Waste:
Waste Planning and Regulation Bureau
Department of Environmental Regulation
2600 Blairstone Road
Tallahassee, FL 32399
904 488 0300

Natural Resources Agency:
Department of Natural Resources
3900 Commonwealth Boulevard
Tallahassee, FL 32399
904 488 1554

Parks:
Division of Recreation and Parks
Department of Natural Resources
3900 Commonwealth Boulevard
Tallahassee, FL 32399
904 488 6131

Superfund, State:
Bureau of Waste Cleanup
Division of Waste Management
2600 Blairstone Road
Tallahassee, FL 32399
904 488 0190

Water Agency:
Division of Water Management
Department of Environmental Regulation
2600 Blairstone Road
Tallahassee, FL 32399
904 488 0130

Climatology:
Institute of Natural Resources
Ecology Building
University of Georgia
Athens, GA 30602
404 542 1555

Fish and Wildlife:
Game and Fresh Water Fish Commission
620 South Meridian Street
Tallahassee, FL 32399
904 488 2975

Geological Survey:
Florida Geological Survey
903 West Tennessee Street
Tallahassee, FL 32304
904 488 4191

Industrial Pre-treatment Program:
Division of Water Facilities
Department of Environmental Regulation
2600 Blairstone Road
Tallahassee, FL 32399
904 487 1855

Nature Preserves Commission:
Florida Natural Areas Inventory
1018 Thomasville Road, Suite 200C
Tallahassee, FL 32303
904 224 8207

Solid Waste:
Solid Waste Section
Division of Waste Management
2600 Blairstone Road
Tallahassee, FL 32399
904 922 6104

Underground Storage Tanks (UST):
Storage Tank Regulation Section
Division of Waste Management
2600 Blairstone Road
Tallahassee, FL 32399
904 488 3935

GEORGIA

Coastal Zone Management:
Coastal Zone Management Program, Ecological Services
Coastal Resources Division, Dept. of Nat. Res.
1 Conservation Way
Brunswick, GA 31523
912 264 7218

Flood Plain Management:
Bureau of Resource Management
Department of Community Affairs
2740 Centerview Drive
Tallahassee, FL 32399
904 487 4915

Groundwater:
Bureau of Drinking Water and Groundwater Resources
Division of Water Facilities
2600 Blairstone Road
Tallahassee, FL 32399
904 488 3601

Mined Land Reclamation:
Bureau of Mine Reclamation
Department of Natural Resources
2051 East Dirac Drive
Tallahassee, FL 32310
904 488 8217

NPDES:
Division of Water Facilities
Department of Environmental Regulation
2600 Blairstone Road
Tallahassee, FL 32399
904 487 1855

Superfund, Federal:
Bureau of Waste Cleanup
Division of Waste Management
2600 Blairstone Road
Tallahassee, FL 32399
904 488 0190

Waste Management Agency
Division of Waste Management
Department of Environmental Regulation
2600 Blairstone Road
Tallahassee, FL 32399
904 487 3299

Air Pollution Agency:
Air Protection Branch
Department of Natural Resources
205 Butler Street, S.E., Room 1162
Atlanta, GA 30334
404 656 6900

Community Right-to-Know:
Program Coordination Branch
Department of Natural Resources
205 Butler Street, S.E., Room 1152
Atlanta, GA 30334
404 656 6905

Dam Safety:
Safe Dams Program
Water Resources Management Branch
4244 International Parkway
Atlanta, GA 30354
404 362 2678

Environmental/Natural Resources Agency:
Department of Natural Resources
205 Butler Street, S.E., Suite 1152
Atlanta, GA 30334
404 656 3500

Forestry:
Georgia Forestry Commission
Department of Natural Resources
P.O. Box 819
Macon, GA 31298
912 751 3480

Hazardous Waste:
Hazardous Waste Management Program
Land Protection Branch
205 Butler Street, S.E., Room 1154
Atlanta, GA 30334
404 656 7802

Natural Resources Agency:
Department of Natural Resources
205 Butler Street, S.E., Room 1252
Atlanta, GA 30334
404 656 3500

Parks:
Parks and Historical Sites Division
Department of Natural Resources
205 Butler Street, S.W., Room 1352
Atlanta, GA 30334
404 656 2753

Superfund, State:
Hazardous Sites Response Program
Hazardous Waste Management Program
205 Butler Street, S.E., Room 1154
Atlanta, GA 30334
404 656 7802

Water Agency:
Water Protection Branch
Department of Natural Resources
205 Butler Street, S.W., East Tower
Atlanta, GA 30334
404 656 4708

Drinking Water:
Drinking Water Program
Water Resources Management Branch
205 Butler Street, S.W., Room 1066
Atlanta, GA 30334
704 656 4807

Fish and Wildlife:
Wildlife Resources Division
Department of Natural Resources
205 Butler Street, S.W., Room 1362
Atlanta, GA 30334
404 656 3523

Geological Survey:
Geologic Survey Branch
Division of Environmental Protection
19 Martin Luther King, Jr. Drive, S.W.
Atlanta, GA 30334
404 656 3214

Industrial Pre-treatment Program:
Municipal Permitting Program
Water Protection Branch
4244 International Parkway, Suite 110
Atlanta, GA 30354
404 362 2680

NPDES:
Municipal Permitting Program
Water Protection Branch
4244 International Parkway, Suite 110
Atlanta, GA 30354
404 362 2680

Solid Waste:
Solid Waste Permitting Program
Land Protection Branch
4244 International Parkway, Suite 104
Atlanta, GA 30354
404 362 2692

Underground Storage Tanks (UST):
Underground Storage Tank Program
Land Protection Branch
4244 International Parkway, Suite 104
Atlanta, GA 30354
404 362 2687

HAWAII

Emergency Response:
Program Coordination Branch
Department of Natural Resources
205 Butler Street, S.E., Room 1152
Atlanta, GA 30334
404 656 6905

Flood Plain Management:
Geologic Survey Branch
Division of Environmental Protection
19 Martin Luther King, Jr. Drive, S.W.
Atlanta, GA 30334
404 656 3214

Groundwater:
Geologic Survey Branch, Division of Environmental
Protection
Department of Natural Resources
19 Martin Luther King, Jr. Drive, S.W.
Atlanta, GA 30334
404 656 3214

Mined Land Reclamation:
Land Protection Compliance Program
Land Protection Branch
4244 International Parkway, Suite 104
Hapeville, GA 30354
404 362 2696

Nuclear Waste/Nuclear Safety:
Corrective Action Program
Hazardous Waste Management Program
205 Butler Street, S.E., Room 1152
Atlanta, GA 30334
404 656 4713

Superfund, Federal:
Facilities Compliance Program
Hazardous Waste Management Program
205 Butler Street, S.E., Room 1154
Atlanta, GA 30334
404 656 7802

Waste Management Agency:
Land Protection Branch, Division of Environmental
Protection
Department of Natural Resources
4244 International Parkway, Suite 104
Atlanta, GA 30354
404 362 2537

Air Pollution Agency:
Clean Air Branch
Environmental Management Division
P.O. Box 3378
Honolulu, HI 96801
808 586 4200

Climatology:
Division of Water Resource Management
Department of Land and Natural Resources
P.O. Box 373
Honolulu, HI 96809
808 548 7533

Dam Safety:
Flood Section
Division of Water and Land Development
P.O. Box 3378
Honolulu, HI 96809
808 587 0217

Fish and Wildlife:
Division of Aquatic Resources
Department of Land and Natural Resources
P.O. Box 621
Honolulu, HI 96801
808 587 0100

Geological Survey:
Geology & Hydrology Section
Commission on Water Resource Management
P.O. Box 373
Honolulu, HI 96809
808 587 0216

Hazardous Waste:
Solid and Hazardous Waste Branch
Environmental Management Division
P.O. Box 3378
Honolulu, HI 96801
808 586 4225

Nature Preserves Commission:
Natural Area Preserve
Division of Forestry and Wildlife, DLNR
South King Street, Suite 132
Honolulu, HI 96813
808 587 0063

Superfund, Federal:
Hazard Evaluation and Emergency Response Office
Deputy Director for Environmental Health
P.O. Box 3378
Honolulu, HI 96801
808 586 4249

Water Agency:
Commission on Water Resource Management
Department of Land and Natural Resources
P.O. Box 621
Honolulu, HI 96809
808 587 0230

Coastal Zone Management:
Coastal Zone Management Program
Office of State Planning
State Capitol, Room 406
Honolulu, HI 96813
808 587 2875

Drinking Water:
Safe Drinking Water Branch
Environmental Management Division
P.O. Box 3378
Honolulu, HI 96801
808 586 4258

Flood Plain Management:
Flood Section
Division of Water and Land Development
P.O. Box 621
Honolulu, HI 96809
808 587 0217

Geological Survey:
Institute of Geophysics
University of Hawaii
2525 Correa Road
Honolulu, HI 96822
808 956 8760

Industrial Pre-treatment Program:
Commission on Water Resource Management
Department of Land and Natural Resources
P.O. Box 621
Honolulu, HI 96809
808 587 0216

Parks:
State Parks Division
Department of Land and Natural Resources
P.O. Box 621
Honolulu, HI 96801
808 587 0300

Superfund, State:
Hazard Evaluation and Emergency Response Office
Deputy Director for Environmental Health
P.O. Box 3378
Honolulu, HI 96801
808 586 4249

IDAHO

Community Right-to-Know:
Hazard Evaluation and Emergency Response Office
Deputy Director for Environmental Health
P.O. Box 3378
Honolulu, HI 96801
808 586 4249

Emergency Response:
Hazard Evaluation and Emergency Response Office
Deputy Director for Environmental Health
P.O. Box 3378
Honolulu, HI 96801
808 586 4249

Forestry:
Division of Forestry and Wildlife
Department of Land and Natural Resources
P.O. Box 621
Honolulu, HI 96809
808 587 0166

Groundwater:
Commission on Water Resource Management
Department of Land and Natural Resources
P.O. Box 621
Honolulu, HI 96809
808 587 0216

Natural Resources Agency:
Department of Land and Natural Resources
1151 Punchbowl Street
Honolulu, HI 96813
808 587 0405

Solid Waste:
Office of Solid Waste Management, Solid and Hazardous Waste Branch
Environmental Management Division
P.O. Box 3378
Honolulu, HI 96801
808 586 4227

Waste Management Agency:
Environmental Management Division
Department of Health
P.O. Box 3378
Honolulu, HI 96801
808 586 4225

Air Pollution Agency:
Air Quality Bureau
Department of Health and Welfare
State House
Boise, ID 83720
208 334 5898

Climatology:
Agricultural Engineering Department
University of Idaho
Moscow, ID 83843
208 885 6182

Drinking Water:
Water Quality Bureau
Department of Health and Welfare
450 West State Street
Boise, ID 83720
208 327 7900

Fish and Wildlife:
Fish and Game Department
600 South Walnut Street
P.O. Box 25
Boise, ID 83707
208 334 5159

Geological Survey:
Bureau of Mines and Geology
University of Idaho
332 Morrill Hall
Moscow, ID 83843
208 885 7991

Mined Land Reclamation:
Department of Lands
1215 West 8th Street
Boise, ID 83720
208 334 3610

Nuclear Waste/Nuclear Safety:
Radiation
Hazardous Materials Bureau
450 West State Street
Boise, ID 83720
208 334 5882

Superfund, Federal:
Policy and Standards
Hazardous Materials Bureau
450 West State Street
Boise, ID 83720
208 334 5879

Waste Management Agency:
Hazardous Materials Bureau
Health and Welfare Department
450 West State Street
Boise, ID 83720
208 334 5879

Community Right-to-Know:
Emergency Response Committee
Air Quality Bureau
1410 North Hilton, 2nd Floor
Boise, ID 83706
208 334 5888

Emergency Response:
Hazardous Materials Bureau
Health and Welfare Department
450 West State Street
Boise, ID 83720
208 334 5879

Flood Plain Management:
National Flood Insurance Program
Department of Water Resources
450 West State Street
Boise, ID 83720
208 327 7993

Groundwater:
Water Quality Bureau
Department of Health and Welfare
450 West State Street
Boise, ID 83720
208 334 5860

Nature Preserves Commission:
Idaho Natural Heritage Program
Department of Fish and Game
600 South Walnut Street, Box 25
Boise, ID 83707
208 334 3402

Parks:
Parks and Recreation Department
2177 Warm Springs Avenue
Boise, ID 83720
208 334 2154

Superfund, State:
IWRAP
Department of Health and Welfare
450 West State Street
Boise, ID 83720
208 334 6664

Water Agency:
Water Resources Department
1301 North Orchard
Boise, ID 83720
208 327 7900

Dam Safety:
Water Resources Department
1301 North Orchard
Boise, ID 83720
208 327 7900

Energy:
Energy Division
Water Resources Department
450 West State Street
Boise, ID 83720
208 327 7968

Forestry:
Forestry and Fire
Department of Lands
1215 West 8th Street
Boise, ID 83720
208 334 3280

Hazardous Waste:
Hazardous Materials Bureau
Health and Welfare Department
450 West State Street
Boise, ID 83720
208 334 5879

NPDES:
Water Quality Bureau
Department of Health and Welfare
450 West State Street
Boise, ID 83720
208 334 5860

Solid Waste:
Solid Waste
Hazardous Materials Bureau
450 West State Street
Boise, ID 83720
208 334 5879

Underground Storage Tanks (UST):
Water Quality Bureau
Department of Health and Welfare
450 West State Street
Boise, ID 83720
208 334 5845

ILLINOIS

Coastal Zone Management:
Planning
Division of Water Pollution Control
2200 Churchill Road
Springfield, IL 62706
217 782 3362

Drinking Water:
Division of Public Water Supply
Environmental Protection Agency
1340 North Ninth Street
Springfield, IL 62702
217 785 8653

Fish and Wildlife:
Resource Management Office
Department of Conservation
524 South Second Street
Springfield, IL 62706
217 785 8287

Geological Survey:
Illinois Geological Survey
Natural Resources Building
615 East Peabody Drive, Room 121
Champaign, IL 61820
217 333 5111

Industrial Pre-treatment Program:
Permits, Industrial
Division of Water Pollution Control
2200 Churchill Road
Springfield, IL 62706
217 782 1696

Nature Preserves Commission:
Nature Preserves Commission
Department of Conservation
524 South Second Street
Springfield, IL 62706
217 785 2963

Parks:
Land Management Division
Department of Conservation
524 South Second Street
Springfield, IL 62706
217 782 1395

Air Pollution Agency:
Division of Air Pollution Control
Environmental Protection Agency
1340 North Ninth Street
Springfield, IL 62702
217 782 7326

Community Right-to-Know:
Emergency Management
Environmental Protection Agency
2200 Churchill Road
Springfield, IL 62706
217 785 0380

Emergency Response:
Emergency Management
Environmental Protection Agency
2200 Churchill Road
Springfield, IL 62706
217 785 0380

Flood Plain Management:
Local Flood Plain Program
Division of Water Resources
201 West Center Court
Schaumburg, IL 60196
708 705 4341

Groundwater:
Groundwater
Division of Public Water Supply
1340 North Ninth Street
Springfield, IL 62702
217 785 4787

Mined Land Reclamation:
Abandoned Mined Lands Reclamation Council
928 South Spring
Springfield, IL 62704
217 782 0588

NPDES:
Permits
Division of Water Pollution Control
2200 Churchill Road
Springfield, IL 62706
217 782 0610

Solid Waste:
Solid Waste and Renewable Resources
Department of Energy and Natural Resources
325 West Adams Street, Room 300
Springfield, IL 62704
217 785 2800

Climatology:
Illinois State Water Survey
2204 Griffith Drive
Champaign, IL 61820
217 333 0729

Dam Safety:
Dam Safety Section, Water Resources Division
Department of Transportation
2300 South Dirksen Parkway
Springfield, IL 62764
217 782 3863

Energy:
Energy Conservation Office
Department of Conservation
524 South Second Street
Springfield, IL 62706
217 785 2800

Forestry:
Forest Resources Division
Department of Conservation
524 South Second Street
Springfield, IL 62706
217 782 2361

Hazardous Waste:
Hazardous Waste Research and Information Center
Department of Energy and Natural Resources
1808 Woodfield Road
Savoy, IL 61874
217 333 8940

Natural Resources Agency:
Department of Conservation
524 South Second Street
Springfield, IL 62706
217 782 6302

Nuclear Waste/Nuclear Safety:
Department of Nuclear Safety
1035 Outer Park Drive, 5th Floor
Springfield, IL 62704
217 785 9900

Superfund, Federal:
Federal Site Management, Remedial Project
Management
Division of Land Pollution
2200 Churchill Road
Springfield, IL 62706
217 782 6760

Superfund, State:
State Site Management, Remedial Project
Management
Division of Land Pollution Control
2200 Churchill Road
Springfield, IL 62706
217 782 6760

Water Agency:
Division of Water Pollution Control
Environmental Protection Agency
2200 Churchill Road
Springfield, IL 62706
217 782 1654

Climatology:
Agronomy Department
Purdue University
West Lafayette, IN 47907
317 494 8105

Drinking Water:
Office of Water Management
Department of Environmental Management
P.O. Box 6015, 105 South Meridian Street
Indianapolis, IN 46225
317 233 4222

Enforcement:
Enforcement Sect., Haz. Waste Mgt. Branch
Office of Solid and Hazardous Waste Management
P.O. Box 6015, 105 South Meridian Street
Indianapolis, IN 46225
317 233 5529

Forestry:
Forestry Division
Land, Forest and Wildlife Resources Bureau
613 State Office Building
Indianapolis, IN 46204
317 232 4105

Hazardous Waste:
Hazardous Waste Management Branch
Office of Solid and Hazardous Waste Management
P.O. Box 6015, 105 South Meridian Street
Indianapolis, IN 46225
317 232 4518

Nature Preserves Commission:
Nature Preserves Division
Land, Forest and Wildlife Resources Bureau
616 State Office Building
Indianapolis, IN 46204
317 232 4052

Underground Storage Tanks (UST):
Leaking Underground Storage Tanks
Division of Land Pollution Control
2200 Churchill Road
Springfield, IL 62706
217 782 6761

INDIANA

Community Right-to-Know:
Emergency Response Section, Office of
Environmental Response
Department of Environmental Management
P.O. Box 6015, 105 South Meridian Street
Indianapolis, IN 46225
317 243 5057

Emergency Response:
Emergency Response Section, Office of
Environmental Response
Department of Environmental Management
P.O. Box 6015, 105 South Meridian Street
Indianapolis, IN 46225
317 243 5057

Fish and Wildlife:
Fish & Wildlife Division
Department of Natural Resources
State Office Building
Indianapolis, IN 46204
317 232 4091

Geological Survey:
Indiana Geological Survey
611 North Walnut Grove
Bloomington, IN 47405
812 855 9350

Mined Land Reclamation:
Division of Reclamation
Bureau of Mine Reclamation
201 West Main Steet
Jasonville, IN 47438
812 665 2207

NPDES:
Enforcement Section
Office of Water Management
P.O. Box 6015, 105 South Meridian Street
Indianapolis, IN 46225
317 232 8432

Waste Management Agency:
Division of Land Pollution Control
Environmental Protection Agency
2200 Churchill Road
Springfield, IL 62706
217 782 6760

Air Pollution Agency:
Office of Air Management
Department of Environmental Management
P.O. Box 6015, 105 South Meridian Street
Indianapolis, IN 46225
317 232 5586

Dam Safety:
Division of Water
Department of Natural Resources
2475 Directors Row
Indianapolis, IN 46241
317 232 4163

Energy:
Division of Energy Policy
Department of Commerce
One North Capitol, Suite 700
Indianapolis, IN 46204
317 232 8946

Flood Plain Management:
Planning Section, Water Division
Department of Natural Resources
2475 Directors Row
Indianapolis, IN 46421
317 232 4178

Groundwater:
Groundwater Section
Office of Water Management
P.O. Box 6015, 105 South Meridian Street
Indianapolis, IN 46225
317 233 4166

Natural Resources Agency:
Department of Natural Resources
608 State Office Building
Indianapolis, IN 46204
317 232 4021

Nuclear Waste/Nuclear Safety:
Office of Solid and Hazardous Waste Management
Department of Environmental Management
P.O. Box 6015, 105 South Meridian Street
Indianapolis, IN 46225
317 232 3210

Parks:
State Parks Division
Land, Forest and Wildlife Resources Bureau
616 State Office Building
Indianapolis, IN 46204
317 232 4124

Superfund, State:
Office of Environmental Response
Department of Environmental Management
P.O. Box 6015, 105 South Meridian Street
Indianapolis, IN 46225
317 243 5057

Water Agency:
Water Division
Department of Natural Resources
2475 Directors Row
Indianapolis, IN 46241
317 232 4160

Air Pollution Agency:
Air Quality Bureau
Environmental Protection Division
Wallace State Office Bldg., 900 E. Grand
Des Moines, IA 50319
515 281 8852

Dam Safety:
Water Quality Section
Surface and Groundwater Protection Bureau
Wallace State Office Bldg., 900 E. Grand
Des Moines, IA 50319
515 281 5029

Energy:
Energy and Geological Resources Division
Department of Natural Resources
Wallace State Office Bldg., 900 E. Grand
Des Moines, IA 50319
515 281 4308

Flood Plain Management:
Flood Insurance Program
Water Quality Section
Wallace State Office Bldg., 900 E. Grand
Des Moines, IA 50319
515 281 8942

Groundwater:
Water Supply Section
Surface and Groundwater Protection Bureau
Wallace State Office Bldg., 900 E. Grand
Des Moines, IA 50319
515 281 8877

Solid Waste:
Solid Waste Management Branch
Office of Solid and Hazardous Waste Management
P.O. Box 6015, 105 South Meridian Street
Indianapolis, IN 46225
317 232 4473

Underground Storage Tanks (UST):
Underground Storage Tank Section
Office of Water Management
5500 W. Bradbury
Indianapolis, IN 46241
317 240 6215

Water Shortage Response:
Water Division
Department of Natural Resources
2475 Directors Row
Indianapolis, IN 46241
317 232 4222

Climatology:
Climatology Bureau
Department of Agriculture and Land Stewardship
Wallace State Office Building
Des Moines, IA 50321
515 281 4062

Drinking Water:
Water Supply Section
Surface and Groundwater Protection Bureau
Wallace State Office Bldg., 900 E. Grand
Des Moines, IA 50319
515 281 8877

Environmental/Natural Resource Agency:
Department of Natural Resources
Des Moines, IA 50319
515 281 5385

Forestry:
Forest and Forestry Division
Department of Natural Resources
Wallace State Office Bldg., 900 E. Grand
Des Moines, IA 50319
515 281 8656

Hazardous Waste:
Solid Waste Bureau
Environmental Protection Division
Wallace State Office Bldg., 900 E. Grand
Des Moines, IA 50319
515 281 8934

Superfund, Federal:
Office of Environmental Response
Department of Environmental Management
P.O. Box 6015, 105 South Meridian Street
Indianapolis, IN 46225
317 243 5057

Waste Management Agency:
Office of Solid and Hazardous Waste Management
Department of Environmental Management
P.O. Box 6015, 105 South Meridian Street
Indianapolis, IN 46225
317 232 3210

IOWA

Community Right-to-Know:
Emergency Management Division
Department of Public Defense
Hoover Building, Level A, Room 29
Des Moines, IA 50319
515 281 3231

Emergency Response.
Field Evaluation and Emergency Response Bureau
Environmental Protection Division
Wallace State Office Bldg., 900 E. Grand
Des Moines, IA 50319
515 281 8883

Fish and Wildlife:
Fish and Wildlife Division
Department of Natural Resources
Wallace State Office Bldg., 900 E. Grand
Des Moines, IA 50319
515 281 5145

Geological Survey:
Geological Survey Bureau, Energy and Geological Resources Division
Department of Natural Resources
123 N. Capitol Street
Iowa City, IA 52240
319 335 1575

Industrial Pre-treatment Program:
Waste Water Permits Section
Environmental Protection Division
Wallace State Office Bldg., 900 E. Grand
Des Moines, IA 50319
515 281 8884

Mined Land Reclamation:
Division of Soil Conservation
Department of Agriculture and Land Stewardship
Wallace State Office Bldg., 900 E. Grand
Des Moines, IA 50319
515 281 5851

NPDES:
Waste Water Permits Section
Environmental Protection Division
Wallace State Office Bldg., 900 E. Grand
Des Moines, IA 50319
515 281 8877

Solid Waste:
Solid Waste Bureau
Environmental Protection Division
Wallace State Office Bldg., 900 E. Grand
Des Moines, IA 50319
515 281 4968

Underground Storage Tanks (UST):
Waste Water Permits Section
Surface and Groundwater Protection Bureau
Wallace State Office Bldg., 900 E. Grand
Des Moines, IA 50319
515 281 8135

KANSAS

Community Right-to-Know:
Right-to-Know Section
Bureau of Air and Radiation
740 Forbes Field
Topeka, KS 66620
913 296 1688

Emergency Response:
Bureau of Environmental Remediation
Division of Environment
740 Forbes Field
Topeka, KS 66620
913 296 1660

Flood Plain Management:
Water Structures Section
Division of Water Resources
109 S.W. Ninth Street, Suite 202
Topeka, KS 66612
913 296 2933

Natural Resources Agency:
Department of Natural Resources
Wallace State Office Bldg., 900 E. Grand
Des Moines, IA 50319
515 281 5385

Nuclear Waste/Nuclear Safety:
Bureau of Environmental Health
Department of Public Health
Lucas State Office Building
Des Moines, IA 50319
515 281 4928

Superfund, Federal:
Solid Waste Bureau
Environmental Protection Division
Wallace State Office Bldg., 900 E. Grand
Des Moines, IA 50319
515 281 8900

Waste Management Agency:
Solid Waste Bureau
Environmental Protection Division
Wallace State Office Bldg., 900 E. Grand
Des Moines, IA 50319
515 281 8934

Air Pollution Agency:
Bureau of Air and Radiation
Division of Environment
740 Forbes Field
Topeka, KS 66620
913 296 1593

Dam Safety:
Water Structures Section
Division of Water Resources
109 S.W. Ninth Street, Suite 202
Topeka, KS 66612
913 296 2933

Energy:
Energy Programs Section
Corporation Commission
1500 S.W. Arrowhead Road
Topeka, KS 66604
913 271 3349

Forestry:
State and Extension Forestry
Kansas State University
2610 Claflin Road
Manhattan, KS 66502
913 537 7050

Nature Preserves Commission:
Parks and Recreation Bureau
Department of Natural Resources
Wallace State Office Bldg., 900 E. Grand
Des Moines, IA 50319
515 281 8524

Parks:
Parks and Recreation Bureau
Department of Natural Resources
Wallace State Office Bldg., 900 E. Grand
Des Moines, IA 50319
515 281 5886

Superfund, State:
Solid Waste Bureau
Environmental Protection Division
Wallace State Office Bldg., 900 E. Grand
Des Moines, IA 50319
515 242 5087

Water Agency:
Surface and Groundwater Protection Bureau
Environmental Protection Division
Wallace State Office Bldg., 900 E. Grand
Des Moines, IA 50319
515 281 8869

Climatology:
Kansas State University
211 Umberger Hall
Manhattan, KS 66506
913 532 6814

Drinking Water:
Public Water Section
Bureau of Water
740 Forbes Field
Topeka, KS 66620
913 296 5503

Fish and Wildlife:
Fish and Wildlife Division
Department of Wildlife and Parks
Route 2, Box 54A
Pratt, KS 67124
316 672 5911

Geological Survey:
Kansas Geological Survey
University of Kansas
1930 Constant Avenue
Lawrence, KS 66046
913 864 3965

Groundwater:
Public Water Section
Bureau of Water
740 Forbes Field
Topeka, KS 66620
913 296 5503

Mined Land Reclamation:
Surface Mining Section
Division of Environment
P.O. Box 1418
Pittsburg, KS 66762
316 231 8540

Nuclear Waste/Nuclear Safety:
Bureau of Air and Radiation
Division of Environment
740 Forbes Field
Topeka, KS 66620
913 296 1593

Superfund, Federal:
Bureau of Environmental Remediation
Division of Environment
740 Forbes Field
Topeka, KS 66620
913 296 1662

Waste Management Agency:
Bureau of Waste Management
Division of Environment
740 Forbes Field
Topeka, KS 66620
913 296 1603

Air Pollution Agency:
Division for Air Quality
Department for Environmental Protection
803 Schenkel Lane
Frankfort, KY 40601
502 564 3382

Dam Safety:
Dam Safety and Flood Plain Compliance Section
Water Resources Branch
14 Reilly Road, Ft. Boone Plaza
Frankfort, KY 40601
502 564 3410

Energy:
Division of Energy
Department for Natural Resources
691 Teton Trail
Frankfort, KY 40601
502 564 7192

Hazardous Waste:
Hazardous Waste Section
Bureau of Waste Management
740 Forbes Field
Topeka, KS 66620
913 296 1608

Natural Resources Agency:
Department of Wildlife and Parks
Landon State Office Building
900 Jackson Street, Suite 502
Topeka, KS 66612
913 296 2281

Parks:
Parks Division
Department of Wildlife and Parks
Route 2, Box 54A
Pratt, KS 67124
316 672 5911

Superfund, State:
Bureau of Environmental Remediation
Division of Environment
740 Forbes Field
Topeka, KS 66620
913 296 1662

Water Agency:
Bureau of Water
Division of Environment
740 Forbes Field
Topeka, KS 66620
913 296 5500

Climatology:
Department of Geography and Geology
Western Kentucky University
Bowling Green, KY 42101
502 745 4555

Drinking Water:
Drinking Water Branch
Division of Water
14 Reilly Road, Ft. Boone Plaza
Frankfort, KY 40601
502 564 3410

Environmental/Natural Resource Agency:
Natural Resources and Environmental Protection Cabinet
Capital Plaza Tower
Frankfort, KY 40601
502 564 3350

Industrial Pre-treatment Program:
Industrial Programs Section
Bureau of Water
740 Forbes Field
Topeka, KS 66620
913 296 5547

NPDES:
Industrial Programs Section
Bureau of Water
740 Forbes Field
Topeka, KS 66620
913 296 5547

Solid Waste:
Solid Waste Section
Bureau of Waste Management
740 Forbes Field
Topeka, KS 66620
913 296 1594

Underground Storage Tanks (UST):
Storage Tanks Section
Bureau of Environmental Remediation
740 Forbes Field
Topeka, KS 66620
913 296 1678

KENTUCKY

Community Right-to-Know:
Freedom of Information Requests
Program Planning and Administration Branch
14 Reilly Road, Ft. Boone Plaza
Frankfort, KY 40601
502 564 6716

Emergency Response:
Environmental Response Team
Field Operations Branch
14 Reilly Road, Ft. Boone Plaza
Frankfort, KY 40601
502 564 2150

Fish and Wildlife:
Division of Fisheries
Department of Fish and Wildlife Resources
#1 Game Farm Road
Frankfort, KY 40601
502 564 3596

Fish and Wildlife:
Division of Wildlife
Department of Fish and Wildlife Resources
#1 Game Farm Road
Frankfort, KY 40601
502 564 4406

Geological Survey:
Kentucky Geological Survey
University of Kentucky
228 Mining and Mineral Resources Bldg.
Lexington, KY 40506
606 257 5863

Industrial Pre-treatment Program:
Pre-Treatment Section
KPDES Branch, Division of Water
14 Reilly Road, Ft. Boone Plaza
Frankfort, KY 40601
502 564 3410

Nature Preserves Commission:
Kentucky State Nature Preserves Commission
Nat. Resources & Environmental Protection Cabinet
801 Schenkel Lane
Frankfort, KY 40601
502 564 2886

Parks:
Parks Department
Tourism Cabinet
500 Mero Street, Capital Plaza Tower
Frankfort, KY 40601
502 564 2172

Superfund, State:
Uncontrolled Sites Branch
Division of Waste Management
14 Reilly Road, Ft. Boone Plaza
Frankfort, KY 40601
502 564 6716

Water Agency:
Division of Water
Department for Environmental Protection
14 Reilly Road, Ft. Boone Plaza
Frankfort, KY 40601
502 564 3410

Climatology:
Department of Geography and Anthropology
Louisiana State University
Baton Rouge, LA 70803
504 388 6184

Flood Plain Management:
Flood Plain Management Section
Water Resources Branch
14 Reilly Road, Ft. Boone Plaza
Frankfort, KY 40601
502 564 3410

Groundwater:
Groundwater Branch
Division of Water
14 Reilly Road, Ft. Boone Plaza
Frankfort, KY 40601
502 564 3410

Mined Land Reclamation:
Natural Resources & Environmental Protection
Cabinet
Capitol Plaza Tower
Frankfort, KY 40601
502 564 3350

NPDES:
KPDES Branch
Division of Water
14 Reilly Road, Ft. Boone Plaza
Frankfort, KY 40601
502 564 3410

Solid Waste:
Solid Waste Branch
Division of Waste Management
14 Reilly Road, Ft. Boone Plaza
Frankfort, KY 40601
502 564 6716

Underground Storage Tanks (UST):
Underground Storage Tanks Branch
Division of Waste Management
14 Reilly Road, Ft. Boone Plaza
Frankfort, KY 40601
502 564 6716

LOUISIANA

Coastal Zone Management:
Coastal Restoration and Management Office
Department of Natural Resources
P.O. Box 44124
Baton Rouge, LA 70804
504 342 7591

Forestry:
Division of Forestry
Department for Natural Resources
627 Comanche Trail
Frankfort, KY 40601
502 564 4496

Hazardous Waste:
Hazardous Waste Branch
Division of Waste Management
14 Reilly Road, Ft. Boone Plaza
Frankfort, KY 40601
502 564 6716

Natural Resources Agency:
Department for Natural Resources
Nat. Resources & Environmental Protection Cabinet
107 Mero Street
Frankfort, KY 40601
502 564 2184

Nuclear Waste/Nuclear Safety:
Radiation Control Branch, Division of Community
Safety
Department of Health Services
275 East Main Street
Frankfort, KY 40601
502 564 3700

Superfund, Federal:
Uncontrolled Sites Branch
Division of Waste Management
14 Reilly Road, Ft. Boone Plaza
Frankfort, KY 40601
502 564 6716

Waste Management Agency:
Division of Waste Management
Department for Environmental Protection
14 Reilly Road, Ft. Boone Plaza
Frankfort, KY 40601
502 564 6716

Air Pollution Agency:
Air Quality and Radiation Protection Division
Department of Environmental Quality
P.O. Box 82135
Baton Rouge, LA 70884
504 765 0102

Community Right-to-Know:
Emergency Response Sect., Office of the Secretary
Department of Environmental Quality
P.O. Box 82263
Baton Rouge, LA 70884
504 765 0634

Dam Safety:
Chief Engineer's Office
Department of Transportation and Development
P.O. Box 94245
Baton Rouge, LA 70804
504 379 1244

Energy:
Energy Division
Department of Natural Resources
P.O. Box 94396
Baton Rouge, LA 70804
504 342 4500

Forestry:
Office of Forestry
Department of Agriculture and Forestry
P.O. Box 631
Baton Rouge, LA 70821
504 925 4500

Hazardous Waste:
Hazardous Waste Branch, Solid and Hazardous
Waste Division
Department of Environmental Quality
P.O. Box 82178
Baton Rouge, LA 70884
504 765 0249

Natural Resources Agency:
Department of Natural Resources
P.O. Box 94396
Baton Rouge, LA 70804
504 342 4500

Nuclear Waste/Nuclear Safety:
Radiation Protection Branch
Air Quality and Radiation Protection Division
P.O. Box 82135
Baton Rouge, LA 70884
504 765 0634

Superfund, Federal:
Inactive & Abandoned Sites Div., Office of
the Secretary
Department of Environmental Quality
P.O. Box 82263
Baton Rouge, LA 70884
504 765 0487

Waste Management Agency:
Solid and Hazardous Waste Division
Department of Environmental Quality
P.O. Box 82178
Baton Rouge, LA 70884
504 765 0249

Drinking Water:
Safer Drinking Water Program
Department of Health and Hospitals
P.O. Box 60630
New Orleans, LA 70160
504 568 5101

Fish and Wildlife:
Department of Wildlife and Fisheries
P.O. Box 98000
Baton Rouge, LA 70898
504 765 2800

Geological Survey:
Louisiana Geological Survey
Department of Natural Resources
P.O. Box G, University Station
Baton Rouge, LA 70893
504 388 5320

Industrial Pre-treatment Program:
Legal Affairs and Enforcement Division
Department of Environmental Quality
P.O. Box 82215
Baton Rouge, LA 70884
504 765 0236

Nature Preserves Commission:
The Nature Conservancy
P.O. Box 4125
Baton Rouge, LA 70821
504 338 1040

Parks:
State Parks Office
Culture, Recreation and Tourism Department
P.O. Box 44426
Baton Rouge, LA 70804
504 342 8111

Superfund, State:
Inactive & Abandoned Sites Div., Office of
the Secretary
Department of Environmental Quality
P.O. Box 82263
Baton Rouge, LA 70884
504 765 0487

Water Agency:
Water Resources Division
Department of Environmental Quality
P.O. Box 82215
Baton Rouge, LA 70884
504 765 0634

Emergency Response:
Emergency Response Sect., Office of the Secretary
Department of Environmental Quality
P.O. Box 82263
Baton Rouge, LA 70884
504 765 0634

Flood Plain Management:
Field Management Section
Department of Urban and Community Affairs
P.O. Box 44455
Baton Rouge, LA 70804
504 935 3725

Groundwater:
Groundwater Protection Section
Water Resources Division
P.O. Box 82215
Baton Rouge, LA 70884
504 765 0634

Mined Land Reclamation:
Office of Conservation
Department of Natural Resources
P.O. Box 94275
Baton Rouge, LA 70804
504 342 5540

NPDES:
Permits Section
Water Resources Division
P.O. Box 82215
Baton Rouge, LA 70884
504 765 0634

Solid Waste:
Solid Waste Branch, Solid and Hazardous Waste
Division
Solid and Hazardous Waste Division
P.O. Box 82178
Baton Rouge, LA 70884
504 765 0333

Underground Storage Tanks (UST):
Underground Storage Tank Section
Solid and Hazardous Waste Division
P.O. Box 82178
Baton Rouge, LA 70884
504 765 0243

MAINE

Coastal Zone Management:
Coastal Program
State Planning Office
State House Station 38
Augusta, ME 04333
207 289 3261

Drinking Water:
Division of Health Engineering
Department of Human Services
State House Station 11
Augusta, ME 04333
207 289 5694

Fish and Wildlife:
Inland Fisheries and Wildlife Department
State House Station 41
Augusta, ME 04333
207 289 3371

Geological Survey:
Maine Geological Survey
Conservation Department
State House Station 22
Augusta, ME 04333
207 289 2801

Industrial Pre-treatment Program:
Licensing and Enforcement Division
Water Quality Control Bureau
State House Station 17
Augusta, ME 04333
207 289 3901

NPDES:
Licensing and Enforcement Division
Water Quality Control Bureau
State House Station 17
Augusta, ME 04333
207 289 3901

Solid Waste:
Bureau of Solid Waste
Department of Environmental Protection
State House Station 17
Augusta, ME 04333
207 582 8740

Air Pollution Agency:
Air Quality Control Bureau
Department of Environmental Protection
State House Station 17
Augusta, ME 04333
207 289 2437

Community Right-to-Know:
Maine Emergency Management Agency
Defense and Veterans Services Department
State House Station 33
Augusta, ME 04333
207 289 4080

Emergency Response:
Response Services Division
Oil and Hazardous Materials Control Bureau
State House Station 17
Augusta, ME 04333
207 289 2651

Flood Plain Management:
Office of Comprehensive Planning
Department of Economic and Community
Development
State House Station 59
Augusta, ME 04333
207 289 6823

Groundwater:
Water Quality Control Bureau
Department of Environmental Protection
State House Station 17
Augusta, ME 04333
207 289 3901

Mined Land Reclamation:
Public Lands Bureau
Maine Geological Survey
State House Station 22
Augusta, ME 04333
207 289 2801

Nuclear Waste/Nuclear Safety:
Oil and Hazardous Materials Control Bureau
Department of Environmental Protection
State House Station 17
Augusta, ME 04333
207 289 2651

Superfund, Federal:
Licensing and Enforcement Division
Oil and Hazardous Materials Control Bureau
State House Station 17
Augusta, ME 04333
207 289 2651

Climatology:
University of Maine
491 College Avenue
Orono, ME 04473
207 581 3880

Dam Safety:
Land Quality Control Bureau
Department of Environmental Protection
State House Station 17
Augusta, ME 04333
207 289 2111

Energy:
Energy Conservation Division
Department of Economic and Community
Development
State House Station 53
Augusta, ME 04333
207 289 6000

Forestry:
Bureau of Forestry
Conservation Department
State House Station 22
Augusta, ME 04333
207 289 2791

Hazardous Waste:
Oil and Hazardous Materials Control Bureau
Department of Environmental Protection
State House Station 17
Augusta, ME 04333
207 289 2651

Natural Resources Agency:
Department of Environmental Protection
State House Station 17
Augusta, ME 04333
207 289 2811

Parks:
Parks and Recreation Bureau
Conservation Department
State House Station 19
Augusta, ME 04333
207 289 3821

Superfund, State:
Licensing and Enforcement Division
Oil and Hazardous Materials Control Bureau
State House Station 17
Augusta, ME 04333
207 289 2651

Underground Storage Tanks (UST):
Oil and Hazardous Materials Control Bureau
Department of Environmental Protection
State House Station 17
Augusta, ME 04333
207 289 2651

MARYLAND

Coastal Zone Management:
Coastal Resources Division, Tidewater Administration
Department of Natural Resources
Tawes State Office Building
Annapolis, MD 21401
410 974 2784

Drinking Water:
Water Supply Program
Water Management Administration
2500 Broening Highway
Baltimore, MD 21224
410 631 3702

Fish and Wildlife:
Fisheries Division, Forest, Park and Wildlife Service
Department of Natural Resources
Tawes State Office Building
Annapolis, MD 21401
410 974 3558

Groundwater:
Individual Septic Systems and Wells Program
Water Management Administration
2500 Broening Highway
Baltimore, MD 21224
410 631 3652

Mined Land Reclamation:
Bureau of Mines
Water Resources Administration
69 Hill Street
Frostburg, MD 21532
410 689 6104

Nuclear Waste/Nuclear Safety:
Toxics Registry Division
Waste Management Administration
2500 Broening Highway
Baltimore, MD 21224
410 631 3800

Waste Management Agency:
Waste Management Agency
State House Station 154
Augusta, ME 04333
207 289 5300

Air Pollution Agency:
Air and Radiation Management Administration
Department of the Environment
2500 Broening Highway
Baltimore, MD 21224
410 631 3255

Community Right-to-Know:
Toxics Registry Division
Waste Management Administration
2500 Broening Highway
Baltimore, MD 21224
410 631 3800

Emergency Response:
Emergency Response Division
Environmental Response and Restoration
2103 Annapolis Road
Baltimore, MD 21030
410 333 2950

Forestry:
Forest, Park and Wildlife Service
Department of Natural Resources
Tawes State Office Building
Annapolis, MD 21401
410 974 3776

Hazardous Waste:
Hazardous Waste Program
Waste Management Administration
2500 Broening Highway
Baltimore, MD 21224
410 631 3343

Natural Resources Agency:
Department of Natural Resources
Tawes State Office Building
Annapolis, MD 21401
410 974 3041

Parks:
Parks Operation, Forest, Park and Wildlife Service
Department of Natural Resources
Tawes State Office Building
Annapolis, MD 21401
410 974 3771

Water Agency:
Water Quality Control Bureau
Department of Environmental Protection
State House Station 17
Augusta, ME 04333
207 289 3901

Climatology:
University of Maryland
1123A, Jull Hall
College Park, MD 20742
301 405 7223

Dam Safety:
Dam Safety Division, Water Resources Administration
Department of Natural Resources
Tawes State Office Building, D-3
Annapolis, MD 21401
410 974 2101

Energy:
Maryland Energy Administration
Department of Housing and Community Development
45 Calvert Street, Room 202
Annapolis, MD 21401
410 974 2511

Geological Survey:
Maryland Geological Survey
Department of Natural Resources
711 West 40th Street, Suite 440
Baltimore, MD 21211
410 554 5503

Industrial Pre-treatment Program:
Pretreatment and Enforcement Division
Water Management Administration
2500 Broening Highway
Baltimore, MD 21224
410 631 3621

NPDES:
Surface Discharge Permits Division
Water Management Administration
2500 Broening Highway
Baltimore, MD 21224
410 631 3671

Solid Waste:
Solid Waste Program
Waste Management Administration
2500 Broening Highway
Baltimore, MD 21224
410 631 3318

Superfund, Federal:
Emergency Response Division
Environmental Response and Restoration
2500 Broening Highway
Baltimore, MD 21224
410 631 3442

Waste Management Agency:
Waste Management Administration
Department of the Environment
2500 Broening Highway
Baltimore, MD 21224
410 631 3304

Air Pollution Agency:
Air Quality Control Division, Bureau of Waste Prevention
Department of Environmental Protection
1 Winter Street, 3rd Floor
Boston, MA 02108
617 292 5593

Community Right-to-Know:
Emergency Response and Right to Know Unit
Department of Public Health
150 Tremont Street
Boston, MA 02111
617 727 7035

Emergency Response:
Emergency Response Section
Waste Site Clean-Up Bureau
1 Winter Street, 5th Floor
Boston, MA 02108
617 292 5851

Flood Plain Management:
Division of Water Resources
100 Cambridge Street
Boston, MA 02202
617 292 3267

Groundwater:
Regulatory Branch, Division of Water Pollution Control
Bureau of Resource Protection
1 Winter Street, 7th Floor
Boston, MA 02108
617 292 5893

Natural Resources Agency:
Department of Environmental Management
Executive Office of Environmental Affairs
100 Cambridge Street
Boston, MA 02202
617 727 3163

Superfund, State:
Emergency Response Division
Environmental Response and Restoration
2500 Broening Highway
Baltimore, MD 21224
410 631 3438

Water Agency:
Water Management Administration
Department of the Environment
2500 Broening Highway
Baltimore, MD 21224
410 631 3567

Climatology:
Division of Water Resources
Department of Environmental Management
496 Park Street
North Reading, MA 01864
617 275 8860

Dam Safety:
Dam Safety Program, Division of Planning and Development
Dept. of Environmental Mgt./Resource Conservation
100 Cambridge Street, 14th Floor
Boston, MA 02202
617 727 3160

Energy:
Division of Energy Resources
Department of Economic Affairs
100 Cambridge Street, Room 1500
Boston, MA 02202
617 727 4732

Forestry:
Bureau of Forestry
Environmental Management Department
100 Cambridge Street, 19th Floor
Boston, MA 02202
617 727 3180

Hazardous Waste:
Hazardous Waste Division, Bureau of Waste Prevention
Department of Environmental Protection
1 Winter Street, 7th Floor
Boston, MA 02108
617 292 5853

Nature Preserves Commission:
Natural Heritage and Endangered Species Program
Division of Fisheries and Wildlife
100 Cambridge Street, 19th Floor
Boston, MA 02202
617 727 9194

Underground Storage Tanks (UST):
Oil Control Program
Waste Management Administration
2500 Broening Highway
Baltimore, MD 21224
410 631 3324

MASSACHUSETTS

Coastal Zone Management:
Coastal Zone Management
Executive Office of Environmental Affairs
100 Cambridge Street, Room 2006
Boston, MA 02202
617 727 9530

Drinking Water:
Water Quality Section, Division of Water Supply
Bureau of Resource Protection
1 Winter Street, 9th Floor
Boston, MA 02108
617 292 5529

Fish and Wildlife:
Division of Fisheries and Wildlife
Dept. of Fisheries, Wildlife and Environmental Mgt
100 Cambridge Street, Room 1902
Boston, MA 02202
617 727 3155

Geological Survey:
Environmental Quality Engineering
Executive Office of Environmental Affairs
100 Cambridge Street, 20th Floor
Boston, MA 02202
617 292 5690

Industrial Pre-treatment Program:
Industrial Wastewater Division
Bureau of Waste Prevention
1 Winter Street, 7th Floor
Boston, MA 02108
617 292 5665

NPDES:
Division of Water Pollution Control, Bureau of Resource Protection
Department of Environmental Protection
P.O. Box 4062
Grafton, MA 02211
508 792 7470

Nuclear Waste/Nuclear Safety:
Radiation Control Program
Department of Public Health
305 South Street
Jamaica Plain, MA 02130
617 727 6214

Superfund, State:
Waste Site Clean-up Bureau
Hazardous Waste Division
1 Winter Street, 5th Floor
Boston, MA 02108
617 292 5819

Water Agency:
Division of Water Pollution Control, Bureau of
Resource Protection
Department of Environmental Protection
1 Winter Street, 7th Floor
Boston, MA 02108
617 292 5647

Climatology:
MDA/Climatology Division
Michigan State University
Natural Science Building, Room 417
East Lansing, MI 48824
517 373 8338

Dam Safety:
Dam Safety Unit, Water Management Section
Land and Water Management Division
P.O. Box 30028
Lansing, MI 48909
517 335 3171

Environmental/Natural Resources Agency:
Department of Natural Resources
P.O. Box 30028
Lansing, MI 48909
517 373 2329

Forestry:
Forest Management Division
Department of Natural Resources
P.O. Box 30028
Lansing, MI 48909
517 373 1275

Hazardous Waste:
Hazardous Waste Permit Section
Waste Management Division
P.O. Box 30241
Lansing, MI 48909
517 373 0530

Parks:
Bureau of Parks and Recreation
Environmental Management Department
100 Cambridge Street, 19th Floor
Boston, MA 02202
617 727 3180

Underground Storage Tanks (UST):
Regulatory Branch
Division of Water Pollution Control
1 Winter Street, 3rd Floor
Boston, MA 02108
617 292 5886

MICHIGAN

Coastal Zone Management:
Great Lakes Office
Department of Natural Resources
P.O. Box 30028
Lansing, MI 48909
517 373 3588

Drinking Water:
Division of Water Supply
Department of Public Health
P.O. Box 30195, 3423 North Logan Street
Lansing, MI 48909
517 335 9216

Fish and Wildlife:
Wildlife Division
Department of Natural Resources
P.O. Box 30028
Lansing, MI 48909
517 373 1263

Geological Survey:
Geological Survey Division
Department of Natural Resources
P.O. Box 30256
Lansing, MI 48909
517 334 6907

Industrial Pre-treatment Program:
Pre-Treatment Field Support Unit
Surface Water Quality Division
P.O. Box 30028
Lansing, MI 48909
517 322 1300

Solid Waste:
Division of Solid Waste Management
Department of Environmental Protection
1 Winter Street, 4th Floor
Boston, MA 02108
617 292 5939

Waste Management Agency:
Bureau of Waste Prevention
Department of Environmental Protection
1 Winter Street, 3rd Floor
Boston, MA 02108
617 292 5939

Air Pollution Agency:
Air Quality Division
Bureau of Environmental Protection
P.O. Box 30028
Lansing, MI 48909
517 373 7023

Community Right-to-Know:
Title III Unit
Environmental Response Division
P.O. Box 30028
Lansing, MI 48909
517 373 8481

Emergency Response:
Environmental Hazard Control Unit
Environmental Response Division
P.O. Box 30028
Lansing, MI 48909
517 373 8174

Flood Plain Management:
Land and Water Protection Section
Land and Water Management Division
P.O. Box 30028
Lansing, MI 48909
517 373 3930

Groundwater:
Groundwater Permits Program
Waste Management Division
P.O. Box 30241
Lansing, MI 48909
517 373 2730

Mined Land Reclamation:
Policy, Procedures and Special Services Unit
Geological Survey Division
P.O. Box 30256
Lansing, MI 48909
517 334 6976

Natural Resources Agency:
Department of Natural Resources
P.O. Box 30028
Lansing, MI 48909
517 373 2329

Nuclear Waste/Nuclear Safety:
Division of Radiological Health
Department of Public Health
P.O. Box 30195, 3423 North Logan Street
Lansing, MI 48909
517 335 8200

Superfund, Federal:
Superfund Section
Environmental Response Division
P.O. Box 30028
Lansing, MI 48909
517 335 3393

Waste Management Agency:
Waste Management Division
Department of Natural Resources
P.O. Box 30241
Lansing, MI 48909
517 373 2730

Air Pollution Agency:
Air Quality Division
Pollution Control Agency
520 Lafayette Road
St. Paul, MN 55155
612-296-7331

Community Right-to-Know:
Superfund Unit, Site Response Section
Ground Water and Solid Waste Division
520 Lafayette Road
St. Paul, MN 55155
612 296 7397

Emergency Response:
Tank and Spills Section
Hazardous Waste Division
520 Lafayette Road
St. Paul, MN 55155
612 643 3439

Flood Plain Management:
Permits and Land Use Section
Division of Waters
500 Lafayette Road
St. Paul, MN 55146
612 296 0440

Nature Preserves Commission:
Wilderness and Natural Areas Council
Wildlife Division
P.O. Box 30028
Lansing, MI 48909
517 373 1263

Parks:
Parks Division
Department of Natural Resources
P.O. Box 30028
Lansing, MI 48909
517 373 1270

Superfund, State:
307 Section
Environmental Responnse Division
P.O. Box 30028
Lansing, MI 48909
517 335 3397

Water Agency:
Surface Water Quality Division
Department of Natural Resources
P.O. Box 30028
Lansing, MI 48909
517 373 1949

Climatology:
Department of Natural Resources
University of Minnesota
S-325 Borlang Hall
St. Paul, MN 55108
612 296 4214

Dam Safety:
Dam Safety
Division of Waters
500 Lafayette Road
St. Paul, MN 55155
612 296 0525

Energy:
Energy Division
Department of Public Service
150 East Kellogg Boulevard, Room 790
St. Paul, MN 55101
612 296 0407

Forestry:
Forestry Division
Department of Natural Resources
500 Lafayette Road
St. Paul, MN 55155
612 296 4484

NPDES:
Permits Section
Surface Water Quality Division
P.O. Box 30028
Lansing, MI 48909
517 373 8088

Solid Waste:
Technical Services Section
Waste Management Division
P.O. Box 30241
Lansing, MI 48909
517 335 3293

Underground Storage Tanks (UST):
Leaking Underground Storage Tank Section
Environmental Response Division
P.O. Box 30028
Lansing, MI 48909
517 373 1230

MINNESOTA

Coastal Zone Management:
Permits and Land Use Section
Division of Waters
500 Lafayette Road
St. Paul, MN 55155
612 296 0440

Drinking Water:
Engineering Unit, Water Supply and Well Management
Department of Health
717 Delaware Street, S.E.
Minneapolis, MN 55440
612 623 5227

Fish and Wildlife:
Fish and Wildlife Division
Department of Natural Resources
500 Lafayette Road
St. Paul, MN 55155
612 297 1308

Geological Survey:
State Geological Survey
2642 University Avenue
St. Paul, MN 55114
612 627 4780

Groundwater:
Ground Water and Technical Analysis Unit
Division of Waters
500 Lafayette Road
St. Paul, MN 55155
612 296 0434

Mined Land Reclamation:
Mined Land Reclamation
Minerals Division
1525 3rd Avenue, East
Hibbing, MN 55746
218 262 6767

NPDES:
Permits Unit, Regulatory Compliance Section
Water Quality Division
520 Lafayette Road
St. Paul, MN 55155
612 296 7713

Superfund, Federal:
Site Response Section
Ground Water and Solid Waste Division
520 Lafayette Road
St. Paul, MN 55155
612 296 7290

Waste Management Agency:
Office of Waste Management
1350 Energy Lane
St. Paul, MN 55108
612 296 7333

Air Pollution Agency:
Air Division
Office of Pollution Control
P.O. Box 10385
Jackson, MS 39209
601 961 5171

Community Right-to-Know:
Mississippi Emergency Response Commission
P.O. Box 4501
Jackson, MS 39296
601 960 9005

Emergency Response:
Emergency Branch
Hazardous Waste Division
P.O. Box 10385
Jackson, MS 39209
601 961 5079

Hazardous Waste:
Hazardous Waste Section
Hazardous Waste Division
520 Lafayette Road
St. Paul, MN 55155
612 643 3402

Natural Resources Agency:
Department of Natural Resources
500 Lafayette Road
St. Paul, MN 55155
612 296 2549

Parks:
Parks and Recreation Division
Department of Natural Resources
500 Lafayette Road
St. Paul, MN 55155
612 296 2270

Superfund, State:
Superfund Unit, Site Response Section
Ground Water and Solid Waste Division
520 Lafayette Road
St. Paul, MN 55155
612 296 7397

Water Agency:
Water Division
Natural Resources Department
500 Lafayette Road
St. Paul, MN 55155
612 296 4810

Climatology:
Department of Geology and Geography
Drawer 5167, Mississippi State University
Miss. State, MS 39762
601 325 3915

Dam Safety:
Division of Permitting and Monitoring
Office of Land and Water Resources
P.O. Box 10631
Jackson, MS 39209
601 961 5204

Energy:
Division of Energy
Department of Economic and Community Development
510 George Street
Jackson, MS 39202
601 359 6600

Industrial Pre-treatment Program:
Municipal Wastewater Treatment Section
Water Quality Division
520 Lafayette Road
St. Paul, MN 55155
612 296 7230

Nature Preserves Commission:
Scientific and Natural Areas
Fish and Wildlife Division
500 Lafayette Road
St. Paul, MN 55155
612 297 2357

Solid Waste:
Ground Water and Solid Waste Division
Pollution Control Agency
520 Lafayette Road
St. Paul, MN 55155
612 296 7340

Underground Storage Tanks (UST):
Ground Water and Technical Analysis Unit
Division of Waters
500 Lafayette Road
St. Paul, MN 55155
612 296 0433

MISSISSIPPI

Coastal Zone Management:
Bureau of Marine Resources
Department of Wildlife, Fisheries and Parks
2620 Beach Boulevard
Biloxi, MS 39531
601 385 5860

Drinking Water:
Division of Water Supply
Department of Health
P.O. Box 1700
Jackson, MS 39215
601 960 7518

Environmental/Natural Resource Agency:
Department of Environmental Quality
P.O. Box 20305, 2380 Highway 80 West
Jackson, MS 39289
601 961 5000

Flood Plain Management:
Mississippi Emergency Management Agency
P.O. Box 4501, 1410 Riverside Drive
Jackson, MS 39296
601 352 9100

Groundwater:
Groundwater Division
Office of Pollution Control
P.O. Box 10385
Jackson, MS 39209
601 961 5119

Mined Land Reclamation:
Division of Mining and Reclamation
Office of Geology
P.O. Box 20307
Jackson, MS 39289
601 961 5515

NPDES:
Municipal Permits Section, Permit Compliance
Branch
Office of Pollution Control
P.O. Box 10385
Jackson, MS 39209
601 961 5159

Solid Waste:
Solid Waste Branch
Groundwater Division
P.O. Box 10385
Jackson, MS 39209
601 961 5171

Underground Storage Tanks (UST):
UST Section
Groundwater Division
P.O. Box 10385
Jackson, MS 39209
601 961 5171

MISSOURI

Community Right-to-Know:
Laboratory Services Program
Environmental Quality Division
2010 Missouri Boulevard
Jefferson City, MO 65102
314 751 7928

Forestry:
Forestry Commission
301 N. Lamar Street
Jackson, MS 39201
601 359 1386

Hazardous Waste:
Hazardous Waste Division
Department of Environmental Quality
P.O. Box 10385
Jackson, MS 39209
601 961 5171

Natural Resources Agency:
Department of Wildlife, Fisheries and Parks
P.O. Box 451
Jackson, MS 39205
601 362 9212

Nuclear Waste/Nuclear Safety:
Radiological Health Division
Department of Health
P.O. Box 1700
Jackson, MS 39215
601 354 6657

Superfund, Federal:
Superfund Branch
Hazardous Waste Division
P.O. Box 10385
Jackson, MS 39209
601 961 5171

Waste Management Agency:
Office of Pollution Control
Department of Environmental Quality
P.O. Box 10631
Jackson, MS 39209
601 961 5171

Air Pollution Agency
Air Pollution Control Program
Environmental Quality Division
P.O. Box 176
Jefferson City, MO 65102
314 751 4817

Dam Safety:
Dams and Reservoirs Safety Program
Geology and Land Survey Division
P.O. Box 250, 111 Fairgrounds Road
Rolla, MO 65401
314 364 1752

Geological Survey:
Office of Geology
Department of Environmental Quality
P.O. Box 20307
Jackson, MS 39289
601 961 5500

Industrial Pre-treatment Program:
Pre-Treatment Sect., Industrial Wastewater Branch
Surface Water Division
P.O. Box 10385
Jackson, MS 39209
601 961 5171

Nature Preserves Commission:
Wildlife Heritage Program
Department of Wildlife, Fisheries and Parks
P.O. Box 451
Jackson, MS 39205
601 362 9212

Parks:
Bureau of Parks and Recreation
Department of Wildlife, Fisheries and Parks
P.O. Box 23093
Jackson, MS 39225
601 364 2010

Superfund, State:
Superfund Branch
Hazardous Waste Division
P.O. Box 10385
Jackson, MS 39209
601 961 5171

Water Agency:
Office of Pollution Control
Department of Natural Resources
P.O. Box 10631
Jackson, MS 39209
601 961 5171

Climatology:
Department of Atmospheric Science
University of Missouri
701 Hitt Street
Columbia, MO 65211
314 882 6591

Drinking Water:
Water and Wastewater Operators Certification and
Training
Field Services
P.O. Box 176
Jefferson City, MO 65102
314 751 0678

Emergency Response:
Environmental Emergency Response Unit
Field Services Section
2010 Missouri Boulevard
Jefferson City, MO 65102
314 751 7929

Fish and Wildlife:
Fisheries Division
Department of Conservation
P.O. Box 180
Jefferson City, MO 65102
314 751 4115

Geological Survey:
Geology and Land Survey Division
Department of Natural Resources
P.O. Box 250, Fairgrounds Road
Rolla, MO 65401
314 364 1752

Industrial Pre-treatment Program:
Permits Section
Water Pollution Control Program
P.O. Box 176
Jefferson City, MO 65102
314 751 6996

Nature Preserves Commission:
Field Operations Program
Natural History Section
P.O. Box 176
Jefferson City, MO 65102
314 751 8660

Parks:
Parks, Recreation and Historical Preservation
Department of Natural Resources
P.O. Box 176
Jefferson City, MO 65102
314 751 2479

Superfund, State:
Superfund Section
Waste Management Program
P.O. Box 176
Jefferson City, MO 65102
314 751 3176

Water Agency:
Water Pollution Control Program
Environmental Quality Division
P.O. Box 176
Jefferson City, MO 65102
314 751 1300

Energy:
Energy Division
Department of Natural Resources
P.O. Box 176
Jefferson City, MO 65102
314 751 4000

Flood Plain Management:
Flood Plain Management Section
Water Resources Planning Program
P.O. Box 176
Jefferson City, MO 65102
314 751 1237

Groundwater:
Water Resources Planning Program
Geology and Land Survey Division
P.O. Box 250, 111 Fairgrounds Road
Rolla, MO 65401
314 364 1752

Mined Land Reclamation:
Land Reclamation Program
Environmental Quality Division
P.O. Box 176
Jefferson City, MO 65102
314 751 4041

NPDES:
Permits Section
Water Pollution Control Program
P.O. Box 176
Jefferson City, MO 65102
314 751 6825

Solid Waste:
Solid Waste Section
Waste Management Program
P.O. Box 176
Jefferson City, MO 65102
314 751 3176

Underground Storage Tanks (UST):
Planning Section
Water Pollution Control Program
P.O. Box 176
Jefferson City, MO 65102
314 751 6825

MONTANA

Environmental/Natural Resources Agency:
Department of Natural Resources
P.O. Box 176
Jefferson City, MO 65102
314 751 4422

Forestry:
Forestry Division
Department of Conservation
P.O. Box 180
Jefferson City, MO 65102
314 751 4115

Hazardous Waste:
Hazardous Waste Section
Waste Management Program
P.O. Box 176
Jefferson City, MO 65102
314 751 3176

Natural Resources Agency:
Department of Natural Resources
P.O. Box 176, 205 Jefferson Street
Jefferson City, MO 65102
314 751 4422

Nuclear Waste/Nuclear Safety:
Administrative Unit
Waste Management Program
P.O. Box 176
Jefferson City, MO 65102
314 751 4810

Superfund, Federal:
Superfund Section
Waste Management Program
P.O. Box 176
Jefferson City, MO 65102
314 751 3176

Waste Management Agency:
Waste Management Program
Environmental Quality Division
P.O. Box 176
Jefferson City, MO 65102
314 751 3176

Air Pollution Agency:
Air Quality Bureau
Environmental Sciences Division
Cogswell Building
Helena, MT 59620
406 444 3454

Climatology:
Plant and Soil Science Department
Montana State University
Bozeman, MT 59717
406 994 5067

Drinking Water:
Drinking Water Subdivision
Water Quality Bureau
Cogswell Building
Helena, MT 59620
406 444 2406

Fish and Wildlife:
Wildlife Division
Department of Fish, Wildlife and Parks
1420 E. 6th Avenue
Helena, MT 59620
406 444 2612

Geological Survey:
Bureau of Mines and Geology
West Park Street
Butte, MT 59701
406 496 4181

Industrial Pre-treatment Program:
Permits Section
Water Quality Bureau
Cogswell Building
Helena, MT 59620
406 444 2406

NPDES:
Permits Section
Water Quality Bureau
Cogswell Building
Helena, MT 59620
406 444 2406

Solid Waste:
Solid Waste Program
Superfund, Solid Waste and Junk Vehicles
Cogswell Building
Helena, MT 59620
406 444 2821

Underground Storage Tanks (UST):
UST Section
Solid and Hazardous Waste Bureau
Cogswell Building
Helena, MT 59620
406 444 2821

Community Right-to-Know:
Solid and Hazardous Waste Bureau
Environmental Sciences Division
Cogswell Building
Helena, MT 59620
406 444 2821

Emergency Response:
Solid and Hazardous Waste Bureau
Environmental Sciences Division
Cogswell Building
Helena, MT 59620
406 444 2821

Flood Plain Management:
Flood Plain Management Section
Water Resources Division
1520 E. 6th Avenue
Helena, MT 59620
406 444 6654

Groundwater:
Groundwater Section
Water Quality Bureau
Cogswell Building
Helena, MT 59620
406 444 2406

Mined Land Reclamation:
Reclamation Division
Department of State Lands
Capitol Station
Helena, MT 59620
406 444 2074

Nuclear Waste/Nuclear Safety:
Occupational Health Bureau
Environmental Sciences Division
Cogswell Building
Helena, MT 59620
406 444 3671

Superfund, Federal:
Superfund, Solid Waste and Junk Vehicles Section
Solid and Hazardous Waste Bureau
Cogswell Building
Helena, MT 59620
406 444 4067

Waste Management Agency:
Solid and Hazardous Waste Bureau
Environmental Sciences Division
Cogswell Building
Helena, MT 59620
406 444 2821

Dam Safety:
Water Resources Division
Department of Natural Resources and Conservation
1520 E. 6th Avenue
Helena, MT 59620
406 444 6816

Energy:
Energy Division
Department of Natural Resources and Conservation
1520 E. 6th Avenue
Helena, MT 59620
406 444 6697

Forestry:
Forestry Division
Department of State Lands
2705 Spurgin Road
Missoula, MT 59801
406 542 4300

Hazardous Waste:
Hazardous Waste Section
Solid and Hazardous Waste Bureau
Cogswell Building
Helena, MT 59620
406 444 2821

Natural Resources Agency:
Department of Natural Resources and Conservation
1520 E. 6th Avenue
Helena, MT 59620
406 444 6699

Parks:
Parks Division
Department of Fish, Wildlife and Parks
1420 E. 6th Avenue
Helena, MT 59620
406 444 3750

Superfund, State:
Superfund, Solid Waste and Junk Vehicles Section
Solid and Hazardous Waste Bureau
Cogswell Building
Helena, MT 59620
406 444 5827

Water Agency:
Water Resources Division
Department of Natural Resources and Conservation
1520 E. 6th Avenue
Helena, MT 59620
406 444 6603

NEBRASKA

Community Right-to-Know:
Underground Storage Tanks and Emergency
Response Section
Department of Environmental Quality
P.O. Box 98922
Lincoln, NE 68509
402 471 0001

Emergency Response:
Underground Storage Tanks and Emergency
Response Section
Department of Environmental Quality
P.O. Box 98922
Lincoln, NE 68509
402 471 4239

Forestry:
Forestry, Fisheries and Wildlife Department
University of Nebraska
101 Plant Industry Building
Lincoln, NE 68583
402 472 2944

Hazardous Waste:
Air and Waste Management Division
Department of Environmental Quality
P.O. Box 98922
Lincoln, NE 68509
402 471 0001

Nature Preserves Commission:
State Historical Parks Division
Game and Parks Commission
P.O. Box 30370
Lincoln, NE 68503
402 464 0641

Parks:
Parks Division
Game and Parks Commission
P.O. Box 30370
Lincoln, NE 68503
402 464 0641

Superfund, State:
Hazardous Waste Section
Air and Waste Management Division
P.O. Box 98922
Lincoln, NE 68509
402 471 0001

Air Pollution Agency:
Air and Waste Management Division
Department of Environmental Quality
P.O. Box 98922
Lincoln, NE 68509
402 471 0001

Dam Safety:
Engineering Division
Department of Water Resources
P.O. Box 94676
Lincoln, NE 68509
402 471 2363

Fish and Wildlife:
Wildlife Division
Game and Parks Commission
P.O. Box 30370
Lincoln, NE 68503
402 464 0641

Geological Survey:
Conservation and Survey Division
University of Nebraska
113 Nebraska Hall
Lincoln, NE 68588
402 472 3471

Industrial Pre-treatment Program:
Permits and Compliance Section
Water Quality Division
P.O. Box 98922
Lincoln, NE 68509
402 471 4239

NPDES:
UST and Emergency Response Section
Department of Environmental Quality
P.O. Box 98922
Lincoln, NE 68509
402 471 4239

Solid Waste:
Integrated Waste Management Section
Air and Waste Management Division
P.O. Box 98922
Lincoln, NE 68509
402 471 4210

Underground Storage Tanks (UST):
UST and Emergency Response Section
Department of Environmental Quality
P.O. Box 98922
Lincoln, NE 68509
402 471 3343

Climatology:
CAMAC
University of Nebraska
237 Chase Hall (0728)
Lincoln, NE 68583
402 472 6706

Drinking Water:
Surface Water Section
Water Quality Division
P.O. Box 98922
Lincoln, NE 68509
402 471 4700

Flood Plain Management:
Engineering Branch
Department of Water Resources
P.O. Box 94676
Lincoln, NE 68509
402 471 2363

Groundwater:
Ground Water Section
Water Quality Division
P.O. Box 98922
Lincoln, NE 68509
402 471 4230

Natural Resources Agency:
Natural Resources Commission
P.O. Box 94876
Lincoln, NE 68509
402 471 2081

Nuclear Waste/Nuclear Safety:
Division of Radiological Health
Department of Health
P.O. Box 95007
Lincoln, NE 68509
402 471 2168

Superfund, Federal:
Hazardous Waste Section
Air and Waste Management Division
P.O. Box 98922
Lincoln, NE 68509
402 471 0001

Waste Management Agency:
Air and Waste Management Division
Department of Environmental Quality
P.O. Box 98922
Lincoln, NE 68509
402 471 0001

NEVADA

Water Agency:
Department of Water Resources
P.O. Box 94676
Lincoln, NE 68509
402 471 2363

Climatology:
Geography Department
College of Arts and Sciences
University of Nevada - Reno
Reno, NV 89557
702 784 6995

Drinking Water:
Public Health Engineering, Community Health
Services, Health Division
Department of Human Resources
505 East King Street, Room 103
Carson City, NV 89710
702 687 4750

Environmental/Natural Resources Agency:
Department of Conservation and Natural Resources
123 Nye Lane, Room 230
Carson City, NV 89710
702 687 4360

Forestry:
Forestry Division
Department of Conservation and Natural Resources
333 West Nye Lane
Carson City, NV 89710
702 687 4350

Hazardous Waste:
Bureau of Waste Management
Division of Environmental Protection
333 West Nye Lane
Carson City, NV 89710
702 687 5872

Natural Resources Agency:
Department of Conservation and Natural Resources
333 West Nye Lane
Carson City, NV 89710
702 687 4360

Nuclear Waste/Nuclear Safety:
Radiological Health Section, Health Division
Department of Human Resources
505 East King Street, Room 202
Carson City, NV 89710
702 687 5394

Community Right-to-Know:
Division of Emergency Management
Department of Military
2525 South Carson Street
Carson City, NV 89710
702 687 4240

Emergency Response:
Division of Emergency Management
Department of Military
2525 South Carson Street
Carson City, NV 89710
702 687 4240

Fish and Wildlife:
Department of Wildlife
P.O. Box 10678
Reno, NV 89520
702 688 1599

Geological Survey:
Bureau of Mines and Geology
University of Nevada, Reno
Reno, NV 89557
702 784 6691

Industrial Pre-treatment Program:
Enforcement Branch
Bureau of Water Pollution Control
333 West Nye Lane
Carson City, NV 89710
702 687 5870

Nature Preserves Commission:
Nevada Natural Heritage Program
Division of State Parks
333 West Nye Lane
Carson City, NV 89710
702 687 4245

Parks:
Division of State Parks
Department of Conservation and Natural Resources
333 West Nye Lane
Carson City, NV 89710
702 687 4370

Air Pollution Agency:
Bureau of Air Quality
Division of Environmental Protection
333 West Nye Lane
Carson City, NV 89710
702 687 5065

Dam Safety:
Water Planning Division
Department of Conservation and Natural Resources
333 West Nye Lane
Carson City, NV 89710
702 687 4380

Energy:
Energy and Community Development
Office of Community Services
1100 East Williams
Carson City, NV 89710
702 687 4990

Flood Plain Management:
Division of Engineering Management
Department of Military
2525 South Carson Street
Carson City, NV 89710
702 687 4250

Groundwater:
Groundwater Section
Division of Environmental Protection
333 West Nye Lane
Carson City, NV 89710
702 687 5870

Mined Land Reclamation:
Bureau of Mining Regulation/Reclamation
333 West Nye Lane
Carson City, NV 89710
702 687 4675

NPDES:
Permits and Grants Branch
Bureau of Water Pollution Control
333 West Nye Lane
Carson City, NV 89710
702 687 5870

Solid Waste:
Planning/Compliance and Enforcement Branch
Bureau of Waste Management
333 West Nye Lane
Carson City, NV 89710
702 687 5872

Superfund, State:
Superfund Branch
Bureau of Waste Management
333 West Nye Lane
Carson City, NV 89710
702 687 5872

Water Agency:
Bureau of Water Quality Planning
Division of Environmental Protection
333 West Nye Lane
Carson City, NV 89710
702 687 5883

Climatology:
Department of Geography
University of New Hampshire
James Hall
Durham, NH 03824
603 862 1719

Dam Safety:
Dam Operations
Bureau of Water Resources
64 North Main Street
Concord, NH 03302
603 271 3406

Energy:
Governor's Energy Office
2 1/2 Beacon Street
Concord, NH 03301
603 271 2711

Forestry:
Forest and Lands Division
Resources and Economic Development Department
105 Loudon Road, Box 856
Concord, NH 03301
603 271 2214

Hazardous Waste:
Hazardous Waste Compliance Section
Waste Management Compliance Bureau
6 Hazen Drive
Concord, NH 03301
603 271 2942

Nature Preserves Commission:
Natural Heritage Inventory Program
Resources and Economic Development Department
105 Loudon Road, Box 856
Concord, NH 03301
603 271 3623

Underground Storage Tanks (UST):
UST/LUST/CLAIMS Branch
Bureau of Waste Management
333 West Nye Lane
Carson City, NV 89710
702 687 5872

NEW HAMPSHIRE

Coastal Zone Management:
Coastal Zone Management
Office of State Planning
2 1/2 Beacon Street
Concord, NH 03301
603 271 2155

Drinking Water:
Water Supply Engineering Bureau
Water Supply and Pollution Control Division
Health & Human Services Bldg, 6 Hazen Dr
Concord, NH 03301
603 271 3503

Fish and Wildlife:
Fish and Game Department
34 Bridge Street
Concord, NH 03301
603 271 3512

Geological Survey:
Water Resources Division
6 Hazen Drive
Concord, NH 03301
603 271 3400

Industrial Pre-treatment Program:
Water Quality and Permit Compliance Bureau
Water Supply and Pollution Control Division
Health & Human Services Bldg, 6 Hazen Dr
Concord, NH 03301
603 271 3503

NPDES:
Water Quality and Permit Compliance Bureau
Water Supply and Pollution Control Division
Health & Human Services Bldg, 6 Hazen Dr
Concord, NH 03301
603 271 3503

Waste Management Agency:
Bureau of Waste Management
Division of Environmental Protection
333 West Nye Lane
Carson City, NV 89710
702 687 5872

Air Pollution Agency:
Air Resources Division
Department of Environmental Services
64 North Main St., Caller Box 2033
Concord, NH 03302
603 271 1370

Community Right-to-Know:
New Hampshire Office of Emergency Management
State Office South
107 Pleasant Street
Concord, NH 03301
603 271 2231

Emergency Response:
Division of Enforcement, Department of Safety
James H. Hayes Building
Hazen Drive
Concord, NH 03301
603 271 3339

Flood Plain Management:
Office of Emergency Management
107 Pleasant Street, State Ofc. Park S.
Concord, NH 03301
603 271 2231

Groundwater:
Groundwater Protection Bureau
Water Supply and Pollution Control Division
Health & Human Services Bldg, 6 Hazen Dr
Concord, NH 03301
603 271 3503

Natural Resources Agency:
Resources and Economic Development Department
105 Loudon Road, Box 856
Concord, NH 03301
603 271 2411

Nuclear Waste/Nuclear Safety:
Radiological Health Bureau, Division of Public Health Services
Department of Health and Human Services
Hazen Drive
Concord, NH 03301
603 271 4588

Parks:
Parks and Recreation Division
Resources and Economic Development Department
105 Loudon Road, Box 856
Concord, NH 03301
603 271 3255

Superfund, State:
Waste Management Division
Department of Environmental Services
6 Hazen Drive
Concord, NH 03301
603 271 2906

Water Agency:
Water Resources Division
Department of Environmental Services
64 North Main Street
Concord, NH 03302
603 271 3406

Climatology:
Department of Meteorology and Physical
Oceanography
Cook College, Rutgers University
P.O. Box 231
New Brunswick, NJ 08903
201 932 9520

Dam Safety:
Division of Coastal Resources
Dept. of Environmental Protection and Energy
401 East State Street, CN 402
Trenton, NJ 08625
609 292 2795

Energy:
Division of Energy, Planning and Conservation
Board of Public Utilities
#2 Gateway Center
Newark, NJ 07102
201 648 2264

Forestry:
Forestry Service, Parks and Forestry Division
Dept. of Environmental Protection and Energy
401 East State Street, CN 402
Trenton, NJ 08625
609 292 2520

Hazardous Waste:
Hazardous Waste Division
Division of Waste Management
401 East State Street, CN 402
Trenton, NJ 08625
609 292 9120

Solid Waste:
Solid Waste Compliance Section
Waste Management Division
6 Hazen Drive
Concord, NH 03301
603 271 2925

Underground Storage Tanks (UST):
Groundwater Protection Bureau
Water Supply and Pollution Control Division
Health & Human Services Bldg, 6 Hazen Dr
Concord, NH 03301
603 271 3503

NEW JERSEY

Coastal Zone Management:
Division of Coastal Resources
Dept. of Environmental Protection and Energy
401 East State Street, CN 402
Trenton, NJ 08625
609 292 2795

Drinking Water:
Bureau of Safe Drinking Water
Division of Water Resources
401 East State Street, CN 402
Trenton, NJ 08625
609 292 5550

Fish and Wildlife:
Division of Fish, Game and Wildlife
Dept. of Environmental Protection and Energy
401 East State Street, CN 402
Trenton, NJ 08625
609 292 9410

Geological Survey:
New Jersey Geological Survey
Dept. of Environmental Protection and Energy
401 East State Street, CN 402
Trenton, NJ 08625
609 292 1185

Natural Resources Agency:
Natural Resources
Dept. of Environmental Protection and Energy
401 East State Street, CN 402
Trenton, NJ 08625
609 292 2885

Superfund, Federal:
Waste Management Engineering Bureau
Waste Management Division
6 Hazen Drive
Concord, NH 03301
603 271 2909

Waste Management Agency:
Waste Management Division
Department of Environmental Services
6 Hazen Drive
Concord, NH 03301
603 271 2906

Air Pollution Agency:
Air Quality Management and Surveillance Element
Division of Environmental Quality
401 East State Street, CN 402
Trenton, NJ 08625
609 292 6710

Community Right-to-Know:
Release Prevention and Emergency Response
Division of Environmental Quality
401 East State Street, CN 402
Trenton, NJ 08625
609 984 3219

Emergency Response:
Release Prevention and Emergency Response
Division of Environmental Quality
401 East State Street, CN 402
Trenton, NJ 08625
609 984 3219

Flood Plain Management:
Division of Coastal Resources
Dept. of Environmental Protection and Energy
401 East State Street, CN 402
Trenton, NJ 08625
609 292 2795

Groundwater:
Bureau of Groundwater Quality Management
Division of Water Resources
401 East State Street, CN 402
Trenton, NJ 08625
609 292 5262

Nature Preserves Commission:
Office of Natural Lands Management
Division of Parks and Forestry
401 East State Street, CN 402
Trenton, NJ 08625
609 984 1339

NPDES:
Construction and Connection Permits
Division of Water Resources
401 East State Street, CN 402
Trenton, NJ 08625
609 984 4429

Solid Waste:
Division of Solid Waste Management
Dept. of Environmental Protection and Energy
401 East State Street, CN 402
Trenton, NJ 08625
609 530 8591

Waste Management Agency:
Division of Waste Management
Dept. of Environmental Protection and Energy
401 East State Street, CN 402
Trenton, NJ 08625
609 292 9120

Air Pollution Agency:
Bureau of Air Quality
Environment Department
P.O. Box 26110
Santa Fe, NM 87502
505 827 0042

Drinking Water:
Drinking Water Section, Groundwater and Toxic
Sites Bureau
Water and Waste Management Division
P.O. Box 26110
Santa Fe, NM 87502
505 827 2945

Fish and Wildlife:
Department of Game and Fish
P.O. Box 25112
Santa Fe, NM 87504
505 827 7899

Geological Survey:
Mining and Minerals Division
Energy, Minerals and Natural Resources Dept.
2040 South Pacheo Street
Santa Fe, NM 87505
505 827 5970

Industrial Pre-treatment Program:
Surface Water Quality Bureau
Water and Waste Management Division
P.O. Box 26110
Santa Fe, NM 87502
505 827 0187

Nuclear Waste/Nuclear Safety:
Low Level Radioactive Waste Siting Board
Radiation Protection Programs
401 East State Street, CN 027
Trenton, NJ 08625
609 987 6375

Superfund, Federal:
Division of Hazard Site Mitigation
Dept. of Environmental Protection and Energy
401 East State Street, CN 402
Trenton, NJ 08625
609 984 2962

Water Agency:
Division of Water Resources
Dept. of Environmental Protection and Energy
401 East State Street, CN 402
Trenton, NJ 08625
609 292 1637

Community Right-to-Know:
Emergency Management Bureau
Department of Public Safety
P.O. Box 1628
Santa Fe, NM 87504
505 827 9236

Emergency Response:
Water and Waste Management Division
Environment Department
P O Box 26110
Santa Fe, NM 87502
505 827 2850

Flood Plain Management:
Technical Division
State Engineer's Office
P.O. Box 25102, 101 Bataan Memorial Bldg
Santa Fe, NM 87504
505 827 6140

Groundwater:
Groundwater Bureau
Water and Waste Management Division
P.O. Box 26110
Santa Fe, NM 87502
505 827 2900

Mined Land Reclamation:
Abandoned Mined Lands Bureau
Mining and Minerals Division
2040 South Pacheo Street
Santa Fe, NM 87505
505 827 5970

Parks:
State Park Service
Division of Parks and Forestry
401 East State Street, CN 402
Trenton, NJ 08625
609 292 2772

Underground Storage Tanks (UST):
Bureau of Underground Storage Tanks
Division of Water Resources
401 East State Street, CN 402
Trenton, NJ 08625
609 984 3156

NEW MEXICO

Dam Safety:
Design & Construction Section
State Engineer's Office
P.O. Box 25102, 101 Bataan Memorial Bldg
Santa Fe, NM 87504
505 827 0187

Energy:
Energy, Minerals, and Natural Resources Dept.
2040 South Pacheo Street
Santa Fe, NM 87505
505 827 5950

Forestry:
Forestry and Resources Conservation Division
Energy, Minerals and Natural Resources Dept.
P.O. Box 1948
Santa Fe, NM 87504
505 827 5830

Hazardous Waste:
Hazardous and Radiological Waste Bureau
Water and Waste Management Division
P.O. Box 26110
Santa Fe, NM 87502
505 827 4363

Natural Resources Agency:
Energy, Minerals and Natural Resources Dept.
2040 South Pacheo Street
Santa Fe, NM 87505
505 827 5950

Nature Preserves Commission:
Habitat, Environment, and Lands Division
Game and Fish Department
P.O. Box 25112
Santa Fe, NM 87504
505 827 7882

Parks:
Park and Recreation Division
Energy, Minerals and Natural Resources Dept.
2040 South Pacheo Street
Santa Fe, NM 87504
505 827 7811

Superfund, State:
Superfund Section, Groundwater and Toxic Sites
Bureau
Water and Waste Management Division
P.O. Box 26110
Santa Fe, NM 87502
505 827 0048

Water Agency:
Water and Waste Management Division
Environment Department
P.O. Box 26110
Santa Fe, NM 87502
505 827 2850

Climatology:
Atmospheric Science Unit
Cornell University
1177 Bradfield Hall
Ithaca, NY 14853
607 255 1749

Dam Safety:
Dam Safety Section, Flood Protection Bureau
Division of Water
50 Wolf Road
Albany, NY 12233
518 457 5557

Energy:
Office of Energy
2 Rockefeller Plaza
Albany, NY 12223
518 473 4376

Flood Plain Management:
Bureau of Flood Protection
Division of Water
50 Wolf Road
Albany, NY 12233
518 457 3157

NPDES:
Surface Water Quality Bureau
Water and Waste Management Division
P.O. Box 26110
Santa Fe, NM 87502
505 827 0187

Solid Waste:
Solid Waste Bureau
Water and Waste Management Division
P.O. Box 26110
Santa Fe, NM 87502
505 827 0169

Underground Storage Tanks (UST):
Underground Storage Tank Bureau
Water and Waste Management Division
P.O. Box 26110
Santa Fe, NM 87502
505 827 2932

NEW YORK

Coastal Zone Management:
Bureau of Flood Protection
Division of Water
50 Wolf Road
Albany, NY 12233
518 457 3157

Drinking Water:
Bureau of Public Water Supply Protection
Department of Health
2 University Place, Western Avenue
Albany, NY 12203
518 458 6731

Environmental/Natural Resources Agency:
Department of Environmental Conservation
50 Wolf Road
Albany, NY 12233
518 457 3446

Forestry:
Forest Resource Management Office
Division of Land and Forest
50 Wolf Road
Albany, NY 12233
518 457 2475

Nuclear Waste/Nuclear Safety:
Water and Waste Management Division
Environment Department
P.O. Box 26110
Santa Fe, NM 87502
505 827 2850

Superfund, Federal:
Superfund Section, Groundwater and Toxic Sites
Bureau
Water and Waste Management Division
P.O. Box 26110
Santa Fe, NM 87502
505 827 0048

Waste Management Agency:
Water and Waste Management Division
Environment Department
P.O. Box 26110
Santa Fe, NM 87502
505 827 2850

Air Pollution Agency:
Division of Air Resources
Department of Environmental Conservation
50 Wolf Road, Room 128
Albany, NY 12233
518 457 7230

Community Right-to-Know:
Division of Hazardous Waste Remediation
Office of Environmental Remediation
50 Wolf Road
Albany, NY 12233
518 457 0730

Emergency Response:
Bureau of Spill Response
Division of Construction Management
50 Wolf Road
Albany, NY 12233
518 457 3891

Fish and Wildlife:
Division of Fish and Wildlife
Department of Environmental Conservation
50 Wolf Road
Albany, NY 12233
518 457 5690

Geological Survey:
New York State Geological Survey
Department of Education
3140 Cultural Education Center
Albany, NY 12230
518 474 5816

Groundwater:
Bureau of Water Quality Management
Division of Water
50 Wolf Road
Albany, NY 12233
518 457 3656

Natural Resources Agency:
Department of Environmental Conservation
50 Wolf Road
Albany, NY 12233
518 457 3446

Nuclear Waste/Nuclear Safety:
Bureau of Radiation
Division of Hazardous Substances Regulation
50 Wolf Road, 2nd Floor
Albany, NY 12233
518 457 2225

Superfund, Federal:
Bureau of Hazardous Site Control
Division of Hazardous Waste Remediation
50 Wolf Road
Albany, NY 12233
518 457 8807

Waste Management Agency:
Office of Environmental Remediation
Department of Environmental Conservation
50 Wolf Road
Albany, NY 12233
518 457 1415

Air Pollution Agency:
Air Quality Section
Division of Environmental Management
P.O. Box 27687
Raleigh, NC 27611
919 733 3340

Community Right-to-Know:
SARA, Title III, Div. of Emergency Management
Department of Crime Control and Public Safety
116 West Jones Street
Raleigh, NC 27603
919 733 3865

Emergency Response:
Division of Emergency Management
Department of Crime Control and Public Safety
116 West Jones Street
Raleigh, NC 27603
919 733 3867

Hazardous Waste:
Division of Hazardous Waste Remediation
Office of Environmental Remediation
50 Wolf Road
Albany, NY 12233
518 457 5861

Nature Preserves Commission:
New York Natural Heritage Program
700 Troy-Schenectady Road
Latham, NY 12110
518 783 3932

Parks:
Off. of Parks, Recreation & Historic Preservation
Empire State Plaza, Agency Building 1
Albany, NY 12238
518 474 0443

Superfund, State:
Bureau of Hazardous Site Control
Division of Hazardous Waste Remediation
50 Wolf Road
Albany, NY 12233
518 457 8807

Water Agency:
Division of Water
Office of Environmental Quality
50 Wolf Road
Albany, NY 12233
518 457 6674

Climatology:
Department of Marine, Earth and Atmospheric
Sciences
North Carolina State University
Raleigh, NC 27650
919 737 7243

Dam Safety:
Land Quality Section
Division of Environmental Management
P.O. Box 27687
Raleigh, NC 27611
919 733 4574

Energy:
Division of Energy
Department of Commerce
430 North Salisbury Street
Raleigh, NC 27603
919 733 2230

Mined Land Reclamation:
Mining Section, Bureau of Resource Management
and Development
Division of Mineral Resources
50 Wolf Road
Albany, NY 12233
518 457 0100

NPDES:
Bureau of Wastewater Facilities and Operations
Division of Water
50 Wolf Road
Albany, NY 12233
518 457 5968

Solid Waste:
Division of Solid Waste
Office of Environmental Quality
50 Wolf Road
Albany, NY 12233
518 457 6603

Underground Storage Tanks (UST):
Bureau of Information and Bulk Storage
Division of Water
50 Wolf Road
Albany, NY 12233
518 457 7463

NORTH CAROLINA

Coastal Zone Management:
Division of Coastal Management
Dept. of Environment, Health and Nat. Resources
P.O. Box 27687
Raleigh, NC 27611
919 733 2293

Drinking Water:
Public Water Supply
Division of Environmental Management
P.O. Box 27687
Raleigh, NC 27611
919 733 2321

Environmental/Natural Resources Agency:
Department of Environment, Health, and Natural
Resources
P.O. Box 27687
Raleigh, NC 27611
919 733 4984

Fish and Wildlife:
Wildlife Resources Commission
Dept. of Environment, Health and Nat. Resources
P.O. Box 27687
Raleigh, NC 27611
919 733 3391

Geological Survey:
Geological Survey
Division of Land Resources
P.O. Box 27687
Raleigh, NC 27611
919 733 2423

Industrial Pre-treatment Program:
Water Quality Section
Division of Environmental Management
P.O. Box 27687
Raleigh, NC 27611
919 733 5083

Nature Preserves Commission:
North Carolina Natural Heritage
Division of State Parks and Recreation
P.O. Box 27687
Raleigh, NC 27611
919 733 7701

Parks:
Parks and Recreation
Dept. of Environment, Health and Nat. Resources
P.O. Box 27687
Raleigh, NC 27611
919 733 4181

Superfund, State:
Superfund Unit, Hazardous Waste Section
Division of Solid Waste Management
P.O. Box 27687
Raleigh, NC 27611
919 733 2801

Water Agency:
Division of Water Resources
Dept. of Environment, Health and Nat. Resources
P.O. Box 27687
Raleigh, NC 27611
919 733 4064

Climatology:
Soil Sciences Department
North Dakota State University
P.O. Box 5638
Fargo, ND 58105
701 237 8576

Flood Plain Management:
Division of Community Assistance
Dept. of Environment, Health and Nat. Resources
P.O. Box 27687
Raleigh, NC 27611
919 733 2850

Groundwater:
Groundwater Section
Division of Environmental Management
P.O. Box 27687
Raleigh, NC 27611
919 733 3221

Mined Land Reclamation:
Land Quality Section
Division of Land Resources
P.O. Box 27687
Raleigh, NC 27611
919 733 4574

NPDES:
Water Planning
Division of Environmental Management
P.O. Box 27687
Raleigh, NC 27611
919 733 7015

Solid Waste:
Solid Waste Section
Division of Solid Waste Management
P.O. Box 27687
Raleigh, NC 27611
919 733 0692

Underground Storage Tanks (UST):
Groundwater Section
Division of Environmental Management
P.O. Box 27687
Raleigh, NC 27611
919 733 3221

NORTH DAKOTA

Community Right-to-Know:
Environmental Program and Emergency Response
Environmental Engineering Section
1200 Missouri Avenue, Box 5520
Bismarck, ND 58502
701 221 5166

Forestry:
Forest Resources
Dept. of Environment, Health and Nat. Resources
P.O. Box 27687
Raleigh, NC 27611
919 733 2162

Hazardous Waste:
Hazardous Waste Section
Division of Solid Waste Management
P.O. Box 27687
Raleigh, NC 27611
919 733 2178

Natural Resources Agency:
Department of Environment, Health and Natural Resources
P.O. Box 27687
Raleigh, NC 27611
919 733 4984

Nuclear Waste/Nuclear Safety:
Division of Radiation Protection
Dept. of Environment, Health and Nat. Resources
P.O. Box 27687
Raleigh, NC 27611
919 733 4283

Superfund, Federal:
Superfund Unit, Hazardous Waste Section
Division of Solid Waste Management
P.O. Box 27687
Raleigh, NC 27611
919 733 2801

Waste Management Agency:
Division of Solid Waste Management
Dept. of Environment, Health and Nat. Resources
P.O. Box 27687
Raleigh, NC 27611
919 733 4996

Air Pollution Agency:
Environmental Engineering Division
Environmental Health Section
1200 Missouri Avenue, Box 5520
Bismarck, ND 58502
701 221 5188

Dam Safety:
Dam Safety Section, Water Development Division
State Water Commission
900 East Boulevard
Bismarck, ND 58505
701 224 2750

Drinking Water:
Drinking Water Program
Municipal Facilities Division
1200 Missouri Avenue, Box 5520
Bismarck, ND 58502
701 221 5210

Fish and Wildlife:
Game and Fish Department
100 North Bismarck Expressway
Bismarck, ND 58501
701 221 6300

Geological Survey:
North Dakota Geological Survey
Industrial Commission
600 E. Boulevard
Bismarck, ND 58505
701 224 2969

Industrial Pre-treatment Program:
Wastewater Facility/Permits
Water Quality Division
1200 Missouri Avenue, Box 5520
Bismarck, ND 58502
701 221 5210

Nature Preserves Commission:
Natural Heritage Inventory, Division of Natural
Resources and Trails
Department of Parks and Recreation
604 E. Boulevard
Bismarck, ND 58505
701 224 4887

Parks:
Department of Parks and Recreation
604 E. Boulevard
Bismarck, ND 58505
701 224 4887

Superfund, State:
Waste Management Division
Environmental Health Section
1200 Missouri Avenue, Box 5520
Bismarck, ND 58502
701 224 2366

Water Agency:
Water Quality Division
Environmental Health Section
1200 Missouri Avenue, Box 5520
Bismarck, ND 58502
701 221 5210

Emergency Response:
Environmental Program and Emergency Response
Environmental Engineering Section
1200 Missouri Avenue, Box 5520
Bismarck, ND 58502
701 221 5166

Flood Plain Management:
Water Development Division
State Water Commission
900 East Boulevard
Bismarck, ND 58505
701 224 2750

Groundwater:
Groundwater Protection Program
Water Quality Division
1200 Missouri Avenue, Box 5520
Bismarck, ND 58502
701 221 5210

Mined Land Reclamation:
Reclamation Division
Public Service Commission
State Capitol Building, 12th Floor
Bismarck, ND 58505
701 224 2400

NPDES:
Wastewater Facility/Permits
Water Quality Control Division
1200 Missouri Avenue, Box 5520
Bismarck, ND 58502
701 221 5210

Solid Waste:
Waste Management Division
Environmental Health Section
1200 Missouri Avenue, Box 5520
Bismarck, ND 58502
701 221 5166

Underground Storage Tanks (UST):
Underground Storage Tank Program
Waste Management Division
1200 Missouri Avenue, Box 5520
Bismarck, ND 58502
701 221 5166

OHIO

Energy:
Energy Development Impact Office
Land Department
918 E. Divide
Bismarck, ND 58501
701 224 3188

Forestry:
University of North Dakota, Bottineau
1st and Brander
Bottineau, ND 58318
701 228 2277

Hazardous Waste:
Hazardous Waste Program
Waste Management Division
1200 Missouri Avenue, Box 5520
Bismarck, ND 58502
701 221 5166

Natural Resources Agency:
Natural Resources Division
Game and Fish Department
100 North Bismarck Expressway
Bismarck, ND 58501
701 221 6325

Nuclear Waste/Nuclear Safety:
Environmental Engineering Division
Environmental Health Section
1200 Missouri Avenue, Box 5520
Bismarck, ND 58502
701 221 5166

Superfund, Federal:
Hazardous Waste Program
Waste Management Division
1200 Missouri Avenue, Box 5520
Bismarck, ND 58502
701 221 5166

Waste Management Agency:
Waste Management Division
Environmental Health Section
1200 Missouri Avenue, Box 5520
Bismarck, ND 58502
701 221 5166

Air Pollution Control:
Division of Air Pollution Control
Environmental Protection Agency
Box 1049, 1800 Watermark
Columbus, OH 43266
614 644 2270

Climatology:
Department of Geography
Ohio State University
103 Bricker Hall
Columbus, OH 43210
614 292 2514

Dam Safety:
Dam Safety, Division of Water
Department of Natural Resources
Fountain Square, Building E-3
Columbus, OH 43224
614 265 6731

Energy:
Office of Energy Conservation
Department of Development
30 East Broad Street, 24th Floor
Columbus, OH 43266
614 466 6797

Forestry:
Division of Forestry
Department of Natural Resources
Fountain Square, Building C-3
Columbus, OH 43224
614 265 6694

Hazardous Waste:
Division of Hazardous Waste Management
Division of Solid and Hazardous Waste Mgt
Box 1049, 1800 Watermark
Columbus, OH 43266
614 644 2934

Natural Resources Agency:
Department of Natural Resources
Fountain Square, Building D-3
Columbus, OH 43224
614 265 6875

Parks:
Division of Parks and Recreation
Department of Natural Resources
Fountain Square, Building C-3
Columbus, OH 43224
614 265 6511

Superfund, State:
Office of Emergency and Remedial Response
Environmental Protection Agency
Box 1049, 1800 Watermark
Columbus, OH 43266
614 644 2260

Coastal Zone Management:
Division of Water
Department of Natural Resources
Fountain Square, Building E
Columbus, OH 43224
614 265 6712

Drinking Water:
Division of Public Water Supply
Environmental Protection Agency
Box 1049, 1800 Watermark
Columbus, OH 43266
614 644 2752

Fish and Wildlife:
Division of Wildlife
Department of Natural Resources
Fountain Square, Building C-4
Columbus, OH 43224
614 265 6305

Geological Survey:
Division of Geological Survey
Department of Natural Resources
Fountain Square, Building B-2
Columbus, OH 43224
614 265 6605

Industrial Pre-treatment Program:
Pretreatment/Certification Section
Division of Water Pollution Control
Box 1049, 1800 Watermark
Columbus, OH 43266
614 644 2001

Nature Preserves Commission:
Natural Heritage Program, Division of Natural Areas
& Preserves
Department of Natural Resources
Fountain Square, Building F
Columbus, OH 43224
614 265 6466

Solid Waste:
Division of Solid Waste Management
Box 1049, 1800 Watermark
Columbus, OH 43266
614 644 3135

Underground Storage Tanks (UST):
RCRA Permits
Division of Solid and Hazardous Waste Mgt
Box 1049, 1800 Watermark
Columbus, OH 43266
614 644 2944

Community Right-to-Know:
Office of Emergency and Remedial Response
Environmental Protection Agency
Box 1049, 1800 Watermark
Columbus, OH 43266
614 644 2260

Emergency Response:
Office of Emergency and Remedial Response
Environmental Protection Agency
Box 1049, 1800 Watermark
Columbus, OH 43266
614 644 3196

Flood Plain Management:
Environmental Planning and Review Section
Division of Water Quality Planning and Assessment
Box 1049, 1800 Watermark
Columbus, OH 43266
614 644 3076

Groundwater:
Division of Ground Water
Environmental Protection Agency
Box 1049, 1800 Watermark
Columbus, OH 43266
614 644 2905

Mined Land Reclamation:
Division of Reclamation
Department of Natural Resources
Fountain Square, Building B-3
Columbus, OH 43224
614 265 6638

NPDES:
Permits Section
Division of Water Pollution Control
Box 1049, 1800 Watermark
Columbus, OH 43266
614 644 2001

Superfund, Federal:
Office of Emergency and Remedial Response
Environmental Protection Agency
Box 1049, 1800 Watermark
Columbus, OH 43266
614 644 2260

Waste Management Agency:
Division of Solid Waste Management
Environmental Protection Agency
Box 1049, 1800 Watermark
Columbus, OH 43266
614 644 2958

Appendix C

OKLAHOMA

Water Agency:
Division of Water Pollution Control
Environmental Protection Agency
Box 1049, 1800 Watermark
Columbus, OH 43266
614 644 2001

Climatology:
Oklahoma Climatological Survey
University of Oklahoma
Sarkey's Energy Ctr., 100 E. Boyd, #1210
Norman, OK 73019
405 325 2541

Drinking Water:
Public Water Supplies
Water Quality Services, 0207
1000 N.E. 10th Street
Oklahoma City, OK 73152
405 271 5205

Fish and Wildlife:
Department of Wildlife Conservation
1801 North Lincoln Street
Oklahoma City, OK 73105
405 521 3851

Geological Survey:
Oklahoma Geological Survey
University of Oklahoma
100 E. Boyd, Room N131
Norman, OK 73019
405 325 3031

Industrial Pre-treatment Program:
Water Pollution Control Division
Water Resources Board
600 N. Harvey, P.O. Box 150
Oklahoma City, OK 73101
405 231 2541

Nature Preserves Commission:
Oklahoma Natural Heritage Inventory
Oklahoma Biological Survey
2001 Priestly Avenue, Building 605
Norman, OK 73019
405 325 1985

Parks:
Parks Division
Oklahoma Tourism and Recreation Department
500 Will Rogers Building
Oklahoma City, OK 73105
405 521 3411

Community Right-to-Know:
Environmental Health Services, 0200
Department of Health
1000 N.E. 10th Street
Oklahoma City, OK 73152
405 271 8056

Emergency Response:
Environmental Health Services, 0200
Department of Health
1000 N.E. 10th Street
Oklahoma City, OK 73152
405 271 8056

Flood Plain Management:
Planning and Development Division
Water Resources Board
600 N. Harvey, P.O. Box 150
Oklahoma City, OK 73101
405 231 2533

Groundwater:
Water Management Division
Water Resources Board
600 N. Harvey, P.O. Box 150
Oklahoma City, OK 73101
405 231 2574

Mined Land Reclamation:
Mines Department
4040 North Lincoln Boulevard, Suite 107
Oklahoma City, OK 73105
405 521 3859

NPDES:
Water Pollution Control Division
Water Resources Board
600 N. Harvey, P.O. Box 150
Oklahoma City, OK 73101
405 231 2541

Solid Waste:
Solid Waste Management Services, 0206
Environmental Health Services
1000 N.E. 10th Street
Oklahoma City, OK 73152
405 271 7159

Air Pollution Agency:
Air Quality Services
Environmental Health Services
1000 N.E. 10th Street
Oklahoma City, OK 73152
405 271 5220

Dam Safety:
Water Management Division
Water Resources Board
600 N. Harvey, P.O. Box 150
Oklahoma City, OK 73101
405 231 2536

Energy:
Governor's Office
125 NW 6th Street
Oklahoma City, OK 73102
405 235 4204

Forestry:
Forestry Services
Department of Agriculture
2800 North Lincoln Boulevard
Oklahoma City, OK 73105
405 521 3864

Hazardous Waste:
Hazardous Waste Management Services, 0205
Environmental Health Services
1000 N.E. 10th Street
Oklahoma City, OK 73152
405 271 5338

Natural Resources Agency:
Oklahoma Tourism and Recreation Department
500 Will Rogers Building
Oklahoma City, OK 73105
405 521 2413

Nuclear Waste/Nuclear Safety:
Hazardous Waste Management Services, 0205
Environmental Health Services
1000 N.E. 10th Street
Oklahoma City, OK 73152
405 271 8056

Superfund, Federal:
Solid Waste Management Services, 0206
Environmental Health Services
1000 N.E. 10th Street
Oklahoma City, OK 73152
405 271 7159

Underground Storage Tanks (UST):
Compliance & Enforcement Sect., Water Quality
Water Resources Board
P.O. Box 53585
Oklahoma City, OK 73152
405 271 2549

Air Pollution Agency:
Division of Air Quality
Department of Environmental Quality
811 Southwest 6th Avenue
Portland, OR 97204
503 229 5397

Community Right-to-Know:
Office of the State Fire Marshal
3000 Market Street Plaza, NE
Salem, OR 97310
503 378 3473

Emergency Response:
Spill Response Section
Division of Hazardous and Solid Waste
811 Southwest 6th Avenue
Portland, OR 97204
503 229 5373

Flood Plain Management:
Department of Land Conservation and Development
1175 Court Street, N.E.
Salem, OR 97310
503 373 0050

Groundwater:
Planning and Monitoring Section
Division of Water Quality
811 Southwest 6th Avenue
Portland, OR 97204
503 229 5284

Mined Land Reclamation:
Department of Geology
910 State Office Building
Portland, OR 97201
503 229 5580

NPDES:
Industrial Waste Section
Division of Water Quality
811 Southwest 6th Avenue
Portland, OR 97204
503 229 6099

Water Agency:
Water Resources Board
P.O. Box 150
Oklahoma City, OK 73101
405 231 2500

Climatology:
Department of Atmospheric Sciences
Oregon State University
Strand Agriculture Hall, Room 326
Corvallis, OR 97331
503 737 5705

Dam Safety:
Department of Water Resources
Department of Environmental Quality
3850 Portland Road, N.E.
Salem, OR 97310
503 378 2907

Energy:
Department of Energy
625 Marion Street, NE
Salem, OR 97310
503 378 4128

Forestry:
Department of Forestry
2600 State Street
Salem, OR 97310
503 378 2511

Hazardous Waste:
Waste Reduction and Technical Assistance
Division of Solid and Hazardous Waste
811 Southwest 6th Avenue
Portland, OR 97204
503 229 6585

Natural Resources Agency:
Department of Land Conservation and Development
1175 Court Street, N.E.
Salem, OR 97310
503 378 4928

Nuclear Waste/Nuclear Safety:
Division of Siting and Regulation
Department of Energy
625 Marion Street, N.E.
Salem, OR 97310
503 378 6469

OREGON

Coastal Zone Management:
Planning and Monitoring Section
Division of Water Quality
811 Southwest 6th Avenue
Portland, OR 97204
503 229 5284

Drinking Water:
Public Drinking Water System
Division of Health
State Office Building, Room 608
Portland, OR 97201
503 229 6302

Fish and Wildlife:
Department of Fish and Wildlife
P.O. Box 59
Portland, OR 97207
503 229 5405

Geological Survey:
Department of Geology and Mineral Industries
910 State Office Building
Portland, OR 97201
503 229 5580

Industrial Pre-treatment Program:
Industrial Waste Section
Division of Water Quality
811 Southwest 6th Avenue
Portland, OR 97204
503 229 5325

Nature Preserves Commission:
Oregon Natural Heritage Program
Oregon Field Office
1205 Northwest 25th Avenue
Portland, OR 97210
503 229 5078

Parks:
Division of Parks and Recreation
Department of Transportation
525 Trade Street, S.E.
Salem, OR 97310
503 378 5019

Solid Waste:
Solid Waste Section
Division of Hazardous and Solid Waste
811 Southwest 6th Avenue
Portland, OR 97204
503 229 5782

Underground Storage Tanks (UST):
LUST Program
Division of Hazardous and Solid Waste
811 Southwest 6th Avenue
Portland, OR 97204
503 229 5733

PENNSYLVANIA

Community Right-to-Know:
Community Right-to-Know
Pennsylvania Emergency Management Agency
P.O. Box 3321
Harrisburg, PA 17105
717 783 7388

Emergency Response:
Emergency Response
Department of Environmental Resources
P.O. Box 2063, Fulton Building
Harrisburg, PA 17120
717 787 5027

Flood Plain Management:
Flood Plain Management Division, Bureau of
Community Planning
Department of Community Affairs
Forum Building, 5th Floor
Harrisburg, PA 17120
717 787 7403

Groundwater:
Pennsylvania Geological Survey
Department of Environmental Resources
9th Floor, Executive House, Box 2357
Harrisburg, PA 17120
717 787 2169

Mined Land Reclamation:
Bureau of Mining and Reclamation
Environmental Protection Deputate
P.O. Box 2063
Harrisburg, PA 17120
717 787 5103

Superfund, Federal:
Program Development Section
Division of Environmental Cleanup
811 Southwest 6th Avenue
Portland, OR 97204
503 229 5072

Waste Management Agency:
Division of Hazardous and Solid Waste
Department of Environmental Quality
811 Southwest 6th Avenue
Portland, OR 97204
503 229 5356

Air Pollution Agency:
Bureau of Air Quality Control
Environmental Protection Deputate
P.O. Box 2357, 101 South Second Street
Harrisburg, PA 17105
717 787 9702

Dam Safety:
Bureau of Dams and Waterway Management
Department of Environmental Resources
P.O. Box 8554
Harrisburg, PA 17105
717 541 7900

Energy:
Governor's Energy Council
P.O. Box 8010, 116 Pine Street
Harrisburg, PA 17101
717 783 9982

Forestry:
Bureau of Forestry
Office of Resource Management
P.O. Box 1467, 2150 Herr Street
Harrisburg, PA 17103
717 787 2703

Hazardous Waste:
Division of Permits
Bureau of Waste Management
P.O. Box 2063, Fulton Building
Harrisburg, PA 17120
717 787 7381

Nature Preserves Commission:
Pennsylvania Natural Diversity Inventory
Bureau of Forestry
P.O. Box 1467, 2150 Herr Street
Harrisburg, PA 17103
717 787 3444

Superfund, State:
Program Development Section
Division of Environmental Cleanup
811 Southwest 6th Avenue
Portland, OR 97204
503 229 5072

Water Agency:
Division of Water Quality
Department of Environmental Quality
811 Southwest 6th Avenue
Portland, OR 97204
503 229 5324

Coastal Zone Management:
Division of Coastal Zone Management
Bureau of Water Resources Management
P.O. Box 8761
Harrisburg, PA 17105
717 783 9500

Drinking Water:
Bureau of Community Environmental Control
Environmental Protection Deputate
P.O. Box 2357
Harrisburg, PA 17120
717 787 9035

Fish and Wildlife:
Game Commission
20001 Elmerton Avenue
Harrisburg, PA 17110
717 787 3633

Geological Survey:
Pennsylvania Geological Survey
Department of Environmental Resources
9th Floor, Executive House, Box 2357
Harrisburg, PA 17120
717 787 2169

Industrial Pre-treatment Program:
Division of Permits and Compliance
Bureau of Water Quality Management
P.O. Box 2063, Fulton Building
Harrisburg, PA 17120
717 787 8184

NPDES:
Division of Permits and Compliance
Bureau of Water Quality Management
P.O. Box 2063, Fulton Building
Harrisburg, PA 17120
717 787 8184

Nuclear Waste/Nuclear Safety:
Bureau of Radiation Protection
Environmental Protection Deputate
P.O. Box 2063, Fulton Building
Harrisburg, PA 17120
717 787 2480

Superfund, Federal:
Hazardous Sites Cleanup Program
Bureau of Waste Management
P.O. Box 2063, Fulton Building
Harrisburg, PA 17120
717 783 7816

Waste Management Agency:
Bureau of Waste Management
Environmental Protection Deputate
P.O. Box 2063, Fulton Building
Harrisburg, PA 17120
717 787 9870

Air Pollution Control:
Air Section
Division of Air and Hazardous Materials
291 Promenade Street
Providence, RI 02908
401 277 2808

Community Right-to-Know:
Occupational Safety Division
Department of Labor
220 Elmwood Avenue
Providence, RI 02908
401 457 1829

Emergency Response:
Emergency Response Section
Division of Air and Hazardous Materials
291 Promenade Street
Providence, RI 02908
401 277 2797

Flood Plain Management:
Wetlands Section
Division of Groundwater and Freshwater Wetlands
291 Promenade Street
Providence, RI 02908
401 277 6820

Groundwater:
Groundwater Protection Program
Division of Groundwater and Freshwater Wetlands
291 Promenade Street
Providence, RI 02908
401 277 2234

Parks:
Bureau of State Parks
Office of Resource Management
P.O. Box 1467
Harrisburg, PA 17120
717 787 6640

Superfund, State:
Hazardous Sites Cleanup Program
Bureau of Waste Management
P.O. Box 2063, Fulton Building
Harrisburg, PA 17120
717 783 7816

Water Agency:
Bureau of Water Resources Management
Department of Environmental Resources
P.O. Box 8761
Harrisburg, PA 17105
717 541 7800

Climatology:
Department of Plant Sciences
University of Rhode Island
Room 313, Woodward Hall
Kinston, RI 02881
401 792 4549

Dam Safety:
Dam Safety
Division of Groundwater and Freshwater Wetlands
291 Promenade Street
Providence, RI 02908
401 277 2306

Energy:
Public Utilities Commission
100 Orange Street
Providence, RI 02903
401 277 3500

Forestry:
Division of Forest Environment, Administration Office
Department of Environmental Management
P.O. Box 851, 1037 Hartford Pike
North Scituate, RI 02857
401 647 3367

Hazardous Waste:
Industrial Compliance Section
Division of Air and Hazardous Materials
291 Promenade Street
Providence, RI 02908
401 277 2797

Solid Waste:
Bureau of Waste Management
Environmental Protection Deputate
P.O. Box 2063, Fulton Building
Harrisburg, PA 17120
717 787 9870

Underground Storage Tanks (UST):
Division of Permits and Compliance
Bureau of Water Quality Management
P.O. Box 2063, Fulton Building
Harrisburg, PA 17120
717 787 8184

RHODE ISLAND

Coastal Zone Management:
Division of Coastal Resources
Department of Environmental Management
22 Hayes Street
Providence, RI 02908
401 277 3429

Drinking Water (SDWA):
Division of Water Quality
Department of Health
Canon Building, Davis Street
Providence, RI 02908
401 277 6867

Fish and Wildlife:
Division of Fish and Wildlife
Department of Environmental Management
4808 Tower Hill Road
Wakefield, RI 02879
401 789 3094

Geological Survey:
University of Rhode Island
Department of Geology
Green Hall, Room 103
Kingston, RI 02881
401 792 2265

Industrial Pre-treatment Program:
Permits and Industrial Pretreatment
Division of Water Resources
291 Promenade Street
Providence, RI 02908
401 277 6519

Natural Resources Agency:
Department of Environmental Management
9 Hayes Street
Providence, RI 02908
401 277 2771

Nuclear Waste/Nuclear Safety:
Division of Occupational Health and Radiation
Control
Department of Health
Canon Building, Davis Street
Providence, RI 02908
401 277 2438

Superfund, Federal:
Emergency Response Section
Division of Air and Hazardous Materials
291 Promenade Street
Providence, RI 02908
401 277 2797

Waste Management Agency:
Division of Air and Hazardous Materials
Department of Environmental Management
291 Promenade Street
Providence, RI 02908
401 277 2797

Air Pollution Agency:
Air Quality Control Bureau
Environmental Quality Control Office
2600 Bull Street
Columbia, SC 29201
803 734 4750

Community Right-to-Know:
Division of Waste Assessment and Emergency
Response
Department of Health and Environmental Control
2600 Bull Street
Columbia, SC 29201
803 734 5189

Emergency Response:
Division of Waste Assessment and Emergency
Response
Department of Health and Environmental Control
2600 Bull Street
Columbia, SC 29201
803 734 5189

Flood Plain Management:
Water Resources Commission
3830 Forest Drive, P.O. Box 4440
Columbia, SC 29240
803 758 2514

Nature Preserves Commission:
Rhode Island Heritage Program
Department of Environmental Management
22 Hayes Street
Providence, RI 02908
401 277 2776

Parks:
Division of Parks and Recreation, Administration
Office
Department of Environmental Management
2321 Hartford Avenue
Johnston, RI 02919
401 277 2632

Superfund, State:
Emergency Response Section
Division of Air and Hazardous Materials
291 Promenade Street
Providence, RI 02908
401 277 2797

Water Agency:
Division of Water Resources
Department of Environmental Management
291 Promenade Street
Providence, RI 02908
401 277 3961

Climatology:
State Climatology Office
1201 Main Street, Suite 1110
P.O. Box 4440
Columbia, SC 29240
803 737 0800

Dam Safety:
Division of Dams and Reservoirs Safety
Land Resources Commission
2221 Devine Street, Suite 222
Columbia, SC 29205
803 734 9100

Energy:
Energy, Agriculture and Natural Resources
Office of Governor
1205 Pendleton Street
Columbia, SC 29201
803 734 0445

Forestry:
Forestry Commission
P.O. Box 21707
Columbia, SC 29221
803 737 8800

NPDES:
Permits and Industrial Pretreatment
Division of Water Resources
291 Promenade Street
Providence, RI 02908
401 277 6519

Solid Waste:
Solid Waste Section
Division of Air and Hazardous Materials
291 Promenade Street
Providence, RI 02908
401 277 2797

Underground Storage Tanks (UST):
Groundwater Protection Program
Division of Groundwater and Freshwater Wetlands
291 Promenade Street
Providence, RI 02908
401 277 2234

SOUTH CAROLINA

Coastal Zone Management:
South Carolina Coastal Council
1201 Main Street, Suite 1520
Columbia, SC 29201
803 737 0880

Drinking Water:
Drinking Water Program, Environmental Quality
Control
Department of Health and Environmental Control
2600 Bull Street
Columbia, SC 29201
803 734 5310

Fish and Wildlife:
Wildlife and Marine Resources Department
R. C. Dennis Building, Box 167
Columbia, SC 29203
803 734 4007

Geological Survey:
Geological and Geodetic Surveys
Budget and Control Board
Harbison Forest Road
Columbia, SC 29210
803 737 9440

Groundwater:
Division of Hydrology
Water Resources Commission
1201 Main Street, Suite 1100
Columbia, SC 29201
803 737 0800

Mined Land Reclamation:
Division of Mining and Reclamation
Land Resources Commission
2221 Devine Street, Suite 222
Columbia, SC 29205
803 737 9100

NPDES:
Division of Industrial and Agricultural Wastewater
Environmental Quality Control Office
2600 Bull Street
Columbia, SC 29201
803 734 5300

Solid Waste:
Bureau of Solid and Hazardous Waste Management
Department of Health and Environmental Control
2600 Bull Street
Columbia, SC 29201
803 734 5200

Underground Storage Tanks (UST):
Ground Water Protection
Department of Health and Environmental Control
2600 Bull Street
Columbia, SC 29201
803 734 5331

Hazardous Waste:
Bureau of Solid and Hazardous Waste Management
Department of Health and Environmental Control
2600 Bull Street
Columbia, SC 29201
803 734 5200

Natural Resources Agency:
Energy, Agriculture and Natural Resources
Office of Governor
1205 Pendleton Street
Columbia, SC 29201
803 734 0445

Nuclear Waste/Nuclear Safety:
Bureau of Radiological Health
Department of Health and Environmental Control
2600 Bull Street
Columbia, SC 29201
803 734 4700

Superfund, Federal:
Site Engineering and Screening
Department of Health and Environmental Control
2600 Bull Street
Columbia, SC 29201
803 734 5177

Waste Management Agency:
Environmental Quality Control Office
Department of Health and Environmental Control
2600 Bull Street
Columbia, SC 29201
803 734 5360

Industrial Pre-treatment Program:
Division of Industrial and Agricultural Wastewater
Department of Health and Environmental Control
2600 Bull Street
Columbia, SC 29201
803 734 5300

Nature Preserves Commission:
Heritage Trust Section
Department of Wildlife and Marine Resources
R. C. Dennis Building, Box 167
Columbia, SC 29202
803 734 3912

Parks:
Parks, Recreation and Tourism
Department of Parks, Recreation and Tourism
1205 Pendleton Street
Columbia, SC 29201
803 734 0166

Superfund, State:
Site Engineering and Screening
Department of Health and Environmental Control
2600 Bull Street
Columbia, SC 29201
803 734 5177

Water Agency:
Water Resources Commission
1201 Main Street, Suite 1100
Columbia, SC 29201
803 737 0800

SOUTH DAKOTA

Air Pollution Agency:
Division of Environmental Regulation
Department of Environment and Natural Resources
Joe Foss Bldg., 523 E. Capitol Avenue
Pierre, SD 57501
605 773 3351

Climatology:
Engineering Department
South Dakota State University
Brookings, SD 57007
605 688 5141

Community Right-to-Know:
Ground Water Quality Program
Department of Environment and Natural Resources
Joe Foss Bldg., 523 E. Capitol Avenue
Pierre, SD 57501
605 773 3296

Dam Safety:
Division of Water Rights
Department of Environment and Natural Resources
Joe Foss Bldg., 523 E. Capitol Avenue
Pierre, SD 57501
605 773 3352

Drinking Water:
Drinking Water Office
Division of Land and Water Quality
Joe Foss Bldg., 523 E. Capitol Avenue
Pierre, SD 57501
605 773 3754

Emergency Response:
Ground Water Quality Program
Department of Environment and Natural Resources
Joe Foss Bldg., 523 E. Capitol Avenue
Pierre, SD 57501
605 773 3296

Energy:
Governor's Office of Economic Development
711 E. Wells Avenue
Pierre, SD 57501
605 773 5032

Environmental/Natural Resources Agency:
Department of Environment and Natural Resources
Joe Foss Bldg., 523 E. Capitol Avenue
Pierre, SD 57501
605 773 3151

Fish and Wildlife:
Wildlife Division
Department of Game, Fish, and Parks
Joe Foss Bldg., 523 E. Capitol Avenue
Pierre, SD 57501
605 773 3381

Geological Survey:
Division of Geological Survey
Department of Environment and Natural Resources
USD Science Center
Vermillion, SD 57069
605 677 5227

Industrial Pre-treatment Program:
Point Source Control Program
Department of Environment and Natural Resources
Joe Foss Bldg., 523 E. Capitol Avenue
Pierre, SD 57501
605 773 3351

Nature Preserves Commission:
Natural Heritage Database, Wildlife Division
Department of Game, Fish, and Parks
Joe Foss Bldg., 523 E. Capitol Avenue
Pierre, SD 57501
605 773 4345

Parks:
Parks and Recreation Division
Department of Game, Fish, and Parks
Joe Foss Bldg., 523 E. Capitol Avenue
Pierre, SD 57501
605 773 3391

Superfund, State:
Ground Water Quality Office
Department of Environment and Natural Resources
Joe Foss Bldg., 523 E. Capitol Avenue
Pierre, SD 57501
605 773 3296

Water Agency:
Division of Water Resources Management
Department of Environment and Natural Resources
Joe Foss Bldg., 523 E. Capitol Avenue
Pierre, SD 57501
605 773 4216

Climatology:
Tennessee Valley Authority
310 Evans Building
Knoxville, TN 37902
615 632 4222

Flood Plain Management:
Emergency and Disaster Services Division
Department of Military and Veterans Affairs
2823 West Main
Rapid City, SD 57702
605 399 6200

Groundwater:
Ground Water Quality Program
Department of Environment and Natural Resources
Joe Foss Bldg., 523 E. Capitol Avenue
Pierre, SD 57501
605 773 3296

Mined Land Reclamation:
Surface Mining Office
Department of Environment and Natural Resources
Joe Foss Bldg., 523 E. Capitol Avenue
Pierre, SD 57501
605 773 4201

NPDES:
Point Source Control Program
Department of Environment and Natural Resources
Joe Foss Bldg., 523 E. Capitol Avenue
Pierre, SD 57501
605 773 3351

Solid Waste:
Office of Waste Management
Department of Environment and Natural Resources
Joe Foss Bldg., 523 E. Capitol Avenue
Pierre, SD 57501
605 773 3153

Underground Storage Tanks (UST):
Ground Water Quality Program
Department of Environment and Natural Resources
Joe Foss Bldg., 523 E. Capitol Avenue
Pierre, SD 57501
605 773 3296

TENNESSEE

Community Right-to-Know:
Tennessee Emergency Response Council
C/O Tennessee Emergency Management Agency
3041 Sidco
Nashville, TN 37204
800 258 3300

Forestry:
Forestry Division
Department of Agriculture
445 East Capitol
Pierre, SD 57501
605 773 3623

Hazardous Waste:
Office of Waste Management
Department of Environment and Natural Resources
Joe Foss Bldg., 523 E. Capitol Avenue
Pierre, SD 57501
605 773 3153

Natural Resources Agency:
Department of Game, Fish and Parks
Joe Foss Bldg., 523 E. Capitol Avenue
Pierre, SD 57501
605 773 3387

Nuclear Waste/Nuclear Safety:
Point Source Control Program
Department of Environment and Natural Resources
Joe Foss Bldg., 523 E. Capitol Avenue
Pierre, SD 57501
605 773 3351

Superfund, Federal:
Ground Water Quality Office
Department of Environment and Natural Resources
Joe Foss Bldg., 523 E. Capitol Avenue
Pierre, SD 57501
605 773 3296

Waste Management Agency:
Office of Waste Management
Department of Environment and Natural Resources
Joe Foss Bldg., 523 E. Capitol Avenue
Pierre, SD 57501
605 773 3153

Air Pollution Agency:
Division of Air Pollution Control
Environment and Conservation Department
701 Broadway, Room 100 Customs House
Nashville, TN 37243
615 532 0554

Dam Safety:
Safe Dams Section
Division of Water Supply
701 Broadway, Room 100 Customs House
Nashville, TN 37243
615 532 0154

Drinking Water:
Division of Water Supply
701 Broadway, Room 100 Customs House
Nashville, TN 37243
615 532 0191

Environmental/Natural Resources Agency:
Department of Environment and Conservation
701 Broadway, Room 100 Customs House
Nashville, TN 37243
615 532 0109

Forestry:
Division of Forestry
Environment and Conservation Department
701 Broadway, Room 100 Customs Office
Nashville, TN 37243
615 370 0720

Hazardous Waste:
Hazardous Waste Management Section
Division of Solid Waste Management
701 Broadway, Room 100 Customs House
Nashville, TN 37243
615 532 0841

Natural Resources Agency:
Environment and Conservation Department
701 Broadway, Room 100 Customs House
Nashville, TN 37243
615 532 0109

Nuclear Waste/Nuclear Safety:
Division of Radiological Health
Environment and Conservation Department
701 Broadway, Room 100 Customs House
Nashville, TN 37243
615 532 0364

Superfund, Federal:
Division of Superfund
Environment and Conservation Department
701 Broadway, Room 100 Customs House
Nashville, TN 37243
615 741 3011

Water Agency:
Division of Water Pollution Control
Environment and Conservation Department
701 Broadway, Room 100 Customs House
Nashville, TN 37243
615 741 0654

Emergency Response:
Tennessee Emergency Response Council
C/O Tennessee Emergency Management Agency
3041 Sidco
Nashville, TN 37204
800 258 3300

Fish and Wildlife:
Wildlife Resources Agency
P.O. Box 40747
Nashville, TN 37204
615 781 6500

Geological Survey:
Division of Geology
Environment and Conservation Department
701 Broadway, Room 100 Customs House
Nashville, TN 37243
615 532 1500

Industrial Pre-treatment Program:
Municipal Facilities Section
Division of Water Pollution Control
701 Broadway, Room 100 Customs House
Nashville, TN 37243
615 532 0649

Nature Preserves Commission:
Division of Ecological Services
Environment and Conservation Department
701 Broadway, Room 100 Customs House
Nashville, TN 37243
615 532 0431

Parks:
Bureau of Parks
Environment and Conservation Department
701 Broadway, Room 100 Customs House
Nashville, TN 37243
615 532 0001

Underground Storage Tanks (UST):
Division of Underground Storage Tanks
Environment and Conservation Department
701 Broadway, Room 100 Customs House
Nashville, TN 37243
615 532 0945

TEXAS

Energy:
Division of Energy
Department of Economic and Community
Development
320 6th Avenue North, 8th Floor
Nashville, TN 37243
615 741 2994

Flood Plain Management:
Local Planning Division
Department of Economic and Community Affairs
320 6th Avenue North, 8th Floor
Nashville, TN 37243
615 741 2211

Groundwater:
Division of Groundwater Protection
Environment and Conservation Department
701 Broadway, Room 100 Customs House
Nashville, TN 37243
615 532 0761

Mined Land Reclamation:
Division of Land Reclamation
Environment and Conservation Department
305 West Springdale Avenue
Knoxville, TN 37917
615 594 6203

NPDES:
Industrial Facilities Section
Division of Water Pollution Control
701 Broadway, Room 100 Customs House
Nashville, TN 37243
615 532 0649

Solid Waste:
Solid Waste Management Section
Division of Solid Waste Management
701 Broadway, Room 100 Customs House
Nashville, TN 37243
615 532 0804

Waste Management Agency:
Division of Solid Waste Management
Environment and Conservation Department
701 Broadway, Room 100 Customs House
Nashville, TN 37243
615 532 0780

Air Pollution Agency:
Air Control Board
6330 Highway 290 East
Austin, TX 78723
512 908 1100

Climatology:
Meteorology Department
Texas A&M University
College Station, TX 77843
409 845 7671

Dam Safety:
Water Rights Section
Office of Water Resources Management
P.O. Box 13087
Austin, TX 78711
512 463 8575

Energy:
Public Utility Commission
7800 Shoal Creek Boulevard, Suite 400N
Austin, TX 78757
512 458 0291

Flood Plain Management:
Water Rights Section
Office of Water Resources Management
P.O. Box 13087
Austin, TX 78711
512 463 8575

Groundwater:
Groundwater Assessment Team
Water Commission
P.O. Box 13087
Austin, TX 78711
512 463 8308

Mined Land Reclamation:
Surface Mining and Reclamation Division
Railroad Commission
P.O. Drawer 12967
Austin, TX 78711
512 463 6900

NPDES:
Watershed Management Division
Water Commission
P.O. Box 13087
Austin, TX 78711
512 462 7742

Solid Waste:
Municipal Solid Waste Division
Water Commission
P.O. Box 13087
Austin, TX 78711
512 908 6692

Coastal Zone Management:
Coastal Division
General Land Office
1700 North Congress Avenue
Austin, TX 78701
512 463 5059

Drinking Water:
Drinking Water Utilities Division
Department of Health
1100 West 49th Street
Austin, TX 78756
512 371 6319

Environmental/Natural Resources Agency:
Texas Natural Resource and Conservation
Commission
P.O. Box 13087
Austin, TX 78711
512 463 7901

Forestry:
Texas Forest Service
Texas A&M, 302 Systems Administration Building
College Station, TX 77843
409 845 2641

Hazardous Waste:
Industrial Hazardous Waste Division
Water Commission
P.O. Box 13087
Austin, TX 78711
512 908 2334

Natural Resources Agency:
Water Commission
P.O. Box 13087
Austin, TX 78711
512 463 7791

Nuclear Waste/Nuclear Safety:
Bureau of Radiation Control
Department of Health
1212 East Anderson Lane
Austin, TX 78756
512 834 6688

Superfund, Federal:
Division of Pollution Cleanup
Water Commission
P.O. Box 13087
Austin, TX 78711
512 908 2454

Community Right-to-Know:
Energy & Hazardous Materials Prog., Governors
Div. of Emergency Mgmt.
Department of Public Safety
P.O. Box 4087
Austin, TX 78773
512 465 2138

Emergency Response:
Emergency Response Unit, Field Operations Div.
Water Commission
P.O. Box 13087
Austin, TX 78711
512 908 2510

Fish and Wildlife:
Department of Parks and Wildlife
4200 Smith School Road
Austin, TX 78744
512 389 4802

Geological Survey:
Bureau of Economic Geology
University of Texas, Balcomes Research Center
Building 130, Box X, University Station
Austin, TX 78713
512 471 1534

Industrial Pre-treatment Program:
Industrial Permit Section
Water Commission
P.O. Box 13087
Austin, TX 78711
512 463 8201

Nature Preserves Commission:
Natural Heritage Program
Department of Parks and Wildlife
4200 Smith School Road
Austin, TX 78744
512 448 4311

Parks:
Parks Division
Department of Parks and Wildlife
4200 Smith School Road
Austin, TX 78744
512 389 4866

Superfund, State:
Division of Pollution Cleanup
Water Commission
P.O. Box 13087
Austin, TX 78711
512 908 2454

Underground Storage Tanks (UST):
Petroleum Storage Tank Division
Water Commission
P.O. Box 13087
Austin, TX 78711
512 908 2106

UTAH

Community Right-to-Know:
Division of Environmental Response and
Remediation
Department of Environmental Quality
150 North 1950 West
Salt Lake City, UT 84114
801 536 4100

Emergency Response:
Division of Environmental Response and
Remediation
Department of Environmental Quality
150 North 1950 West
Salt Lake City, UT 84114
801 536 4100

Flood Plain Management:
National Flood Insurance Program
Comprehensive Emergency Mgmt., Public Safety
Dept.
4501 South 2700 West
Salt Lake City, UT 84119
801 533 5271

Groundwater:
Groundwater Section
Division of Water Quality
288 North 1460 West, P.O. Box 114870
Salt Lake City, UT 84114
801 538 6146

Mined Land Reclamation:
Division of Oil, Gas and Mining
Department of Natural Resources
355 West North Temple, Suite 350
Salt Lake City, UT 84180
801 538 5340

NPDES:
Permits and Compliance Section
Division of Water Quality
288 North 1460 West, P.O. Box 114870
Salt Lake City, UT 84114
801 538 6146

Waste Management Agency:
Industrial Hazardous Waste Division
Water Commission
P.O. Box 13087
Austin, TX 78711
512 908 2334

Air Pollution Agency:
Division of Air Quality
Department of Environmental Quality
150 North 1950 West
Salt Lake City, UT 84114
801 536 4000

Dam Safety:
Dam Safety, Division of Water Rights
Department of Natural Resources
1636 West North Temple
Salt Lake City, UT 84116
801 538 7240

Energy:
Utah Energy Office
Department of Natural Resources
355 West North Temple, Suite 350
Salt Lake City, UT 84180
801 538 5428

Forestry:
Division of State Lands & Forestry
Department of Natural Resources
355 West North Temple, Suite 400
Salt Lake City, UT 84180
801 538 5508

Hazardous Waste:
Division of Solid and Hazardous Waste
Department of Environmental Quality
288 North 1460 West
Salt Lake City, UT 84114
801 538 6170

Natural Resources Agency:
Department of Natural Resources
1636 West North Temple
Salt Lake City, UT 84116
801 538 7200

Nuclear Waste/Nuclear Safety:
Division of Radiation Control
Department of Environmental Quality
150 North 1950 West
Salt Lake City, UT 84144
801 536 4250

Water Agency:
Water Commission
P.O. Box 13087
Austin, TX 78711
512 463 7791

Climatology:
Utah State University
UMC-48
Logan, UT 84322
801 750 2190

Drinking Water:
Division of Drinking Water
Department of Environmental Quality
288 North 1460 West, P.O. Box 1148330
Salt Lake City, UT 84114
801 538 6163

Fish and Wildlife:
Division of Wildlife Resources
Department of Natural Resources
1596 West North Temple
Salt Lake City, UT 84116
801 538 4700

Geological Survey:
Geological Survey Division
Department of Natural Resources
2363 South Foothill Drive
Salt Lake City, UT 84109
801 467 7970

Industrial Pre-treatment Program:
Industrial Permit and Compliance Section
Division of Water Quality
288 North 1460 West, P.O. Box 114870
Salt Lake City, UT 84114
801 538 6146

Nature Preserves Commission:
Resource Management
Natural Heritage Prog., Dept. of Natural Resources
1636 West North Temple
Salt Lake City, UT 84116
801 538 7200

Parks:
Division of Parks and Recreation
Department of Natural Resources
1636 West North Temple, Room 116
Salt Lake City, UT 84116
801 538 7200

Solid Waste:
Solid Waste Section
Division of Solid and Hazardous Waste
288 North 1460 West
Salt Lake City, UT 84114
801 538 6170

Underground Storage Tanks (UST):
Division of Environmental Response and
Remediation
Department of Environmental Quality
150 North 1950 West
Salt Lake City, UT 84114
801 536 4100

VERMONT

Community Right-to-Know:
Division of Occupational and Radiological Health
Department of Health
Administration Building, 10 Baldwin St
Montpelier, VT 05602
802 828 2886

Emergency Response:
Technical Services Section
Hazardous Materials Management Division
West Building, 103 South Main Street
Waterbury, VT 05676
802 244 8702

Flood Plain Management:
Flood Plain Management
Division of Water Quality
10 North Bldg., 103 South Main Street
Waterbury, VT 05676
802 244 6951

Groundwater:
Groundwater Management
Division of Water Quality
10 North Bldg., 103 South Main Street
Waterbury, VT 45676
802 244 6951

Natural Resources Agency:
Agency of Natural Resources
Center Building, 103 South Main Street
Waterbury, VT 05676
802 244 7347

Superfund, Federal:
Division of Environmental Response and
Remediation
Department of Environmental Quality
150 North 1950 West
Salt Lake City, UT 84114
801 536 4100

Waste Management Agency:
Division of Solid and Hazardous Waste
Department of Environmental Quality
288 North 1460 West
Salt Lake City, UT 84114
801 538 6170

Air Pollution Agency:
Air Pollution Control Division
Department of Environmental Conservation
103 South Main Street, Building 3 South
Waterbury, VT 05676
802 244 8731

Dam Safety:
Division of Agency Facilities
Department of Environmental Conservation
Building 1 South, 103 South Main Street
Waterbury, VT 05676
802 244 8755

Energy:
Department of Public Service
120 State Street
Montpelier, VT 05602
802 828 2393

Forestry:
Division of Forestry
Department of Forests, Parks and Recreation
10 South Bldg., 103 South Main Street
Waterbury, VT 05676
802 244 8711

Hazardous Waste:
Hazardous Materials Management Division
Department of Environmental Conservation
West Building, 103 South Main Street
Waterbury, VT 05676
802 244 8702

Nature Preserves Commission:
Vermont Natural Heritage Program
103 South Main Street
Waterbury, VT 05676
802 244 7340

Superfund, State:
Division of Environmental Response and
Remediation
Department of Environmental Quality
150 North 1950 West
Salt Lake City, UT 84114
801 536 4100

Water Agency:
Division of Water Quality
Department of Environmental Quality
288 North 1460 West, P.O. Box 114870
Salt Lake City, UT 84114
801 538 6146

Climatology:
Plant and Soil Science, University of Vermont
208 Hills Building
Burlington, VT 05401
802 656 3131

Drinking Water:
Environmental Health Division
Health Department
P.O. Box 70
Burlington, VT 05402
802 863 7223

Fish and Wildlife:
Fish and Wildlife Department
Agency of Natural Resources
10 South Bldg., 103 South Main Street
Waterbury, VT 05676
802 244 7331

Geological Survey:
Agency of Natural Resources
103 South Main Street, Center Building
Waterbury, VT 05676
802 244 5164

Industrial Pre treatment Program:
Water Pollution Control
Division of Public Facilities
10 North Bldg., 103 South Main Street
Waterbury, VT 05676
802 244 8744

NPDES:
Division of Permits, Compliance and Protection
Department of Environmental Conservation
10 North Bldg., 103 South Main Street
Waterbury, VT 05676
802 244 5674

Nuclear Waste/Nuclear Safety:
Hazardous Waste Management
Hazardous Materials Management Division
Center Building, 103 South Main Street
Waterbury, VT 05676
802 244 5164

Superfund, Federal:
Hazardous Sites Management
Hazardous Materials Management Division
West Building, 103 South Main Street
Waterbury, VT 05676
802 244 8702

Waste Management Agency:
Department of Environmental Conservation
Agency of Natural Resources
1 South Building, 103 South Main Street
Waterbury, VT 05676
802 244 8755

Air Pollution Agency:
Division of Air Pollution Control
Department of Environmental Quality
P.O. Box 10089
Richmond, VA 23240
804 786 6035

Community Right-to-Know:
Community Right-to-Know
Division of Waste Management
101 North 14th Street, 11th Floor
Richmond, VA 23219
804 225 2631

Emergency Response:
Department of Emergency Services
310 Turner Road
Richmond, VA 23225
804 674 2497

Flood Plain Management:
Flood Plain Programs, Division of Soil and Water
Conservation
Department of Conservation and Recreation
203 Governor Street
Richmond, VA 23219
804 371 6136

Groundwater:
Office of Water Resource Management
Division of Water
P.O. Box 11143, 211 North Hamilton St.
Richmond, VA 23230
804 367 0411

Parks:
Department of Environmental Conservation
Agency of Natural Resources
10 South Bldg., 103 South Main Street
Waterbury, VT 05676
802 244 8711

Superfund, State:
Hazardous Waste Section
Hazardous Materials Management Division
West Building, 103 South Main Street
Waterbury, VT 05676
802 244 8702

Water Agency:
Division of Water Quality
Department of Environmental Conservation
10 North Bldg., 103 South Main Street
Waterbury, VT 05676
802 244 6951

Climatology:
Department of Environmental Sciences
University of Virginia
Clark Hall
Charlottesville, VA 22903
804 924 0549

Dam Safety:
Dam Safety and Flood Plain Pgm, Div. of Soil and
Water Conservation
Department of Conservation and Recreation
203 Governor Street
Richmond, VA 23219
804 371 7536

Energy:
Division of Energy
Department of Mines, Minerals and Energy
2201 West Broad Street
Richmond, VA 23220
804 367 0979

Forestry:
Department of Forestry
P.O. Box 3758
Charlottesville, VA 22903
804 977 6555

Hazardous Waste:
Division of Technical Services
Division of Waste Management
101 North 14th Street, 11th Floor
Richmond, VA 23219
804 225 2667

Solid Waste:
Division of Solid Waste Management
Department of Environmental Conservation
Laundry Building, 103 South Main Street
Waterbury, VT 05676
802 244 7831

Underground Storage Tanks (UST):
Management and Prevention Section
Hazardous Materials Management Division
West Building, 103 South Main Street
Waterbury, VT 05676
802 244 8702

VIRGINA

Coastal Zone Management:
Coastal and Ocean Projects
Council on the Environment
Room 903, Ninth Street Office Building
Richmond, VA 23219
804 257 4500

Drinking Water:
Office of Water Programs
Department of Health
109 Governor Street
Richmond, VA 23219
804 786 6277

Fish and Wildlife:
Department of Game and Inland Fisheries
P.O. Box 11104, 4010 West Broad Street
Richmond, VA 23230
804 367 1000

Geological Survey:
Division of Mineral Resources
Department of Mines, Minerals and Energy
P.O. Box 3667
Charlottesville, VA 22903
804 293 5121

Industrial Pre-treatment Program:
Office of Engineering Applications
Division of Water
P.O. Box 11143, 211 North Hamilton St.
Richmond, VA 23230
804 367 6389

Mined Land Reclamation:
Division of Mine Land Reclamation
Department of Mines, Minerals and Energy
622 Powell Avenue, P.O. Drawer U
Big Stone Gap, VA 24219
703 523 2925

NPDES:
Office of Water Resource Management
Division of Water
P.O. Box 11143, 211 North Hamilton St.
Richmond, VA 23230
804 367 1868

Solid Waste:
Division of Technical Services
Division of Waste Management
101 North 14th Street, 11th Floor
Richmond, VA 23219
804 225 2667

Underground Storage Tanks (UST):
Office of Water Resource Management
Division of Water
P.O. Box 11143, 211 North Hamilton St
Richmond, VA 23230
804 367 0411

WASHINGTON

Natural Resources Agency:
Office of Natural Resources
P.O. Box 1475
Richmond, VA 23212
804 786 0044

Nuclear Waste/Nuclear Safety:
Nuclear Waste Section
Division of Waste Management
101 North 14th Street, 11th Floor
Richmond, VA 23219
804 225 2667

Superfund, Federal:
Division of Administrative and Special Programs
Division of Waste Management
101 North 14th Street, 11th Floor
Richmond, VA 23219
804 225 2811

Waste Management Agency:
Waste Management Division
Monroe Building, 11th Floor
101 North 14th Street
Richmond, VA 23219
804 225 2667

Air Pollution Agency:
Air Quality Program
Department of Ecology
MS PV-11
Olympia, WA 98503
206 459 6255

Nature Preserves Commission:
Virginia Natural Heritage Program
Department of Conservation and Recreation
1100 Washington Building
Richmond, VA 23219
804 786 2121

Parks:
Division of State Parks
Department of Conservation and Recreation
1201 Washington Building
Richmond, VA 23219
804 786 2132

Superfund, State:
Division of Administrative and Special Programs
Division of Waste Management
101 North 14th Street, 11th Floor
Richmond, VA 23219
804 225 2811

Water Agency:
Division of Water
Department of Environmental Quality
P.O. Box 11143, 211 North Hamilton St.
Richmond, VA 23230
804 367 0056

Climatology:
Atmospheric Science Department
University of Washington
AK-40
Seattle, WA 98195
206 543 0448

Coastal Zone Management:
Shorelands and Coastal Zone Management Program
Water and Shorelands
MS PV-11
Olympia, WA 98504
206 459 6777

Drinking Water:
Groundwater Unit
Water Quality Program
MS PV-11
Olympia, WA 98504
206 438 8199

Fish and Wildlife:
Department of Wildlife
600 North Capitol Way
Olympia, WA 98504
206 753 5710

Community Right-to-Know:
Hazardous Waste Information and Planning
Solid and Hazardous Waste Program
MS PV-11
Olympia, WA 98504
206 438 7252

Emergency Response:
Toxics Cleanup Program
Department of Ecology
MS PV-11
Olympia, WA 98504
206 438 3007

Flood Plain Management:
Flood Plain Management Section
Water Quality Program
MS PV-11
Olympia, WA 98504
206 459 6791

Dam Safety:
Dam Safety Section
Water Resources Program
MS PV-11
Olympia, WA 98504
206 459 6046

Energy:
Washington State Energy Office
809 Legion Way, SE FA-11
Olympia, WA 98509
206 586 5000

Forestry:
Division of Forest Land Management
Department of Natural Resources
Blomberg Road MS MQ-11
Olympia, WA 98504
206 753 0671

Geological Survey:
Division of Geology and Earth Resources
Department of Natural Resources
Rowesix, MS PY-12
Olympia, WA 98504
206 459 6372

Industrial Pre-treatment Program:
Point Source Pollution Section
Water Quality Program
MS PV-11
Olympia, WA 98504
206 438 7040

Nature Preserves Commission:
Washington Natural Heritage Program
Department of Natural Resources
MS EX-13
Olympia, WA 98504
206 902 1650

Parks:
State Parks and Recreation Commission
7150 Cleanwater Lane
Olympia, WA 98504
206 753 5757

Superfund, State:
Toxics Cleanup Program
Department of Ecology
MS PV-11
Olympia, WA 98504
206 438 3007

Water Agency:
Water and Shorelands
Department of Ecology
MS PV-11
Olympia, WA 98504
206 436 7090

Climatology:
Division of Forestry
West Virginia University
337 Perceival Hall
Morgantown, WV 26506
304 293 3411

Drinking Water:
Environmental Engineering Division
Office of Environmental Health Services
815 Quarrier Street, Morrison Building
Charleston, WV 25301
304 558 2981

Groundwater:
Groundwater Unit
Water Quality Program
MS PV-11
Olympia, WA 98504
206 438 8199

Mined Land Reclamation:
Division of Geology and Earth Resources
Department of Natural Resources
Rowesix, MS PY-12
Olympia, WA 98504
206 459 6372

NPDES:
Point Source Pollution Section
Water Quality Program
MS PV-11
Olympia, WA 98504
206 438 8702

Solid Waste:
Solid and Hazardous Waste Program
Department of Ecology
MS PV-11
Olympia, WA 98504
206 459 6259

Underground Storage Tanks (UST):
Underground Storage Tank Section, Toxics Cleanup
Program
Department of Ecology
MS PV-11
Olympia, WA 98504
206 438 7999

WEST VIRGINIA

Community Right-to-Know:
Natural Resources Division
Commerce, Labor and Environmental Resources
Dept.
Capitol Complex, Building 3
Charleston, WV 25305
304 348 2754

Emergency Response:
Compliance/Monitoring/Enforcement Section
Office of Waste Management
1356 Hansford Street
Charleston, WV 25301
304 558 5989

Hazardous Waste:
Solid and Hazardous Waste Program
Waste Management
MS PV-11
Olympia, WA 98504
206 459 6316

Natural Resources Agency:
Department of Natural Resources
201 Cherberg Building
Olympia, WA 98504
206 753 5317

Nuclear Waste/Nuclear Safety:
Nuclear and Mixed Waste Program
Waste Management
MS PV-11
Olympia, WA 98504
206 438 7020

Superfund, Federal:
Toxics Cleanup Program
Department of Ecology
MS PV-11
Olympia, WA 98504
206 438 3007

Waste Management Agency:
Waste Management
Department of Ecology
MS PV-11
Olympia, WA 98504
206 459 6029

Air Pollution Agency:
Office of Air Quality
Division of Environmental Protection
1558 Washington Street East
Charleston, WV 25311
304 558 3286

Dam Safety:
Dam Safety Branch
Office of Water Resources
1201 Greenbrier Street
Charleston, WV 25311
304 558 0320

Energy:
Division of Environmental Protection
Commerce, Labor and Environmental Resources
Dept.
10 McJunkin Road
Nitro, WV 25143
304 759 0515

Environmental/Natural Resources Agency:
Commerce, Labor, and Environmental Resources
Department
State Capitol Building
Charleston, WV 25305
304 558 3255

Fish and Wildlife:
Wildlife Resources Section
Division of Natural Resources
Capitol Complex, Building 3
Charleston, WV 25305
304 558 2771

Flood Plain Management:
Program and Technical Support
Office of Water Resources
1201 Greenbrier Street
Charleston, WV 25311
304 558 2108

Forestry:
Division of Forestry
Commerce, Labor and Environmental Resources
Dept.
1900 Kanawha Blvd. East, State Capitol
Charleston, WV 25305
304 558 2788

Geological Survey:
Geological and Economic Survey
Mount Chatau Research Center
P.O. Box 879
Morgantown, WV 26507
304 594 2331

Groundwater:
Groundwater Program
Program and Technical Support Branch
1201 Greenbrier Street
Charleston, WV 25311
304 558 2108

Hazardous Waste:
Hazardous Waste Section
Office of Waste Management
1356 Hansford Street
Charleston, WV 25301
304 558 5393

Mined Land Reclamation:
Abandoned Mined Land and Reclamation Section
Mining and Reclam. Div., Div. of Env. Protection
10 McJunkin Road
Nitro, WV 25143
304 759 0530

Natural Resources Agency:
Division of Natural Resources
Commerce, Labor and Environmental Resources
Dept.
Capitol Complex, Building 3
Charleston, WV 25305
304 558 2754

Nature Preserves Commission:
Natural Heritage Program
Wildlife Resources Section
P.O. Box 67
Elkins, WV 26241
304 637 0245

NPDES:
Permits Branch
Office of Water Resources
1201 Greenbrier Street
Charleston, WV 25311
304 558 0375

Parks:
Division of Tourism and Parks
Commerce, Labor and Environmental Resources
Dept.
1900 Kanawha Blvd., East, Building 6
Charleston, WV 25305
304 558 2200

Solid Waste:
Solid Waste Management Section
Office of Waste Management
1356 Hansford Street
Charleston, WV 25301
304 558 6350

Superfund, Federal:
Site Investigation/Response Section
Office of Waste Management
1356 Hansford Street
Charleston, WV 25301
304 558 2745

Superfund, State:
Site Investigation/Response Section
Office of Waste Management
1356 Hansford Street
Charleston, WV 25301
304 558 2745

Underground Storage Tanks (UST):
Underground Storage Tank Section
Office of Waste Management
1356 Hansford Street
Charleston, WV 25301
304 558 6371

Waste Management Agency:
Office of Waste Management
Division of Environmental Protection
1356 Hansford Street
Charleston, WV 25301
304 558 5929

Water Agency:
Office of Environmental Health Services
Bureau of Public Health
815 Quarrier Street, Morrison Building
Charleston, WV 25301
304 558 2981

WISCONSIN

Air Pollution Agency:
Bureau of Air Management
Division of Environmental Quality
P.O. Box 7921
Madison, WI 53707
608 266 0603

Climatology:
University of Wisconsin Extension
1225 West Dayton Street
Madison, WI 53706
608 263 2374

Coastal Zone Management:
Lake Management Section
Bureau of Water Resources Management
P.O. Box 7921
Madison, WI 53707
608 266 0502

Community Right-to-Know:
Emergency Government Division
Department of Administration
4802 Sheboython Avenue
Madison, WI 53707
608 266 3232

Dam Safety:
Dam Safety/Floodplain Management Section
Bureau of Water Regulation and Zoning
P.O. Box 7921
Madison, WI 53707
608 266 1926

Drinking Water:
Public Water Supply Section
Bureau of Water Supply
P.O. Box 7921
Madison, WI 53707
608 267 7651

Environmental/Natural Resources Agency:
Department of Natural Resources
P.O. Box 7921
Madison, WI 53702
608 266 2121

Forestry:
Forestry Bureau
Resource Management Division
P.O. Box 7921
Madison, WI 53707
608 266 0842

Hazardous Waste:
Hazardous Waste Management Section
Bureau of Solid and Hazardous Waste Management
P.O. Box 7921
Madison, WI 53707
608 266 7055

Natural Resources Agency:
Natural Resources Department
P.O. Box 7921
Madison, WI 53707
608 266 2121

Nuclear Waste/Nuclear Safety:
Radiation Protection Unit, Bureau of Public Health,
Div. of Health
Department of Health and Social Services
P.O. Box 309
Madison, WI 53701
608 267 4792

Superfund, Federal:
Emergency and Remedial Response Section
Bureau of Solid and Hazardous Waste Management
P.O. Box 7921
Madison, WI 53707
608 267 3540

Waste Management Agency:
Bureau of Solid and Hazardous Waste Management
Division for Environmental Quality
P.O. Box 7921
Madison, WI 53707
608 266 1327

Emergency Response:
Environmental Response and Repair Section
Bureau of Solid and Hazardous Waste Management
P.O. Box 7921
Madison, WI 53707
608 267 7562

Fish and Wildlife:
Bureau of Wildlife Management
Resource Management Division
P.O. Box 7921
Madison, WI 53707
608 266 2193

Geological Survey:
Wisconsin Geological Survey
University of Wisconsin
3817 Mineral Point Road
Madison, WI 53705
608 262 1705

Industrial Pre-treatment Program:
Permits and Pre-treatment Section
Bureau of Waste Water Management
P.O. Box 7921
Madison, WI 53707
608 266 7721

Nature Preserves Commission:
Bureau of Endangered Resources
Resource Management Division
P.O. Box 7921
Madison, WI 53707
608 266 2625

Parks:
Parks and Recreation Bureau
Resource Management Division
P.O. Box 7921
Madison, WI 53707
608 266 2181

Superfund, State:
Emergency and Remedial Response Section
Bureau of Solid and Hazardous Waste Management
P.O. Box 7921
Madison, WI 53707
608 266 2699

Water Agency:
Bureau of Water Resources Management
Division for Environmental Quality
P.O. Box 7921
Madison, WI 53707
608 266 8631

Energy:
Energy and Intergovernmental Relations Division
Department of Administration
P.O. Box 7868
Madison, WI 53707
608 266 8234

Flood Plain Management:
Dam Safety/Flood Plain Management Section
Bureau of Water Regulation and Zoning
P.O. Box 7921
Madison, WI 53707
608 266 1926

Groundwater:
Groundwater Management Section
Bureau of Water Resources Management
P.O. Box 7921
Madison, WI 53707
608 267 9350

Mined Land Reclamation:
Mine Reclamation Section
Bureau of Solid and Hazardous Waste Management
P.O. Box 7921
Madison, WI 53707
608 266 2050

NPDES:
Permits and Pre-treatment Section
Bureau of Waste Water Management
P.O. Box 7921
Madison, WI 53707
608 266 7721

Solid Waste:
Solid Waste Management Section
Bureau of Solid and Hazardous Waste Management
P.O. Box 7921
Madison, WI 53707
608 266 0520

Underground Storage Tanks (UST):
Environmental Response and Repair Section
Bureau of Solid and Hazardous Waste Management
P.O. Box 7921
Madison, WI 53707
608 267 7562

WYOMING

Dam Safety:
Wyoming State Engineer
Herschler Building, 4th Floor East
Cheyenne, WY 82002
307 777 7354

Fish and Wildlife:
Game and Fish Commission
5400 Bishop Boulevard
Cheyenne, WY 82002
307 777 4601

Geological Survey:
Wyoming Geological Survey
P.O. Box 3008, University Station
Laramie, WY 82071
307 766 2286

Mined Land Reclamation:
Abandoned Mine Land Program, Land Quality
Division
Department of Environmental Quality
122 West 25th St., Herschler Building
Cheyenne, WY 82002
307 777 6191

Solid Waste:
Solid Waste Management Division
Department of Environmental Quality
122 West 25th St., Herschler Building
Cheyenne, WY 82002
307 777 7752

Underground Storage Tanks (UST):
Water Quality Division
Department of Environmental Quality
122 W. 25th St., Herschler Bldg.
Cheyenne, WY 82002
307 777 7781

Air Pollution Agency:
Air Quality Division
Department of Environmental Quality
122 West 25th St., Herschler Building
Cheyenne, WY 82002
307 777 7391

Drinking Water:
Environmental Health, Health and Medical Services
Division
Department of Health and Social Services
Hathaway Building, Room 482
Cheyenne, WY 82002
307 777 7957

Flood Plain Management:
Disaster and Civil Defense
Office of the Adjutant General
P.O. Box 1709
Cheyenne, WY 82003
307 777 7566

Groundwater:
Ground Water Operations
Water Quality Division
122 West 25th St., Herschler Building
Cheyenne, WY 82002
307 777 7781

NPDES:
Review Analysis
Water Quality Division
122 West 25th St., Herschler Building
Cheyenne, WY 82002
307 777 7781

Superfund, Federal:
Solid Waste Management Division
Department of Environmental Quality
122 West 25th St., Herschler Building
Cheyenne, WY 82002
307 777 7752

Waste Management Agency:
Department of Environmental Quality
122 West 25th St., Herschler Building
Cheyenne, WY 82002
307 777 7938

Community Right-to-Know:
State Emergency Response Commission
P.O. Box 1709
Cheyenne, WY 82003
307 777 7566

Emergency Response:
Oil and Hazardous Response
Water Quality Division
122 West 25th St., Herschler Building
Cheyenne, WY 82002
307 777 7781

Forestry:
Forestry Division
Public Lands Commission
Herschler Building
Cheyenne, WY 82002
307 777 7586

Hazardous Waste:
Solid Waste Management Division
Department of Environmental Quality
122 West 25th St., Herschler Building
Cheyenne, WY 82002
307 777 7752

Parks:
Recreation Commission
122 West 25th St., Herschler Building
Cheyenne, WY 82002
307 777 6310

Superfund, State:
Solid Waste Management Division
Department of Environmental Quality
122 West 25th St., Herschler Building
Cheyenne, WY 82002
307 777 7752

Water Agency:
Water Quality Division
Department of Environmental Quality
122 West 25th St., Herschler Building
Cheyenne, WY 82002
307 777 7781

D FREEDOM OF INFORMATION

Sample Open Records Request

Jane Q. Public
123 Main Street
Anywhere, KY 12345

September 3, 1992

Ann E. Over, County Judge/Executive
1 Main Street
Needmore, KY 54321

Dear Ms. Over:

I am writing to request copies (or inspection) of the following records:

> 1. All correspondence between you or any other representative of Wayout County and any representative of We Waste It Landfill Company.
>
> 2. All other documents in your possession or custody relating to We Waste It Landfill Company.
>
> 3. The solid waste management plan for Wayout County.

Please call (or write) me if the cost of copies is over $2.00, so I can inspect the records and select those to be copied. If any of the documents described are not in your possession or custody, but you are aware of such documents, please advise me which agency or person has the document.

If you withhold any documents please describe them in detail and your reasons for withholding them. I expect a reply within 3 working days per KRS 61.872 (citation is for Kentucky only, other states may have similar provisions). Thank you for your attention to this matter.

Sincerely,

Jane Q. Public

102 Main Street
Anytown, Kentucky 40000
(502) 444-4444

September 3, 1992

Freedom of Information Officer
Anytown Army Depot
Anytown, Kentucky 40001

Dear FOIA Officer:

This will request disclosure of copies of materials available from your agency under the Freedom of Information Act and regulations of your agency. Specifically, the information I am requesting is as follows:

[Insert the descriptions of documents you request (see example below)]
All documents and reports comprising or relating to the RCRA Facility Assessment performed on the site or sites known as the Anytown Army Depot or on any property under the authority of the commanding officers of the Anytown Army Depot.

All environmental data relating to sampling and analysis of soils, surface water, groundwater, sediments, soil water, or soil gases performed at the site or sites known as the Anytown Army Depot or on any property under the authority of the commanding officers of the Anytown Army Depot.

Please note that I would like to exclude from this request the following documents, which were already provided to me in response to a previous FOIA request:

-Report DRXTH-AS-CR-82186, Rapid Response Environmental Surveys, Anytown Facility, Final Report and Appendices, 28 February 1983;
-Report DRXTH-AS-CR-82164, Rapid Response Environmental Surveys, Anytown Facility, Appendices, 5 November 1982;
-Environmental Assessment Draft, Assessment Current Operation, Anytown Depot Activity, 31 October 1978.

Under present regulations and case law pertaining to the Freedom of Information Act, I believe that these documents are available to me and other members of the public. They are not exempt from disclosure under present interpretations of the Act, and must therefore be released. Your agency is believed to have custody of these documents, but if it does not I would request prompt notice of their current location.

If any portion of this request is denied, I request a detailed statement of the reasons for the withholding and an index or similar statement of the nature of the withheld documents. To expedite this request, I would be willing to discuss specific instances of deletion or other exemption claims in advance of a final decision by the agency. If you contend that any document requested is not available for inspection because it is in preliminary or draft form, please state the date the document is anticipated to be in final form, and the date the document was made available to you in its present form. In the event of deletions I request that a reason be provided for each partial denial of access.

I am prepared to pay reasonable costs for locating the requested file and reproducing it. As you know, the amended Act permits you to reduce or waive the fee if it "is in the public interest because furnishing the information can be considered as primarily benefiting the public." I am requesting this information on behalf of the Concerned Citizens of Anytown, a non profit membership association, formed for the purpose of gathering and disseminating to the public factual information regarding the environment in and around Anytown. The Concerned Citizens of Anytown intend to use this information to disseminate to the public information about the regulatory compliance status of the facility, and does not stand to gain any monetary benefit through the use of this information. I therefore believe that this request plainly fits the above category, and I ask that you waive any fees. If the fees are not waived, please call before incurring any expense if the amount will exceed one hundred dollars.

As provided in the amended Act, I will expect to receive a reply within ten working days. Thank you in advance for your assistance in this matter.

Sincerely,

Jane Doe,
For the Concerned Citizens of Anytown

E FEDERAL LAW SUMMARIES

Emergency Planning and Community Right-to-Know Act (EPCRA)

EPCRA, or the Emergency Planning and Community Right-to-Know law, has two themes. The Community right-to-know portion of the law gives citizens and government the right to have information on hazardous chemicals in their communities. The planning portion of the law requires local governments to create local emergency plans.

The law requires the creation of a state emergency response commission (SERC) which must designate emergency planning districts. The SERC must appoint, supervise, and coordinate Local Emergency Planning Committees (LEPCs). The public participation process is left up to the LEPCs.

An emergency plan must be developed that includes the following:

1. Identification of facilities subject to the requirements of this law that are within the emergency planning district; identification of routes likely to be used for transporting substances on the list of extremely hazardous substances referred to in section 302(a); and identification of additional facilities, such as hospitals or natural gas facilities, that contribute or are subject to additional risks due to their proximity to these facilities.

2. Methods and procedures to be followed by facility owners and operators and local emergency and medical personnel in responding to any release of various chemicals.

3. Identification of a community emergency coordinator and facility emergency coordinators, who shall make determinations necessary to implement the plan.

4. Procedures by the facility emergency coordinators and the community emergency coordinator to provide reliable, effective, and timely notification to persons designated in the emergency plan, and to the public, that a release has occurred (consistent with the emergency notification requirements of section 304).

5. Methods for determining the occurrence of a release, and the area or population likely to be affected by such release.

6. A description of emergency equipment and facilities in the community (including each facility in the community subject to the requirement of this subtitle), and the persons responsible for such equipment and facilities.

7. Evacuation plans, including provision for a precautionary evacuation and alternative traffic routes.

8. Training programs, including schedules for training of local emergency response and medical personnel.

9. Methods and schedules for exercising the emergency plan.

The LEPCs have considerable flexibility to develop their own local plan, including making it more stringent than EPCRA requires.

Facilities must report spills in excess of certain thresholds of any chemicals on a hazardous substances list. Material Safety Data Sheets (MSDSs - see Appendix F) have been required by the Occupational Safety and Health Act (OSHA) to be available for all hazardous chemicals used at a facility. EPCRA requires MSDSs to be submitted to the SERCs and LEPCs and available to the public.

Section 313 is probably the best known part of EPCRA. This part of the law requires that information about releases of approximately 320 toxic chemicals be made available to the public. The reporting requirements apply to a facility with at least 10 full-time employees, classified in Standard Industrial Classification Codes 20-39 (see Appendix G), and manufactured, imported, processed or otherwise used at least 10,000 pounds of the toxic chemicals.

Citizen suits may be brought against facility owners and operators, EPA, governors, and state Emergency Response Commissions. Violations for which suits may be brought include: failure to submit proper forms and notices, failure of EPA to timely publish regulations and forms, and failure to provide a mechanism for making the information available to the public.

Clean Water Act

The Clean Water Act is the basic law controlling water pollution. In 1972, Congress set the goal of eliminating all discharges of pollutants into the waters of the United States by 1985. Obviously, this goal has not been met. But it explains the name of what is probably the most important aspect of the Act: the National Pollutant Discharge Elimination System (NPDES) permit. All discharges of pollutants into streams, lakes and rivers are required to have an NPDES (or state) permit. The idea of the act was to get all the dischargers permitted and then gradually crank the discharge limits down to zero pollution, closed loop systems. In reality, permits continue to be issued. The act also sought to make all rivers, lakes and streams "fishable and swimmable."

In order to meet these goals, the federal EPA is required to publish water quality "criteria." Based on the type of stream or lake, and on the goals of protecting human health, welfare, and aquatic life, these are numbers for each pollutant of concern. States must adopt these or stricter numbers into their own laws or regulations. There are then two kinds of effluent standards that are applied to wastewater being discharged pursuant to a permit: water quality based standards, and technology based standards. Water quality based limits are based on back-calculating the amount of pollution each discharge can contribute to the stream or river without exceeding the water quality standards. Technology-based standards are based on the degree of pollution reduction that other companies in a given industry are achieving nationwide. Both must be considered in issuing a permit, and the stricter of the two will govern. In addition, the toxicity of all the pollutants in a discharge combined may be limited through the use of biomonitoring. In biomonitoring, the wastewater (straight and diluted) is tested to see if fish and water insects can live in it for a certain period of time. Depending on the flow of the receiving stream, the discharge might be required to sustain aquatic life in undiluted effluent (wastewater discharge) or with some degree of dilution. The biomonitoring is supposed to provide a check on whether the limits for the individual pollutants are strict enough to protect aquatic life when taken together in the whole discharge.

States have to submit their requirements to the EPA for approval. If approved, they become the primary permitting and enforcement agency for their territory, although EPA retains oversight authority.

Local governments can operate publicly owned treatment works. Industries that discharge to such treatment works are not required to obtain permits from the federal or state governments. Instead, the local government is required to have a state or EPA approved "pretreatment" program. Under a pretreatment program, local governments are supposed to issue and enforce permits for discharges from industries to the treatment works with limitations that will ensure that the treatment plant, in turn, can comply with its own permit.

The Clean Water Act also regulates wetlands. A permit is required prior to filling any wetland (there may be waivers for small areas), and the person filling in the wetland is supposed to create new wetlands to replace those destroyed.

In addition, the Clean Water Act provides funding for construction of sewage treatment plants, requires a report to Congress on which water bodies in a state are polluted in excess of water quality standards, and puts in place programs to control nonpoint source pollution.

Clean Air Act

In 1963, Congress passed the first Clean Air Act, although government programs to improve air quality date back to 1955. It has been amended several times, most recently in 1990.

Section 109 of the act requires EPA to establish national ambient air quality standards for air pollutants which endanger public health or welfare. Ambient air standards exist for carbon monoxide, particulates, sulfur dioxide, nitrogen dioxide, hydrocarbons, ozone, and lead. Each state is required to develop a state implementation plan (SIP) for how it will comply with the standards, including "emission limitations, schedules, and timetables for compliance with such limitations."

The law also addresses stationary sources (industry, smokestacks) and mobile sources (cars). In areas where the ambient air (air all around us) quality standards have been exceeded —nonattainment areas—new pollutant sources may be prohibited. Mobile sources—cars and light trucks—have to meet certain standards.

A number of the amendments of the Clean Air Act were enacted to extend deadlines that could not be met.

Title III of the Act provides for the regulation of 189 toxic air pollutants. Emitters of these chemicals will be required to install the "maximum available control technology," upon full implementation of the 1990 Act.

Acid rain is addressed in title IV of the Act. It provides for the reduction of sulphur dioxide and nitrogen oxide emissions.

Resource Conservation and Recovery Act
(RCRA)

The Resource Conservation and Recovery Act was passed in 1976, and amended by the Hazardous and Solid Waste Amendments (HSWA, pronounced Hiss-wah in the Midwest, and Hazwah in the East) in 1984. Subtitle C of RCRA applies to hazardous wastes. In response to numerous reports and studies showing toxic waste was being secretly dumped (in midnight dumping) all over the U.S., Congress established an elaborate "cradle-to-grave" tracking system for hazardous wastes - from point of creation to point of final disposal. It also required EPA to establish standards for the operation of hazardous waste landfills, incinerators, storage and other treatment and disposal facilities, and for the handling of hazardous waste by those who create it (generators). Unlike CERCLA, which applies to sites regardless of when the hazardous substances were disposed of, RCRA applies only to sites where hazardous wastes were handled after the effective date of EPA's implementing regulations, November 19, 1980. Because so many currently regulated hazardous waste facilities also had old problem areas on their sites, in 1984 Congress gave EPA authority to require corrective action at those old contaminated areas, as long as they were on sites that were subject to RCRA because of other hazardous waste treatment, storage or disposal activities.

In the hazardous waste area, RCRA allows states to take over the primary role in enforcing the federal system. This is called state "authorization." In order to be authorized (which takes the federal government out of the direct day-to-day regulation of industries generating and handling hazardous waste, and gives the state federal money to carry out the program), the state laws must be at least as stringent as the federal standards, and state laws are expressly allowed to be more stringent.

RCRA also has provisions dealing with solid waste, found in Subtitle D. EPA has promulgated a set of standards that are a minimum for states to follow. The states must promulgate their own solid waste regulations that meet these federal standards as a minimum.

Comprehensive Environmental Response, Compensation, and Liability Act (CERCLA - Superfund)

The Comprehensive Environmental Response, Compensation, and Liability Act (CERCLA) was passed by Congress in 1980, and amended by the Superfund Amendments and Reauthorization Act (SARA) in 1986 (EPCRA, which is part of SARA, is summarized elsewhere in this Appendix). CERCLA was intended to provide for cleanup of abandoned toxic dumpsites and includes a provision for EPA to promulgate a list of hazardous substances, and quantities of those substances which must be reported to the federal EPA if released to the environment in reportable quantities. It also established standards for who would be responsible for cleanup of toxic sites (owners of contaminated sites, or anyone who "arranged for disposal" of any hazardous substance, including generators, transporters, and brokers). All responsible parties are "jointly and severally" liable for cleanup, meaning any one party can be held responsible for the whole mess, even if it only generated a fraction of the waste. Such a party can sue other responsible parties for their share of the costs. EPA has broad enforcement powers, which include spending its own money from the "Superfund" to perform cleanup and suing responsible parties to get the money back, issuing orders (106 orders) ordering companies to take action to alleviate an imminent threat, and entering into agreements (called consent decrees) with responsible parties for them to voluntarily perform the work.

Congress also required EPA to establish the National Priorities List. Sites are placed on the list based on a score (Hazard Ranking System, or HRS score) which is supposed to reflect how big a danger the site is to public health and the environment. EPA was also required to promulgate a set of regulations called the National Contingency Plan (40 CFR 300 et. seq.) which describes in more detail the procedures for performing site investigations and cleanup. The act also required that key elements of the cleanup plan be subject to notice and public comment.

CERCLA also gives some rights to private parties. In addition to contribution actions (who pays and how much) which may be brought by one responsible party against another, people who have suffered damages as a result of a release of hazardous substances may bring an action for damages. Costs of cleaning up someone else's mess can be recovered, as can costs of medical monitoring to detect future harm from exposure.

CERCLA also gives some rights to the states. Federal cleanups are supposed to meet or exceed all appropriate state standards. States can enter into agreements with EPA ("cooperative agreements") to take over all or part of the Superfund site evaluation and cleanup process for federally listed sites. In addition, states often have their own laws that allow them to obtain some kind of cleanup for non-NPL sites.

Surface Mining Control and Reclamation Act of 1977 (SMCRA)

The Surface Mining Control and Reclamation Act (or SMCRA) was passed to control the environmental effects of strip mining of coal and the surface effects of underground mining of coal. The act requires any person or company who intends to mine coal to get a permit before conducting any surface or underground operation. For underground mines, the permit is simply to make sure that the mining operation does not cause the surface to cave in (or subside), causing damage to houses, roads, buildings, and even making streams or rivers disappear. For strip (or surface) mining, the company is required by law to file a reclamation plan, showing how they will return the land to useful condition. In general, companies are required to return the surface of the land to about the same shape it originally had (called approximate original contours). Along with their reclamation plan, companies are required to post a bond, which is supposed to mean that enough money is guaranteed to be available to reclaim the site properly, even if the company goes out of business or skips town. The bond is not to be released until the company has satisfactorily completed the reclamation of the land.

The law provides that the Office of Surface Mining is ultimately responsible for the administration and enforcement of the law. If a state can demonstrate that it has an equally stringent set of laws and regulations, and that it has the capability, it may apply for and receive primacy, which means it has the primary role in implementing and enforcing the law within its boundary, with the federal agency providing oversight of the program.

The surface mining law also requires that the public be notified (through the newspaper) when the company applies for a permit; prior to blasting; and prior to the state or federal government releasing the bond. Any home-owner within a half mile radius of the permit area has the right to request a pre-blast survey from the company prior to the blasting operations. This is to establish a record of the condition of the property, so that if someone's house is damaged by the blasting activity, it can be more easily proven, and the company can be required to pay for the damage. In addition, the public can submit written comments, or request a permit conference on permit applications, and may comment or object to bond releases.

The surface mining law also provides that individuals or companies that are in violation of the law at any site should not be allowed to get a permit on any other site until the violations are cleared up. It also contains a provision allowing people to petition for lands to be declared unsuitable for mining, based on environmental, historical, or land-use reasons. The permit also provides that money be made available to reclaim abandoned mine lands, and to respond to emergencies caused by abandoned mine sites.

Safe Drinking Water Act

In 1974 Congress passed the Safe Drinking Water Act to protect drinking water. This Act requires EPA to set, and public drinking water supplies to meet, regulations concerning Maximum Contaminant Levels (MCLs) of a number of pollutants. The Act also requires public water supplies to meet certain treatment requirements such as filtration.

The law requires drinking water supplies to test and control a number of potential contaminants (Appendix D). These contaminants include toxic organic chemicals, pesticides, metals, and some compounds that are created in the purification process itself. It should be noted that these standards are based on health risk assessments and the feasibility of attaining those standards, including cost and treatment technology considerations. This means that exemptions for meeting the standard can be allowed. Currently, a set of primary standards and a set of contaminants are being reviewed for inclusion in the regulations.

Another part of the law seeks to protect groundwater by controlling the underground injection of wastes. Underground injectors must obtain a permit and cannot cause MCLs to be exceeded in the groundwater. They must also add monitoring wells at these sites to watch for contamination.

The law also calls for state wellhead protection programs. A wellhead protection program should protect the surface and subsurface area that, if contaminated, could pollute a water well, spring, or well field supplying a public water supply.

F_{ORMS}

EPA Form R (Part II. Chemical-specific information) / pages 293-294

Form R is actually nine pages. The two example pages included here show the identification of a chemical used by a company and where it goes. Other sheets include company and other information.

MSDS Safety Sheets / pages 295-296

MSDS or Material Safety Data Sheets are available to employees upon request and give information about the hazards of a chemical.

EPA FORM R

⊕EPA United States Environmental Protection Agency	**EPA FORM R** **PART II. CHEMICAL-SPECIFIC INFORMATION**	TRI FACILITY ID NUMBER
		Toxic Chemical, Category, or Generic Name Acetoue

SECTION 1. TOXIC CHEMICAL IDENTITY   (Important: DO NOT complete this section if you complete Section 2 below.)

1.1	CAS Number (Important: Enter only one number exactly as it appears on the Section 313 list. Enter category code if reporting a chemical category.) 67-64-1
1.2	Toxic Chemical or Chemical Category Name (Important: Enter only one name exactly as it appears on the Section 313 list.) Acetoue
1.3	Generic Chemical Name (Important: Complete only if Part I, Section 2.1 is checked "yes." Generic Name must be structurally descriptive.)

SECTION 2. MIXTURE COMPONENT IDENTITY   (Important: DO NOT complete this section if you complete Section 1 above.)

2.1	Generic Chemical Name Provided by Supplier (Important: Maximum of 70 characters, including numbers, letters, spaces, and punctuation.)

SECTION 3. ACTIVITIES AND USES OF THE TOXIC CHEMICAL AT THE FACILITY
(Important: Check all that apply.)

3.1	Manufacture the toxic chemical:	a. ☐ Produce b. ☐ Import	If produce or import: c. ☐ For on-site use/processing d. ☐ For sale/distribution e. ☐ As a byproduct f. ☐ As an impurity
3.2	Process the toxic chemical:	a. ☐ As a reactant b. ☐ As a formulation component	c. ☐ As an article component d. ☐ Repackaging
3.3	Otherwise use the toxic chemical:	a. ☒ As a chemical processing aid b. ☐ As a manufacturing aid	c. ☐ Ancillary or other use

---

SECTION 4. MAXIMUM AMOUNT OF THE TOXIC CHEMICAL ON-SITE AT ANY TIME DURING THE CALENDAR YEAR

4.1	04	(Enter two-digit code from instruction package.)	

EPA Form 9350-1(Rev. 12/4/93) - Previous editions are obsolete.

⊕EPA
United States
Environmental Protection
Agency

EPA FORM R

PART II. CHEMICAL-SPECIFIC INFORMATION (CONTINUED)

TRI FACILITY ID NUMBER

Chemical, Category, or Generic Name

ACETONE

SECTION 8. SOURCE REDUCTION AND RECYCLING ACTIVITIES

All quantity estimates can be reported using up to two significant figures.		Column A 1992 (pounds/year)	Column B 1993 (pounds/year)	Column C 1994 (pounds/year)	Column D 1995 (pounds/year)
8.1	Quantity released *	5320	5680	6250	6900
8.2	Quantity used for energy recovery on-site	0	0	0	0
8.3	Quantity used for energy recovery off-site	4400	23200	22000	23000
8.4	Quantity recycled on-site	4500	3090	3350	3690
8.5	Quantity recycled off-site	0	0	0	0
8.6	Quantity treated on-site	76300	110600	122000	134000
8.7	Quantity treated off-site	10	22	24	26
8.8	Quantity released to the environment as a result of remedial actions, catastrophic events, or one-time events not associated with production processes (pounds/year)		162		
8.9	Production ratio or activity index		1.04		

8.10	Did your facility engage in any source reduction activities for this chemical during the reporting year? If not, enter "NA" in Section 8.10.1 and answer Section 8.11.				
	Source Reduction Activities [enter code(s)]	Methods to Identify Activity (enter codes)			
8.10.1	NA	a.	b.	c.	
8.10.2		a.	b.	c.	
8.10.3		a.	b.	c.	
8.10.4		a.	b.	c.	

8.11	Is additional optional information on source reduction, recycling, or pollution control activities included with this report? (Check one box)	YES ☐ NO ☒

* Report releases pursuant to EPCRA Section 329(8) including "any spilling, leaking, pumping, pouring, emitting, emptying, discharging, injecting, escaping, leaching, dumping, or disposing into the environment." Do not include any quantity treated on-site or off-site.

MSDS Safety Sheet

Material Safety Data Sheet
May be used to comply with
OSHA's Hazard Communication Standard,
29 CFR 1910.1200. Standard must be
consulted for specific requirements.

U.S. Department of Labor
Occupational Safety and Health Administration
(Non-Mandatory Form)
 Form Approved
 OMB No. 1218-0072

IDENTITY *(As Used on Label and List)*

Note: *Blank spaces are not permitted. If any item is not applicable, or no information is available, the space must be marked to indicate that.*

Section I

Manufacturer's Name	Emergency Telephone Number
Address *(Number, Street, City, State, and ZIP Code)*	Telephone Number for Information
	Date Prepared
	Signature of Preparer *(optional)*

Section II — Hazardous Ingredients/Identity Information

Hazardous Components (Specific Chemical Identity; Common Name(s))	OSHA PEL	ACGIH TLV	Other Limits Recommended	% *(optional)*

Section III — Physical/Chemical Characteristics

Boiling Point		Specific Gravity (H$_2$O = 1)	
Vapor Pressure (mm Hg.)		Melting Point	
Vapor Density (AIR = 1)		Evaporation Rate (Butyl Acetate = 1)	

Solubility in Water

Appearance and Odor

Section IV — Fire and Explosion Hazard Data

Flash Point (Method Used)		Flammable Limits	LFL	UFL

Extinguishing Media

Special Fire Fighting Procedures

Unusual Fire and Explosion Hazards

(Reproduce locally)

OSHA 174, Sept. 1985

Section V — Reactivity Data

Stability	Unstable		Conditions to Avoid
	Stable		

Incompatibility (*Materials to Avoid*)

Hazardous Decomposition or Byproducts

Hazardous Polymerization	May Occur		Conditions to Avoid
	Will Not Occur		

Section VI — Health Hazard Data

Route(s) of Entry: Inhalation?   Skin?   Ingestion?

Health Hazards (*Acute and Chronic*)

Carcinogenicity: NTP?   IARC Monographs?   OSHA Regulated?

Signs and Symptoms of Exposure

Medical Conditions
Generally Aggravated by Exposure

Emergency and First Aid Procedures

Section VII — Precautions for Safe Handling and Use

Steps to Be Taken in Case Material Is Released or Spilled

Waste Disposal Method

Precautions to Be Taken in Handling and Storing

Other Precautions

Section VIII — Control Measures

Respiratory Protection (*Specify Type*)

Ventilation	Local Exhaust		Special
	Mechanical (*General*)		Other

Protective Gloves		Eye Protection

Other Protective Clothing or Equipment

Work/Hygienic Practices

☆ U.S.G.P.O.: 1986-491-529/45775

G SIC CODES

Standard Industrial Classification Codes 20-39 / pages 298-302

20 Food and Kindred Products

2011 Meat packing plants
2013 Sausages and other prepared meat products
2016 Poultry dressing plants
2017 Poultry and egg processing
2021 Creamery butter
2022 Cheese, natural and processed
2023 Condensed and evaporated milk
2024 Ice cream and frozen desserts
2026 Fluid milk
2032 Canned specialties
2033 Canned fruits vegetables, preserves, jams and jellies
2034. Dried and dehydrated fruits, vegetables, and soup mixes
2035 Pickled fruit and vegetables, vegetable sauces and seasonings, and salad dressings
2037 Froren fruits, fruit juices and vegetables
2038 Frozen specialties
2041 Flour and other grain mill products
2043 Cereal breakfast foods
2044 Rice milling
2045 Blended and prepared flour
2046 Wet corn milling
2047 Dog, cat and other pet food
2048 Prepared feeds and feed ingredients for animals and fowls, n.e.c.*
2051 Bread and other bakery products, except cookies and crackers
2052 Cookies and crackers
2061 Cane sugar, except refining only
2062 Cane sugar refining
2063 Beet sugar
2065 Candy and other confectionery products
2066 Chocolate and cocoa products
2067 Chewing gum
2074 Cottonseed oil mills
2075 Soybean oil mills
2076 Vegetable oil mills, except corn, cottonseed, and soybean
2077 Animal and marine fats and oils
2079 Shortening, table oils, margarine and other edible fats and oils, n.e.c.*
2082 Malt beverages
2083 Malt
2084 Wines, brandy, and brandy spirits
2085 Distilled, rectified, and blended liquors
2086 Bottled and canned soft drinks and carbonated waters
2087 Flavoring extracts and flavoring syrups, n.e.c.*
2091 Canned and cured fish and seafoods
2092 Fresh or frozen packaged fish and seafoods
2095 Roasted coffee
2097 Manufactured ice
2098 Macaroni, spaghetti, vermicelli and noodles
2099 Food preparations, n.e.c.*

21 Tobacco Manufacturers

2111 Cigarettes
2121 Cigars
2131 Tobacco (chewing and smoking) and snuff
2141 Tobacco stemming and redrying

22 Textile Mill Products

2211 Broad woven fabric mills, cotton
2221 Broad woven fabric mills, man-made fiber and silk
2231 Broad woven fabric mills, wool (including dyeing and finishing)
2241 Narrow fabrics and other smallwares mills: cotton, wool, silk, and man-made
2251 Women's full length and knee length hosiery
2252 Hosiery, except women's full length and knee length hosiery
2253 Knit outerwear mills
2254 Knit underwear mills
2257 Circular knit fabric mills
2258 Wrap knit fabric mills
2259 Knitting mills, n.e.c.*
2261 Finishers of broad woven fabrics of cotton
2262 Finishers of broad woven fabrics of man-made fiber and silk
2269 Finishers of textiles, n.e.c.*
2271 Woven carpets and rugs
2272 Tufted carpets and rugs
2279 Carpets and rugs, n.e.c.*
2281 Yarn spinning mills; cotton, man-made fibers and silks
2282 Yarn texturizing, throwing, twisting, and winding mills; cotton, man-made fibers and silk
2283 Yarn mills, wool, including carpet and rug yarn
2284 Thread mills
2291 Felt goods, except woven felts and hats
2292 Lace goods
2293 Paddings and upholstery filling
2294 Processed waste and recovered fibers and flock
2295 Coated fabrics, not rubberized
2296 Tire cord and fabric
2297 Nonwoven fabrics
2298 Cordage and twine
2299 Textile goods, n.e.c.*

23 Apparel and Other Finished Products made from Fabrics and Other Similar Materials

2311 Men's, youth's, and boys' suits, coats and overcoats
2321 Men's, and boys' shirts (except work shirts), and nightwear
2322 Men's, youth's, and boys' underwear
2323 Men's, youth's, and boys' neckwear
2327 Men's, youth's, and boys' separate trousers
2328 Men's, youth's, and boys' work clothing
2329 Men's, youth's, and boys' clothing, n.e.c.*
2331 Women's, misses', and juniors' blouses, waists, and shirts
2335 Women's, misses', and juniors' dresses
2337 Women's, misses', and juniors' suits, skirts, and coats
2339 Women's, misses', and juniors', outerwear, n.e.c.*
2341 Women's, misses', children's, underwear and nightwear

2342 Corsets and allied garments
2351 Millinery
2352 Hats and caps, except millinery
2361 Girls', children's and infants' dresses, blouses, waists and shirts
2363 Girls', children's and infants' coats and suits
2369 Girls', children's and infants' outerwear, n.e.c.*
2371 Fur goods
2381 Dress and work gloves, except knit and all leather
2584 Robes and dressing gowns
2385 Raincoats and other waterproof outer garments
2386 Leather and sheep lined clothing
2387 Apparel belts
2389 Apparel and accessories, n.e.c,*
2391 Curtains and draperies
2392 Housefurnishings, except curtains and draperies
2393 Textile bags
2394 Canvas and related products
2395 Pleating, decorative and novelty stitching, and tucking for the trade
2396 Automotive trimmings, apparel findings, and related products
2397 Schiffli machine embroideries
2399 Fabricated textile products, n.e.c.*

24 Lumber and Wood Products, Except Furniture

2411 Logging camps and logging contractors
2421 Sawmills and planing mills, general
2426 Hardwood dimension and flooring mills
2429 Special products sawmills, n.e.c.*
2431 Millwork
2434 Wood kitchen cabinets
2435 Hardwood veneer and plywood
2436 Softwood veneer and plywood
2439 Structural wood members, n.e.c.*
2441 Nailed and lock corner wood boxes and shook
2448 Wood pallets and skids
2449 Wood containers, n.e.c.*
2451 Mobile homes
2452 Prefabricated wood buildings and components
2491 Wood preserving
2492 Particleboard
2499 Wood products, n.e.c.*

25 Furniture and Fixtures

2511 Wood household furniture, except upholstered
2512 Wood household furniture, upholstered
2514 Metal household furniture
2515 Mattresses and bedsprings
2517 Wood television, radio, phonograph, and sewing machine cabinets
2519 Household furniture, n.e.c.*
2521 Wood office furniture
2522 Metal office furniture
2531 Public building and related furniture
2541 Wood partitions, shelving, lockers, and office and store fixtures

2542 Metal partitions, shelving, lockers and office and store fixtures
2591 Drapery hardware and window blinds and shades
2599 Furniture and fixtures, n.e.c.*

26 Paper and Allied Products

2611 Pulp mills
2621 Paper mills, except building paper mills
2631 Paperboard mills
2641 Paper coating and glazing
2642 Envelopes
2643 Bags, except textile bags
2645 Die cut paper and paperboard and cardboard
2646 Pressed and molded pulp goods
2647 Sanitary paper products
2648 Stationery, tablets and related products
2649 Converted paper and paperboard products, n.e.c.*
2651 Folding paperboard boxes
2652 Set-up paperboard boxes
2653 Corrugated and solid fiber boxes
2654 Sanitary food containers
2655 Fiber cans, tubes, drums, and similar products
2661 Building paper and building board mills

27 Printing, Publishing, and Allied Industries

2711 Newspapers: publishing, publishing and printing
2721 Periodicals: publishing, publishing and printing
2731 Books: publishing, publishing and printing
2732 Book printing
2741 Miscellaneous publishing
2751 Commercial printing, letterpress, and screen
2752 Commercial printing, lithographic
2753 Engraving and plate printing
2754 Commercial printing, gravure
2761 Manifold business forms
2771 Greeting card publishing
2782 Blankbooks, looseleaf binders and devices
2789 Bookbinding and related work
2791 Typesetting
2793 Photoengraving
2794 Electrotyping and stereotyping
2795 Lithographic plate making and related services

28 Chemicals and Allied Products

2812 Alkalies and chlorine
2813 Industrial gases
2816 Inorganic pigments
2819 Industrial inorganic chemicals, n.e.c.*
2821 Plastics materials, synthetic resins, and non-vulcanizable elastomers
2822 Synthetic rubber (vulcanizable elastomers)
2823 Cellulosic man-made fibers
2824 Synthetic organic fibers, except cellulosic
2831 Biological products
2833 Medicinal chemicals and botanical products
2834 Pharmaceutical preparations
2841 Soap and other detergents except specialty cleaners

2842 Specialty cleaning, polishing, and sanitation preparations
2843 Surface active agents, finishing agents, sulfonated oils and assistants
2844 Perfumes, cosmetics, and other toilet preparations
2851 Paints, varnishes, lacquers, enamels, and allied products
2861 Gum and wood chemicals
2865 Cyclic (coal tar) crudes, and cyclic intermediates, dyes, and organic pigments (lakes and toners)
2869 Industrial organic chemicals, n.e.c.*
2873 Nitrogenous fertilizers
2874 Phosphatic fertilizers
2875 Fertilizers, mixing only
2879 Pesticides, and agricultural chemicals, n.e.c.*
2891 Adhesives and sealants
2892 Explosives
2893 Printing ink
2895 Carbon black
2899 Chemical and chemical preparations, n.e.c.*

29 Petroleum Refining and Related Industries
2911 Petroleum refining
2951 Paving mixtures and blocks
2952 Asphalt felts and coatings
2992 Lubricating oils and greases
2999 Products of petroleum and coal, n.e.c.*

30 Rubber and Miscellaneous Plastics Products
3011 Tires and inner tubes
3021 Rubber and plastic footwear
3031 Reclaimed rubber
3041 Rubber and plastic hose and belting
3069 Fabricated rubber products, n.e.c.*
3079 Miscellaneous plastics products

31 Leather and Leather Products
3111 Leather tanning and finishing
3131 Boot and shoe cut stock and findings
3142 House slippers
3143 Men's footwear, except athletic
3144 Women's footwear, except athletic
3149 Footwear, except rubber, n.e.c.*
3151 Leather gloves and mittens
3161 Luggage
3171 Women's handbags and purses
3172 Personal leather goods, except women's handbags and purses
3199 Leather goods, n.e.c.*

32 Stone, Clay, Glass and Concrete Products
3211 Flat glass
3221 Glass containers
3229 Pressed and blown glass and glassware, n.e.c.*
3231 Glass products, made of purchased glass
3241 Cement, hydraulic
3251 Brick and structural clay tile
3253 Ceramic wall and floor tile
3255 Clay refractories
3259 Structural clay products, n.e.c.*
3261 Vitreous china plumbing fuctures and china and earthenware fittings and bathroom accessories
3262 Vitreous china table and kitchen articles
3263 Fine earthenware (whitewear) table and kitchen articles
3264 Porcelain electrical supplies
3269 Pottery products, n.e.c.*
3271 Concrete block and brick
3272 Concrete products, except block and brick
3.273 Ready mixed concrete
3274 Lime
3275 Gypsum products
3281 Cut stone and stone products
3291 Abrasive products
3292 Asbestos products
3293 Gaskets, packing and sealing devices
3295 Minerals and earths, ground or otherwise treated
3296 Mineral wool
3297 Nonclay refractories
3299 Nonmetallic mineral products, n.e.c.*

33 Primary Metal Industries
3312 Blast furnaces (including coke ovens), steel works, and rolling mills
3313 Electrometallurgical products
3315 Steel wire drawing and steel nails and spikes
3316 Cold rolled steel sheet, strip and bars
3317 Steel pipe and tubes
3321 Gray iron foundries
3322 Malleable iron foundries
3324 Steel investment foundries
3325 Steel foundries, n.e.c.*
3331 Primary smelting and refining of copper
3332 Primary smelting and refining of lead
3333 Primary smelting and refining of zinc
3334 Primary production of aluminum
3339 Primary smelting and refining of nonferrous metals, n.e.c.*
3341 Secondary smelting and refining of nonferrous metals
3351 Rolling, drawing, and extruding of copper
3353 Aluminum sheet, plate, and foil
3354 Aluminum extruded products
3355 Aluminum rolling and drawing, n.e.c.*
3356 Rolling, drawing, and extruding of nonferrous metals, except copper and aluminum
3357 Drawing and insulating of nonferrous wire
3361 Aluminum foundries (castings)
3362 Brass, bronze, copper, copper base alloy foundries (castings)
3369 Nonferrous foundries (castings), n.e.c.*
3398 Metal heat treating
3399 Primary metal products, n.e.c.*

34 Fabricated Metal Products, except Machinery and Transportation Equipment

3411 Metal cans
3412 Metal shipping barrels, drums, kegs, pails
3421 Cutlery
3423 Hand and edge tools, except machine tools and hand saws
3425 Hand saws and saw blades
3429 Hardware, n.e.c.*
3431 Enameled iron and metal sanitary ware
3432 Plumbing fixture fittings and trim (brass goods)
3433 Heating equipment, except electric and warm air furnaces
3441 Fabricated structural metal
3442 Metal doors, sash, frames, molding and trim
3443 Fabricated plate work (boiler shops)
3444 Sheet metal work
3446 Architectural and ornamental metal work
3448 Prefabricated metal buildings and components
3449 Miscellaneous metal work
3451 Screw machine products
3452 Bolts, nuts, screws, rivets and washers
3462 Iron and steel forgings
3463 Nonferrous forgings
3465 Automotive stampings
3468 Crowns and closures
3469 Metal stampings, n.e.c.*
3471 Electroplating, plating, polishing, anodizing and coloring
3479 Coating, engraving and allied services, n.e.c.*
3482 Small arms ammunition
3483 Ammunition, except for small arms, n.e.c.*
3484 Small arms
3489 Ordnance and accessories, n.e.c.*
3493 Steel springs, except wire
3494 Valves and pipe fittings, except plumbers' brass goods
3495 Wire springs
3496 Miscellaneous fabricated wire products
3497 Metal foil and leaf
3498 Fabricated pipe and fabricated pipe fittings
3499 Fabricated metal products, n.e.c.*

35 Machinery, except Electrical

3511 Steam, gas and hydraulic turbines and turbine generator set units
3519 Internal combustion engines, n.e.c.*
3523 Farm machinery and equipment
3524 Garden tractors and lawn and garden equipment
3531 Construction machinery and equipment
3532 Mining machinery and equipment, except oil field machinery and equipment
3533 Oil field machinery and equipment
3534 Elevators and moving stairways
3535 Conveyors and conveying equipment
3536 Hoists, industrial cranes and monorail systems
3537 Industrial trucks, tractors, trailers and stackers
3541 Machine tools, metal cutting types
3542 Machine tools, metal forming types
3544 Special dies and tools, die sets, jigs and fixtures and industrial molds
3545 Machine tool accessories and measuring devices
3546 Power driven hand tools
3547 Rolling mill machinery and equipment
3549 Metalworking machinery, n.e.c.*
3551 Food products machinery
3552 Textile machinery
3553 Woodworking machinery
3554 Paper industries machinery
3555 Printing trades machinery and equipment
3559 Special industry machinery, n.e.c.*
3561 Pumps and pumping equipment
3562 Ball and roller bearings
3563 Air and gas compressors
3564 Blowers and exhaust and ventilation fans
3565 Industrial patterns
3566 Speed changers, industrial high speed drives and gears
3567 Industrial process furnaces and ovens
3568 Mechanical power transmission equipment, n.e.c.*
3569 General industrial machinery and equipment, n.e.c.*
3572 Typewriters
3573 Electronic computing equipment
3574 Calculating and accounting machines, except electronic computing equipment
3576 Scales and balances, except laboratory
3579 Office machines, n.e.c.*
3581 Automatic merchandising machines
3582 Commercial laundry, dry cleaning and pressing machines
3585 Air conditioning and warm air heating equipment and commercial and industrial refrigeration equipment
3586 Measuring and dispensing pumps
3589 Service industry machines, n.e.c.*
3592 Carburetors, pistons piston rings and valves
3599 Machinery, except electrical, n.e.c.*

36 Electrical and Electronic Machinery Equipment and Supplies

3612 Power, distribution and specialty transformers
3613 Switchgear and switchboard apparatus
3621 Motor and generators
3622 Industrial controls
3623 Welding apparatus, electric
3624 Carbon and graphite products
3629 Electrical industrial appliances, n.e.c.*
3631 Household cooking equipment
3632 Household refrigerators and home and farm freezers
3633 Household laundry equipment
3634 Electrical housewares and fans
3635 Household vacuum cleaners
3636 Sewing machines
3639 Household appliances, n.e.c.*
3641 Electric lamps
3643 Current carrying wiring devices
3644 Noncurrent carrying wiring devices
3645 Residential electric lighting fixtures

3646 Commercial, industrial and institutional electric lighting fixtures
3647 Vehicular lighting equipment
3648 Lighting equipment, n.e.c.*
3651 Radio and television receiving sets, except communication types
3652 Phonograph records and pre-recorded magnetic tape
3661 Telephone and telegraph apparatus
3662 Radio and television transmitting, signaling and detection equipment and apparatus
3671 Radio and television receiving type electron tubes, except cathode ray
3672 Cathode ray television picture tubes
3673 Transmitting, industrial and special purpose electron tubes
3674 Semiconductors and related devices
3675 Electronic capacitors
3676 Resistors, for electronic applications
3677 Electronic coils, transformers and other inductors
3678 Connectors, for electronic applications
3679 Electronic components, n.e.c.*
3691 Storage batteries
3692 Primary batteries, dry and wet
3693 Radiographic X-ray, fluoroscopic X-ray, therapeutic X-ray and other X-ray apparatus and tubes; electromedical and electrotherapeutic apparatus
3694 Electric equipment for internal combustion engines
3699 Electric machinery, equipment and supplies, n.e.c.*

37 Transportation Equipment
3711 Motor vehicles and passenger car bodies
3713 Truck and bus bodies
3714 Motor vehicle parts and accessories
3715 Truck trailers
3716 Motor homes
3721 Aircraft
3724 Aircraft engines and engine parts
3728 Aircraft parts and auxiliary equipment, n.e.c.*
3731 Ship building and repairing
3732 Boat building and repairing
3743 Railroad equipment
3751 Motorcycles, bicycles and parts
3761 Guided missiles and space vehicles
3764 Guided missile and space vehicle propulsion units and propulsion unit parts
3769 Guided missile and space vehicle parts and. auxiliary equipment, n.e.c.*
3792 Travel trailers and campers
3796 Tanks and tank components
3799 Transportation equipment, n.e.c.*

38 Measuring, Analyzing and Controlling Instruments: Photographic, Medical and Optical Goods Watches and Clocks
3811 Engineering, laboratory, scientific and research instruments and associated equipment
3822 Automatic controls for regulating residential and commercial environments and appliances

3823 Industrial instruments for measurement, display and control of process variables; and related products
3824 Totalizing fluid meters and counting devices
3825 Instruments for measuring and testing of electricity and electrical signals
3829 Measuring and controlling devices, n.e.c.*
3832 Optical instruments and lenses
3841 Surgical and medical instruments and apparatus
3842 Orthopedic, prosthetic and surgical appliances and supplies
3843 Dental equipment and supplies
3851 Ophthalmic goods
3861 Photographic equipment and supplies
3873 Watches, clocks, clockwork, operated devices and parts

39 Miscellaneous Manufacturing Industries
3911 Jewelry, precious metal
3914 Silverware, platedware and stainless steelware
3915 Jewelers' findings and materials and lapidary work
3931 Musical instruments
3942 Dolls
3944 Games, toys and children's vehicles; except dolls and bicycles
3949 Sporting and athletic goods, n.e.c.*
3951 Pens, mechanical pencils and parts
3952 Lead pencils, crayons and artists' materials
3953 Marking devices
3955 Carbon paper and inked ribbons
3961 Costume jewelry and costume novelties, except precious metal
3962 Feathers, plumes and artificial trees and flowers
3963 Buttons
3964 Needles, pins, hooks and eyes and similar notions
3991 Brooms and brushes
3993 Signs and advertising displays
3995 Burial caskets
3996 Linoleum, asphalted-felt-base and other hard surface floor coverings, n.e.c.*
3999 Manufacturing industries, n.e.c.*

*"Not elsewhere classified" indicated by "n.e.c."

APPENDIX H LISTS OF REGULATED CHEMICALS

TCLP List
(toxicity characteristic leach procedure)

HWNO[1]	Constituents	CASNO[2]	Regulatory Level (mg/L)
D016	Acrylonitrile	107-13-1	5.0
D004	Arsenic	7440-38-2	5.0
D005	Barium	7440-39-3	100.0
D019	Benzene	71-43-2	0.07
D020	Bis(2-chloroethyl) ether	111-44-4	0.05
D006	Cadmium	7440-43-9	1.0
D021	Carbon disulfide	75-15-0	14.4
D022	Carbon tetrachloride	58-23-5	0.07
D023	Chlordane	54-74-9	0.03
D024	Chlorobenzene	108-90-7	1.4
D025	Chloroform	67-66-3	0.07
D007	Chromium	1333-82-0	5.0
D026	o-Cresol	95-46-7	10.0
D027	m-Cresol	106-39-4	10.0
D028	p-Cresol	106-44-5	10.0
D016	2,4-D	94-75-7	1.4
D029	1,2-Dichlorobenzene	96-50-1	4.3
D030	1,4-Dichlorobenzene	106-46-7	10.8
D031	1,2-Dichloroethane	107-08-2	0.40
D032	1,1-Dichloroethylene	75-35-4	0.1
D033	2,4-Dinitrotoluene	121-14-2	0.13
D012	Endrin	72-20-8	0.003
D034	Heptachlor (and its hydroxide)	76-44-2	0.001
D035	Hexachlorobenzene	118-74-1	0.13
D036	Hexachlorobutadiene	87-68-3	0.72
D037	Hexachloroethane	67-72-1	4.3
D038	Isobutanol	78-83-1	36.0
D008	Lead	7439-92-1	5.0
D013	Lindane	58-89-9	0.06
D009	Mercury	7439-97-6	0.2
D014	Methoxychlor	72-43-5	1.4
D039	Methylene chloride	75-09-2	8.6
D040	Methly ethyl ketone	78-93-3	7.2
D041	Nitrobenzene	96-95-3	0.13
D042	Pentachlorophenol	87-86-5	3.6
D043	Phenol	106-95-2	14.4
D044	Pyridine	110-86-1	5.0
D010	Selenium	7782-49-2	1.0
D011	Silver	7440-22-4	5.0
D045	1,1,2,2-Tetrachloroethane	630-20-6	10.0
D046	1,1,2,2-Tetrachloroethane	79-34-5	1.3
D047	Tetrachloroethylene	127-18-4	0.1
D048	2,3,4,6-Tetrachlorophenol	58-90-2	1.5
D049	Toluene	106-88-3	14.4
D015	Toxaphene	8001-35-2	0.07
D050	1,1,1-Trichloroethane	71-55-6	30.0
D051	1,1,2-Trichloroethane	79-00-5	1.2
D052	Trichloroethylene	79-01-6	0.07
D053	2,4,5-Trichlorophenol	95-95-4	5.8
D054	2,4,6-Trichlorophenol	88-06-2	0.30
D017	2,4,5-TP (Silvex)	93-76-5	0.14
D066	Vinyl chloride	75-01-4	0.05

[1] EPA Hazardous Waste Code number
[2] Chemical Abstracts Service (CAS) number

Federal Ambient Water Quality Criteria

Chemical Name	Maximum Allowable Level(µg/l)	Basis for Concern
Acenaphthene	20	taste & odor
Acrolein	320	toxic effects
Acrylonitrile	0.058	carcinogen
Aldrin/Dieldrin	0.000074	carcinogen
Antimony	146	toxic effects
Arsenic	.0022	carcinogen
Asbestos	30,000 fibers/l	carcinogen
Benzene	0.66	carcinogen
Benzidine	0.00012	carcinogen
Beryllium	0.0068	carcinogen
bis (2-chloro isopropyl)ether	34.7	toxic effects
bis (chloromethyl) ether	.0000004	carcinogen
bis (2-chlorethyl) ether	0.03	carcinogen
Cadmium	10	toxic effects
Carbon Tetrachloride	0.40	carcinogen
Chlordane	0.00046	carcinogen
Chlorinated naphthalenes	None	
Chlorobenzene	None	
Chloroform	0.19	carcinogen
2-Chlorophenol	0 1	taste & odor
3-Chlorophenol	0.1	taste & odor
4-Chlorophenol	0.1	taste & odor
Chromium III	170	toxic effects
Chromium IV	50	toxic effects
Copper	1000	taste & odor
Cyanides	200	toxic effects
DDT	0.000024	carcinogen
Dichlorobenzenes[a]	400	toxic effects
Dichlorobenzidine	0.0	carcinogen
1,1 dichloroethane	None	
1,2 dichloroethane	0.94	carcinogen
1,1-dichloroethylene	0.033	carcinogen
1,2-dichloroethylene	None	
2,3-dichlorophenol	0.04	taste & odor
2,4-dichlorophenol	3090	toxic effects
	0.3	taste & odor
2,5-dichlorophenol	0.5	taste & odor
2,6-dichlorophenol	0.2	taste & odor
3,4-dichlorophenol	0.3	taste & odor
Dichloropropanes	NA	
Dichloropropenes	87	toxic effects
2,4-dimethylphenol	400	taste & odor
Dibutyl phthalate	34,000	taste & odor
Di-2-ethylhexyl phthalate	15,000	carcinogen
Diethyl phthalate	350,000	toxic effects
Dimethyl phthalate	313,000	toxic effects
2,4-dinitro-o-cresol	13.4	toxic effects
Dinitrophenols	70	toxic effects
2,4-Dinitrotoluene	0.11	carcinogen
1,2-Diphenylhydrazine	0.00042	carcinogen
Endosulphan	74	toxic effects
Endrin	1	toxic effects
Ethylbenzene	1400	toxic effects
Fluoranthene	42	toxic effects
Haloethers[b]	NA	
Halomethanes[c]	0.19	carcinogen
Heptachlor	0.00028	carcinogen
Hexachlorobenzene	0.00072	carcinogen

Chemical Name	Maximum Allowable Level(μg/l)	Basis for Concern
Hexachlorobutadiene	0.45	carcinogen
Hexachlorocyclohexane		
alpha-hexachloro-cyclohexane	0.0092	carcinogen
beta-hexachloro-cyclohexane	0.0163	carcinogen
gamma-hexachloro-cyclohexane	0.0186	carcinogen
tech-hexachloro-cyclohexane	0.0123	carcinogen
Hexachloroethane	1.9	carcinogen
Hexachlorocyclopentadiene	206	toxic effects
Isophorone	5200	toxic effects
Lead	50	toxic effects
Mercury	0.144	toxic effects
2-methyl-4-chlorophenol	1,800	taste & odor
3-methyl-4-chlorophenol	3,000	taste & odor
3-methyl-6-chlorophenol	20	taste & odor
Monochlorobenzene	488	toxic effects
	20	taste & odor
Monochloroethane	NA	
Monochlorophenols	0.1	taste & odor
Mononitrophenol	NA	
Naphthalene	NA	toxic effects
Nickel	13.4	toxic effects
Nitrobenzene	19,800	toxic effects
	30	taste & odor
N-nitrosodi-n-butylamine	0.0064	carcinogen
N-nitrosodiethylamine	0.0008	carcinogen
N-nitrosodimethylamine	0.0014	carcinogen
N-nitrosodiphenylamine	4.9	carcinogen
N-nitrosopyrrolidine	0.016	carcinogen
Pentachloroethane	NA	
Pentachlorobenzene	74	toxic effects
Pentachlorophenol	1010	toxic effects
	30	taste & odor
Phenol	3500	toxic effects
Polychlorinated biphenyls	0.000079	carcinogen
Polynuclear aromatic hydro-carbons	0.0028	carcinogen
Selenium	10	toxic effects
Silver	50	toxic effects
1,2,4,5-tetrachlorobenzene	38	toxic effects
1,1,1,2-tetrachloroethane	NA	
1,1,2,2,-tetrachloroethane	0.17	carcinogen
Tetrachloroethylene	0.80	carcinogen
2,3,4,6-tetrachlorophenol	1	taste & odor
Thallium	13	toxic effects
Toluene	14,300	toxic effects
Toxaphene	.00071	carcinogen
Trichlorobenzene	NA	
1,1,1-trichloroethane	18,400	toxic effects
1,1,2-trichloroethane	0.6	carcinogen
Trichloroethylene	2.7	carcinogen
2,4,5-trichlorophenol	2,600	toxicity
	1.0	taste & odor
2,4,6-trichlorophenol	1.2	carcinogen
Trinitrophenols	NA	
Vinyl chloride	2.0	carcinogen
Zinc	5000	toxic effects

ª Includes any combination of 1,2-dichloro; 1,3-dichloro; and 1,4-dichlorobenzene.

ᵇ Includes any combination of chlorophenyl phenyl ethers; bromophenyl ethers; and polychlorinated diphenyl ethers.

ᶜIncludes any combination of chloromethane, bromoethane, methylene chloride, bromoform, bromodischloromethane, trichlorofluoromethane, and dichlorodifluoromethane. *(Environmental Defense Fund)*

Threshold Limit Values (TLVs) for Chemicals in Air

Chemical Name	TLV ppm	MODIFIED TLV mg/m³	TLV* ppb	μg/m³
Acctaldehyde	100	180	238	428
Acetone	1000	2400	2380	5714
Acrolein	0.1	0.25	0.2	0.6
Aldrin	—	0.25	—	0.6
Allyl chloride	1	3	2.4	7.1
Arsenic & soluble compounds as As	—	0.2	—	0.5
Benzene	10	30	23.8	71.4
Benzyl chloride	1	5	2.4	11.9
Beryllium	—	0.002	—	0.005
Bromoform	0.5	5	1.2	11.9
Cadmium dust & salts	—	0.05	—	0.12
Carbon tetrachloride	5	30	11.9	71.4
Chlordane	—	0.5	—	1.2
Chlorinated camphene	—	0.5	—	1.2
Chlorobenzene (Monochlorobenzene)	75	350	178	833
Chloroform	10	50	23.8	119
bis-Chloromethyl ether	0.001	0.005	0.002	0.001
Chromium metal	—	0.5	—	1.2
Chromium (II) compounds, as Cr	—	0.5	—	1.2
Chromium (III) compounds, as Cr	—	0.5	—	1.2
Chromium (VI) compounds, as Cr ;	—	0.05	—	0.1
Coal tar pitch volatiles, as benzene solubles	—	0.2	—	0.5
Cresol	5	22	11.9	52.4
DDT (Dichlorodiphenyl- trichloroethane)	—	1	—	2.4
o-Dichlorobenzene	50	300	119	714
p-Dichlorobenzene	75	450	178	1.1
Dichloro- difluoromethane	1000	4950	2381	11785
1,l-Dichloroethane	200	810	476	1928
Dichloropropene	1	5	2.4	11.9
Dieldrin	—	0.25	—	0.6
Diethyl phthalate	—	5	—	11.9
1,1-Dimethylhydrazine	0.5	1	1.2	2.4
Dimethyl sulfate	0.1	0.5	0.2	1.2
Dinitrotoluene	—	1.5	—	3.6
Dioxane	25	90	59.5	214
Endosulfan	—	0.1	—	0.2

Chemical Name	TLV		TLV*	
	ppm	mg/m3	ppb	µg/m3
Endrin	—	0.1	—	0.2
Epichlorohydnn	2	10	4.8	23.8
Ethyl benzene	100	435	238	1035
Ethylene dichloride	10	40	23.8	95.2
Ethylene oxide	10	20	23.8	47.6
Ethyleneimine	0.5	1	1.2	2.4
Fluorine	1	2	2.4	4.8
Formaldehyde	2	3	2.4	7.1
Heptachlor	—	0.5	—	1.2
Hexachlorocyclo-pentadiene	0.01	0.1	0.02	0.2
Heptachloroethane	1	10	2.4	23.8
Hexane (n-hexane)	100	360	238	857
Isophorone	5	25	11.9	59.5
Lindane	—	0.5	—	1.2
Maleic anhydride	0.25	1	0.6	2.4
Manganese & compounds, as Mn	—	5	—	11.9
Methyl chloroform	350	1900	833	4524
Methylene chloride	100	360	238	857
Methyl iodide	2	10	4.8	23.8
Naphthalene	10	50	23.8	119
Nickel	—	0.1	—	0.2
Nitrobenzene	1	5	2.4	11.9
Pentachlorophenol	—	0.5	—	1.2
Perchloroethylene	100	670	238	1595
Phosgene	0.1	0.4	0.2	0.9
Propylene dichloride	75	350	178	833
Propylene oxide	20	50	47.6	119
1,1,2,2-Tetrachloroethane	5	35	11.9	83.3
Toluene	100	375	238	893
1,2,4-Trichlorobenzene	5	40	11.9	95.2
1,1,2-Trichloroethane	10	45	23.8	107
Trichloroethylene	100	535	238	1274
Trichlorofluoromethane	1000	5600	2380	13333
Vinyl chloride	5	10	—	23.8
Vinylidene chloride	10	40	23.8	95.2
Xylene	100	435	238	1036

*This value incorporates a safety factor to modify the TLV value. The safety factor was suggested for use in an EPA publication entitled Multimedia Environmental Goals for Environmental Assessment, EPA 600-7-77-136a, p. 61 The modification is necessary because TLV values were developed for 8-hour exposures, 40 hours per week, for a working population. Acceptable exposure levels must be lower for people who breathe these chemicals all day every day and for people who are young, old, or sick We suggest you compare the date in the report to these safety values instead of the TLV values. Reminder: the safety valuc number looks larger than the TLV number but really is not; the units are different. (*Environmental Defense Fund*)

Federal Drinking Water Guidelines

Chemical	Highest Safe Level (Units = μg/l)	Type of Guideline
Arsenic	50	Standard
Barium	1000	Standard
Cadmium	10	Standard
Carbofuran	5	Chronic SNARL*
Carbon Tetrachloride	20	10-day SNARL
Chlordane	8	Chronic SNARL
Chromium (Hexavalent)	50	Standard
Cis-1,2-dichloroethylene	70	Chronic SNARL
Coliform bacteria	<1/100 mL	Standard
1,1-dichloroethylene	400	10-day SNARL
Endrin	0.2	Standard
Ethylene Glycol	5500	Chronic SNARL
Lindane	4	Standard
Lead	50	Standard
Mercury	2	Standard
Methoxychlor	100	Standard
Methyl Ethyl Ketone	750	10-day SNARL
Methylene Chloride	150	Chronic SNARL
n-Hexane	4000	10-day SNARL
Nitrate	10,000	Standard
Radionuclides		
Radium 226 & 228 (total)	5 pCi/L (picocuries/liter)	Standard
Gross alpha particle activity	15 pCi/L (picocuries/liter)	Standard
Gross beta particle activity	4 millirem (calculated)	Standard
Selenium	10	Standard
Silver	50	Standard
Tetrachloroethylene	3.5	Chronic SNARL
Trans-1,2-dichloroethylene	270	10-day SNARL
Toxaphene	5	Standard
Total Trihalomethanes**	100	Standard
1,1,1 Trichloroethane	1000	Chronic SNARL
Trichloroethylene	4.5	Chronic SNARL
2,4,5-Trichlorophenoxy-Propionic acid	10	Chronic SNARL
2,4,-D	100	Standard
Xylenes	620	Chronic SNARL

*SNARLS (Suggested No Adverse Response Levels) have been developed by EPA for some chemicals without formal drinking water standards. Ten-day SNARLs are the highest levels suggested for a 10-day exposure. Chronic Snarls are the highest levels suggested for indefinite exposure. When chemicals do not have a chronic SNARL, the 10-day SNARL is reported.

**Total Trihalomethanes is the sum of the concentrations of bromodichloromethane, dibromochloromethane, bromoform, and chloroform.

APPENDIX

I CHEMICALS OF CONCERN

List of Chemicals of Concern* / pages 311-317

The following categories of potential adverse human health effects are used in the Chemicals of Concern table.

Carcinogens (C) Chemicals in this category are those that can cause cancer in humans, like benzene (which can cause leukemia), and those that are thought possibly to cause cancer in humans because they cause cancer in other animals.

Genetic and Chromosomal Mutagens (GC) These are chemicals that can cause the genes (DNA) in a sperm or an egg to be mutated or changed. Those changes can then be passed along to a baby. Changes to other cells in the body, such as cells in your liver, can also occur.

Developmental toxicity (DT) These are chemicals that affect the development of a baby inside its mother. Being exposed to such chemicals can cause miscarriages and physical defects to the baby.

Reproductive toxicity (RT) These are chemicals that can damage the ability of men and women to reproduce.

Acute Toxicity (AT) Short term exposures, either through the lungs, mouth, or skin, can cause death.

Chronic Toxicity (CT) Exposure over a long period can cause damage other than cancer, such as lung, liver, or kidney problems.

Nervous System Toxicants (N) These include chemicals such as solvents and glues that cause problems with the brain and nervous system. These effects can be either temporary or permanent.

Ecological and environmental concerns relate to how a chemical harms wildlife and plants, whether a chemical stays in the environment, and whether it accumulates in the food chain. There are three categories for the chemicals listed in the following table.

Environmental Toxicity (ET) These chemicals can harm wildlife when released to the water, air, or onto the land.

Bioaccumulative (B) This means a chemical becomes more and more concentrated in the food chain. For example, an insect will have a low level of chemical, a mouse that eats insects will have a higher level, and the hawk that eats mice will have an even higher level.

Persistent (P) This means that it is stable and does not break down very easily once it enters the environment.

*Information for this Appendix from U.S. EPA, Region IV

310

Chemicals of Concern

Chemical Abstract Service (CAS) NUMBER	CHEMICAL NAME	Human Health							Ecological			Toxicity Index Profile
		C	GC	DT	RT	AT	CT	N	ET	B	P	(TIP)
000075070	ACETALDEHYDE	X				X			X			3
000060355	ACETAMIDE	X									X	2
000067641	ACETONE						X		X		X	3
000075058	ACETONITRILE			X	X	X	X				X	5
000053963	2-ACETYLAMINOFLUORENE	X										1
000107028	ACROLEIN					X	X		X	X		4
000079061	ACRYLAMIDE	X	X		X	X	X	X	X			7
000079107	ACRYLIC ACID					X	X		X			3
000107131	ACRYLONITRILE	X		X	X	X	X		X		X	7
000309002	ALDRIN			X	X	X	X	X	X	X		7
000107186	ALLYL ALCOHOL*		X			X	X		X			4
000107051	ALLYL CHLORIDE			X		X	X	X	X			5
000134327	ALPHA-NAPHTHYLAMINE	X										1
007429905	ALUMINUM (FUME OR DUST)											
001344281	ALUMINUM OXIDE						X					1
000117793	2-AMINOANTHRAQUINONE	X					X					2
000060093	4-AMINOAZOBENZENE	X										1
000092671	4-AMINOBIPHENYL	X										1
000082280	1-AMINO-2-METHYLANTHRA-QUINONE	X										1
006484522	AMMOMIUM NITRATE (SOLUTION)						X					1
007783202	AMMOMIUM SULFATE (SOLUTION)								X			1
007664417	AMMONIA					X	X		X			3
000062533	ANILINE					X	X		X		X	4
000120127	ANTHRACENE						X		X	X	X	4
007440360	ANTIMONY				X		X			X		3
ANTIMONY	ANTIMONY COMPOUNDS				X		X			X		3
007440382	ARSENIC	X		X		X	X	X	X	X		7
ARSENIC C	ARSENIC COMPOUNDS	X		X		X	X	X	X	X		7
001332214	ASBESTOS (FRIABLE)	X					X					2
007440393	BARIUM			X			X					2
BARIUM CO	BARIUM COMPOUNDS			X			X					2
000098873	BENZAL CHLORIDE						X					1
000055210	BENZAMIDE*		X									1
000071432	BENZENE	X		X	X		X		X		X	6
000092875	BENZIDINE	X				X	X		X			4
000098077	BENZOIC TRICHLORIDE (BENZOTRICHLORI	X		X			X					3
000098884	BENZOYL CHLORIDE			X		X	X		X			4
000094360	BENZOYL PEROXIDE*						X					1
000100447	BENZYL CHLORIDE			X		X	X	X	X			5
007440417	BERYLLIUM	X				X	X					3
BERYLLIUM	BERYLLIUM COMPOUNDS	X				X	X					3
000091598	BETA-NAPHTHYLAMINE	X										1
000057578	BETA-PROPIOLACTONE	X	X			X						3
000092524	BIPHENYL			X			X		X			3
000108601	BIS(2-CHLORO-1-METHYL-ETHYL) ETHER					X	X					2
000111444	BIS(2-CHLOROETHYL) ETHER					X	X	X			X	4
000103231	BIS(2-ETHYLHEXYL) ADIPATE			X								1
000542881	BIS(CHLOROMETHYL) ETHER	X					X					2
000353593	BROMOCHLORODIFLUORO-METHANE*					X		X			X	3

Chemical Abstract Service (CAS) NUMBER	CHEMICAL NAME	Human Health							Ecological			Toxicity Index Profile (TIP)
		C	GC	DT	RT	AT	CT	N	ET	B	P	
000075252	BROMOFORM (TRIBROMO-METHANE)						X	X	X			3
000074839	BROMOMETHANE (METHYL BROMIDE)					X	X	X	X		X	5
000075638	BROMOTRIFLUOROMETHANE*					X		X			X	3
000106990	1,3-BUTADIENE	X		X	X		X	X	X			6
000141322	BUTYL ACRYLATE								X			1
000085687	BUTYL BENZYL PHTHALATE						X		X			2
000106887	1,2-BUTYLENE OXIDE*		X									1
000123728	BUTYRALDEHYDE								X			1
004680788	C.I. ACID GREEN 3											
000569642	C.I. BASIC GREEN 4					X			X			2
000989388	C.I. BASIC RED 1	X										1
016071866	C.I. DIRECT BROWN 95	X					X					2
001937377	C.I. DIRECT BLACK 38	X					X					2
002602462	C.I. DIRECT BLUE 6	X		X			X					3
002832408	C.I. DISPERSE YELLOW 3											
003761533	C.I. FOOD RED 5	X										1
000081889	C.I. FOOD RED 15	X					X					2
003118976	C.I. SOLVENT ORANGE 7*								X	X		2
000842079	C.I. SOLVENT YELLOW 14	X										1
000492808	C.I. SOLVENT YELLOW 34 (AURAMINE)	X										1
000097563	C.I. SOLVENT YELLOW 3	X									X	2
000128665	C.I. VAT YELLOW	X										1
007440439	CADMIUM	X		X	X	X	X		X	X		7
CADMIUM C	CADMIUM COMPOUNDS	X		X	X	X	X		X	X		7
000156627	CALCIUM CYANAMIDE					X	X					2
000133062	CAPTAN		X	X	X	X	X		X		X	7
000063252	CARBARYL [1-NAPHTHALENOL METHYLCARB			X	X	X	X	X	X	X	X	8
000075150	CARBON DISULFIDE			X	X		X	X	X		X	6
000056235	CARBON TETRACHLORIDE	X		X		X	X	X	X		X	7
000463581	CARBONYL SULFIDE						X					1
000120809	CATECHOL						X		X			2
000133904	CHLORAMBEN											
000057749	CHLORDANE			X	X	X	X	X		X	X	7
010049044	CHLORIDE DIOXIDE			X	X							2
CHLORINAT	CHLORINATED PHENOLS	X							X		X	3
007782505	CHLORINE					X	X		X			3
000079118	CHLOROACETIC ACID					X						1
000532274	2-CHLOROACETOPHENONE					X						1
000108907	CHLOROBENZENE				X		X		X			3
000510156	CHLOROBENZILATE				X		X		X		X	4
000075003	CHLOROETHANE (ETHYL CHLORIDE)											
000067663	CHLOROFORM	X		X	X	X	X		X		X	7
000074873	CHLOROMETHANE (METHYLCHLORIDE)			X	X		X				X	4
000107302	CHLOROMETHYL METHYL ETHER	X			X							2
CHLOROPHE	CHLOROPHENOLS	X							X		X	3
000126998	CHLOROPRENE		X	X	X	X	X	X				6
001897456	CHLOROTHALONIL						X	X	X		X	4
007440473	CHROMIUM	X				X	X		X			4
CHROMIUM	CHROMIUM COMPOUNDS	X				X	X		X			4
007440484	COBALT						X					1
COBALT CO	COBALT COMPOUNDS						X					1
007440508	COPPER			X	X				X	X		4
COPPER CO	COPPER COMPOUNDS			X	X				X	X		4

Chemical Abstract Service (CAS) NUMBER	CHEMICAL NAME	Human Health							Ecological			Toxicity Index Profile
		C	GC	DT	RT	AT	CT	N	ET	B	P	(TIP)
008001589	CREOSOTE	X		X			X		X	X	X	6
001319773	CRESOL (MIXED ISOMERS)					X	X		X			3
000098828	CUMEME					X	X		X			3
000080159	CUMEME HYDROPEROXIDES					X			X			2
000135206	CUPFERRON	X										1
CYANIDE C	CYANIDE COMPOUNDS			X		X	X	X	X			5
000110827	CYCLOHEXANE								X			1
000094757	2,4-D [ACETIC ACID,2,4, DICHLORO-PHE			X	X	X	X		X			5
001163195	DECADROMODIPHENYL OXIDE			X			X			X	X	4
000117817	DI-(2-ETHYLHEXYL) PHTHALATE (DEPH)	X	X	X	X	X	X		X	X		8
002303164	DIALLATE			X					X		X	3
000615054	2,4-DIAMINOANISOLE	X										1
039156417	2,4-DIAMINOANISOLE SULFATE	X										1
000101804	4,4-DIAMINODIPHENYL ETHER	X					X					2
000095807	2,4-DIAMINOTOLUENE	X	X									2
025376458	DIAMINOTOLUENE (MIXED ISOMERS)	X	X				X					3
000334883	DIAZOMETHANE											
000132649	DIBENZONFURAN*						X			X	X	3
000096128	1,2-DIBROMO-3-CHLORO-PROPANE (DBCP)	X		X	X	X	X		X		X	7
000106934	1,2-DIBROMOETHANE (ETHYLENE DIBROMI	X	X	X	X	X	X		X		X	8
000124732	DIBROMOTETRAFLUORO-ETHANE (HALON)*					X		X			X	3
000084742	DIBUTYL PHTHALATE			X	X		X		X	X		5
000095501	1,2-DICHLOROBENZENE					X	X		X	X		4
000541731	1,3-DICHLOROBENZENE								X			1
000106467	1,4-DICHLOROBENZENE	X					X		X	X	X	5
025321226	DICHLOROBENZENE (MIXED ISOMERS)	X					X		X	X		4
000091941	3,3-DICHLOROBENZIDINE	X										1
000075274	DICHLOROBROMOMETHANE										X	1
000075718	DICHLORODIFLUOROMETHANE*					X		X			X	3
000107062	1,2-DICHLOROETHANE (ETHYLENE DICHLO	X	X	X	X		X				X	6
000540590	1,2-DICHLOROETHYLENE*							X				1
000075092	DICHLOROMETHANE (METHYLENE CHLORIDE)	X					X				X	3
000120832	2,4-DICHLOROPHENOL								X			1
000078875	1,2-DICHLOROPROPANE								X			1
000078886	2,3-DICHLOROPROPENE*		X								X	2
000542756	1,3-DICHLOROPROPYLENE	X				X	X		X		X	5
000076142	DICHLOROTETRAFLUORO-ETHANE(CFC-114)*					X		X			X	3
000062737	DICHLORVOS			X	X	X			X		X	5
000115322	DICOFOL					X				X		2
001464535	DIEPOXYBUTANE	X	X			X						3
000111422	DIETHANOLAMINE								X			1
000084662	DIETHYL PHTHALATE								X			1
000064675	DIETHYL SULFATE	X	X									2
000119904	3,3'-DIMETHOXYBENZIDINE	X					X					2
000060117	4-DIMETHYLAMINOAZO-BENZENE	X				X	X			X		4
000119937	3,3'-DIMETHYLBENZINE (O-TOLIDINE)	X										1
000057147	1,1-DIMETHYL HYDRAZINE	X				X	X	X	X			5
000105679	2,4-DIMETHYLPHENOL								X			1

Chemical Abstract Service (CAS) NUMBER	CHEMICAL NAME	Human Health							Ecological			Toxicity Index Profile (TIP)
		C	GC	DT	RT	AT	CT	N	ET	B	P	(TIP)
000131113	DIMETHYL PHTHALATE					X			X			2
000077781	DIMETHYL SULFATE	X	X			X	X	X	X		X	7
000079447	DIMETHYLCARBAMYL CHLORIDE	X				X						2
000534521	4,6-DINITRO-O-CRESOL					X	X		X		X	4
000051285	2,4-DINITROPHENOL			X	X	X	X		X			5
000121142	2,4-DINITROTOLUENE				X		X	X	X			4
000606202	2,6-DINITROTOLUENE					X	X	X	X			4
025321146	DINITROTOLUENE (MIXED ISOMERS)				X	X	X	X	X			5
000123911	1,4-DIOXANE	X										1
000122667	1,2-DIPHENYLHYDRAZINE (HYDRAZOBENZE	X					X		X			3
000106898	EPICHLOROHYDRIN	X	X		X	X	X	X	X		X	8
000110805	2-ETHOXYETHANOL			X	X		X					3
000140885	ETHYL ACRYLATE	X		X			X		X		X	5
000541413	ETHYL CHLOROFORMATE					X						1
000100414	ETHYLBENZENE			X	X		X		X		X	5
000074851	ETHYLENE						X					1
000107211	ETHYLENE GLYCOL						X					1
000075218	ETHYLENE OXIDE	X	X	X	X	X	X	X	X		X	9
000096457	ETHYLENE THIOUREA	X	X	X	X		X			X		6
000151564	ETHYLENEIMINE (AZIRIDINE)	X	X		X	X	X		X		X	7
002164172	FLUOMETURON						X		X			2
000050000	FORMALDEHYDE	X	X			X	X	X	X			7
000076131	FREON 113						X					1
GLYCOL ET	GLYCOL ETHERS			X	X		X					3
000076448	HEPTACHLOR			X		X	X	X	X	X	X	7
000087683	HEXACHLORO-1,3-BUTADIENE			X		X	X	X	X	X	X	7
000118741	HEXACHLOROBENZENE	X		X	X	X	X	X	X	X	X	9
000077474	HEXACHLOROCYCLOPENTADIENE			X	X	X	X	X	X	X	X	8
000067721	HEXACHLOROETHANE			X	X		X		X			4
001335871	HEXACHLORONAPHTHALENE*						X		X	X	X	4
000680319	HEXAMETHYLPHOSPHORAMIDE	X	X				X					3
000302012	HYDRAZINE	X				X	X		X			4
010034932	HYDRAZINE SULFATE	X					X		X			3
007647010	HYDROCHLORIC ACID					X	X					2
000074908	HYDROGEN CYANIDE					X	X		X			3
007664393	HYDROGEN FLUORIDE			X	X	X	X	X				5
000123319	HYDROQUINONE					X	X		X			3
000078842	ISOBUTYRALDEHYDE						X					1
000067630	ISOPROPYL ALCOHOL	X					X	X				3
000080057	4,4-ISOPROPYLIDENEDIPHENOL*					X		X	X	X		4
000120581	ISOSAFROLE*	X										1
007439921	LEAD	X		X	X		X	X	X	X	X	8
LEAD COMP	LEAD COMPOUNDS	X		X	X		X	X	X	X	X	8
000058899	LINDANE	X		X	X	X	X		X	X	X	8
000108394	m-CRESOL						X		X			2
000099650	m-DINITROBENZENE*			X	X	X	X					4
000108383	m-XYLENE			X		X	X		X		X	5
000108316	MALEIC ANHYDRIDE					X	X		X			3
012427382	MANEB			X	X	X	X		X		X	6
007439965	MANGANESE				X	X	X	X			X	5
MANGANESE	MANGANESE COMPOUNDS				X	X	X	X			X	5
007439976	MERCURY			X	X	X	X	X	X	X	X	8
MERCURY C	MERCURY COMPOUNDS			X	X	X	X	X	X	X	X	8
000067561	METHANOL						X					1
000072435	METHOXYCHLOR			X	X		X		X	X	X	7
000109864	2-METHOXYETHANOL			X	X		X					3
000096333	METHYL ACRYLATE					X	X		X			3

Chemical Abstract Service (CAS) NUMBER	CHEMICAL NAME	Human Health							Ecological			Toxicity Index Profile
		C	GC	DT	RT	AT	CT	N	ET	B	P	(TIP)
000101144	4,4'-METHYLENEBIS (2-CHLORO ANALIN	X										1
000101611	4,4'-METHYLENEBIS (N,N-DIMETHYL)						X					1
000101779	4,4-METHYLENEDIANILINE	X					X					2
000078933	METHYL ETHYL KETONE			X	X		X	X			X	5
000060344	METHYL HYDRAZINE					X	X			X	X	4
000074884	METHYL IODIDE	X						X			X	3
000108101	METHYL ISOBUTYL KETONE						X	X				2
000624839	METHYL ISOCYANATE			X	X		X				X	4
000080626	METHYL METHACRYLATE			X	X		X					3
001634044	METHYL TERT-BUTYL ETHER*					X		X			X	3
000074953	METHYLENE BROMIDE							X				1
000101688	METHYLENEBIS(PHENYLISO-CYANATE)						X	X				2
000090948	MICHLER'S KETONE	X										1
001313275	MOLYBDENUM TRIOXIDE					X	X	X				3
000076153	MONOCHLOROPENTAFLUO-ROETHANE*					X		X			X	3
000505602	MUSTARD GAS	X					X					2
000071363	n-BUTYL ALCOHOL						X					1
000117840	n-DIOCTYL PHTHALATE					X	X			X		3
000088755	2-NITROPHENOL						X	X	X			3
000079469	2-NITROPROPANE	X		X	X	X	X					5
000684935	N-NITROSO-N-METHYLUREA	X	X	X		X						4
000759739	N-NITROSO-N-ETHYLUREA	X	X	X	X							4
000924163	N-NITROSODI-N-BUTYLAMINE	X										1
000621647	N-NITROSODI-N-PROPYLAMINE	X									X	2
000055185	N-NITROSODIETHYLAMINE	X	X	X	X	X						5
000062759	N-NITROSODIMETHYLAMINE	X	X			X						3
000086306	N-NITROSODIPHENYLAMINE						X		X			2
004549400	N-NITROSOMETHYLVINYLAMINE	X	X			X						3
000059892	N-NITROSOMORPHOLINE	X	X	X			X					4
016543558	N-NITROSONONICOTINE	X										1
000100754	N-NITROSOPIPERIDINE	X	X			X	X		X			5
000091203	NAPHTHALENE			X			X		X	X		4
007440020	NICKEL	X		X	X	X	X		X			6
NICKEL CO	NICKEL COMPOUNDS	X		X	X	X	X		X			6
007697372	NITRIC ACID						X					1
000139139	NITRILOTRIACETIC ACID	X					X					2
000098953	NITROBENZENE				X	X	X		X			4
000092933	4-NITROBIPHENYL	X										1
001836755	NITROFEN	X		X	X		X	X	X			6
000051752	NITROGEN MUSTARD	X	X	X	X	X						5
000099592	5-NITRO-o-ANISIDINE	X										1
000055630	NITROGLYCERIN								X			1
000100027	4-NITROPHENOL					X	X	X	X			4
000121697	N,N-DIMETHYLANILINE						X	X				2
000134292	o-ANISIDINE HYDROCHLORIDE	X					X	X				3
000090040	o-ANISIDINE	X					X	X				3
000095487	o-CRESOL					X	X	X	X			4
000528290	o-DINITROBENZENE*					X	X	X				3
000095534	o-TOLUIDINE	X					X		X			3
000636215	o-TOLUIDINE HYDROCHLORIDE	X										1
000095476	o-XYLENE			X	X		X		X		X	5
002234131	OCTACHLORONAPHTHALENE			X					X			2
020816120	OSMIUM TETROXIDE					X						1
000104949	p-ANISIDINE*					X	X					2
000120718	p-CRESIDINE	X										1
000106445	p-CRESOL					X			X			2

Appendix I

Chemical Abstract Service (CAS) NUMBER	CHEMICAL NAME	Human Health							Ecological			Toxicity Index Profile
		C	GC	DT	RT	AT	CT	N	ET	B	P	(TIP)
000100254	p-DINITROBENZENE*		X			X	X	X				4
000156105	p-NITROSODIPHENYLAMINE	X										1
000106503	p-PHENYLENEDIAMINE		X			X	X		X			4
000106423	p-XYLENE			X	X				X		X	4
000056382	PARARTHION			X	X	X	X		X			5
000087865	PENTACHLOROPHENOL (PCP)			X	X	X	X		X	X	X	7
000079210	PERACETIC ACID					X	X					2
000108952	PHENOL			X		X	X		X	X	X	6
000090437	2-PHENYLPHENOL			X	X	X						3
000075445	PHOSGENE					X					X	2
007664382	PHOSPHORIC ACID*								X			1
007723140	PHOSPHORUS (YELLOW OR WHITE)					X	X	X	X			4
000085449	PHTHALIC ANHYDRIDE						X	X	X			3
000088891	PICRIC ACID								X			1
POLYBROMI	POLYBROMINATED BIPHENYLS	X		X	X	X	X					5
001336363	POLYCHLORINATED BI-PHENYLS (PCBs)	X		X	X	X	X					5
001120714	PROPANE SULTONE	X										1
000123386	PROPIONALDEHYDE						X		X			2
000114261	PROPOXUR						X					1
000115071	PROPYLENE (PROPENE)*							X	X			2
000075569	PROPYLENE OXIDE	X	X	X	X	X	X	X	X		X	9
000075558	PROPYLENEIMINE	X				X						2
000110861	PYRIDINE						X		X		X	3
000091225	QUINOLINE					X	X		X		X	4
000106514	QUINONE					X			X			2
000082688	QUINTOZENE [PENTA-CHLORONITROBENZENE			X	X				X	X		4
000081072	SACCHARIN	X	X	X	X							4
000094597	SAFROLE	X			X		X					3
000078922	sec-BUTYL ALCOHOL*					X		X				2
007782492	SELENIUM			X	X		X		X			4
SELENIUM	SELENIUM COMPOUNDS			X	X		X		X			4
007440224	SILVER						X					1
SILVER CO	SILVER COMPOUNDS						X					1
001310732	SODIUM HYDROXIDE (SOLUTION)								X			1
000100425	STYRENE	X	X	X			X		X			5
000096093	STYRENE OXIDE	X		X	X							3
007664939	SULFURIC ACID					X	X		X			3
000100210	TEREPHTHALIC ACID							X			X	2
000075650	tert-BUTYL ALCOHOL*					X	X	X				3
000079345	1,1,2,2-TETRACHLOROETHANE	X		X			X	X	X		X	6
000127184	TETRACHLOROETHYLENE	X		X	X		X	X	X		X	7
000961115	TETRACHLORVINPHOS*					X	X					2
THALLIUM	THALLIUM COMPOUNDS*		X		X		X	X	X	X	X	7
007440280	THALLIUM*		X		X		X	X	X	X	X	7
000062555	THIOACETAMIDE	X	X				X					3
000062566	THIOUREA	X		X	X	X						4
000139651	4,4'-THODIANILINE	X			X							2
001314201	THORIUM DIOXIDE			X	X							2
007550450	TITANIUM TETRACHLORIDE					X						1
000108883	TOLUENE			X	X				X			3
000584849	TOLUENE-2,4-DIISOCYANATE	X				X	X		X			4
000091087	TOLUENE-2,6-DIISOCYANATE	X				X	X					3
026471625	TOLUENEDIISOCYANATE (MIXED ISOMERS)					X	X		X			3
008001352	TOXAPHENE	X		X	X	X	X	X	X	X	X	9
000068768	TRIAZIQUONE	X	X		X							3

Chemical Abstract Service (CAS) NUMBER	CHEMICAL NAME	Human Health							Ecological			Toxicity Index Profile
		C	GC	DT	RT	AT	CT	N	ET	B	P	(TIP)
000052686	TRICHLORFON			X	X	X	X		X		X	6
000120821	1,2,4-TRICHLOROBENZENE			X			X		X	X	X	5
000079005	1,1,2-TRICHLOROETHANE						X		X		X	3
000071556	1,1,1-TRICHLOROETHANE (METHY:CHLOR)			X	X		X	X			X	5
000079016	TRICHLOROETHYLENE			X	X		X	X			X	5
000075694	TRICHLOROFLUOROMETHANE*			X			X			X		3
000095954	2,4,5-TRICHLOROPHENOL	X					X		X			3
000088062	2,4,6-TRICHLOROPHENOL	X					X		X		X	3
001582098	TRIFLURALIN			X	X		X		X	X		5
000095636	1,2,4-TRIMETHYLBENZENE								X			1
000126727	TRIS(2,3-DIBROMOPROPYL) PHOSPHATE	X	X	X	X							4
000051796	URETHANE (ETHYL CARBAMATE)	X										1
007440622	VANADIUM (FUME OR DUST)*						X				X	2
000108054	VINYL ACETATE						X		X			2
000593602	VINYL BROMIDE	X					X					2
000075014	VINYL CHLORIDE	X	X	X	X	X	X				X	7
000075354	VINYLIDENE CHLORIDE			X	X	X	X		X			5
001330207	XYLENE (MIXED ISOMERS)			X	X		X		X			4
000087627	2,6-XYLIDINE						X					1
007440666	ZINC (FUME OR DUST)			X			X		X		X	4
ZINC COMP	ZINC COMPOUNDS			X			X		X		X	4
012122677	ZINEB			X			X		X		X	4

INDEX TO KEY TERMS

This index gives the term and only the page number where it is best defined or described. The same words may be used in other parts of the book.